Conflict, Cooperation and Institutions in International Water Management

ADVANCES IN ECOLOGICAL ECONOMICS

Series Editor: Jeroen C.J.M. van den Bergh, *Professor of Environmental Economics, Vrije Universiteit, Amsterdam, The Netherlands*

Founding Editor: Robert Costanza, *Gund Professor of Ecological Economics and Director, Gund Institute for Ecological Economics, University of Vermont, USA*

This important series makes a significant contribution to the development of the principles and practices of ecological economics, a field which has expanded dramatically in recent years. The series provides an invaluable forum for the publication of high quality work and shows how ecological economic analysis can make a contribution to understanding and resolving important problems.

The main emphasis of the series is on the development and application of new original ideas in ecological economics. International in its approach, it includes some of the best theoretical and empirical work in the field with contributions to fundamental principles, rigorous evaluations of existing concepts, historical surveys and future visions. It seeks to address some of the most important theoretical questions and gives policy solutions for the ecological problems confronting the global village as we move into the twenty-first century.

Titles in the series include:

Economic Growth, Material Flows and the Environment
New Applications of Structural Decomposition Analysis and Physical Input–Output Tables
Rutger Hoekstra

Joint Production and Responsibility in Ecological Economics
On the Foundations of Environmental Policy
Stefan Baumgärtner, Malte Faber and Johannes Schiller

Frontiers in Ecological Economic Theory and Application
Edited by Jon D. Erickson and John M. Gowdy

Socioecological Transitions and Global Change
Trajectories of Social Metabolism and Land Use
Edited by Marina Fischer-Kowalski and Helmut Haberl

Conflict, Cooperation and Institutions in International Water Management
An Economic Analysis
Ines Dombrowsky

Conflict, Cooperation and Institutions in International Water Management
An Economic Analysis

Ines Dombrowsky

Department of Economics
Helmholtz Centre for Environmental Research – UFZ, Leipzig, Germany

ADVANCES IN ECOLOGICAL ECONOMICS

Edward Elgar
Cheltenham, UK • Northampton, MA, USA

Figure 7.1 (p. 225) reprinted with kind permission of *Administrative Science Quarterly*, 36 (2), 284. © Johnson Graduate School of Management, Cornell University

Published by
Edward Elgar Publishing Limited
Glensanda House
Montpellier Parade
Cheltenham
Glos GL50 1UA
UK

Edward Elgar Publishing, Inc.
William Pratt House
9 Dewey Court
Northampton
Massachusetts 01060
USA

A catalogue record for this book
is available from the British Library

Library of Congress Cataloguing in Publication Data

Dombrowsky, Ines, 1968–
    Conflict, cooperation, and institutions in international water management : an economic analysis / Ines Dombrowsky.
        p. cm. — (Advances in ecological economics series)
    Includes bibliographical references (p.) and index.
    1. Water-supply—Economic aspects. 2.
Water-supply—Management—International cooperation. I. Title.
        HD1691.D66 2007
        333.91—dc22

                                                                2007000733

ISBN 978 1 84720 341 0

Printed and bound in Great Britain by MPG Books Ltd, Bodmin, Cornwall

Contents

List of Figures

List of Tables

List of Boxes

List of Abbreviations

AD	Anno Domini
BC	Before Christ
BS	Battle of the Sexes game
C	cooperate
CBW	German-Czech Commission on Boundary Waters
CC	Cooperative outcome
CCRN	Central Commission for Rhine Navigation
CH	Chicken game
CPR	Common Pool Resource
D	defect
DD	Joint defection
DL	Deadlock game
EU	European Union
FAO	Food and Agriculture Organization of the United Nations
GWP	Global Water Partnership
i.i.o.	italics in the original
ibid.	ibidem (at the same place)
IBWC	International Boundary and Water Commission United States and Mexico
ICPE	International Commission for the Protection of the Elbe
ICPO	International Commission for the Protection of the Oder against Pollution
ICPR	International Commission for the Protection of the Rhine
ICWE	International Conference on Water and the Environment
IDGEC	Institutional Dimensions of Global Environmental Change
IJC	International Joint Commission United States and Canada
IKGB	Internationale Gewässerschutzkommission für den Bodensee
IKSE	Internationale Kommission zum Schutz der Elbe
ILA	International Law Association
ILC	International Law Commission
IRBO	International River Basin Organization
ISR-JOR JWC	Joint Water Committee Israel and Jordan
ISR-PAL JWC	Joint Water Committee Israel and Palestinian Authority
IWRM	Integrated Water Resources Management

JSET	Joint Supervision and Enforcement Teams
km^2	square kilometers
km^3	cubic kilometers
LAWA	Working Group of the Federal States on Water Problems, Germany
$m^3/c*a$	cubic meters per capita and year
MRC	Mekong River Commission
N	Nash equilibrium
N.d.	No date
NBI	Nile Basin Initiative
NGO	Non Governmental Organization
OMVS	Organization for the Development of the Senegal River
P	Pareto optimum
P+	Aggregated welfare optimum
P+*	Qualified Pareto optimum
PC	Game of Pure Coordination
PD	Prisoner's Dilemma game
PIC	Permanent Indus Commission
PWC	Permanent Water Commission Namibia and South Africa
R&D	Research and development
RBM	River Basin Management
RBO	River Basin Organization
SADC	Southern African Development Community
TCE	Transaction Cost Economics
TFDD	Transboundary Freshwater Dispute Database
UFZ	Helmholtz Centre for Environmental Research - UFZ
UN	United Nations
UNCED	United Nations Conference on Environment and Development
UNDP	United Nations Development Programme
UNEP	United Nations Environment Programme
USA/US	United States of America
WTO	World Trade Organization
WWC	World Water Council

Preface

This book is concerned with the nexus of conflict, cooperation and institutions in the management of international water resources. Particular emphasis is put on the role of institutions in bringing cooperation about. It is a slightly revised version of my PhD thesis which was accepted by the Department of Economics of the Martin-Luther-University Halle-Wittenberg in June 2006. The dissertation was written at the Helmholtz Centre for Environmental Research – UFZ, Leipzig, where I had the opportunity to obtain UFZ doctoral as well as project funding. The financial support by and the excellent working conditions at UFZ are greatly appreciated.

The topic of international water resources management has accompanied me for more than a decade. Trained as an environmental engineer, I first dealt with it when I wrote my Master thesis on water problems in the Middle East in 1994. I then had the opportunity to work on transboundary water issues in the Jordan River Basin with the Deutsche Gesellschaft für Technische Zusammenarbeit (GTZ) from 1995 to 1997 and in the Nile River Basin with the World Bank from 1997 to 2001. The work on the Jordan and the Nile, and in particular the interaction with a large number of colleagues and representatives of governments in the two basins, were deeply impressive experiences, and I learned a lot about water resources management, international negotiations, facilitation and institutions. At the same time the feeling persisted that it would be useful to know more about these issues at a theoretical level. I was wondering in what way the social sciences and economics would be able to inform the design of institutions for international water management. The idea came up to write the book which I would like to have read in support of the process on the Nile.

I am not sure that I have succeeded in this endeavor, but I have certainly learned a lot about what economics can contribute. One insight is that – at least in the given context – economic theory is particularly helpful in explaining and predicting outcomes. Policy prescriptions can be derived to the extent that they contribute towards the realization of gains of cooperation.

Overall this book can be understood as an economic contribution to a multi-disciplinary discourse on international water management. It was written with the intention to be comprehensible for economists and non-economists alike. At the same time, by taking hydrological and legal aspects into account, the study itself features interdisciplinary elements. Its results are driven both by theoretical and empirical insights.

A great number people encouraged me to pursue a PhD and supported me throughout the process. I am very grateful to Prof. Bernd Hansjürgens, Head of the Department of Economics at UFZ and professor of economics at the Martin-Luther-University Halle-Wittenberg, for supervising the thesis, for his genuine interest in the topic, for his trust and moral support, for repeated discussions on the research question, the structure and parts of the dissertation and for his elaborate and constructive comments on the entire manuscript.

I furthermore thank Prof. Marlies Ahlert (Martin-Luther-University Halle-Wittenberg) and Prof. Volkmar Hartje (Technical University of Berlin) for agreeing to serve as additional reviewers of the dissertation. The dialogue with Volkmar Hartje, especially in the early stage of the process, helped me to decide which road to go in approaching the topic. Marlies Ahlert provided valuable feedback on game theory. I would also like to thank Prof. Robert Holländer (University of Leipzig) and Prof. Tony Allan (King's College London) for their interest in my progress.

My former colleagues at the World Bank and GTZ, in particular David Grey, Barbara Miller, Ashok Subramanian, Inger Andersen, Claudia Sadoff, Astrid Hillers, Vahid Alvian, Ulrich Küffner and Dedo Geinitz as well as Waltina Scheumann at the Technical University Berlin played an important role in getting me started. Barbara kept reminding me that a PhD is only 10 percent inspiration and 90 percent perseverance, although I am still not quite sure whether this is really true. The work on the Nile and Jordan continued to be a huge source of inspiration, and the two basins remained important test cases.

Many colleagues at UFZ provided substantive support and encouraged me throughout the process. Ingo Bräuer, Christoph Görg, Bernd Klauer, Frank Messner, Hennning Nuissl, Cornelia Ohl, Johannes Schiller and Heidi Wittmer commented on earlier drafts and parts of the manuscript. In particular Heidi and Johannes followed the process very closely, which meant a lot to me. Heidi always had an open ear to discuss strategic questions and problems related to empirical research. Johannes was not only a very thoughtful and analytically rigorous discussion partner when it came to substance, but also helped me to reflect the process of writing a dissertation. Our work retreat in Spain in October 2004 was much fun and an important step towards getting into a sustainable writing mode. I owe a special thanks to all my friends who endured long discussions about my dissertation. In this context I would in particular like to mention Oliver Zwirner, Anke Jentsch, Sabine Kannengiesser, Catherine Mann-Grabowski, and Nadia Mazouz. My brother Mirko, in a heroic effort, read the first version of the manuscript in search of typing errors and improved the English. Sabine Linke helped me to bring the manuscript into book format. I am very grateful to all of you!

Finally, I would like to thank my parents, Bruni and Klaus Dombrowsky, for their love, trust and encouragements.

Ines Dombrowsky
Leipzig, October 2006

1. Introduction

Two hundred and sixty three river basins on earth cross international boundaries (Wolf et al. 1999: 389; UNEP 2002). These international river basins cover about 45 percent of the total land area on earth. Some of these river basins are shared by two, others by several riparian countries. River basins are used for many different purposes, including water abstraction for domestic uses, agricultural and industrial production, transport, hydropower generation and wastewater disposal. In addition they constitute habitats for fish and water-related ecosystems and these ecosystems perform important functions for human health, nutrition and recreation.

Whenever a water resource is international, uses in one country may have repercussions on possible uses in other countries. In the case of transboundary rivers upstream users may affect downstream users; in the case of border rivers, shared lakes or aquifers users may mutually affect each other. In some cases the use of international waters is unproblematic, however, as populations grow, and water extractions for productive uses and wastewater discharges rise, competing claims over shared water may increasingly lead to disputes or even conflict among riparian countries.

Against this background the last two decades have witnessed a growing public and scientific debate about conflict and cooperation and adequate strategies and institutions in the management of international waters. The underlying debate has focused on two main issues. First it is disputed whether water may rather be seen as a cause of conflict or as a cause of cooperation. While some predict that water may increasingly become a cause of conflict and possibly war, others stress that water may also serve as a catalyst for cooperation. Second there is a discourse on adequate approaches to foster cooperation. In this context the concepts of Integrated Water Resources Management (IWRM) and River Basin Management (RBM) are being promoted as instruments for a sustainable resource use. IWRM calls for the integrated management of different water uses within the hydrological confines of a river basin. Often it is also argued that it would be desirable to set up new organizational units, so called River Basin Organizations for this purpose. More generally institutions are assumed to play an important role to bring cooperation about.

The discourse on conflict and cooperation raises the question under which conditions cooperation is in the interest of the riparian countries involved, and how institutions must be designed to bring cooperation about. The discourse on Integrated Water Resources Management raises more detailed design questions with respect to the expedient membership, substantive scope and form of international water management institutions.

In view of these discourses this book will address the nexus of conflict, cooperation and institutions in the management of international waters. It will primarily do so from an economic perspective, arguing that economics has something to contribute to the understanding of the conditions under which cooperation and the set up of institutions can be expected as well as to the analysis of the economic effects of alternative institutional arrangements. In taking this economic perspective special attention will be paid to the different types of water uses and the physical behavior of the resource in different geophysical environments as well as to the role of the legal framework conditions. As such this book can be seen at the interface of hydrology, law and economics.

In the context of this book international waters are freshwater resources crossing or constituting international boundaries including international rivers, lakes and aquifers. Transboundary or successive rivers are those crossing a boundary between countries or federal states (Caflisch 1998: 5). Border or contiguous rivers are those constituting a boundary between countries or states. Conflict can be understood as a situation in which the status quo allocation of the resource is contested. Cooperation takes place if the actors involved choose strategies that allow them to realize gains of cooperation. Institutions are humanly devised rules that constrain human interaction, including the rules that constitute organizations. Management can be understood as the regime of actions that modify resource flows and stocks (e.g. Ostrom 1990).

The remainder of this introductory chapter will proceed as follows. Section 1.1 will introduce into the ongoing discourses on conflict and cooperation and integrated water resources management in order to develop the research question in a more systematic fashion. Section 1.2 will revisit the state of the economic literature. Section 1.3 will present conceptual foundations for an economic analysis of conflict, cooperation and institutions providing a terminological and methodological basis of this book. Section 1.4 will summarize the study's objectives and approach and Section 1.5 will present the plan of the book.

1.1 THE POLICY PROBLEM

As argued above there are different professional and scholarly discourses ongoing that address the management of international waters, informed by contributions from a wide range of different disciplines including hydrology, ecology, engineering, geography, political science, economics and law. In the following section these ongoing multi-disciplinary policy discourses will be presented as a starting point in order to develop this book's research question and to put the research question into its policy context. Thus the purpose of this section is to identify the policy problem and to translate the policy problem into a research question. It will be argued that (1) our understanding of conflict, cooperation and the nature and role of institutions in the management of international waters remains incomplete, and (2) there is a lack of economic thinking in the prevailing discourses. This motivates an economic analysis of conflict, cooperation and institutions in international water management.

Section 1.1.1 will provide evidence of international river basins worldwide as a basis for this book. Section 1.1.2 will address the discourse on conflict and cooperation on international waters and Section 1.1.3 the debate on integrated water resources management. Section 1.1.4 will discuss research implications.

1.1.1 International River Basins Worldwide

The Oregon State University has identified a total of 263 river basins that cross international boundaries (Wolf et al. 1999; UNEP 2002).[1] They define a river basin as 'the area which contributes hydrologically (including both surface- and groundwater) to a first-order stream, which, in turn, is defined by its outlet to the ocean or to a terminal (closed) lake or inland sea' (Wolf et al. 1999: 389). A river basin is international 'if any perennial tributary crosses the political boundaries of two or more nations' (ibid.). Approximately 40 percent of the world's population lives in international river basins. They account for an estimated 60 percent of the global

---

[1] In 1958, the United Nations identified 166 major river basins (UN 1958, in Gleick 2000: 27). The 1978 'Register of International Rivers', compiled by the Department of Economic and Social Affairs of the United Nations, listed 214 international waterways (UN 1978). Wolf et al. (1999) have sought to update this register based on a new mapping of watersheds, taking account of geopolitical changes across the world. In 1999, they counted 261 international river basins. Their updated web-version of 2002 contains 263 international river basins (http://www.transboundarywaters.orst.edu/publications/register/tables/IRB_table_4.html (15 June 2005)).

freshwater flow and, as mentioned above, cover 45 percent of the earth's land surface.

Out of these 263 international rivers, according to a count carried out in the context of this book, 87 are shared by three or more countries. One basin, the Danube, has 17 riparian countries. The Congo and Niger are shared by eleven, the Nile by ten and the Rhine and Zambezi River Basins by nine countries. Thirteen river basins – the Amazon, Ganges-Brahmaputra, Lake Chad, Tarim, Aral Sea, Jordan, Kura-Araks, Mekong, Tigris-Euphrates, Volga, La Plata, Neman and Vistula Basins – are shared by between five and eight riparian countries. A total of 145 countries share rivers with other countries. While some of these countries have only a smaller part of their territory in an international river basin, 21 countries are located with more than 99.5 percent of their entire territory within international river basins. A number of countries share several river basins: Russia shares 30 river basins, Argentina and Chile 19 each, China and the USA 18 each and Canada and Guinea each share 14 rivers.[2] The river basins identified vary hugely in size. The Amazon, the Congo, Mississippi and the Nile Basin exceed 3 million square kilometers (km²). Some large international river basins include several international sub-basins which are not separately accounted for in Wolf et al.'s database.

The above shows that first that the phenomenon of international waters is relatively widespread and some countries are significantly affected, either because they are by and large located in international river basins or because they share several international waters, and second that the nature of these international waters varies greatly. As mentioned above, potential competing claims at international waters have given rise to a discourse on conflict and cooperation.

1.1.2   The Discourse on Conflict and Cooperation on International Waters

The discourse on conflict and cooperation on international waters has been stimulated by predictions that the wars of the 21st century would be on water. In the article 'Water Wars', Starr (1991: 17) refers to estimates by the US intelligence services 'that there were at least 10 places in the world where war could break out over dwindling shared water, the majority in the Middle East'. Gleick (1993) argues that in view of an increasing demand for a fixed amount of water supply, tensions over water are likely to increase, including the possibility of violent conflict in some regions, such as the Middle East

---

[2] Derived from: http://www.transboundarywaters.orst.edu (2 May 2003).

and southern and central Asia. Elhance (1999: 4) posits that conflict between states is likely when 'severe scarcities of an *essential, nonsubstitutable, and shared resource*, such as freshwater, are experienced or anticipated by one or more states' (italics in the original (i.i.o.)), although he does not necessarily refer to violent conflict. Homer-Dixon (1994: 19) concludes that the renewable resource most likely to stimulate violent conflict is river water. In a later study he qualified this statement, arguing that wars over river water between upstream and downstream neighbors are only likely in a narrow set of circumstances (Homer-Dixon 1999: 139-141). Klare (2001) counts water among the resources giving rise to a 'new geography of conflict'. He argues while the use of force in solving water disputes has been rare so far, 'the growing pressure on vital supplies, combined with the paucity of vital water-sharing agreements, will create more frequent clashes' (Klare 2001: 60). The likelihood of water wars has been reinforced by spokespersons of international organizations. At a meeting in Stockholm in August 1995, Ismail Serageldin, then the World Bank's Vice President for Environmentally Sustainable Development, declared that the 'wars of the next century will be over water', not oil.[3] Most of these authors also build their arguments on the rhetoric of statesmen which have threatened to go to war over water (e.g., Levi Eshkol of Israel, King Hussein of Jordan or Ansat Saddat and Boutros Boutros Ghali of Egypt).[4]

In essence the above authors take a neo-Malthusian stand, positing a linear relationship between population and economic growth on the one hand and water scarcity on the other. It is argued that water is essential for life and water resources are finite and unevenly distributed. As populations grow, water scarcity increases, which may increasingly lead to conflict, and ultimately to war.

However other scholars have questioned the water war hypothesis on empirical grounds and argue that international waters (as well as world markets), in principle also offer opportunities for cooperation. Sadoff and Grey (2002) seek to identify opportunities for cooperation on international

---

[3] Ismail Serageldin: 'Earth Faces Water Crisis', Press Release, World Bank, Washington DC, 6 August 1995 (in Homer-Dixon 1999: 228) or *New York Times*, 10 August 1995 (in Wolf 1998: 253). A more recent World Bank publication emphasizes the cooperation potential at international waters (Sadoff et al. 2002).

[4] Before the Six-Day-War between Israel and its Arab neighbours in 1967, Prime Minister Levi Eshkol had declared that 'water is a question of life for Israel', and that therefore 'Israel would act to ensure that the waters continue to flow' (in Gleick 1993: 85). After the historic peace treaty with Israel in 1979, Anwar Sadat declared: 'The only matter that could take Egypt to war again is water' (in Starr 1990: 19). In 1988, when he was Egypt's Foreign Minister, Boutros Boutros Ghali claimed that 'the next war in our region will be over the waters of the Nile, not politics' (in Klare 2001: 59). According to Starr (1990: 23) King Hussein suggested in 1990 that water disputes could lead to war.

rivers, distinguishing benefits for the river, from the river and beyond the river as well as reduced costs because of the river. Wolf (1998) rejects the 'myth' of water wars, arguing that the last war that has been fought on water alone was a war between the two Mesopotamian city states of Lagash and Umma in 3100 before Christ (BC). Turton (2000: 166) asserts that '[w]ater scarcity, as both a necessary and sufficient condition for going to war, is an almost non-existent phenomenon'. He emphasizes the necessity to distinguish between water as a cause of war, which is highly unlikely, and water as a target of war, for which many examples can be found. With regard to the Middle East Allan (1996) argues that since the 1960s, water scarcity in countries, such as Israel or Egypt has been alleviated through food imports. In this case the water deficit has been met by the import of 'virtual water' in the form of food staple.

On the basis of a systematic analysis of cooperative and conflicting events on transboundary river basins Wolf et al. (2003) identified a total of 1 831 transboundary events on international watercourses between 1950 and 2000, out of which two thirds were classified as cooperative and only one third as conflictive. Since 1948 they singled out a total of 37 incidents of acute conflict which involved violence, 30 of which had taken place between Israel and its neighbors prior to 1970. Cooperative events, on the other hand, included a total of 157 international water treaties that have been signed between 1950 and 2000. The authors find that (1) overall cooperation appears to be more likely than conflict. (2) According to their analysis water stress alone is not a significant indicator of water dispute. Instead they posit that the likelihood of conflict is related to the institutional capacity to deal with rapid physical or institutional change, on the basis that overall basins without treaties were significantly more conflictive than basins with treaties (Wolf et al. 2003: 45).[5]

Other empirical analyses tend to remain more pessimistic. Toset et al. (2000) carried out a large N-study, in which they tested whether dyads of contiguous countries that share a river have more conflict behavior than other contiguous dyads. Their results 'provide some support for the idea that shared river dyads have a higher frequency of dispute outbreaks than other contiguous dyads' (Toset et al. 2000: 990). Sigman (2002) showed that, outside the European Union, gauging stations upstream of international borders feature higher pollution levels than other stations, indicating that upstream riparians tend to be unwilling to reduce transboundary pollution.

---

[5] While Wolf et al.'s (2003) research suggests that institutions are an important explanatory variable for cooperation, they do not tell us *under which conditions* institutions can be expected to come about and *how* they should be designed in order to foster cooperation.

The above discussion shows that the issue of conflict and cooperation remains an issue of debate. Overall the above mentioned empirical analyses have certainly contributed towards putting the water wars hypothesis into perspective. Even if we cannot predict the future, past experience indicates that states rarely go to war over water. However at the same time it would be wrong to assume that the use of water between states is non-conflictive and that cooperation is straight forward. Instead many water uses are conflictive at a non-violent level, and it is prima facie not clear how such conflicts can be resolved and cooperation be brought about. A particular problem is presented by the upstream-downstream relationship at transboundary rivers, where the upstream riparian has no immediate interest in cooperation.

Given this unresolved tension between conflict and cooperation in the management of international waters this book will address the relationship of conflict and cooperation from an economic perspective. It will maintain that an economic analysis of the incentives of the actors involved can shed light on this tension by indicating potential gains of cooperation, but also by identifying the factors that inhibit cooperation.

Before doing so the concepts of Integrated Water Resources and River Basin Management shall be introduced. This shall be done for a number of reasons. First these concepts can be said to reflect the mainstream of an ongoing multi-disciplinary policy discourse on how water resources in general, and international waters in particular, should be managed. Second they are explicitly perceived as a policy response on how conflicts can be avoided. And third they point at different dimensions of institutional design in the management of international waters such as membership, scope and form.

1.1.3 Integrated Water Resources Management as a Response to Conflict?

The concepts of Integrated Water Resources and River Basin Management have been promoted as central answers to the question of how conflicts can be avoided and water resources, including international waters, should be managed. For instance Wolf (1997: 362) argues:

> Integrated, international water management is best implemented before conflicts arise within a watershed. Such an institutional framework for conflict resolution helps preclude data disputes and provides a pattern of cooperation in the absence of the intense political tensions of a flashpoint (i.i.o.).

The following will (1) introduce into these concepts, (2) reinforce their significance by a review of policy recommendations of international water conferences, (3) ask for empirical evidence in the management of international waters and (4) review the reception of IWRM for international water management in the social sciences in order to further develop this book's research question.

The Concepts of Integrated Water Resources and River Basin Management

One answer to the question of how water resources, including international waters, should be managed is the concept of Integrated Water Resources Management (IWRM). IWRM has evolved as a response to traditional approaches to water resources management which primarily relied on narrow engineering and sectoral solutions (e.g. Hartje 2002). It calls for more integrated approaches, both at the level of the resource and at an actor level. As such it refers to the integrated management of water quantity and quality, surface water and ground water, water and land resources, human and ecological demands, upstream and downstream uses as well as different water using sectors (e.g. GWP 2000). A broad definition defines IWRM as

> a process which promotes the co-ordinated development and management of water, land and related resources, in order to maximize the resultant economic and social welfare in an equitable manner without compromising the sustainability of vital ecosystems (GWP 2000: 22).

Often IWRM incorporates the concept of River Basin Management (RBM), i.e. the idea that water resources should be managed within the hydrological confines of the catchment area or river basin. River Basin Management can be understood as an institutional response to problems of 'spatial fit', i.e. problems misfit between biophysical – in this case hydrological – and societal boundaries as indicated in Figure 1.1 (IDGEC 1999; Moss 2003). While the concept of River Basin Management is not necessarily new (e.g. Teclaff 1967; Kneese and Bower 1968), it has gained new momentum in the last decades. For instance since December 2000 the establishment of a river basin management approach is a legal requirement of the Water Framework Directive of the European Union (EU 2000). The concept of River Basin Management has been supported by natural scientists, lawyers and often also by economists (e.g. Newson 1992; McCaffrey 2003a; Rogers 1997; Sadoff et al. 2002).[6] For instance Rogers (1997) states:

---

[6] Others principally support IWRM, but are more critical of a narrow focus on the river basin. With reference to the concept of 'virtual water' Allan (2001; 2003) emphasizes the need to look for solutions to water scarce regions at the level of the global economy and beyond the hydrological confines of river basins.

The general economic prescription to deal with externalities is to 'internalize' them. The river basin itself is an ideal unit of analysis to achieve this goal: it can reasonably be assumed most externalities are captured by analysing the river basin as a single unit. This is why the concepts of *integrated river basin planning* and the creation of *river basin commissions* to implement and plan are so popular in the economic and planning literature (Rogers 1997: 45, i.i.o.).

Another interpretation of IWRM puts greater emphasis on the integration of different water using sectors, such as water supply and sanitation, industry, agriculture, nature protection, energy, transport, etc. (e.g. GWP 2000: 26 ff.; World Bank 2004: 13). The reason is that water is a multi-functional resource which entails a whole range of different uses. Competing claims of different water users and water using sectors create problems of horizontal 'institutional interplay' as indicated in the second picture of Figure 1.1. Problems of interplay refer to problems of interaction between different water-related institutions (Moss 2003). In this case the challenge is to coordinate between different water using sectors.

"Problems of fit"

Problems of incompatibility between institutional arrangements and biogeophysical systems

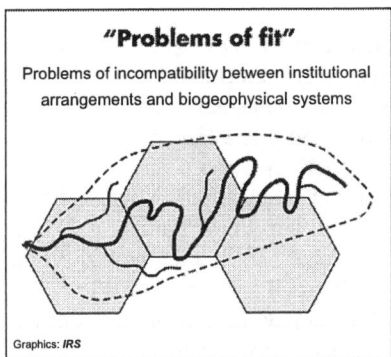

Graphics: *IRS*

"Problems of interplay"

Problems of interaction between different institutions

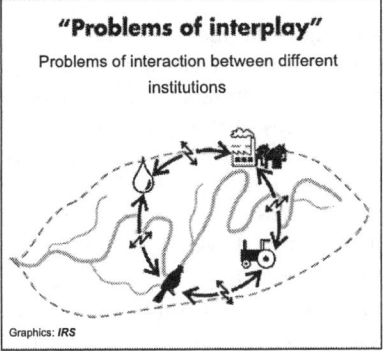

Graphics: *IRS*

Source: After Moss (2003: 35 and 37), graphics provided by and quoted with the permission of the author

Figure 1.1   Problems of Fit and Problems of Interplay

In order to solve problems of fit and problems of interplay there is often an explicit or implicit assumption that it is desirable to establish new organizational units, so called River Basin Organizations (RBOs) which are responsible for the integrated management of water within the hydrological confines of a river basin. Reference is usually made to the Tennessee Valley Authority, the English river authorities, the French basin agencies or the German water associations in the Ruhr area. For instance the report of the World Commission for Water for the 21st Century states: 'If the IWRM principle is adopted, then basin-level systemic management is clearly needed ... Accordingly, governments should set up management agencies at the basin and aquifer levels' (Serageldin et al. 2000: 290).

Thus it can be concluded that IWRM and RBM encompass three main ideas. First the idea is to manage water resources at the level of river basins as opposed to the level of political jurisdictions. Second it is being proposed to integrate different water uses and water using sectors. Third it is often argued that this should be done through the set up of river basin organizations. As such the discourse on IWRM points at different dimensions of institutional design, such as the membership, the substantive scope and the form of respective institutions.

According to the 2004 World Bank Water Resources Sector Strategy IWRM can be perceived as the prevailing policy consensus (World Bank 2004: 28). One indication of this consensus is the repeated reference to IWRM at international water and environment conferences.

Policy recommendations of international conferences

Starting with the so called Dublin Statement of the 1992 International Conference on Water and the Environment in Dublin (ICWE 1992), IWRM has been promoted by international environmental and freshwater conferences of Rio de Janeiro (1992), Paris (1998), The Hague (2000), Bonn (2001), Johannesburg (2002) and Kyoto (2003). It is the central idea of an emerging global policy dialogue on water that is supported by international organizations, such as the United Nations and the World Bank (e.g. World Bank 1993; World Bank 2004) and new global actors, such as the World Water Council (WWC)[7] and the Global Water Partnership (GWP).[8] The following will present a brief analysis of the policy recommendations of the above conferences with respect to the management of international river basins:

---

[7] The World Water Council is a non-profit non-governmental umbrella organization, established in 1996. It is an international water policy 'think tank' dedicated to promote awareness and build political commitment on critical water issues at all levels, including the highest decision-making level and to facilitate efficient and environmentally sustainable water management (http://www.worldwatercouncil.org/about.shtml (29 August 2005)). Together with the respective host country the World Water Council organizes the World Water Forum every three years.

[8] The Global Water Partnership (GWP) was established by the World Bank, the United Nations Development Program (UNDP) and the Swedish International Development Agency (Sida) in 1996 as a working partnership among all organizations involved in water management to 'support countries in the sustainable management of their water resources' (http://www.gwpforum.org/servlet/PSP?ch-StartupName=_about (29 August 2005)).

- The Action Agenda of the 1992 Dublin conference recognizes the role of existing international river organizations in the harmonization of interests and calls for the elaboration of 'integrated management plans, endorsed by all affected governments backed by international agreements' (ICWE 1992: 4). The Conference Report reiterates 'the need for international co-operation and mechanisms at international or regional level to facilitate inter-country agreement on the co-ordination of the management of such resources in an economically and environmentally sound manner' (ICWE 1992: 6). Furthermore it acknowledges that international law has a crucial role to play in the facilitation of agreements.
- Paragraph 18.4 of Agenda 21 of the 1992 United Nations Conference on the Environment and Development in Rio de Janeiro calls riparian states to 'formulate water resources strategies, prepare water resources action programmes and consider, where appropriate, the harmonization of those strategies and action programmes' (UNCED 1992).
- The Ministerial Declaration of the Second World Water Forum in The Hague in 2000 calls states 'to promote peaceful co-operation and develop synergies between different uses of water at all levels, whenever possible, within and, in the case of boundary and trans-boundary water resources, between states concerned, through sustainable river basin management or other appropriate approaches' (WWC 2000: 26). It recognizes that in order 'to achieve integrated water resources management, there is a need for coherent national and, where appropriate, regional and international policies to overcome fragmentation, and for transparent and accountable institutions at all levels' (WWC 2000: 27).
- The 'Bonn Keys' of the International Conference on Freshwater in Bonn in 2001 acknowledge that the design of adequate agreements for transboundary river basin management remains challenging and encourage efforts to 'make existing agreements more vital and valid' (German Federal Government 2001: 6). In doing so they stress the potential for benefit-sharing.
- The Plan of Implementation of the 2002 World Summit on Sustainable Development in Johannesburg calls for the development of 'integrated water resources management and efficiency plans' by the year 2005 (UN 2002: 21). This shall include 'national/regional strategies, plans and programmes with regard to integrated river basin, watershed and groundwater management' (ibid.). International water management is not explicitly addressed; however, it is presumably subsumed under the notion of regional strategies.

These statements reflect that in principle cooperative arrangements for integrated water resources management at the level of international river basins are considered as desirable.[9] As such these statements reflect that IWRM is also recommended for international river basins. However the analysis of the respective documents also shows that overall these conference statements remain desiderata, and there is little indication despite moral appeal how to get there. In particular in large international river basins, integration can be expected to entail considerable complexities, and the question remains whether it is in the interest of the respective riparian states to cooperate and integrate and, if so, what is meant by integration. Therefore the next section will briefly look at empirical evidence for IWRM in international water management.

Empirical evidence of IWRM in international water management

If we look at state practice, it appears that the existing institutional arrangements for the management of water resources are often not fully integrated in the sense that they do not cover the entire river basin, that not all ripiaran states are member states of respective institutional arrangements and that the number of water uses covered by a single agreement remain limited. For a long time many of the large river basins in the world with several riparian countries, such as the Nile with ten riparians, the Zambezi with nine or the Ganges with six, only used to have bilateral agreements in place (e.g. Dombrowsky and Grey 2002; Rogers 1997).[10]

Even in the case of the Rhine Basin, which is generally hailed as one of the great successes of international water management (e.g. Durth 1996; Holtrup 1999), closer inspection reveals great institutional fragmentation, in terms of both spatial coverage and substantive scope (Dombrowsky and Holländer 2004). In the Rhine Basin institutional arrangements emerged in a decentral fashion over time, addressing such diverse issues, such as transboundary navigation, river regulation, energy generation, flood control, fisheries and environmental protection. Many of these arrangements co-exist to date, including the Central Commission for Rhine Navigation (CCRN) with five of the nine riparian states as members and the International Commission for the Protection of the Rhine (ICPR), also with five member

---

[9] A slight shift is noticeable between the 1992 Dublin and the 2001 Bonn conference. While the former still stressed the role of international law, the latter recommends focusing on opportunities for benefit-sharing and thus an economic approach.

[10] In recent years there have been efforts to promote more integrated regimes in the Nile and the Zambezi River Basins. In 1999, nine of the ten Nile riparian countries established the Nile Basin Initiative as an interim arrangement to promote the realization of mutual benefits from water resources development and management (NBI 1999). In 2004, the Zambezi riparians created the Zambezi Watercourse Commission (Wirkus and Böge 2005). Both arrangements were facilitated by international organizations.

states. An all-inclusive basin-wide approach addressing environmental concerns is only now being implemented as a requirement of the European Union Water Framework Directive. At the same time the other regimes continue to co-exist.

With respect to their substantive and geographical scope, based on a review of experiences with river basin management Teclaff (1996) concludes that the majority of international water management institutions are single-purpose and tend to be confined to specific sections of the respective river basins:

> Despite the pronouncements of international organizations, the urging of global and regional agencies, and the recommendations of conferences as to the desirability of a river basin approach to multi-state water management (all within the past half-century), the majority of institutions created during that period have been single-purpose and confined to single waterways and portions of waterways. Some deal only with fisheries, some with pollution, some with water apportionment, power production, or the construction of waterworks. In several instances, their jurisdiction is limited to frontier waters (Teclaff 1996: 384).

Furthermore with respect to organizational aspects of international water management empirical analyses show that international river basin organizations with substantive authority remain rare. In his early legal review of river basin management Teclaff (1967) distinguished between basin or valley authorities 'in control of all stages of water resources management', and planning and coordinating commissions and committees with more attenuated powers (Teclaff 1967: 123 and 143). For international waters he concluded that existing arrangements were limited to commissions and committees (Teclaff 1967: 179). Teclaff (1996) identifies the Organization for the Development of the Senegal River (OMVS) as the first international river basin entity with executive powers (see also McCaffrey 1998). This, however, appears to indicate that international river basin organizations with executive powers tend to be very rare.

While there is still uncertainty with regard to the overall picture, the above appears to indicate a gap between prescription and reality, suggesting that either integrated river basin management is an inadequate concept (at least at the international level), or that states (so far) lack the capacity to 'get it right'. While the global water policy discourse suggests the latter, in particular political scientists have argued for the former.

The reception of IWRM in the social sciences

In particular in the social sciences an emerging critical discourse on the concept of IWRM can be observed. Political scientist Frank Marty (2001) goes so far as to reject IWRM as unrealistic for international water management. Instead he favors what he calls the 'functional model', according to which problems are solved on a case-by-case basis without an overarching framework in place (Marty 2001: 27). The functional model predicts that the majority of international water agreements will be bilateral and narrow in scope, and Marty also suggests that this is how problems should be addressed:

> Judging from the results of this book, it seems to be doubtful whether it is really advisable to call for, or advocate, projects that provide for the integrated managing of an international river or river basin... Many riparian problems, taken by themselves, are so complex already that it seems unwise to increase their complexity even further (Marty 2001: 399).

Similar to Marty (2001) Waterbury (1997) warns that the quest of integrated river basin development in international river basins will prove elusive, and the costs for searching it will be excessive. He also reasons that bilateral, sub-basin accords may be more feasible than basin-wide agreements. However in contrast to Marty (2001) he concedes that bilateral agreements are not necessarily a solution to rival claims in multiparty basins, as two countries may reach agreement at the expense of a third (Waterbury 1997: 285 f.). Having the Nile case in mind he therefore goes so far to suggest proactive unilateral measures, such as pricing reforms in water scarce areas that will be beneficial to the country implementing them irrespectively of the behavior of other co-riaprian countries. His expectation is, though, that unilateral steps will enhance the prospects of international cooperation.

Bernauer (1997) takes a more balanced view, arguing while integrated structures may be more difficult to establish and implement, opportunities for linkages may also improve the possibilities of cooperation, and integrated structures may contribute to better performance:

> Many experts tend to regard integrated-issue river management as the more promising approach, but whether it really performs better than single-issue management depends on a variety of conditions. Integrated management perhaps makes more sense from a ecological viewpoint, and it may also provide more opportunities for issue linkages, which may improve the possibilities of cooperation. On the other hand, integrated management significantly complicates negotiations and poses a greater challenge to the capacity of the actors involved... It seems, that although IRMIs [international river management institutions, ID] designed to manage transboundary rivers in an integrated manner are probably more difficult to establish and operate, they may contribute to better performance or river management (Bernauer 1997: 184 and 192 f.).

From the above it becomes evident that IWRM provides a theoretic-conceptual answer without specifying the conditions under which it can be implemented. Both the question of how much integration can be expected, and the question of how much integration is desirable, remain largely unresolved. While 'full' integration in the sense of a cross-sectorally integrated river basin management approach with an international river basin organization in place may indeed prove elusive, in view of the fact that at least some bilateral water agreements have given rise to substantial conflict by not including affected co-riparians, a narrow normative interpretation of the functional approach, as suggested by Marty's work, at least entails the danger of falling short of problem solving.[11] This, however, means that we need more refined answers to the questions raised above.

1.1.4 Research Implications

The above discussion shows the following:

1. While the discourse on conflict and cooperation has forwarded various theoretical and empirical arguments for both conflict and cooperation, it lacks a rigorous analysis of potential gains of cooperation and of potential factors that inhibit cooperation to come about, even where such gains exists. Therefore an economic analysis of the interests and incentives of the riparian countries involved may contribute towards understanding the interrelationship between conflict and cooperation and may also illuminate the role of institutions in bringing cooperation about. The discourse on conflict and cooperation thus raises the question *under* which conditions it is in the interest of riparian countries to cooperate, and how institutions must be designed in order to realize gains of cooperation. The hypothesis is that institutional change can be expected if the respective actors are able to realize gains of cooperation.

2. While there is a broad consensus on the concept of IWRM, at least in international river basins state practice appears to be far away from the ideal of an integrated water resources management. This means that the question how the membership, the substantive scope and the form of institutional arrangements for international water management should be shaped in order to lead to a 'sustainable' resource management remains an unresolved issue.

---

[11] Given that Marty's (2001) empirical analysis is limited to bilateral negotiations, the empirical test of integrated arrangement in international river basins is still out (see also Bernauer 2002: 12).

- The question of membership asks which of the riparian states sharing a river basin should become members of an international water management institution.
- The question of substantive scope asks which water uses should be covered by a respective agreement.
- The question of form refers to the organizational form of respective institutional arrangements, i.e. whether it suffices that the riparian countries conclude an agreement or whether they should also establish an organization, and if so, what the respective organization should look like.

'Full' integration would be achieved, if all riparian states were members of a formal international river basin organization with substantial discretionary power covering a broad range of different uses.

Answers to these design questions depend on the underlying norm, and they may differ depending on whether one approaches the question from an ethical, legal or an economic perspective. From an economic perspective these questions may be looked at in terms of economic expedience. Integration can be considered as expedient if it makes the actors involved individually or collectively better off.[12, 13] Thus the discourse on IWRM raises the question what may be considered as the economically expedient 'degree of integration' in the management of international waters in terms of membership, substantive scope and form. The term 'degree of integration' is used in order to express that there may be different levels of integration ranging from no integration to 'full' integration.

This book maintains that economics has something to contribute to these questions. Taking an economic approach does not deny that the process of cooperation on international waters is fundamentally of a political nature. However an economic analysis can inform the political process by analyzing the interests and incentives of the actors involved and by identifying possible benefits of, as well as possible obstacles towards, cooperation.

How this can be done will be further discussed in the next two sections. Given that the above questions have so far been developed from an analysis of the predominantly multi-disciplinary policy discourse in the field of international water management, Section 1.2 will review relevant economic contributions to the topic and Section 1.3 will ask what is meant by an economic analysis of institutions.

---

[12] For the differentiation of individual and collective interests see Sections 1.3 and 1.4.

[13] In the use of water cooperation is, in principle, possible at the expense of 'nature'. This book is aware of this problem, and the intention is to analyze 'sustainable' forms of cooperation that take ecological constraints into account.

1.2 STATE OF THE ECONOMIC LITERATURE

A literature review shows that overall economic contributions to the problem of international water management have been comparatively rare, and where they exist little emphasis has been put on the role of institutions.

A number of authors have studied the economics of transboundary water management in particular river basins. An early study is Krutilla's analysis of transboundary river management in the Columbia River Basin (Krutilla 1967). Guariso and Whittington (1987) and Whittington et al. (2005) have analyzed the economics of transboundary water management in the Nile Basin. Rogers (1997) describes the problem of transboundary water management as one of pervasive unidirectional externalities and explores the concepts of Pareto-admissibility, superfairness and the game-theoretic concept of the core towards benefit-sharing among India, Nepal and Bangladesh in the Ganges Basin. He concludes that if a strong river basin authority was in place that could allocate costs and benefits according to the core, there would be no incentives for coalitions to block these allocations.

Others have explored the potential of markets for an efficient allocation of water resources in the Middle East, seeking to demonstrate the benefits of cooperation (Dinar and Wolf 1994; Zeitouni et al. 1994; Fisher 1995; Becker and Zeitouni 1998). Netanyahu (1998) has used a game-theoretic approach to analyze the Israeli-Palestinian conflict on shared transboundary groundwater resources. Richards and Singh (2001) on the other hand have critiqued Fisher's (1995) market approach from the perspective of the New Institutional Economics, arguing that the institutional preconditions for the establishment of water markets in the Middle East are not in place.

At a more general level Barrett (1994b) presents an initial game-theoretic reconstruction of different problem structures in transboundary river management, distinguishing unidirectional and reciprocal externality as well as economy of scale problems. He argues that in order to sustain cooperation agreements must be self-enforcing. As mentioned above Sadoff and Grey (2002) present a typology of benefits of cooperation on international rivers. Whittington et al. (2005: 230) introduce the concept of the 'system value of water' defined 'as the total value generated by water within the river system' as a means to determine the potential benefits of cooperative river basin management.[14]

Durth's (1996) study of the political economy of transboundary water management examines the conditions for cooperation in upstream-

---

[14] In an earlier publication Sadoff et al. (2002: 27) defined the 'system value of water' as the 'aggregate value that a unit of water can generate as it moves through the river system before it is consumed or lost'.

downstream constellations and the role of regional integration for the internalization of negative external effects at international rivers and tests his findings for the Rhine, the Elbe and the Euphrates river basins. He concludes that in the case of negative external effects cooperation can be expected if side-payments are acceptable and if riparian states are able to make binding commitments. The outcome can be expected to be efficient if (1) property rights are well defined and tradable; (2) information is complete and symmetrically distributed, (3) transaction costs are sufficiently low; and if (4) notions of fairness and levels of risk aversions converge. Furthermore cooperation may be easier if a transboundary commission is in place which facilitates the search for mutually acceptable solutions and if there are opportunities for non-governmental actors to participate in the process. Durth argues that these conditions are more likely to be fulfilled in integrated settings.

A number of authors use (cooperative) game theory to determine efficient allocations in river basins with two and more riparians (see also Rogers 1997 above). Kilgour and Dinar (1995; 2001) develop a water sharing model (assuming that property rights are predefined) in order to determine efficient allocations depending on actual hydrological flows. They show that flexible agreements that take account of hydrological variability produce higher welfare levels than allocations based on average flows. They are optimistic that satellite technology will make flexible and enforceable water sharing agreements possible. Barrett (1994b; 1996) proposes a mechanism for reconciling equity and efficiency considerations in a three-country water pollution game, determining efficient allocations under both the legal doctrine of absolute territorial sovereignty and of absolute territorial integrity and splitting the difference between the allocations under the two doctrines for each country.[15] Ambec and Sprumont (2002) present a model for the efficient allocation of a river among N riparian countries that satisfies a lower welfare bound set by the legal doctrine of absolute territorial sovereignty and an upper bound set by the doctrine of absolute territorial integrity for each riparian. These conditions are met by the so called 'downstream incremental distribution vector'. Thus the latter two contributions seek to address the fact that often the legal situation on international rivers is disputed and to reconcile efficiency and equity considerations.

---

[15] The doctrine of absolute territorial sovereignty maintains that a watercourse enjoys exclusive authority of the water resource in its territory. The doctrine of absolute territorial integrity claims that a state is entitled to the unaltered inflow of a river into its state (see Chapter 3).

Those rare economic contributions that explicitly address institutional and organizational aspects of river basin management do not address the problem of international cooperation. Kneese and Bower (1968) have provided an early analysis of the economic rationale for river basin management organizations. Holm (1988) has presented an economic analysis of the French *Agences de Bassin* and the German water association in the Ruhr area. Challen (2000) has used a transaction cost approach for the analysis of the reform of irrigation water rights in Australia. Saleth and Dinar (2004) have presented a volume on the institutional economics of water resources management.

Overall it can be concluded that the economic literature on conflict, cooperation and institutions in international water management remains limited in scope. Most of the existing literature points at potential benefits of cooperation, either in general conceptual terms or in specific river basins, but does not necessarily address how institutions must be shaped to realize these benefits. The literature shows that efficient allocations are possible if property rights are well defined, and if riparians are able to bind themselves, but very few authors acknowledge the difficulty of achieving these cooperation conditions. With the exception of Barrett (1994a) the literature is largely confined to water allocation or water quality problems, but rarely takes account of the spectrum of water uses and the specific problem structures depending on the alignment of hydrological and political boundaries. With the exception of Durth (1996), no economic work on the role of international river basin organizations or other forms of organization could be identified.

This book seeks to close these gaps by revisiting the nexus of conflict, cooperation and institutions and by putting institutional questions of international water management at its center. Before further developing the research question and approach, Section 1.3 will ask what we mean by conflict, cooperation and institutions and by the economic analysis of institutions as a terminological and methodological foundation of this book.

1.3 CONCEPTUALIZING AND ANALYZING INSTITUTIONS

In order to further develop the book's approach and structure this section will present two different theoretical frameworks which may help to organize the thinking about conflict, cooperation and institutions in international water management.

- The first framework – which is referred to as the 'economic approach towards institutions' – distinguishes different types of institutions and different economic approaches towards the analysis of institutions. It asks what kind of institutions we talk about, and what we mean by an economic analysis of institutions (Section 1.3.1).
- The second framework introduces a simple model of the nexus of conflict, cooperation and institutions in the management of international waters. The purpose of this model is to obtain a better procedural understanding of the emergence of institutions through negotiations and of the impact of institutions on the negotiation process. In the framework of this procedural model it will be possible to make predictions under which conditions the establishment of institutions can be expected and how different institutional settings shape the negotiation process (Section 1.3.2).

As such these frameworks offer two different ways to organize the research within this book.

1.3.1   The Economic Approach towards Institutions

From an economic perspective institutions can be understood as humanly devised constraints or the formal and informal rules of the game (North 1990: 3): 'Institutions are the rules of a game in a society or, more formally, are the humanly devised constraints that shape human interaction.'

Examples of institutions include social norms and conventions, property rights, voting rules, informal and formal agreements or enforcement mechanisms. According to Ostrom (1990: 51) institutions are 'rules in use', i.e. those rules that are socially accepted by the actors involved. Hence not all formal agreements are institutions, but only those that effectively bind their signatories.

North (1990: 4 f.) furthermore draws an analytical distinction between institutions and organizations, where institutions are understood as the formal and informal rules of the game, and organizations are understood as the players bound by some common purpose. While this analytical distinction sometimes appears to contradict the colloquial use of the term institution, where 'organizations' are referred to as 'institutions', it is useful when it comes to the analysis of the interaction between institutions and organizations. However while organizations are analytically distinct from institutions, North (1990) also points at the fact that organizations are constituted by rules. One purpose of agreements may thus be to serve as the constitution of an organization. Thus organizations may be conceived as a specific form of institutionalization. While they are constituted by rules, as a whole they are more than institutions.

Agreements on the other hand can be understood as a more general form of institutionalization which may or may not include the set up of an organization. Other purposes of agreements may be to agree on specific action or to define property rights. Agreements may take the form of a formal treaty, a convention, minutes or some other form of contract. They may also be of an informal nature.

An economic analysis is usually carried out under the assumption that individuals pursue their self-interest and that they behave (boundedly) rational in the sense that they make decisions on the basis of cost-benefit (or advantage-disadvantage) calculations (e.g. Pies 2001: 172). Individuals are assumed to maximize their utility according to their preferences within their budgetary restrictions.

Outcomes are usually evaluated in terms of the Pareto or the welfare criterion. An outcome is Pareto efficient if there is no other outcome that makes at least one actor better off without making any other actor worse off. The Pareto criterion does not allow that anybody is made worse off through a policy measure. Whenever a measure meets the Pareto criterion it can be expected to be acceptable to the parties involved. As such the Pareto criterion can be expected to be applied in consensual decision-making. Under the Kaldor-Hicks or welfare criterion outcomes are evaluated for their potential to increase or decrease aggregated net benefits. An outcome is potentially Pareto efficient if it maximizes the aggregated net benefits (or the welfare) of society as a whole and if the winners could potentially compensate the losers. An actual compensation is not required.

This means that under a narrow perspective an economic analysis of institutions seeks to analyze the economic implications of institutions. In other words institutions are analyzed for their expediency, more specifically for their potential to increase efficiency or to realize gains of cooperation. Next to the analysis of the effects of institutions an economic analysis may also be carried out in order to determine the conditions for the formation of institutions. In general institutions are expected to be set up or to change if this allows actors to generate gains of cooperation (e.g. North 1990).

Depending on the aspect to be analyzed the economic analysis of institutions can principally be informed by various theories within the so called New Institutional Economics, including transaction cost economics, property rights theories, contract theory, principal-agent theory, public choice, constitutional economics and others (e.g. Furubotn and Richter 1997; Erlei et al. 1999).

A useful framework which distinguishes different types of institutions and associated levels of analysis is presented by Williamson (1998). This approach will be briefly introduced in order to analyze which theories will be relevant in the context of this book.

Williamson (1998: 25-28) distinguishes four levels in the analysis of institutions, namely (social) embeddedness, the institutional environment, governance structures and resource allocation and employment (Figure 1.2).

1. The level of social embeddedness (L 1) refers to informal institutions, such as norms, customs, mores and traditions. Williamson argues that informal institutions are mainly the subject of social theory. With the exception of some economic historians, most economists take this level as a given. Informal institutions only change over long time intervals in the order of centuries or millennia. According to Williamson the origin of these informal institutions is mainly spontaneous and not the result of deliberate choice.

2. The level of the institutional environment (L 2) mainly refers to the formal rules of the game, in particular political structures, such as the polity, judiciary and the bureaucracy of government as well as the law governing the definition and enforcement of property rights. These rules and structures are mainly the result of the political process. Except for extreme events, such as political or financial crises institutional change takes place in the order of decades or centuries. The analysis of the formal institutional environment is at the heart of the economic theory of property rights which posits that well defined property rights are a key towards the realization of superior economic performance (e.g. Demsetz 1967; Libecap 1989; Bromley 1991). According to Williamson the maxim 'Get the institutional environment right' can be considered as first-order economizing. In other words the political process of shaping the institutional environment creates the conditions under which economic optimization can take place.

3. The level of governance (L 3) deals with governance structures, such as markets, hybrids (contracts), hierarchies, bureaus or – according to Williamson – the 'play of the game'.[16] The analysis of governance structures is at the center of Williamson's transaction cost economics. Governance structures can be considered as the result of economic organization within a given institutional environment. Institutional change takes place in the order of years or decades. The maxim 'Get the governance structure right' is referred to as second-order economizing. The economic analysis of governance structures compares the economic implications of discrete structural alternatives, such as markets or

---

[16] The boundary between L2 and L3 appears to be rather fluent, as Williamson mentions the bureaucracy under L2 and (public) bureaus under L3.

hierarchies, taking all relevant costs, including transaction costs, into account.

4. Level 4 (L4) refers to subject areas of neoclassical economics and agency theory, such as resource allocation and employment. It moves from the comparison of discrete structural alternatives to marginal analysis. Adaptation occurs on a continuous basis. According to Williamson 'Getting the marginal conditions right' can be considered as third-order economizing.

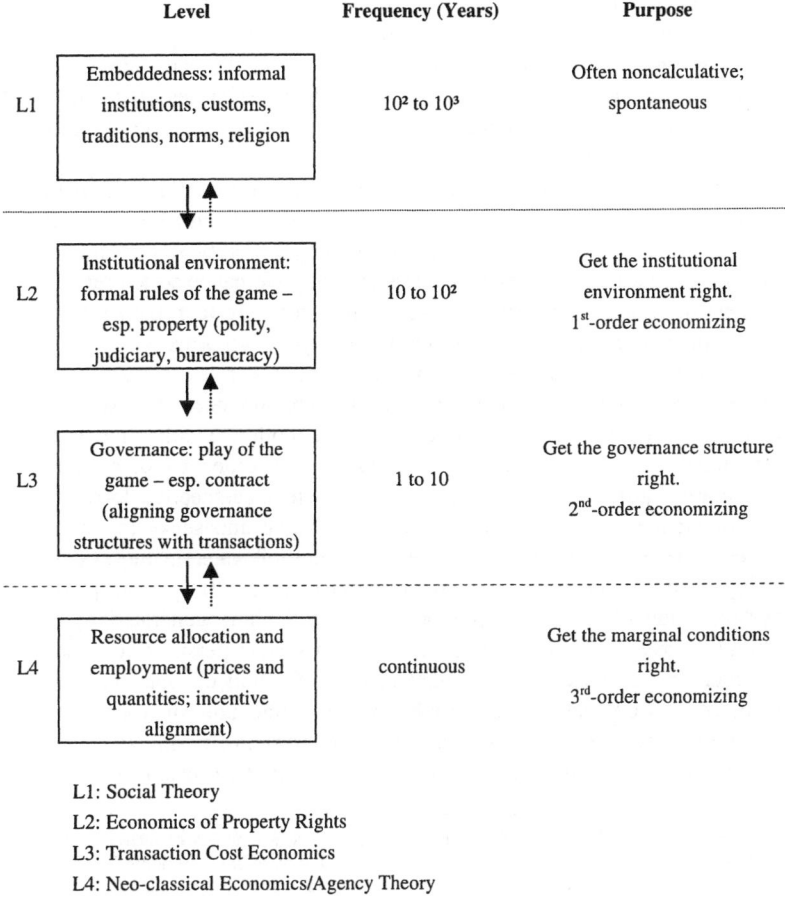

Level	Frequency (Years)	Purpose
L1 Embeddedness: informal institutions, customs, traditions, norms, religion	10^2 to 10^3	Often noncalculative; spontaneous
L2 Institutional environment: formal rules of the game – esp. property (polity, judiciary, bureaucracy)	10 to 10^2	Get the institutional environment right. 1st-order economizing
L3 Governance: play of the game – esp. contract (aligning governance structures with transactions)	1 to 10	Get the governance structure right. 2nd-order economizing
L4 Resource allocation and employment (prices and quantities; incentive alignment)	continuous	Get the marginal conditions right. 3rd-order economizing

L1: Social Theory
L2: Economics of Property Rights
L3: Transaction Cost Economics
L4: Neo-classical Economics/Agency Theory

Source: Williamson 1998: 26, adapted

Figure 1.2   Williamson's Economics of Institutions

This book will follow Williamson's understanding that the New Institutional Economics mainly focuses on the institutional environment and governance structures (L2 and L3), meaning that its two central theories comprise property rights economics and transaction cost economics.

This raises the question of what the implications of the above are, in terms of the theoretical underpinning of this book. Given that in the international system there is no external authority which could define and enforce property rights to international waters, the explicit definition of property rights relies on voluntary negotiations among co-riparian states. In doing so international law provides guidance, but there is no entity that could enforce a solution. This implies that riparian states have to negotiate property rights and efficiency gains simultaneously (Barrett 1996). At the same time riparian countries are also faced with the question whether to set up institutional arrangements – or in Williamson's terminology – specific governance structures that facilitate the cooperation process.

Hence an analysis of institutions for international water management has to address both the level of the institutional environment, i.e. the political process of negotiating agreements that specify property rights and realize benefits at international waters and the level of governance structures, i.e. the process of choosing an expedient governance structure (e.g. the set up of an international organization) that supports the negotiation process.[17]

In analyzing the cooperation potential and the role of institutions in international water management the analyst eventually needs to take a system and an actor-oriented perspective, analyzing both the collective and the individual interests of the actors involved. In order to determine the cooperation potential in a river basin the system perspective looks at the hydrological system (the river basin) as a whole and seeks to determine water allocations that maximize the total value of water in the system. In doing so one may draw upon Whittington et al.'s (2005) concept of the system value of water, understood as the total value generated by water within the river system (Section 1.2). Such a system perspective seeks, for instance to maximize non-consumptive uses of a unit of water (e.g. in the form of hydropower generation) before the same unit of water is used consumptively (e.g. in irrigation). The system perspective allows determining an optimal outcome for all users in the river basin. In economic

---

[17] A one-to-one application of Williamson's framework to the subject of international water management remains difficult. Strictly speaking the negotiation of property rights falls under the level of the institutional environment (L2) and the negotiation of efficiency gains under the level of governance as well as resource allocation (L3 and L4). Furthermore contracts are not limited to L3. Nevertheless Williamson's distinction helps to structure the problem in the sense that it shows that we need to address both the level of the institutional environment and the level of governance structures.

terms this corresponds to a welfare economic perspective, which seeks to maximize the aggregate value for 'society as a whole'. The system or welfare economic perspective asks what is in the collective interest.

The problem with a sole system or welfare economic perspective in international water management is that there is no unitary decision-maker who could impose an optimal solution and, as will be argued in this book, voluntary negotiations among respective riparian countries do not necessarily reach agreements that implement the collectively desirable outcome. Therefore, in addition to a system perspective, it is useful to take an actor-oriented perspective, analyzing the individual interests of the respective riparian countries and their strategic interaction.[18] As such the actor-oriented perspective analyzes the conditions under which the respective 'actors' are able to realize a given cooperation potential within the river basin through voluntary negotiations.[19] In order to do so the respective actors may device institutions as rules which manage possible interaction problems (e.g. Pies 2000). Such an actor-oriented analysis may be supported by the tools of game theory.

In this book the process of negotiating property rights and efficiency gains (L2 and L4) will be addressed in Chapters 5 and 6. In doing so the study will take a game-theoretic perspective but also build upon theories of externalities and public goods and property rights economics. The economic rationale for the set up of international organizations will be addressed in Chapter 7, drawing on Williamson's transaction cost economics and a special version of actor-centered institutionalism.

1.3.2 An Explanatory Model of Conflict, Cooperation and Institutions

With respect to understanding the nexus of conflict, cooperation and institutions in international water management the discourse has so far been dominated by rational choice analysts in political science. LeMarquand (1977) developed a theoretical framework that drew upon theories of public goods and public choice theory and analyzed international water negotiations in the Colorado, Skagit, Columbia and Rhine River Basins. In view of LeMarquand's findings Bernauer (1997) proposed to distinguish between structural, procedural and institutional factors determining conflict and cooperation on international rivers. Building upon these authors Marty

---

[18] The term 'actor-oriented' as opposed to 'game-theoretic' perspective is used in order to contrast this perspective with a 'system' perspective.

[19] Under the actor-oriented perspective it is usually assumed that the cooperation potential is known – however given the complex interdependencies in the use of water, in the absence of a system analysis this may not necessarily be the case.

(2001) proposed an explanatory model of regime[20] formation and effectiveness in international water management, which he tested for five cases of bilateral negotiations on transboundary water projects. He distinguished between problem, process and exogenous factors that determine regime formation and institutional and exogenous factors influencing regime effectiveness. Scharpf (1997) proposed a general theoretical framework for the analysis of policy processes that takes account of the role of the institutional setting within which negotiations occur.

In order to move towards a procedural understanding of the nexus of conflict cooperation and institutions in international water management the following will present a simple explanatory model as presented in Figure 1.3 which is influenced by the above authors.

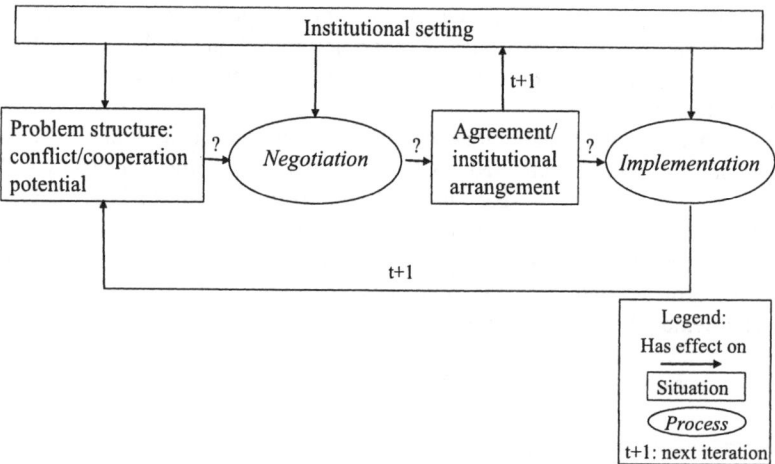

Source: Own presentation

Figure 1.3   Conceptualizing Conflict, Cooperation and Institutions

The starting point is a certain problem structure. The problem structure is the result of the underlying hydrological, economic and political conditions. More specifically the problem structure is constituted by the alignment of hydrological and political boundaries and the respective water uses at hand. The problem structure may give rise to 'conflict', but it may also contain a

---

[20] In international relations international institutions are often referred to as 'regimes'. A widely accepted definition defines international regimes as: 'implicit and explicit principles, norms, rules, and decision-making procedures around which actors' expectations converge in a given area of international relations' (Krasner 1983: 2).

'cooperation' potential. Conflict can be understood as a situation in which the status quo allocation and use of the resource is contested. Conflict over water may strain the broader relations between states, may impact the political economy of a region and may ultimately lead to war. In economic terms it may give rise to missed opportunities for trade and diplomatic or military costs. A cooperation potential is present if there are potential benefits of cooperation, i.e. if a Pareto improvement may be realized by mutually agreeing on a different set of actions.

The conflict or cooperation potential may give rise to negotiations, the purpose of which would be to come up with an agreement that alters the status quo. The parties involved may employ different negotiation strategies, such as confidence building measures, threats, side-payments or issue linkage in order to come up with an agreement. The agreement may be of a formal or an informal nature. It may contain substantive as well as procedural provisions. Substantive provisions may include the specification of property rights or agreement on certain infrastructure measures. Procedural provisions may include the set up of an institutional arrangement, such as an international commission to support future negotiations as well as agreement on decision-making rules. It is expected that the implementation of the agreement will alter the problem structure. The altered problem structure may or may not give rise to a new iteration of negotiations.

This process of conflict and cooperation is furthermore shaped by the institutional setting in which it takes place (Scharpf 1997). The problem-solving capacity of the negotiation and implementation process can be expected to differ depending on whether these negotiations take place under quasi anarchical conditions of the international system without any external enforcement authority in place or, for instance, within a state or hierarchical organization. Furthermore any agreement on institutional arrangements will change the institutional setting in the next iteration.

According to the above model it can be argued that 'cooperation' takes place if the parties involved realize a cooperation potential, i.e. if a cooperation potential exists and if the parties negotiate and implement an agreement that materializes this cooperation potential.

The model is not meant to be deterministic. A cooperation potential will not always lead to negotiations. Negotiations will not always be able to identify a cooperation potential and even if a cooperation potential exists, they may not result in an agreement. Not every agreement will be implemented.

This model has been used to structure the economic analysis of conflict, cooperation and institutions in this book. Chapter 5 will analyze the repercussions of the problem structure on cooperation and institutions. Chapter 6 will address the role of issue linkage as a negotiation strategy for solving unidirectional externality problems. Chapter 7 will analyze the role of international organizations and the institutional setting for the problem-solving capacity of negotiations.

Based on these considerations the next section will summarize the objectives and approach of this book.

1.4   STUDY OBJECTIVES AND APPROACH

This book revisits the nexus of conflict, cooperation and institutions in the management of international waters from an economic perspective. Its primary objective is to analyze the conditions under which cooperation is in the interest of the riparian countries sharing international water resources, and how institutions must be designed in order to realize a given cooperation potential. In view of the concept of Integrated Water Resources Management particular attention is being paid to the expedient degree of institutional integration in terms of membership, substantive scope and form.

In order to do so the study draws upon different theories in economics including theories of public goods and externalities, (non-cooperative) game theory, property rights economics, transaction cost economics and the so called 'actor-centered institutionalism'. These theories have been found useful to explain particular aspects of the cooperation problem and institutional design.

In order to analyze the conditions under which cooperation is in interest of the respective riparian countries the study will distinguish different types of externality problems, depending on the underlying water uses and the alignment of hydrological and political boundaries (Chapter 2). In order to analyze the relationship of problem structure and institutional design these different types of externality problems will be reconstructed on the basis of non-cooperative theory (Chapter 5). In analyzing the conditions for cooperation the study will take the legal framework conditions for international water negotiations and legal perspectives on institutional design into account (Chapter 3).

In principal the expedient degree of integration can be evaluated in terms of the Pareto or the welfare criterion. The Pareto perspective asks if integration makes at least one party better off without making any party worse off. The welfare perspective asks which degree of integration generates the highest welfare for society as a whole. In this book the question of scope will be addressed in view of the Pareto criterion, by analyzing to what extent the linking different water uses can be considered to be in the interest of the riparian states involved (Chapter 6). The question of form will be informed by a comparative analysis of alternative governance structures

(Chapter 7).[21] The empirical review of international water management institutions will describe existing arrangements in terms of their membership arrangements, substantive scope and form (Chapter 4).

From a methodological point of view the study by and large looks at governments as unitary actors, or more precisely, at the scope of action of ministries responsible for water within a government. It assumes that the respective governments seek to maximize their country's welfare under the conditions of international law.[22] It does not focus on sub-national policy processes and the role of non-state actors (which have, for instance, been analyzed by Durth 1996 or Blatter and Ingram 2000). Unless specified otherwise, whenever the study speaks of 'actors', 'parties' or 'players', it refers to riparian countries.

Overall the study is primarily of a theoretical and conceptual nature. This notwithstanding it requires a basic understanding of the object of analysis as a starting point and, in principle, an empirical analysis of the theoretical considerations is also desirable.[23] This empirical starting point and theory check is provided in form of a cross-country review of international water management institutions (Chapter 4). Furthermore the analysis of the cooperation problem in Chapters 5 through 7 will make reference to selected examples as appropriate. These examples draw partly upon prior case studies of the author (e.g. Dombrowsky 1995; Dombrowsky 2003; Dombrowsky and Holländer 2004), they are also informed by other case studies in the literature. The thrust of this book, however, is to improve the theoretical framework. Improving the hypotheses can be seen as a research strategy towards the generation of generalizable knowledge when comparative empirical research is faced with the problem that there are many explanatory

---

[21] Given that Chapter 5 will largely be limited to two-person games, a systematic theoretical treatment of the question of membership will not be provided in this book. This notwithstanding the issue of membership shall be motivated as an economic problem.

[22] These assumptions are not unproblematic as it can be argued that the analysis of composite actors contradicts the economic concept of methodological individualism. Methodological individualism aims at explaining social phenomena as the aggregation of decisions by individuals who make choices according to their preferences and under their respective constraints. It is furthermore questionable whether government representatives actually maximize national welfare. This notwithstanding these simplifications are made in order to explore the inter-country cooperation potential.

[23] Under ideal circumstances an iterative approach would be desirable: empirical phenomena inform the choice of theories, and the hypotheses generated are empirically validated and refined.

variables, but only few comparable cases (Scharpf 1997: 28).[24] Overall this book seeks to:

- contribute to the economic literature on international water management by distinguishing different problem structures in international water management; by analyzing the relationship of problem structure and institutional design; and by moving towards an economic theory of international water management organizations;
- inform the discourse on conflict and cooperation in the social sciences by examining incentives for cooperation and potential factors that inhibit cooperation and by analyzing how institutions must be designed to bring cooperation about; and
- make an economic contribution to the multi-disciplinary policy discourse on Integrated Water Resources Management (IWRM) by examining the expedient substantive scope of respective institutional arrangements and by analyzing alternative forms of organization in international water management.

By taking hydrological and legal constraints into account this book is located at the interface of hydrology, law and economics and can thus be understood as an interdisciplinary contribution.

1.5   PLAN OF THE BOOK

The book is divided into two parts. Part I provides hydro-economic, legal and empirical foundations for an economic analysis of international water management institutions.[25] It introduces the object of the analysis by offering different perspectives on the problem of international water management and institutional design including an economic conceptualization of different problem structures in international water management (Chapter 2), an analysis of legal perspectives on institutional design (Chapter 3) and a cross-country review of international water management institutions as empirical basis (Chapter 4). Part II analyzes the cooperation problem and institutional implications from an economic perspective. Special attention is being given

---

[24] Scharpf (1997: 28) notes for the area of public policy analysis: 'However, since our methods for subjecting hypotheses to quantitative empirical tests are inherently weak, this requires a shift of emphasis in the methodological discussion – away from the dominant focus on the quality of testing procedures and toward *a greater concern for the quality of the hypotheses that we bring to our empirical material*' (i.i.o.).

[25] The term 'hydro-economic' is used in order to signify that in the respective chapter different types of hydrological problems are conceptualized as economic problems.

to the role of problem structure (Chapter 5), the role of issue linkage as a negotiation strategy (Chapter 6) and the role of international organizations (Chapter 7). Figure 1.4 indicates how each of the chapters in Part I provides a distinct foundation for the economic analysis of the cooperation problem and institutions in Part II.

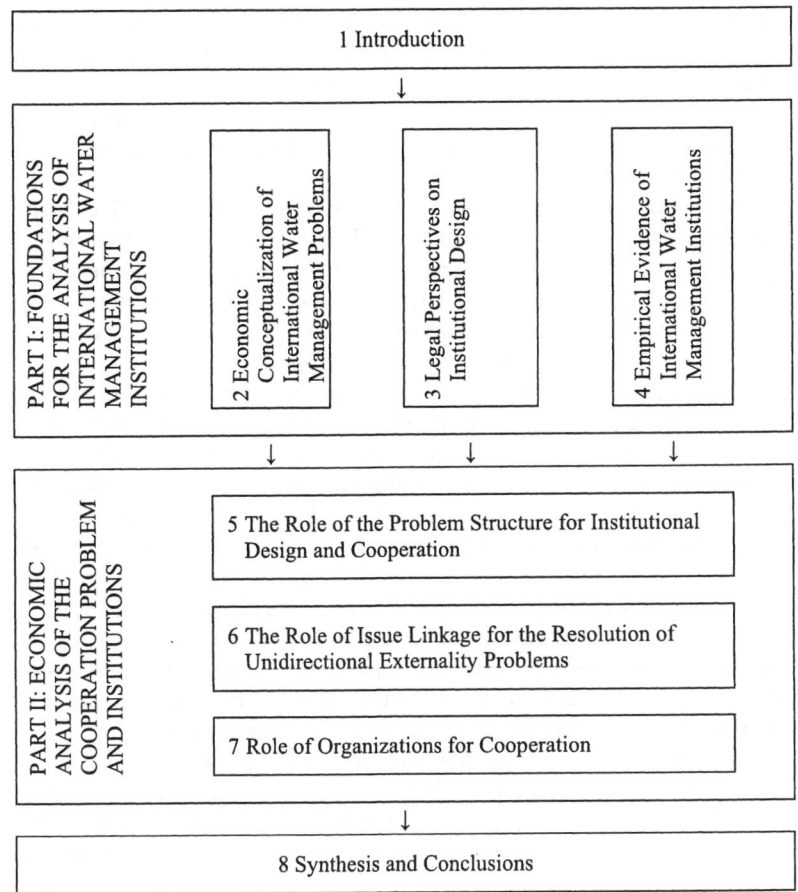

Source: Own presentation

Figure 1.4   Structure of the Book

Chapter 2 provides an economic conceptualization of different problem structures in the management of international water. It describes the multiple functions water plays as an economic resource and identifies different types of externalities in the use of international waters. Depending on the use the chapter distinguishes negative and positive externality problems and depending on the alignment of borders it differentiates between reciprocal and unidirectional externality problems. As such Chapter 2 provides an economic analysis of the resource and conceptualizes the cooperation problem, providing the link between hydrology and economics. The economic analysis of the cooperation problem and of institutions to manage the cooperation problem will be pursued in Part II.

Chapter 3 examines the role of international law in international water negotiations as well as legal perspectives on the design of international water management institutions. It draws upon the law of international watercourses and international institutional law. It shows that there is no external authority that could define property rights to water but that they are themselves subject to negotiation. It furthermore presents legal perspectives on the design of international water management institutions, both at the level of property rights and at the level of organizations. This will allow the contrasting of economic and legal perspectives later on in the book.

Chapter 4 provides empirical evidence in the form of a cross-country review of international water management institutions. It takes stock of the global coverage of international river basins with agreements and organizations and of the variety of the institutional solutions chosen. In analyzing institutional variety special attention is given to the geographical and substantive scope of respective agreements and the forms and functions of associated organizations. Overall the chapter serves as an empirical reference point and partly also as a test for the economic analysis in Part II.

Chapter 5 analyzes the role of the problem structure for the prospects of cooperation and analyzes institutional implications. In a first step it analyzes the relationship between problem structure and institutional design, drawing upon the theory of externalities and non-cooperative game theory. In a second step it takes up the externality problems in the management of international waters identified in Chapter 2 and reconstructs them in a game-theoretic manner. The chapter argues whether cooperation can be expected depends on the underlying problem structure and on the way incentives are restructured by international agreements.

Chapter 6 focuses on the role of issue linkage for the resolution of unidirectional externality problems. Issue linkage may be considered as a negotiation strategy to overcome asymmetric actor constellations. The issues to be linked may stem from different economic sectors, however, given the multi-functionality of water there may also be opportunities for linking different issues within the water sector. The analysis of opportunities for intra-water issue linkage shows to which extent the integration of different water uses is in the interest of the players involved.

Chapter 7 finally addresses the role of international organizations in promoting cooperation on international waters. It draws upon transaction cost economics and actor-centered institutionalism. In contrast to Chapters 5 and 6 the question is not how institutions may emerge from voluntary interaction, but how different institutional settings, including international organizations, can be expected to influence the problem-solving capacity of the actors involved under incomplete information.

Chapter 8 summarizes the main findings and provides a synthesis at two levels. First it revisits the relationship of theoretical and empirical findings in this book (and as such of Chapter 4 and Part II). Second it revisits the interrelationship of law and economics in the analysis of international water management institutions (and as such of Chapter 3 and Part II). It furthermore discusses policy implications and identifies further research needs.

PART I

Foundations for the Analysis of International Water Management Institutions

2. Economic Conceptualization of International Water Management Problems

This chapter seeks to set the scene for the following analyses by presenting an economic conceptualization of water resources management. It describes the multiple functions water plays as an economic resource and identifies different types of externalities in the use of international waters depending on the underlying water uses and the alignment of hydrological and political boundaries. In doing so the chapters seek to develop an economic language with which the complex of water resources management can be described. The resulting typology of problem structures will serve as a starting point for the economic analysis of the cooperation problem in Part II.

This chapter is a response to three observations with respect to the state of the literature. First the literature on water resources management is still dominated by natural scientists and engineers on the on hand (e.g. Cech 2003) and practitioners on the other (e.g. GWP 2000), and economic conceptualizations of water resources management are rare. Second most economic analyses of international water problems only analyze one specific problem, such as a water quantity or a water pollution problem (e.g. Kilgour and Dinar 1995; Durth 1996; Ambec and Sprumont 2002), and only few economists have acknowledged the fact that there may be different economic types of problems in the use of international waters (e.g. Rogers 1993; Barrett 1994b; Sadoff et al. 2002). For an analysis of institutions the latter is significant in so far, as if there are different economic problem structures, this is likely to have implications for institutional design. Third even where different economic types of problems have been acknowledged, these have not necessarily yet been described in a systematic fashion. Therefore this chapter steps back and seeks to identify the range of different problems in the use of international water resources in a systematic manner. As such the chapter lays the ground for a differentiated analysis of institutional responses (Chapter 5) and for dealing with problems that arise from the interaction of different uses (Chapter 6) and as such for addressing institutions and the question of integration later on in the study.

Section 2.1 will characterize water as an economic resource. Section 2.2 will differentiate between different types of externality problems in the use of international waters.

2.1   WATER AS AN ECONOMIC RESOURCE

Water is a renewable natural resource that serves many different functions. Section 2.1.1 will introduce into the hydrological cycle, within which water is made available. Section 2.1.2 will address resource functions, the spectrum of water uses and related infrastructure requirements. Section 2.1.3 will ask for relevant actors in the management of water resources and levels of interaction. As such this section lays the ground for the subsequent analysis of externality problems in the use of international water resources.

2.1.1   The Hydrological Cycle

Freshwater is a renewable resource. It is made available through an ongoing process of precipitation, runoff, storage and evaporation known as the hydrological cycle. The latter describes the movement of water between the land, oceans and the atmosphere or, more abstractly, the stocks, flows and interactions of water as liquid, ice and vapor. Solar energy evaporates water from the oceans and land surface. In the atmosphere water is transported in the form of vapor before it condensates and precipitates as rainfall. Over land rainfall runs off in streams and rivers and finally discharges into the sea or is stored in lakes, the soil, groundwater aquifers or icecaps. There is a net transfer of evaporated water from the oceans to the land and of liquid water from the land to the sea. As such a single water molecule is in permanent movement. Rivers, lakes, aquifers or icecaps constitute different water bodies. The total land area that contributes water to a river is called a river basin (also watershed, drainage basin or catchment area) (Cech 2003: 59). A river basin is delineated by a ridge or drainage divide that marks its boundaries.

The rate of renewal of water resources varies significantly. The average residence time of a water molecule in the atmosphere is about eight days; in deep groundwater aquifers or large glaciers it may be up to hundred thousands of years (Gleick 2000: 20 f.). In some regions freshwater was accumulated a long time ago; this water is known as fossil or non-renewable water.

The total volume of water on earth is estimated at approximately 1.4 billion cubic kilometers (km^3). Of the total amount over 97 percent is saltwater and only 2.5 percent or about 35 million km^3, is freshwater. Of the total freshwater the vast majority is locked in glaciers, permanent snow cover or deep groundwater aquifers. The usable portion of these freshwater resources is estimated to be less than 1 percent or about 200 000 km^3, and even of this amount much is located far away from human settlements (Gleick 2000: 21).

Due to the heterogeneous nature of energy fluxes, land surfaces and the atmosphere water is extremely unevenly distributed in time and space. Some places receive huge quantities of water, while others do not obtain any rain for long periods. Globally the potential water availability is estimated at 7 600 m^3/capita a year (m^3/c*a), varying between 3 920 m^3/c*a in Asia and 82,200 m^3/c*a in Australia and Oceania (Gleick 2000: 217). The average annual freshwater supply including surface water inflows from other countries varies between 0 km^3/year in Bahrain or Malta and 6 950 km^3/year in Brazil (Gleick 2000: 199-202). Inter-temporal variation takes place on every time scale including different inter-seasonal to inter-annual variations. For instance in Asia almost 80 percent of all runoff occurs between May and October. In Australia up to 30 percent of the total runoff may occur in the single month of March (Gleick 2000: 22). The inter-annual coefficient of variation, measured as the standard deviation divided by the mean, varies between 0.08 in Brazil and 0.55 in Portugal (Gleick 2000: 218, selected countries only).

2.1.2 Water Resource Systems, Water Uses and Services

Water is essential for life and a fundamental economic resource. Water resources are used for drinking, basic hygiene and cleaning, agricultural and industrial production, transport, hydropower generation and waste disposal. In addition water resources are habitats for fish and water-related ecosystems and these ecosystems perform important functions for human health, nutrition and recreation. Thus water is a multi-functional resource.

From an economic perspective it is useful to distinguish (1) the resource system and its functions, (2) the appropriation of resource units from the system or water uses and (3) the provision of infrastructure for the appropriation of resource units and for the regulation of the resource system.

The resource system and its functions

Resource systems can be understood as 'stock variables that are capable, under favorable conditions, of producing a maximum quantity of a flow variable without harming the stock or the resource system itself' (Ostrom 1990: 30). Examples of water resource systems are the combined surface water and groundwater systems constituting a river basin, a lake or an isolated groundwater system.

Resource units are 'what individuals appropriate or use from resource systems' (Ostrom 1990: 30). A water resources system produces different streams of resource units (the flow variable), such as a certain water quantity at a certain quality, a certain velocity, a certain self-purification capacity, a certain water storage capacity as well as certain fish stocks and water-dependent ecosystems. As such water resource systems fulfill different water resource functions, i.e. the provision of a certain water quantity for certain uses, the provision of a certain water quality, the regulatory functions of the resource system, the provision of eco-systems, etc.

Often water resource systems are characterized as common pool resources (CPRs), which are characterized by rivalry of consumption and non-excludability of benefits (Ostrom and Ostrom 1977). Rivalry of consumption means that the utilization of a good by one person forecloses its utilization by another person. Non-excludability of benefits means that it is impossible or at least costly to exclude other users from the resource. However strictly spoken, this common pool resource character of water resource systems cannot be generally defined, but only for certain uses (such as water abstraction) and it is questionable whether the criterion of non-excludability applies to rivers.[26]

As mentioned above water is a renewable resource. The amount of resource units that can be appropriated from the resource without harming the stock itself is called the safe yield. In terms of water quantity the safe yield of a freshwater resource is determined by the annual recharge. In the case of groundwater water abstraction beyond the safe yield leads to falling water tables. In some cases this also entails a qualitative deterioration of the resource, e.g. through the intrusion of saltwater in coastal groundwater systems. Hence as long as the average rate of withdrawal does not exceed the safe yield, the resource system is sustained over time.

Appropriation of resource units and water uses

The right to appropriate a resource unit can be understood as a property right to a resource function. Property rights are the rules regulating the use of objects, the capture of income from them and their alienation: 'Property

---

[26] The criterion excludability of benefits can only be usefully be defined on the basis of private law (Grossekettler 1991: 71). Exclusion is always possible on the basis of public law if public authorities have the means to enforce their laws. In the case of rivers upstream riparians may sometimes be in the position to exclude downstream riparians from certain uses. This, however, does not necessarily mean that this exclusion is legally sanctioned.

rights of individuals over assets consist of the rights, or the powers, to consume, obtain income from and alienate these assets' (Barzel 1989: 2).

After water resource units are appropriated, water uses refer to the actual use of resource units for specific purposes. Off-stream water uses include the use of water for drinking, cleaning, agricultural and industrial production and the discharge of wastewater and return flows. In-stream water uses include the use of the water resource system for recreation, navigation, fishing, hydropower generation or the aesthetical appreciation of water resource systems and related ecosystems (Figure 2.1).

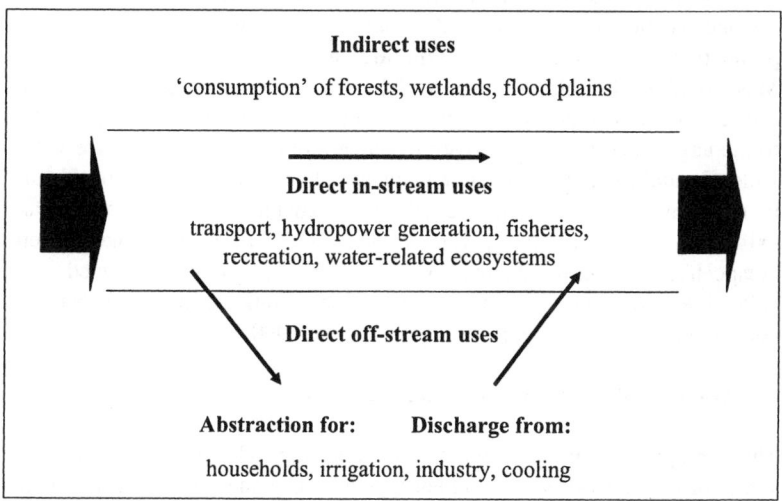

Source: Durth 1996: 25, adapted

Figure 2.1   The Use of Water Resources

Next to these direct water resource uses, indirect water resource uses include uses that affect the resource system indirectly, e.g. though the alteration ('consumption') of forests, wetlands and flood plains within the river basin. These indirect uses mainly affect the regulatory functions of the resource system, both in terms of water quantity and water quality.

The use of water generates a benefit for its user. In some cases it fulfills basic needs essential for life, in others it is used for productive purposes and yet in other cases it serves aesthetic or cultural functions. Under an economic perspective the value of a water resource unit cannot be determined in abstract, but depends on the valuation by a specific user in a specific situation. It may be expressed by the respective individual's willingness-to-pay for the good, which again depends on the individual's preferences and its constraints (e.g. Mitchell and Carson 1989; Hanley and Spash 1993). The unit value of water may differ significantly.[27]

Given these different resource uses there may be competing claims on a resource. There may be competition within a certain use (e.g. water abstraction between upstream and downstream users) and between different uses (e.g. between water abstraction and wastewater discharge, wastewater discharge and fisheries, fisheries and hydropower production, etc.). From a (welfare) economic perspective this competition can be expressed in form of the concept of externalities, understood as the direct (non-monetary) effects of one economic agent's production or consumption activity on the production and consumption possibilities of another economic agent (e.g. Mas-Colell et al. 1995).[28] In view of possible external effects Sadoff et al. (2002: 17-21) distinguish between 'use value' of a resource unit which refers to the aggregated value of a given resource unit to users the 'full use value' which in addition to the use value includes externalities of the use of this unit to other users and the 'full value', which includes non-use (option and existence) values of the given resource unit. From a game-theoretic perspective competing claims to a resource can be characterized as a collective action problem, where individually rational behavior leads to collectively undesirable outcomes (e.g. Ostrom 1990).

Provision of infrastructure or water services

The appropriation of water resource units usually relies on the provision of some form of infrastructure and energy and thus comes at a cost. Examples for water-related infrastructure include bottles and containers, pipelines and distribution systems, treatment plants, dams and reservoirs, dykes, locks, harbors, hydropower plants, fishing equipment, ships, etc. Analogously to the value of water Sadoff et al. (2002: 21-26) distinguish between the 'use costs', 'full use costs' and 'full costs'. For an individual user the 'use costs' of a resource unit comprise the financial costs of providing the unit including capital costs and operation and maintenance costs. However from the perspective of society as a whole, the 'full use costs' include use costs plus use-related externalities and opportunity costs that go along with the provision and use of the respective resource unit (see also Hansjürgens and

---

[27] Sadoff et al. (2002: 18) quote a willingness-to-pay of US$ 3/m³ for small quantities of water for domestic consumption in African cities and of US$ 0.01-0.25/m³ for irrigation purposes.

[28] For a more detailed discussion of the concept of externalities see Section 2.2 and Section 5.1.1.

Messner 2002).[29] The 'full costs' include full use costs plus non-use externalities and opportunity costs.

Often the provision of water infrastructure is carried out collectively, meaning that the respective infrastructure serves a whole group of users. Collectively provided water infrastructure is sometimes also referred to as water service. For instance given that it would be uneconomic for competing providers to run parallel pipelines, water supply and sanitation is usually provided collectively, either by municipal governments on behalf of the population or in the absence of government intervention, users would ideally organize themselves in a 'club' to jointly provide the respective infrastructure (Ostrom and Ostrom 1977; Dombrowsky 2004). Governments usually also organize bulk water supply as well as measures for river regulation and flood control. The provision of water infrastructure may thus raise second order collective action problems in the use of water resources. In addition water-related infrastructure also tends to go along with various externalities (see below).

The above implies that the use of water resources may entail different types of collective action problems. First users have to determine the substractable flow and to determine who has the right to access the resource. Second in view of externalities the question arises what an efficient allocation of a given flow would look like. Third users may have to organize the collective provision of infrastructure for the appropriation of the resource.

At a more abstract level Ostrom et al. (1994) distinguish between appropriation and provision problems. Appropriation problems relate to the allocation of a given flow of resource units among a set of users. In this case the question is what an individual appropriator's efficient level of appropriation is in view of the interdependence created by the resource among a set of users:

> In appropriation problems, the production relationship between yield from the CPR [common pool resource, ID] and the level of inputs required to produce that yield is assumed to be given. The problems to be solved relate to excluding potential beneficiaries and allocating the subtractable flow. This is accomplished by various means, including agreement on the level of appropriation, the method of appropriation, and the allocation of output (Ostrom et al. 1994: 9).

In contrast provision problems pertain to 'creating a resource, maintaining or improving the production capabilities of the resource, or avoiding the destruction of the resource' (Ostrom et al. 1994: 9). Demand-

---

[29] Opportunity costs are the benefits foregone had the resource unit been put to its next-best use.

side provision problems deal with the problem that the combination of individual uses may lead to the collective destruction of the resource. As such it is concerned with determining the total flow that may be appropriated. Supply-side provision problems address the problem of free-riding in the provision of public goods:

> Provision problems focus on the behavioral incentives for appropriators to (a) alter appropriation activities within an existing CPR that alters the productive capacity of the resource, *demand-side* provision, or (b) contribute resources for the provision of maintenance of a CPR, *supply-side* provision (Ostrom et al. 1994: 12, i.i.o.).

Appropriation problems are thus concerned with the flow of the resource and provision problems with the stock of the resource and resource facilities.

2.1.3 Actors in Water Resources Management and Levels of Interaction

Given the multi-functionality of water and the different geographical scales that are involved in the appropriation of resources and the provision of water services, the management of water resources involves a great diversity of different actors. From an economic point of view one may differentiate between different water users (consumers) and different suppliers of water (see Durth 1996).

On the demand side water users can be distinguished according to the different off-stream and in-stream uses of water. Different individuals pursuing the same use can be grouped into user groups or water using sectors. These include the households or the general public, municipalities, industry, agriculture, energy producers, fishers, transport companies, etc. (Table 2.1). Sometimes different individuals organize themselves in interest groups to pursue their respective interests collectively. Such interest groups may include farmer or industrial associations, associations of water works along a river, environmental organizations, etc.

On the supply side it is useful to distinguish between regulators of uses and providers of water services. Given that water is a resource that is being used collectively, within states the right to abstract freshwater and to discharge drainage and wastewater into water bodies is usually granted by the government. Governments thus serve as regulators of property rights to water. Depending on the type of government different levels of government (local/municipal, state, federal) are involved in the water policy process.

For instance in Germany all levels of government – federal, state (Länder), county and municipal – are involved in the water policy process (Kahlenborn and Kraemer 1999; Petry and Dombrowsky N.d.). While the federal government has only framework competencies, the main responsibility for water management is with the German states, mostly located in the state environment and agriculture ministries. The states are responsible for all issues pertaining to water quantity, water quality and flood control, with the exception of navigation, which is under the responsibility of the Federal Ministry of Transport. Municipal governments oversee the provision of water supply and sanitation. In some cases the systems are operated by municipally owned operators; in other cases municipalities regulate the provision of the respective services by private companies or non-profit organizations.[30] In addition there are special administrative bodies for many different tasks. In some regions, local waters are maintained by special water and drainage associations (*Wasser- und Bodenverbände*). The Federal Shipping and Waterways Administration is responsible for providing and maintaining the navigability of rivers. Hydropower infrastructure is often provided by private companies.

Table 2.1   Classification of Water Users

Water uses	Water users
Water abstraction	
Drinking Water	Municipalities, general public, industry
Irrigation	Agriculture/farmers
Process water	Industry
Cooling water	Energy producers
Water discharge	
Drainage water	Agriculture, municipalities, industry
Wastewater	Municipalities, industry
Cooling water	Energy producers
In-stream uses	
Transport	Inland navigation
Hydropower generation	Energy producers
Fisheries	Fishers, fishing industry
Recreation	General public, tourism
Ecology	General public
Indirect uses	
Consumption of forests, wetlands	Spatial planning, municipalities,
and flood plains	forestry, mining, transport, etc.

Source: Durth 1996, adapted

---

[30] In this case public goods are privately produced. Note that there is a distinction between provision and production (e.g. Musgrave et al. 1994).

Given the multi-functionality of water the policy process usually requires horizontal coordination among different states and different line ministries within the administration and vertical coordination among different levels of government. In Germany coordination among the different federal states in water-related legislative and management matters is institutionalized within the Working Group of the Federal States on Water Problems (LAWA).

In the case of negotiations on international waters the German delegation is usually headed by the Federal Ministry of the Environment, which coordinates the interests of the different federal ministries and the different German states involved and represents German interests at the international level.

The management of water resources is thus carried out by governmental actors, private companies, non governmental organization (NGOs) and individuals and over time, roles and responsibilities have shifted. During the first three quarters of the 20th century in many countries water resources management was primarily a government affair. With the general trend towards devolution, decentralization and deregulation, there has recently been a movement towards the devolution of power towards the local level as well as towards increased private sector participation and the involvement of NGOs in water resources management. The ongoing debate on 'effective water governance' centers around clarifying roles and responsibilities in water resources management at various levels of government (multi-level governance) and between government and non-governmental actors (see German Federal Government 2001; Rogers and Hall 2003).

The following will focus on possible problems and the types of externalities that may occur in the management of international waters. The internal policy process will be neglected in order to focus on the transboundary (international) cooperation potential.

2.2   THE USE OF INTERNATIONAL WATER RESOURCES

Often hydrological and political-administrative boundaries do not match. This mismatch is the rule at the level of municipalities and counties. However often water also transcends state or country boundaries. In the latter case one usually speaks of transboundary water resources. As argued above whenever freshwater crosses an international boundary, we are dealing with international water resources. The left image of Figure 1.1 shows a transboundary river basin in a stylized fashion, indicating the river and its tributaries, the hydrological divide constituting the river basin and the intersection of the river and its basin with various neighboring jurisdictions.

As argued in Section 1.1.3 the mismatch of geophysical and political boundaries may create problems of 'spatial fit' in the use of natural resources (IDGEC 1999; Young 2002). Uses in one jurisdiction may lead to 'externalities' or 'spill-overs' in another jurisdiction. An externality is present whenever the production or consumption activities of one economic agent have direct effects on the production or consumption activities of another economic agent. This definition also applies to resource-mediated externalities that are involved in the use of water resources. The presence of externalities implies that scarce resources are used inefficiently; and they may potentially lead to conflict among the respective users.

A number of authors have hinted at the fact that the use of international waters may involve different types of externalities. Rogers (1993) points out that externalities in the use of water may be negative or positive and emphasizes the unidirectional character of externalities in the use of transboundary rivers. Barrett (1994) distinguishes unidirectional and reciprocal externality problems and economy of scale problems in the use of international waters. Marty (2001) distinguishes negative and positive externality problems at transboundary rivers and 'collective problems' at border rivers or shared lakes.[31] Similar distinctions are also drawn by Sadoff et al. (2002), who, in view of the fact that we are faced with diverse externalities, reject the notion of unidirectional externalities and prefer to speak of 'multidirectional externalities'.[32]

Thus while different types of problems have in principle been described in the literature, different authors use different terminology and tend to emphasize different problems and a uniform typology and terminology of international water management problems still appears to be lacking. Therefore the following section will seek to revisit the nature of externality problems in the management of international waters in a systematic fashion. It will draw on the usual distinction of positive and negative externalities (e.g. Feess 1998) and unidirectional and reciprocal externalities (e.g. Mäler 1990) in economics. Depending on the underlying water use Section 2.2.1 will distinguish between negative and positive transboundary externalities. Depending on the alignment of hydrological and political boundaries, Section 2.2.2 will differentiate between unidirectional and reciprocal externalities. Section 2.2.3 will summarize the findings by presenting a typology of problem structures.

---

[31] In my opinion the term 'collective problems' may hide the fact that we are still dealing with externalities, albeit of a reciprocal nature.

[32] While externalities in river management may indeed take effect in multiple directions, it may still be analytically more useful to first isolate each type of externality and to analyze the interplay of simultaneous external effects in a second step (the latter will be done in Chapter 6).

2.2.1   Negative and Positive Transboundary Externalities

Many water uses and use-related water infrastructure measures are associated with physical repercussions on the resource system, which might create costs or sometimes also benefits, for third parties who also wish to use the resource.

Table 2.2 lists physical effects of water uses – or resource appropriation – and of water infrastructure measures – or service provision – on various functions of the water resource system. This resource functions include its capacity to provide a certain water quantity at a certain quality, the regulatory capacity of the resource system and its capacity to maintain water-related eco-systems. The distinction of externalities stemming from resource appropriation and infrastructure provision may partly seem artificial, as most uses involve an infrastructure component, however from an analytical point of view it appears useful to distinguish externalities related to resource appropriation and infrastructure provision problems.

Table 2.2   Effects of Water Uses and Infrastructure Measures on Resource Functions

Effect on	Water quantity	Water quality	Water regulation	Ecology
Water use/resource appropriation				
Water abstraction	(-)			((-))
Wastewater discharge	((+))	(-)		(-)
Hydropower generation				(-)
Navigation				(-)
Recreational uses				(-)
Fisheries				(-)
Consumption of forests, wetlands and flood plains		(-)	(-)	(-)
Infrastructure measures/provision of services				
Water supply systems	(-)			((-))
Wastewater treatment		(+)		(+)
Erection of dams	((+))	((-))	(+/-)	(-)
River channeling	((+))		(+/-)	(-)
Erection of dykes			(-)	(-)
Provision of retention areas	((+))	((+))	(+)	(+)
Ecosystem protection		(+)	(+)	(+)

Source: Own presentation

In terms of resource appropriation the most 'visible' effects are the negative effects of water abstraction on water quantity and of wastewater discharge on water quality. However as Table 2.2 also indicates, many uses that are usually considered as non-consumptive, such as hydropower generation, navigation or recreation may still have negative repercussions on ecosystem functions. When being referred to as non-consumptive, this means that there is no rivalry of consumption with respect to water quantity. Externalities may also stem from indirect water uses, such as changes in land use (e.g. changes in forest covers), many of which affect water quality or the regulatory functions of the system. Except for the water quantity effect of wastewater discharge, which is positive, the effects of resource appropriation tend to be negative.[33]

In contrast the provision of water infrastructure for a particular user or community may have both positive and negative transboundary effects. Wastewater treatment that benefits the population of state A, also benefits the population of the downstream state B.[34] The erection of dams for hydropower generation will often have positive regulatory effects downstream, but may have negative effects on ecosystems. While the erection of dykes brings benefits for the population behind the dyke, it tends to increase the velocity of the flow and flood risks downstream, thus generating negative externalities downstream. In contrast the provision of retention areas for the benefit of community A also has positive regulatory effects for the communities downstream of A.

These examples show that (1) many infrastructure measures in the use of water resources produce different streams of intended and unintended benefits and costs (so called multi-purpose projects) and (2) often the benefits of a certain infrastructure measure are non-excludable, meaning that they also benefit third parties who do not contribute towards the provision of the good.

Given the multi-functionality and fluidity of the resource, the use of transboundary waters thus tends to go along with pervasive negative and positive transboundary externalities (see also Rogers 1993).

---

[33] There are also natural processes that cause negative downstream effects which are often mistaken for externalities, such as the silt fraction in the Blue Nile flood, which stems from the natural erosion of the Ethiopian plateau.

[34] In the case of wastewater treatment a positive externality is provided in order to remedy a negative externality. As such the complex of water pollution and wastewater treatment may be considered as a combined appropriation and provision problem.

2.2.2   Unidirectional and Reciprocal Transboundary Externalities

In his typology of international environmental problems Mäler (1990) distinguishes between unidirectional and reciprocal externality problems. This distinction also applies to externalities in the use of water resources which may be differently distributed, depending on the relation of hydrological and political boundaries and the behavior of water as a liquid in its respective geophysical environment. The nature of the externality problem differs depending on whether the use involves a transboundary river, a border river or a shared lake or a shared aquifer.

In the case of a transboundary or successive river, the border cuts across the river, separating an upstream and a downstream riparian (Figure 2.2a). Given the flow of the water and given the fact that the water is used consecutively and not simultaneously (Waterbury 1994: 40), in this case externalities are unidirectional (Rogers 1993: 118). A unidirectional externality rules out reciprocal effects in the *same* use. While activity X in an upstream country A may affect a downstream country B, the same activity X in the downstream country B does not physically affect the upstream country A.[35] In the case of transboundary rivers most of these negative and positive external effects are directed downstream, however in some cases downstream uses may also have physical effects upstream.[36] An example may be a downstream dam which is located close to a border and which floods upstream (e.g. the Egyptian Aswan High Dam required resettlement in Sudan). Furthermore in the case of some uses, such as navigation or fish migration, it is the downstream riparian who controls the river. Unidirectional externalities by definition imply an asymmetrical actor constellation (Barrett 2003: 52). They are at the heart of upstream-downstream water conflicts.

In contrast rivers which constitute a common border between two parties are called border or contiguous rivers.[37] In the case of contiguous rivers and

---

[35] Although the externality is unidirectional, the externality problem per se is of a reciprocal nature in the Coasean sense. Any decrease of A's level of economic activity generates a benefit to B, but a loss to A.

[36] Some authors point at the fact that downstream states often develop first in a river basin given that they rely on the use of the river for their water supply and economic activity (the classic example being Egypt) (McCaffrey 1993). These downstream riparians are often the more powerful player in the basin, despite the disadvantageous riparian position. By claiming acquired rights they may factually foreclose development upstream and thus cause negative effects upstream (Sadoff et al. 2002: 35), even if these effects are not physically mediated. Whether these claims are legally vindicable is another matter (see Chapter 3).

[37] There are different methods of drawing a boundary along a river. The 'thalweg' may refer to '(i) the succession of deepest points in the river bed; (ii) the main channel used by navigators when travelling downstream; and (iii) the median line of that main channel' (Caflisch 1998: 5). The 'median line' is the line of all equidistant points from the nearest shore on each side.

aquifers, shared lakes or regional seas external effects are reciprocal in the sense that every actor imposes externalities on himself as well as on all other actors that share the resource (Figure 2.3). In this case activity X by party A has an impact on B, and the same activity X by B has an impact on A (e.g. water abstractions by A and B from a shared lake). Activity X furthermore affects the party causing the effects in the same way it affects the other party. This implies that behavior by one party can be reciprocated by the other party. In some idealized cases the distribution of these reciprocal effects is perfectly symmetrical, in others it may by more asymmetrical, depending on the location of the boundary and the respective level of use. Reciprocal externalities create mutual interdependence in the use of the resource, generating a classic collective action problem.

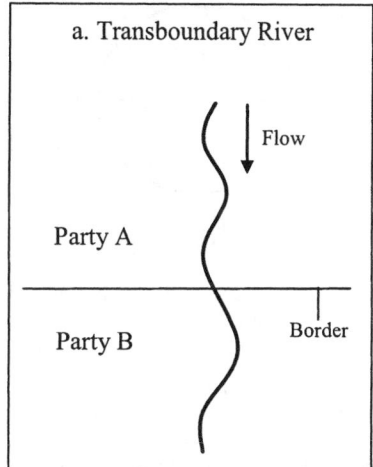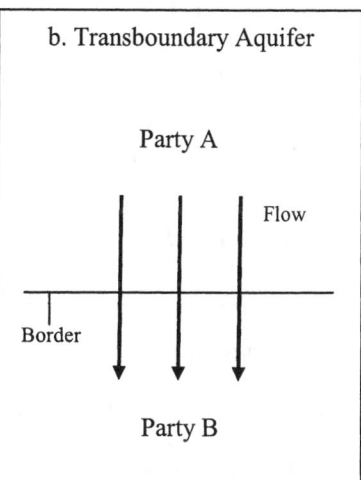

Source: Own presentation

Figure 2.2   Transboundary Rivers and Transboundary Aquifers

In the case of aquifers (Figure 2.2b) the flow is usually also directed, but the aquifer flows at very low velocity and the principle of communicating tubes applies. Also microbiological processes are much slower than in surface water. Aquifers may also be successive or contiguous. While contiguous aquifers can be treated analogously to contiguous river, in the case of transboundary aquifers the nature of external effects depends on the underlying use. In contrast to rivers, water abstraction downstream may cause falling water tables upstream, and the party pumping is always affected in the same way as all other riparians. Water abstraction from aquifers thus represents a case of reciprocal externalities. Water pollution, however, is more directed downstream, and a downstream party is usually not able to affect an upstream party (unless the pumping regime alters the flow of the aquifer). Thus in aquifers the effects of pollution tend to be more unidirectional.

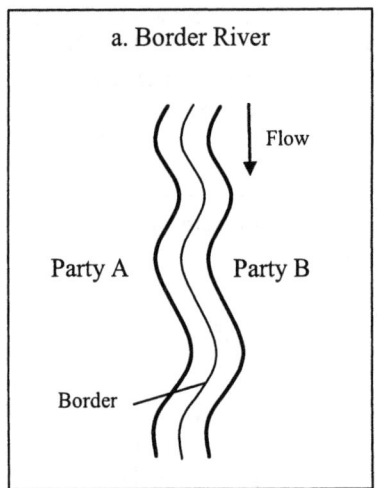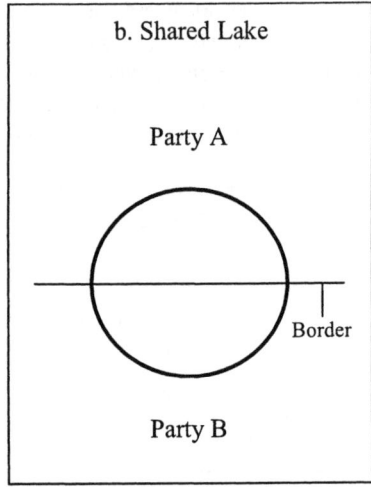

Source: Own presentation

Figure 2.3   Border Rivers and Shared Lakes

While these may be considered the most important basic constellations, in practice we can expect to find mixed forms (see also Toset et al. 2000). For instance two tributaries of the Rio Grande River originate in the USA and one in Mexico. The river then constitutes the common border between the USA and Mexico and finally reenters the USA before it terminates in the Gulf of Mexico. For settings with three riparian countries Kilgour and Dinar (1995) distinguish between the so called I- and Y-geography. In case of the three state I-geography the river is strictly transboundary, flowing from country A in country B and from country B in country C. In the case of the three state Y-geography the river has two tributaries, which originate in countries A and B and which merge in country C. In the case of such mixed forms it obviously matters whether one considers a particular border region only or the entire river basin.

2.2.3   A Typology of International Water Management Problems

The above analysis shows that depending on the respective water use, we may distinguish negative and positive externality problems in the use of international waters, and depending on the alignment of hydrological and political boundaries these externalities may be unidirectional or reciprocal. This implies that from an economic point of view four types of problem structures may be distinguished in the management of international waters (Table 2.3). The first type relates to negative reciprocal externalities. Examples are the water abstraction from a shared lake or aquifer or wastewater discharge into a lake. The second type relates to positive reciprocal externalities. A typical example is the provision of water retention area at a contiguous river. The third type pertains to negative unidirectional externalities. Examples are the upstream abstraction of water or discharge of wastewater. The fourth type addresses positive unidirectional externalities, such as the provision of water storage upstream with water regulation (e.g. flood protection) benefits downstream.

Table 2.3   A Typology of International Water Management Problems

Type of externality	Reciprocal	Unidirectional
Negative	Type 1	Type 3
	E.g.	E.g.
	Water abstraction from a border river/shared lake or aquifer	Upstream water abstraction
		Upstream water pollution
	Wastewater discharge into a border river/shared lake	
Positive	Type 2	Type 4
	E.g.	E.g.
	Wastewater treatment at a border river/shared lake	Upstream wastewater treatment
	Provision of retention area at a border river	Upstream provision of retention area

Source: Own presentation

In the case of unidirectional problems interests and incentives among the respective actors are asymmetrically distributed. In the case of reciprocal externality problems, at least in the ideal case, there is a symmetry of incentives and interests.

From a welfare economic perspective the main problem with externalities is that they lead to an inefficient allocation of scarce resources. A Pareto improvement is possible if a different allocation is feasible that makes at least one actor better off without making any other actor worse off. This raises the question how these external effects can be 'internalized' so that an efficient outcome can be reached. In the language of game theory externalities are an expression of interdependence among actors giving rise to strategic interaction and potential conflict. The economic analysis of how the above different types of externalities can be internalized through the negotiation of agreements and possibly through the set up of organizations will be further pursued in Part II.

Overall the above chapter provided an economic conceptualization of the process of water resources management in general, and of different types international water management problems in particular. Hence water resources management was not presented as a technical or managerial, but as an economic problem. This may sound trivial to an economist, as water constitutes a basic economic resource and performs basic economic functions; however the discourse on water resources management by and large remains dominated by natural scientists and engineers, and only few economists have framed water resources management as an economic problem.

The economic lens on water resources management does not conceptualize the problem in terms of different physical problems and related engineering solutions (such as water quantity, water quality or water regulation problems), but in terms of different types of externality problems depending on the underlying use and the underlying alignment of hydrological and political boundaries. In order to do so this book draws upon the distinction of negative and positive externalities and reciprocal and unidirectional externalities in environmental and resource economics. Part II of this book will argue that these different types of externality problems differ with respect to the institutional requirements in order to manage them in a way that allows for the realization of potential gains of cooperation. Hence the typology developed in this chapter is fundamental to an economic analysis of international water management institutions.

As a further prerequisite for the economic analyses of the cooperation problem and institutions in Part II, Chapter 3 will examine the legal framework conditions for international water negotiations and legal perspectives on institutional design, and Chapter 4 will present empirical evidence of international water management institutions.

3. Legal Perspectives on Institutional Design

This chapter will examine the legal framework conditions for, and the role of, international law in international water negotiations and will present legal perspectives on the design of international water management institutions. As such the chapter serves two main purposes. (1) It specifies the institutional framework conditions under which negotiations on the use of international waters take place. The chapter will show that there is no external authority that could define property rights on international waters, but that they are themselves subject to negotiations. This implies that riparian states have to negotiate property rights and efficiency gains simultaneously. (2) It presents legal perspectives on the design of international water management institutions, both at the level of property rights (the institutional environment) and at the level of organizations (governance structures).[38] This will allow the contrasting of economic and legal perspectives on institutional design later on in the study. A major finding of these comparative legal and economic analyses will be that international law may inform the economic analysis, and the economic analysis may inform international law: International law informs the economic analysis of the externality problem in the management of international waters about customary norms regarding the (initial) definition of property rights and design features of international organizations as reflected by state practice. The economic analysis informs international law about the incentives for interest-based cooperation and expedience considerations in the design of international organizations. In order to get into a position to show how this is the case, international law will be presented in greater detail than what would usually be expected in an economic study.[39]

International law comes in two variants, first in the form of customary law and second in the form of treaties. Customary law emerges from state

---

[38] As will be argued below, these legal considerations are not only of a theoretical nature, but they are informed by the weight of state practice. As such they can be considered as a reflection of actual state behavior and are thus empirically highly relevant.

[39] A very profound treatment of the interrelationship of international customary law and economics in dealing with international environmental problems can be found in Barrett (2003).

practice and is binding on all states. Examples of international customary law are the recognition of 'sovereignty' or the principle of 'borders'. Treaties flow from specific negotiations between countries and are solely binding on their signatories, or more precisely, on those who have ratified the treaties.

Two different directions in international law may inform the design of property rights in the management of international waters and governance structures respectively. The Law of International Watercourses deals with the rights and obligations of watercourse states. As such international watercourse law distills the underlying principles of customary law for property rights negotiations on international waters. The question of institutional arrangements is being touched upon, but it is not at the center of the analysis.

Therefore further insights into the nature and the rights and obligations of international organizations can be gained from International Institutional Law. It is based on an analysis of the commonalities and differences of existing international organizations. As such it provides a basic understanding of the concept and basic features of international organizations. This will serve as an input into the economic analysis of the role of international organizations in Chapter 7.

Section 3.1 will present contributions of the Law of International Watercourses and Section 3.2 of International Institutional Law. Section 3.3 will summarize the findings and will draw conclusions for the economic analysis.

3.1   THE LAW OF INTERNATIONAL WATERCOURSES

Given that customary law emerges from state practice, the discourse on the codification of the law of international watercourses reflects the tension in opinion between riparian states depending on their respective riparian positions and interests. Historically four different principle theories or doctrines have been maintained by riparian states regarding the rights on international waters. (1) The theory of absolute territorial sovereignty maintains that a watercourse state enjoys exclusive authority over the waters of an international watercourse within its territory. (2) According to the theory of absolute territorial integrity a watercourse state has a right to the natural flow of water into its territory. (3) The theory of limited territorial sovereignty maintains that the sovereignty of a state over its territory is limited by the obligation to use the territory in a way that does not cause significant harm to other states. (4) According to the theory of community of interests the physical unity of the watercourse creates a community of interests in the water.

In view of these various, partly contradictory positions the law of international watercourse is an area of international law that has been late to develop (Caflisch 1998). This notwithstanding important steps towards a codification have taken place. In 1911, the Institute of International Law, a non-official expert body of some 130 elected members, adopted the 'Madrid Resolution on International Regulations regarding the Use of International Watercourses'. In 1966, the International Law Association (ILA), an international non governmental organization of about 4000 members, drafted the 'Helsinki Rules' as a comprehensive code of the law of international watercourses with the rule of equitable and reasonable apportionment at its heart, albeit without official standing. This is why in 1970 the UN General Assembly asked the International Law Commission of the United Nations (ILC) to prepare a set of 'Draft Articles' to govern the non-navigational uses of international watercourses. The ILC is responsible for the progressive development of international law and its codification in the United Nations.

The Draft Articles were finalized in 1994. On their basis the Sixth Legal Committee of the UN General Assembly, convening as a 'Working Group of the Whole', negotiated the 'UN Convention on the Law of the Non-navigational Uses of International Watercourses'. The Convention was adopted by the UN General Assembly on 21 May 1997. At the vote in the General Assembly 103 countries voted for the convention, three voted against (Burundi, China and Turkey) and 27 abstained.[40] The convention requires 35 ratifications to enter into force. By 2002, 12 countries had ratified the convention or consented to be bound by the agreement (UNEP 2002: 6). The 1997 UN Convention spells out basic substantive and procedural principles in the use of international watercourses and thus reflects customary norms in the use of international watercourses.

This section presents contributions of the law of international watercourses to the design of international water management institutions. Section 3.1.1 will provide basic definitions. Section 3.1.2 will present the theoretical bases of the law of international watercourses by discussing the above four theories that have been maintained with regard to the allocation of property rights in the use of international watercourses. This discussion will inform the economic analysis of the externality problem in the management of international waters from a legal perspective (see Chapter 5). Section 3.1.2 will furthermore argue that the fourth theory, the theory of

---

[40] Abstentions: Andorra, Argentina, Azerbaijan, Belgium, Bolivia, Bulgaria, Colombia, Cuba, Ecuador, Egypt, Ethiopia, France, Ghana, Guatemala, India, Israel, Mali, Monaco, Mongolia, Pakistan, Panama, Paraguay, Peru, Rwanda, Spain, Tanzania and Uzbekistan. Belgium, Nigeria and Fiji later informed the UN Secretariat that they had intended to vote in favor of the convention, augmenting the affirmative vote to 106 (McCaffrey 2003a: 301).

community of interests, basically represents an economic concept. Section 3.1.3 will address the fundamental rights and obligations of watercourse states as reflected by the 1997 UN Watercourse Convention. The detailed analysis of these principles is of interest for the economic analysis in Part II, as it shows to what extent international law relies on economic arguments, and where it goes beyond them in determining an equitable allocation of property rights to international waters. Section 3.1.4 will analyze the provisions of international watercourse law on organizational aspects. Overall this section draws heavily on McCaffrey (2003a), a recent major volume on the law of international watercourses.

3.1.1   Definitions

The law of international watercourses distinguishes the law of navigational uses and the law of non-navigational uses.[41] The reason is that there has long been a need to codify the rules of navigational uses, while the pressures to deal with conflicts of interests between non-navigational uses emerged much later. Traditionally there had been the view that navigation takes priority over other uses. However as the economic importance of non-navigational uses has significantly increased, this preferred status is not reflected any more in state practice (McCaffrey 2003a: 46-50). The 1997 UN Watercourse Convention states that a priori no use enjoys inherent priority, and conflicts between uses have to be resolved according to the principles of equitable utilization and the obligation not to cause significant harm. This also applies to conflicts between navigational and non-navigational uses (McCaffrey 2003a: 49 f.).

International watercourse law refers to international waters as 'international watercourse'. The choice of the term and its exact definition has itself been a matter of debate, as the exact definition affects the rights and obligations of the riparian states.[42] Article 2 of the 1997 UN Convention defines an international watercourse as follows:

> (a) 'Watercourse' means a system of surface waters and groundwaters constituting by virtue of their physical relationship a unitary whole and normally flowing into a common terminus;

---

[41] While upper riparians are usually in a more powerful position vis-à-vis lower riparians with regard to non-navigational uses, with regard to navigational uses, the power relationship is reversed.

[42] Apparently there was a concern among some states that the alternative term 'international drainage basin' could have resulted in the regulation not only of the use of water, but also of land territory (McCaffrey 2003a: 36 f.).

(b) 'International watercourse' means a watercourse, parts of which are situated in different states.

This definition acknowledges that the watercourse is a system which may consist of different components, such as rivers, tributaries, lakes, aquifers, glaciers, reservoirs and channels which are interrelated with each other. Furthermore it is widely recognized that it refers to both the channel and the water it contains (McCaffrey 2003a: 35).

The term international watercourse does not include confined groundwater. The latter has been defined by the International Law Commission (ILC) as 'groundwater not related to an international watercourse' (McCaffrey 2003a: 37). Again given that the use of groundwater at a larger scale is a fairly recent phenomenon, states have only recently begun to deal with shared groundwater resources. According to McCaffrey (2003a: 433), current practice demonstrates that states tend to apply the principles of the law of international watercourses to confined groundwater too. However the specific characteristics of groundwater, such as its comparatively high vulnerability, raise the question whether this would not justify more stringent protection.

Historically international law furthermore distinguished between contiguous and successive international watercourses. As mentioned in Chapter 1, the former refer to watercourses that form boundaries between states and the latter to those that traverse boundaries. While this is a useful differentiation when it comes to the analysis of particular interest constellations (see Chapters 2 and 5), McCaffrey (2003a: 42) argues that this distinction should not have any legal implications. While the 1971 Declaration of Asunción of the River Plate Basin States imposes more stringent cooperation requirements for contiguous than for successive rivers, according to McCaffrey (2003a: 43), expert bodies and leading commentators have concluded that the legal rules governing both types of watercourses are the same.

Thus different types of uses and resource systems have given rise to different codification processes in international law. However with the possible exception of groundwater, which might require stricter protection, today these different uses and resources are treated on an equal legal basis. This is of interest for the economic analysis of different problem structures in so far, as the underlying legal rules do not differ between the various cases.

3.1.2   Theoretical Bases of International Watercourse Law: Four Theories

As mentioned above, in terms of the positions of riparian states, since the early 20th century international law has distinguished four principle theories, (1) the theory of absolute territorial sovereignty, (2) the theory of absolute territorial integrity, (3) the theory of limited territorial sovereignty and (4) the theory of community of interests. While the first three theories address the rights and obligations of states in a narrow sense, the theory of community of interests asks for the normative consequences of the fact that a watercourse system constitutes a physical unity. In economic terms these different theories reflect different opinions on the allocation of property rights at international waters.

Theory of absolute territorial sovereignty

The theory of absolute territorial sovereignty maintains that a watercourse state enjoys exclusive authority over the waters of an international watercourse within its territory and that in the absence of an agreement, international law places no restrictions upon the use of the watercourse (McCaffrey 2003a: 69). This theory is generally associated with the 'Harmon Doctrine', an opinion given by US Attorney Harmon on the dispute between the USA and Mexico on the Rio Grande waters in 1895. In economic terms the theory of absolute territorial sovereignty corresponds to the laissez-faire rule in the Coase theorem (Coase 1960 and Chapter 5).

The theory of absolute territorial sovereignty is deduced from the principle of territorial sovereignty that states have sovereign authority and therefore complete freedom of action over their territory, including the natural resources within it. However given the flow of water, the question is whether such absolute sovereignty can also be conferred to an international watercourse. Theoretically waters in the territory of a state are those waters in the portion of the international watercourse that are within the borders of the state (at a given point of time). In a successive river, sovereign control over water might be comparatively feasible for an upstream state, although even here attempts to confine water completely are difficult.[43] However in the case of contiguous rivers, the delineation of borders does not give exclusive control over the water in the river channel (McCaffrey 2003a: 70-74). In economic terms even the definition of borders does not guarantee excludability of benefits. Hence a contiguous river has the characteristics of a

---

[43] The flow of a river may, however, largely be stopped through an inter-basin transfer.

common pool resource, which is defined by rivalry of consumption and non-excludability of benefits, and private property rights are difficult to enforce.

From a legal perspective, territorial sovereignty finds its limits where a neighboring state is significantly harmed. In other words the rights of one riparian state are restricted by the rights of the other watercourse states.[44] In the Swiss case Aargau v. Zurich, the Swiss Federal Court in 1878 derived from the principle of sovereignty not an absolute right to dispose of the water, but rather an obligation to recognize the equal sovereignties of the other jurisdictions (McCaffrey 2003a: 331). McCaffrey (2003a: 123 ff.) argues that legal commentators have stopped to support the doctrine since the mid 20th century. He maintains that the theory of absolute territorial sovereignty may be rejected as an anachronism.

According to McCaffrey the doctrine's irrelevance is also supported by the dominant state practice. While it is often argued that upstream states tend to maintain the doctrine of absolute territorial sovereignty, McCaffrey (2003a: 122) cautions whether all statements attributed to the doctrine do indeed support it. Furthermore while some states have at times referred to this doctrine in order to mark a negotiating position (e.g. India, Austria or Chile), no treaty which has flown from such negotiations transports the doctrine. In particular the USA, the country in which the Harmon doctrine was put forward, has never acted according to the doctrine (McCaffrey 1998: 23).[45]

This, however, means that in the management of international waters the laissez-faire rule is not supported by international customary law.

Theory of absolute territorial integrity

The theory of absolute territorial integrity can be seen as the theoretical opposite of the doctrine of absolute territorial sovereignty. It maintains that the upstream state may do nothing which might affect the natural flow of the water into the downstream state. In economic terms the theory of absolute territorial integrity corresponds to the liability rule of the Coase theorem (see Chapter 5).

---

[44] In contrast to economics, which refers to 'property rights', international law speaks of 'rights' and 'obligations'.

[45] The question is, whether there are basins in which upstream states still maintain the doctrine of absolute territorial sovereignty, and in which in consequence no (satisfactory) agreement has been concluded so far. An example might be Turkey. Also even if the weight of existing treaties reflects the doctrine of limited territorial sovereignty, this does not imply that all existing treaties may necessarily be considered as equitable or fair; instead it can be argued they often rather reflect the balance of powers between the respective states. For instance despite an unequal access to water in favor of Israel, the 1994 peace treaty between Israel and Jordan by and large confirms the existing Israeli uses (e.g. Elmusa 1995; Dombrowsky 2003).

Sometimes the theory of absolute territorial integrity is justified by the argument that downstream states cannot physically harm upstream states. However a downstream state maintaining the doctrine of absolute territorial integrity could in fact veto development upstream, and thus 'legally' harm the upstream state – even if that harm is not physically conveyed. As such the doctrine could have extremely negative effects on any water related development in an upstream state.

In principle this doctrine can be rejected for the same reasons as the doctrine of absolute territorial sovereignty. Again McCaffrey questions whether those states that have been attributed to maintain or have maintained this position (e.g. Egypt, Spain, Pakistan or Bolivia) have actually done so or whether their practice de facto reflects this position (McCaffrey 2003a: 130-133).[46] He concludes

> [b]oth doctrines are, in essence, factually myopic and legally "anarchic": they ignore other states' need for and reliance on the waters of an international watercourse, and they deny that sovereignty entails duties as well as rights (McCaffrey 2003a: 135).

Nor does contemporary commentary support the doctrine (McCaffrey 2003a: 123). Hence neither the laissez-faire nor the liability rule of the Coase theorem is supported by international law. Instead international law favors the theory of limited territorial sovereignty.

Theory of limited territorial sovereignty

According to the theory of limited territorial sovereignty, the sovereignty of a state over its territory is limited by the obligation not to use that territory in such a way as to cause significant harm to other states (McCaffrey 2003a: 137). It maintains that watercourse states have rights to use their waters, that those rights are, in principle, equal, and that each state must therefore respect the rights of its co-riparian states. In other words the freedom of one watercourse state is limited by the freedom of the other watercourse state. As such the theory of limited territorial sovereignty represents a compromise between the two extreme doctrines.

---

[46] An example where the US legal advisor maintained a position of absolute territorial integrity is the Trail Smelter case. The Trail Smelter case dealt with sulfur dioxide air pollution from a smelter at Trail, British Columbia, which affected agricultural activities in the US state of Washington. In the end the tribunal recognized the rights of both sides, allowing the smelter to continue operating, subjecting it to emission reduction to avoid unreasonable harm in Washington State. In order to do so, it established a detailed regime for the smelter's operation, taking account of factors such as prevailing winds, climate, growing seasons and called for compensation should it fail to reduce pollution (McCaffrey 2003a: 129f. and 354).

Some commentators explain the doctrine on the basis of neighbourship law which derives neighbourship rights and duties from the physical unity of the watercourse where uses must be compatible with good neighborly relations. Being a good neighbor means both refraining from causing significant physical harm to neighboring states, but also tolerating a certain level of harm emanating from activities in those states (McCaffrey 2003a: 353).

Others found the theory of limited territorial sovereignty on the principle of equity or the doctrine of abuse of rights. According to the abuse of rights doctrine a state's freedom to use its territory would have to be exercised in good faith, and in such a manner as to not to cause unreasonable harm to other states (McCaffrey 2003a: 352). It would thus interpret the doctrine of absolute territorial sovereignty as an abuse of rights.

Today the theory of limited territorial sovereignty represents the prevailing theory of the law of international watercourses, supported by the 'weight' of state practice and by most modern commentators and decisions (McCaffrey 2003a: 137-149).[47] It is also reflected by the Madrid Resolution, the Helsinki Rules and the ILC Draft Articles.

The theory of limited territorial sovereignty has no corresponding initial property rights allocation in Coase's analysis of the externality problem.[48] This, however, implies that international law can inform the economic analysis about fundamental legal – and arguably also ethical – considerations regarding the initial allocation of property rights on international waters. Before discussing the principles underlying the doctrine of limited territorial sovereignty as reflected by the UN Watercourse Convention further, a fourth theory will be presented, the theory of community of interests. It represents a somewhat different theory which asks for the legal implications of the physical unity created by the resource.

---

[47] McCaffrey (2003a) refers to statements of states and agreements in the following cases: the Meuse agreements between Holland and Belgium of 1863 and 1873; the 1906 Boundary Convention between Mexico and the USA; the 1909 Boundary Waters Treaty between Canada and the USA; the 1929 Nile treaty between Egypt and Great Britain on the behalf of the Sudan; the Montevideo Declaration between Bolivia and Chile of 1933; the Johnston plans between Syria, Lebanon, Jordan and Israel in 1955; the 1959 Nile treaty between Egypt and Sudan; the Act of Asunción between Argentina, Brazil and Paraguay of 1971; and the Lake Lanoux arbitration between France and Spain of 1974. Examples of decisions of international courts or tribunals include the Lake Lanoux arbitration in 1974; decision of the International Court of Justice in the Gabčikovo-Nagymaros case in 1997 and outside international waters the Trail Smelter arbitration in 1941.

[48] As will be argued in Chapter 5, in his analysis of the externality problem Coase assumes that either of the two absolute doctrines applies. He argues that from an economic perspective the rule should be chosen that avoids the more serious harm (Coase 1960: 2).

Theory of community of interests

The theory of community of interests maintains that the natural physical unity of a watercourse creates a community of interest or interests in the resource. It is a less well defined concept, although it is not necessarily a new idea, and according to McCaffrey (2003a: 149-171) it may be the direction in which the law of international watercourses will develop.

The theory of community of interests can be said to conform with antic philosophers, the Roman law that considered perennial streams as common or public as well as with natural law theories. According to these interpretations the theory of community of interests is tantamount to the watercourse being the 'common property' of the riparian states. In a number of 18th and 19th century agreements an explicit reference to 'common rivers', or rivers as 'common property', can be found. However 20th century agreements lack such language, although a number of treaties treat the watercourse or related infrastructure as common property, while not necessarily referring to it. An example is the Columbia River Basin Treaty of 1961 which allows the USA to use Canadian territory for water storage. Recently reference to 'shared water resources' has become much more common and is reflected in the Protocol on Shared Watercourse Systems in the Southern African Development Community (SADC) of 1995, or the 1992 agreement between Namibia and South Africa establishing a Permanent Water Commission. The use of the term 'shared waters' can be interpreted as a modern form of emphasizing the common character of international watercourses. Reference to a 'community of interest' is, however, made in the 1929 decision of the Permanent Court of Justice on the jurisdiction of the International Commission for the River Oder. It is also referred to in the 1997 judgment of the International Court of Justice on the Gabčikovo-Nagymaros case.

The theory of community of interests has long been reflected by publicists, however, there appears to be a relatively broad consensus that while states may establish the principle of common property or joint ownership by treaty, customary law by itself does not necessarily create such common property (McCaffrey 2003a: 160 ff.). Huber (1907) rejects the notion that international watercourses are subject to joint ownership because this would imply a restriction of the independence and sovereignty of states (in McCaffrey 2003a: 147). Caflisch (1992: 9) proposes that international rivers should be 'denationalized' and their management be transferred to joint organizations.[49] However he acknowledges that such a condominium

---

[49] In industrial organization such a step would correspond to the set up of a firm (see Coase 1937 and Chapter 7).

can only be established by treaty, but is not necessarily formed by customary law (in McCaffrey 2003a: 164).

McCaffrey (2003a: 167 f.) argues that the fact that a 'community of interests' does not necessarily imply joint ownership is quite obvious in the case of successive rivers, as the upstream riparian might control the flow. But even in the case of contiguous rivers, each state enjoys sovereignty over that portion of the watercourse situated on its side of the boundary. While water molecules move forward and backwards over boundaries, a given water molecule is 'owned' solely by the state in whose territory it is located at a given point in time. According to McCaffrey neighborship law provides a more useful private law analogy than joint or co-ownership. He therefore speaks of an 'extended "neighbourhood"', even if watercourse states are no immediate neighbors, such as in successive rivers with more than two riparian states (McCaffrey 2003a: 170). The implication of these legal considerations for economic theory is that a 'common property regime' is no natural or legal inevitability, but would always be a social construct. Furthermore international lawyers such as McCaffrey prefer to speak of an extended neighbourhood.[50]

McCaffrey makes the case that the theory of community of interests is primarily a positive or descriptive concept. It describes the fact that due to the physical unity of the resource the various riparian states all have interests or even bundles of interests, in the resource system, as such forming a 'community of interests'.[51] At the same time these interests are not necessarily the same, and not all riparian states have necessarily an interest in the entire watercourse. While some interests may be complementary, others may be conflictive. Furthermore these inter-related interests may provide the impetus for some form of collective action and further institutionalization. The latter may be reflected by a regime of joint institutional management of the watercourse. According to McCaffrey (2003a: 159 f.), the establishment of a great number of international water commissions can be interpreted as an expression of the principle of community of interests.

However the theory of community of interests does not in itself entail a legal implication (McCaffrey 2003a: 170 f.). While it can be argued that states with interests in the same watercourse should work together, international law does not require them to do so. In that sense and going beyond McCaffrey's explicit argumentation, the theories of community of

---

[50] It remains unclear whether the economic categories of private or common property rights to international waters are legally appropriate.

[51] McCaffrey (2003a: 165) defines a state's 'interest' in an international watercourse system by the state's 'present and prospective uses of the watercourse as well as its concern for the health of the watercourse system'.

interests and limited territorial sovereignty are not equivalent alternatives, but rather complement each other. Legal obligations that flow from limited territorial sovereignty, such as the obligation to cooperate, reinforce the concept of community of interest, and the concept of community of interests informs legal obligations, such as the balancing of interests according to principle of equitable utilization (McCaffrey 2003a: 152 and 171).

This, however, means that legal theory of community of interests as interpreted by McCaffrey (2003a) in essence represents an economic theory: it describes the interrelated interests of riparian states in the resource, and asks for the rationale for collective action and a possible institutionalization. However if the latter is true, the economic analysis of cooperation and institutions in Part II can be understood as an economic elaboration of the legal theory of community of interests. In this case the economic analysis informs international law.

The next section will further elaborate on principles underlying the doctrine of limited territorial sovereignty as reflected by the UN Watercourse Convention.

3.1.3 Rights and Obligations in the 1997 UN Watercourse Convention

As mentioned above, on 21 May 1997, the UN General Assembly adopted the 'UN Convention on the Law of the Non-Navigational Uses of International Watercourses'.[52] The convention has seven parts, Part I, Introduction; Part II, General Principles; Part III, Planned Measures; Part IV, Protection, Preservation and Management; Part V, Harmful Conditions and Emergency Situations; Part VI, Miscellaneous Provisions and Part VII, Final Clauses.

The Convention can be understood as an embodiment of the theory of limited territorial sovereignty. At the core of the Convention are three substantive obligations, (1) the obligation to utilize an international watercourse in an equitable and reasonable manner (Articles 5-6), (2) the duty to prevent significant harm to other riparian states (Article 7) and (3) the obligation to protect international watercourses and their ecosystems against unreasonable degradation (Articles 20-23). While Articles 5-7 were primarily formulated in view of water allocation problems, Articles 20-23 refer to environmental concerns (McCaffrey 2003a: 310). In addition the convention contains two important procedural obligations, (4) the obligation to provide prior notification of planned measures that might affect other watercourse

---

[52] The text of the Convention is reprinted in Annex 1.

states (Articles 11-19) and (5) the general obligation to cooperate with other watercourse states (Article 8).

While the International Law Commission does not specify which norms reflect the progressive development of international law and which represent a codification of the law, McCaffrey argues that the principles of equitable and reasonable utilization, avoidance of significant harm and prior notification reflect the codification of existing norms. The obligations to protect international watercourses and to cooperate can be understood as emerging principles (McCaffrey 2003a: 316).

While the Convention has not yet entered into force,[53] McCaffrey argues that the fact that it has been negotiated in a forum in which each interested state could participate confers to it a high degree of legitimacy and that it is likely that the Convention will serve as a point of departure for future negotiations (McCaffrey 2003a: 316).

Therefore the Convention's obligations will be reviewed in the following in order to further reflect how international law treats the issue of the (initial) allocation of property rights on international waters, and thus how international law can inform the economic analysis.

Before doing so, a short reference shall be made to Article 4 which deals with the parties to watercourse agreements and as such with legal perspectives on the appropriate membership of international water management institutions. Paragraph 1 of Article 4 provides that every watercourse state is entitled to become a party to a watercourse agreement that applies to the entire international watercourse. Paragraph 2 deals with the participation in agreements that cover only a portion of the watercourse. It provides that states that are significantly affected by such agreements are entitled to participate in consultations, and 'where appropriate, in the negotiation thereof in good faith with a view to becoming a party thereto, to the extent that its use is thereby affected'. According to McCaffrey (2003a: 304), the Working Group negotiating the Convention changed Paragraph 2 of the 1994 Draft Articles to the text quoted above. The 'where appropriate' indicates that an affected party would not in any case be able to become a party, in particular when the respective state is only affected by some provisions of the agreement. As such the rights of affected parties were considerably attenuated. According to McCaffrey (2003a: 305)

---

[53] While 103 (+3) countries voted for the Convention in the General Assembly, a number of countries can be expected to have little incentive to sign and ratify the Convention. Some countries may not have a direct interest, as they do not share international watercourses (such as islands), some countries may be satisfied with existing agreements in place, and some may believe they are better off not to ratify because of ongoing dispute (cp. McCaffrey 2003a: 314).

'[o]nly experience with this provision will tell whether the proper balance was struck between inclusiveness, on the one hand, and the possibility of excluding what might be viewed as undesirable interference by a third state, on the other'.

This caveat notwithstanding, Article 4 implies that although broad participation is encouraged by international law, a basin-wide agreement as called for by the concept of River Basin Management is no legal requirement.

Equitable and reasonable utilization

The obligation to utilize an international watercourse in an equitable and reasonable manner can be understood as the cornerstone of the law of international watercourses. It embodies the theory of limited territorial sovereignty. The principle reflects the legal equality of all watercourse states in their right to use the watercourse (equality of right) as well as the principle of the sovereign equality of states. The fundamental status of the doctrine has recently been confirmed by the decision of the International Court of Justice in the 1997 Gabčikovo-Nagymaros case (McCaffrey 2003a: 325).

Equality of rights, however, does not imply an entitlement to an equal share of water. Instead the principle aims at achieving an equitable balance of uses, needs and interests of the respective riparian states (McCaffrey 1998: 728). In order to support such a reconciliation of interests, Article 6 of the Convention lists a range of factors that should be taken into account in determining an equitable utilization, including natural factors, needs, existing and potential uses, efficiency of use and the availability of alternatives. Existing uses are listed as one factor among others; they are thus 'not absolutely protected by international law but neither do they enjoy no protection at all' (McCaffrey 2003a: 339).

What constitutes an equitable utilization can hardly be established unilaterally, but has to be determined by the respective watercourse states in a process of claim and counter-claim, by balancing the factors that are relevant in a given case. This process may be supported by third-party dispute resolution, such as mediation or, ultimately, arbitration by the International Court of Justice.[54] Balancing the various factors is, however, by no means a simple process. Relevant data are not necessarily available, and there may be information asymmetries among the respective riparian states. Riparian states thus have to enter into a process of sharing of information which might be considered sensitive.

---

[54] The International Court of Justice can only decide cases if all sides to a dispute agree to this procedure.

Also equitable utilization is not a static concept that can be determined once for ever, since what can be considered as equitable may change over time. This means that equitable utilization is not only a rule, but has also to be understood as a process (McCaffrey 2003a: 343). Both information problems and the dynamic nature of the problem are strong arguments for an institutionalization of cooperation.[55] This is also why the convention complements the substantive criterion of equitable utilization by procedural obligations.

The above shows that according to international law 'equitable' means the balancing of uses, needs and interests. There is no a priori criterion, but it needs to be established through a process of claim and counter-claim. In doing so, international law lists factors that should be considered. However this implies that in establishing an equitable utilization economic considerations such as prior investments, needs, efficiency of existing uses and access to alternative sources play an important role. This, however, means that it is not only international law that informs the economic analysis on the underlying customary norms, but what is equitable is among others also being informed by economic considerations. However in contrast to an economic analysis of interests and incentives, international law describes due process from the perspective of the impartial third.

Prevention of significant harm

A second substantive criterion of the convention is the obligation not to cause significant harm to other watercourse states. The no harm rule is a general principle of international and domestic law. The term 'significant' refers to harm that is not minor or trivial, but is less that 'substantial' or 'serious' (McCaffrey 2003a: 369 f.). The no harm rule corresponds to the maxim, *sic utere tuo ut alienum non laedas* (so use your own as not to harm that of others).[56] However in the case of international watercourses, a strict application of the no harm rule could lead to a situation in which it sanctions existing uses and forecloses development opportunities for those riparians who wish to develop their water resources later. This is the reason why the no harm rule alone does not suffice as a principle for the use of international watercourses, and the principle of 'equitable and reasonable utilization' has specifically been developed for international watercourses. The co-existence of the equitable utilization and the no harm rule has led to significant

---

[55] Chapter 7 will review the literature on transaction cost economics in order to discuss whether such an institutionalization may be considered to be in the interest of the riparian states involved.

[56] A famous tribunal decision supporting the no harm rule is the Trail Smelter arbitration between Canada and the USA (see above footnote).

controversy as to their relationship. However the 1997 UN Convention does contribute towards clarifying this relationship. According to Article 6, harm to existing uses is only one factor to be considered among others in the determination of an equitable utilization, and according to Article 7, in determining what constitutes significant harm, the equitable utilization principle has to be taken into account. Paragraph 2 states that where significant harm is caused, the state causing the harm shall 'take all appropriate measures, having due regard for the provision of articles 5 and 6, in consultation with the affected state, to eliminate or mitigate such harm and, where appropriate, to discuss the question of compensation'.

This implies that causing harm is not per se wrongful, but that the state causing the harm and the affected state have to jointly resolve the situation by ensuring that overall each state's utilization is equitable and reasonable vis-à-vis the other state's. This might include the payment of compensation of the harming state to the harmed state to the extent that its harm was not reasonable (McCaffrey 2003a: 309).[57] The provisions of Article 7 imply that it is not factual harm, but legal harm, i.e. harm to a legally protected interest that is prohibited (McCaffrey 2003a: 329).

The fact that in the case of international watercourses the no harm rule refers back to the equitable utilization rule has raised the question whether it at all represents an independent norm or whether it has to be understood as part of the principle of equitable utilization. McCaffrey argues that it does indeed qualify as an independent criterion, given its acceptance as a general principle of domestic and international law, however, that in the case of international watercourses it is not interpreted or applied rigidly in state practice (McCaffrey 2003a: 136). It therefore does not embody an absolute standard or supersede the equitable utilization rule where the two appear to be in conflict with each other. Instead the main function of the no harm rule is

> to trigger discussions over (a) whether and to what extent harm has occurred, and if so, (b) whether the source state exercised due diligence to prevent the harm and (c) whether it is reasonable for the complaining state to insist on being free from the harm (McCaffrey 2003a: 380).

In procedural terms first the affected state has to make a prima facie showing that it has been significantly harmed. Then the burden shifts to the alleged harming state which has to show that it has fulfilled its obligation of

---

[57] The commentary to the Helsinki rules states that while an existing use may have to give way to a new use in order to achieve an equitable utilization, compensation would have to be paid for the impairment or discontinuance of the existing use (McCaffrey 2003a: 321).

due diligence to prevent the harm. Due diligence refers to what could reasonably be expected from the state in question in the circumstances. It may be informed by implicitly or explicitly agreed minimum standards in the respective field (such as environmental thresholds) or in their absence, to what can reasonably be expected of a state, having regard for its capabilities. If the alleged state does not carry this burden, it is responsible for breach of the due diligence obligation. If it has fulfilled its due diligence obligation, it must also establish that its conduct or use is equitable and reasonable (McCaffrey 2003a: 380). Due diligence requires that a state does not simply increase its utilization of water until the other states complain, but that states should enter into negotiations early on in the process of planned changes in the use regime.

Last but not least the no harm rule also proscribes certain forms of serious harm. The no harm rule has particularly been promoted in the context of environmental pollution.[58] In the case of environmental harm, the causing of significant harm may be considered per se inequitable and unreasonable, for instance, when the harm threatens human health or is of irreversible nature.

For the economic analysis it is of interest that it is harm to legally protected interests that is prohibited by the no harm rule. As such international law takes a clear legal stand on who has to compensate whom. This is of interest for the economic discussion of side-payments (see Chapter 5). From a legal perspective the starting point for determining who has to compensate whom is an equitable balance of uses, meaning that the no harm rule refers back to the principle of equitable utilization, but also due diligence considerations play a role.

Protection of ecosystems

In addition to the general obligations of equitable utilization and prevention of significant harm, Articles 20-23 of the Convention contain more detailed

---

[58] A famous statement in this context is Principle 21 of the Stockholm Declaration, adopted at the United Nations Conference on the Human Environment in 1972, reading as follows: 'States have, in accordance with the Charter of the United Nations and the principles of international law, the sovereign right to exploit their own resources pursuant to their own environmental policies, and the responsibility to ensure that activities within their jurisdiction or control do not cause damage to the environment of other States or of areas beyond the limits of national jurisdiction' (in McCaffrey 2003a: 358). On the one hand Principle 21 reflects the tension between the right to act freely within the own territory and the duty not to harm others, on the other hand the no harm requirement seems to be quite strict. According to McCaffrey, commentators have concluded that Principle 21 reflects a due diligence obligation. Principle 21 has been reiterated in various international treaties and declarations, such as in Principle 2 of the Rio Declaration 1992 and can be considered as part of the corpus of international law relating to the environment.

environmental provisions. Article 21, Paragraph 2 requires watercourse states to 'prevent, reduce and control pollution of an international watercourse that may cause significant harm to other watercourse States or to their environment'. In this context 'prevent' refers to new and 'reduce' and 'control' to existing pollution. This distinction is relevant, as states tend to apply more stringent standards for new or increased as compared to existing pollution. While Article 21 lacks any reference to equitable utilization, as argued above, significant pollution harm can be understood as tantamount with being inequitable and unreasonable (McCaffrey 2003a: 385, 393). In that sense it can be concluded that the no significant harm rule is more strictly applied in the case of pollution than in the case of water allocation problems, and new pollution is more strictly treated than existing pollution (McCaffrey 2003a: 365).

Paragraph 3 of Article 21 furthermore hints at good practice in dealing with pollution. Watercourse states 'shall, at the request of any of them, consult with a view to arriving at mutually agreeable measures and methods'. Such measures and methods may include joint water quality standards, pollution abatement technology and lists of prohibited substances. Again in order to do so, it might be expedient to institutionalize cooperation.

In addition to the obligation to prevent significant pollution harm of Article 21, Article 20 reflects an emerging obligation to protect and preserve the ecosystems of international watercourses. This obligation is irrespectively of transboundary effects.

Hence for the economic analysis it is of interest that the no harm rule is more strictly applied in the case of pollution than in the case of water quantity problems, and that there is an emerging obligation to protect ecosystems.

Obligation to cooperate

As mentioned above, in addition to the three main substantive obligations, the convention contains two main procedural obligations. The general obligation to cooperate in Article 8, Paragraph 1, requires watercourse state to 'cooperate on the basis of sovereign equality, territorial integrity, mutual benefit and good faith in order to attain optimal utilization and adequate protection of an international watercourse'. Paragraph 2 underlines the importance of joint mechanisms or commissions for such cooperation.[59] As such Article 8 reflects the fact that in order to achieve an optimal and

---

[59] The role of 'joint management mechanisms' is reinforced by Article 24, Paragraph 1 which encourages the establishment of a joint management mechanism.

sustainable management of a river basin, cooperation will almost inevitably be required.

Whether cooperation is in fact an obligation was controversially discussed in the International Law Commission, but in the end Article 8 became part of the ILC Draft Articles. Some argued that under international law there was no general obligation on States to cooperate, and that cooperation was only a guideline for conduct (McCaffrey 2003a: 401). In contrast McCaffrey (2003a: 403 f.) argues that cooperation is the precondition or underpinning of the substantive obligations of the law of international watercourses, such as equitable utilization and no significant harm, and as such it may also be understood as a general obligation.

With reference to the Prisoner's Dilemma, he points at the fact that in the case of contiguous rivers, boundary lakes or shared aquifers cooperation is often in the reciprocal interest of the involved watercourse states, and that even in the case of successive rivers cooperation can be in the self-interest of the states involved, when options for mutual exchange of concessions exist.[60] However given the fact that such options for linkage do not always exist, in his opinion, makes the role of law and the principle of good faith cooperation all the more significant (McCaffrey 2003a: 399).

This line of argumentation is of particular interest in the context of this book, as it again shows a very close interrelationship of law and economics. Basically it is being argued that often cooperation is in the self-interest of the players involved anyway. However where it is not in the immediate interest of all parties involved, international customary law may inform the parties on how to settle disputed property rights in an equitable manner in order to realize gains of cooperation. The question under which conditions cooperation is in the interest of the players involved will be examined in greater detail in Chapters 5 and 6.

Prior notification

Article 12 deals with the obligation of prior notification. It calls for prior notification if a 'significant' adverse effect can be expected from a planned measure. This implies that in order to prevent dispute, the threshold for notification is lower than significant harm. Articles 13-19 contain detailed procedures for the notification process.

The obligation of prior notification applies to upstream and downstream states alike. Sometimes it has been argued that it would not be required for

---

[60] While McCaffrey points out that communication may provide a solution towards overcoming a Prisoner's Dilemma situation (McCaffrey 2003a: 400), Chapter 5 will argue that communication alone may not suffice to enforce the cooperative solution.

downstream countries since they could not physically harm upstream countries. However a downstream country can 'legally' harm an upstream country by altering the equitable balances of uses between the riparian states. Furthermore some measures downstream may even cause physical harm upstream, such as dams flooding into an upstream country.[61] In view of the obligation of equitable utilization, it is clear that it also is incumbent upon downstream countries to notify upstream states:

> By implementing a water development project, a downstream state is creating 'facts on the ground' which will often alter the equitable balance of uses between the upstream and the downstream states and could thus effectively foreclose future uses by the upstream state. This is clearly an 'adverse effect' and also qualified as 'harm', as Ronald Coase has shown, and as the US Supreme Court has recognized in its interstate apportionment decisions (McCaffrey 2003a: 407).

In addition Article 9 contains the obligation to exchange data and information on a regular basis. It can be seen as a necessary part of the obligations of equitable utilization and prevention of significant harm. Often the exchange of information is perceived as first step of cooperation (McCaffrey 2003a: 412). However empirical evidence indicates that states tend to be careful to provide information early on in the process if they are not certain whether this will result in tangible benefits (e.g. Chenoweth and Feitelson 2001).

Thus the principle of prior notification requires states to notify co-riparian states if a 'significant' adverse effect can be expected from a planned measure, i.e. to take possible negative externalities into account early on in the decision-making process.

So far the main emphasis of the legal analysis has been on the definition of property rights. The next section will revisit the contribution of international watercourse law to the set up of organizations and other mechanisms.

3.1.4 International Watercourse Law and the Institutionalization of Negotiations

As indicated above, the theory of community of interests implies that in many situations it may be expedient to institutionalize negotiations on international waters in the form of commissions or other mechanisms. The set up of joint mechanisms is also encouraged by the 1997 UN Convention. Article 24 Paragraph 1 states: 'Watercourse States shall, at the request of any

---

[61] As mentioned in Section 2.2.1, an example is the Aswan High Dam in Egypt, which floods into Sudan.

of them, enter into consultations concerning the management of an international watercourse, which may include the establishment of a joint management mechanism.'[62] Article 24 is reinforced by Article 8, Paragraph 2 according to which riparian states may set up a joint mechanism to facilitate cooperation in view of the experience gained with such mechanism:

> In determining the manner of such cooperation, watercourse States may consider the establishment of joint mechanisms or commissions, as deemed necessary by them, to facilitate cooperation on relevant measures and procedures in the light of experience gained through cooperation in existing joint mechanisms and commissions in various regions.

However while the UN Convention encourages institutionalization, there is no obligation to do so. McCaffrey (1998: 732) explains with respect to Article 8:

> The purpose of this provision seems to be purely didactic; it imposes no obligations on States. Yet it serves as a helpful reminder that the positive experience gained in a variety of regions of the world can be drawn upon profitably in establishing concrete forms of co-operation between riparian States (McCaffrey 1998: 732).

Instead the law of international watercourses only sets the minimum obligations of states (McCaffrey 1998: 728). At the same time state practice shows that many river basins with international water agreements in place also feature the set up of international water commissions and other joint mechanisms. In 1979, the United Nations Secretariat came up with a list of 90 bi- and multipartite commissions (McCaffrey 2003a: 159). In the context of this book, a total of 86 existing organizations were identified (see Chapter 4):

> The sheer number of commissions and other administrative arrangements that have been established by watercourse States – especially States that use international watercourses most intensively – suggests that such joint institutional mechanisms are a natural and logical outgrowth of heavy reliance upon shared water resources, and the interdependence that is its inevitable by-product (McCaffrey 1998: 735).

---

[62] According to the ILC commentary to Article 24 of the 1994 Draft Articles, the term 'mechanism' was chosen to indicate that the management of international watercourses may also be affected through less formal mechanisms than organizations (ILC 1994: 301). Article 24 is believed by many specialists to be too modest in view of the importance of joint commissions (McCaffrey 2003a: 313).

These commissions and joint mechanisms differ greatly in scope, form and function (see Chapter 4). The ILC commentary to Article 24 concludes that the respective design depends on the circumstances at hand, and argues that it would be wrong to proscribe specific forms of organization:

> The powers vested in the respective commissions are tailored to the subject matter of the individual agreements. Thus, the competence of a joint body may be defined rather specifically where a single watercourse is involved and more generally where the agreement covers an international drainage basin or a series of boundary rivers, lakes and aquifers. Article 24 is cast in terms that are intended to be sufficiently general to be appropriate for a framework agreement. At the same time, the article is designed to provide guidance to watercourse States with regard to the powers and functions that could be entrusted to such joint mechanisms or institutions they may decide to establish (ILC 1994: 302).

Thus while the law of international watercourses recommends the set up of specific mechanisms or organizations, it does not come up with particular recommendations as to how these mechanisms should and could look like. Only Article 4 of the UN Convention makes reference to the question of membership of agreements, but neither does it entail strict legal requirements.

This implies that the questions which factors and considerations influence the design of such organizations, and which form and functions are expedient under which circumstances are largely unresolved. Obviously, international watercourse law presumes that it is expedient to institutionalize cooperation. Given that expediency is an economic category, in Part II this issue will be addressed from an economic perspective. Before doing so, the next section will examine the contribution of international institutional law on the nature and features of international organizations.

3.2   INTERNATIONAL INSTITUTIONAL LAW

So far the terms commission, institutional mechanism and international organization have been used rather loosely. This raises the question when interstate cooperation takes the legal form of an international organization. In order to address this question this section will draw on international institutional law. Again this will be done in view of the question how international law and economic theory can inform each other.

Section 3.2.1 will present a legal definition of international organizations. Section 3.2.2 will discuss important features of international organizations. Section 3.2.3 will conclude this sub-chapter by revisiting the relationship of member states and international organizations.

The legal definition and description of international organizations will be used as a starting point for the economic analysis of the role of international organizations in Chapter 7. The analysis of important features of international organizations will provide a guide for the empirical review of the forms and functions of existing organization in Chapter 4.

3.2.1 Legal Definition of International Organizations

In general there is no universally accepted definition of what constitutes an international organization. The authors of an encyclopedic volume on international institutional law define public international organizations as: 'forms of cooperation founded on an international agreement creating at least one organ with a will of its own, established under international law' (Schermers and Blokker 1995: 23). This means that there are three elements to a public international organization.

The first element requires that an international organization be established by the means of an international agreement. The agreement will be concluded between at least two states, and usually takes the form of a treaty. In addition to states, often other international organizations may also become a party to an international organization.

The second element requires that the international organization has at least one organ with a will distinct from the will of its member states. The 'distinct will' is the legal criterion that distinguishes an organ from an agreement:

> The requirement that the organ in question have a will of its own distinguishes organizations from bilateral and multilateral treaties, whereby parties lay down a common will, which remains their own, however, and is not entrusted to a newly created body. This requirement is of a legal nature; in practice it is often difficult for organizations to develop and maintain an identity of their own (Schermers and Blokker 1995: 30).

The distinct will reflects the tension – and problematic relationship – between the international organization and its sovereign members:

> In one way, the international organization is little more than the tool in the hands of the member states, and viewed from this perspective, the distinct will of the organization is little more than a legal fiction. Yet, the international organization, in order to justify its *raison d'être* and its somewhat special status in international law, must insist on having such a distinct will. For, otherwise, it becomes indistinguishable from other forms of cooperation (Klabbers 2002: 12 f., i.i.o.).

According to the third element, the international organization has to be established under international law. This requirement is usually fulfilled when there is an international agreement, unless the agreement specifies otherwise (Schermers and Blokker 1995: 31).

Thus international organizations are established by international agreement under international law and are composed of at least one organ with a distinct will from its member states. While there are exceptions to these rules, from a legal perspective, the above definition distinguishes public international organizations from international corporations and international non governmental organizations, which are usually established under domestic law.[63]

3.2.2   Key Features of International Organizations

The following will portray key design features of international organizations as described by international institutional law, including (1) membership and the rights and obligations of members, (2) the organs of international organizations, (3) the legal status and the power of international organizations, (4) decision-making mechanisms and (5) monitoring and enforcement mechanisms.

These design features reflect empirically relevant aspects of institutional design. They will be revisited in the analysis of specific international river basin organizations in Chapter 4 and inform the economic analysis in Part II.[64]

Membership and rights and obligations of members

Participation in an international organization is usually determined by the need to cooperate. A state may become a member of an international organization through participation in its creation or through subsequent admission. The constitutions of many international organizations enter into force once a certain number of founding states have ratified the underlying agreement (Schermers and Blokker 1995: 59 f.).[65]

There are different ways to end the membership within an international organization. (1) A member may withdraw from the organization. (2) The

---

[63] An example of a water-related international entity which does not have the status of a public international organization is the *Donaukraftwerk-Jochenstein AG*, established by the Federal Republic of Germany, the Free State of Bavaria and Austria in 1952 (Schermers and Blokker 1995: 31). Article 5, Paragraph 1 of the agreement creates the Donaukraftwerk-Jochenstein AG as a joint-stock company under German law.

[64] Chapter 4 will also consider specific functions and financing arrangements.

[65] Barrett (2003) provides an economic reconstruction of the rationale of the so called minimum participation clause.

organization may expel the member. (3) The member or (4) the organization may cease to exist (Schermers and Blokker 1995: 82).

Members have individual and collective rights and obligations (Schermers and Blokker 1995: 108-112). Individual obligations include the duty to cooperate. All member states together collectively control the powers of an international organization. They can modify and even dissolve the organization regardless of the constitutional provisions. They are the masters of the treaty *(Herren der Verträge)*. Single governments and delegations, however, are bound by the provisions of the constitution, unless they obtain a special waiver or approval by all member states. Otherwise they have the option to leave the organization.

Thus states participate in international organizations on voluntary terms; however, once they join an organization this also entails obligations. It will be argued in Chapter 5 that from an economic perspective the rationale for the participation in an (international) organization relies on a cost-benefit calculus (Olson 1965; Barrett 2003).

Organs

Most international organizations are composed of more than one organ. An organ is formed by delegates of two or more states, and must not depend on any particular state (Schermers and Blokker 1995: 29 f.). Different organs may perform distinct functions, and sometimes also check each other. Distinctions are drawn between policy-making and administrative, and between plenary and non-plenary organs. In plenary organs all member states are represented, whereas in non-plenary organs they are not.

The majority of international organizations feature at least one plenary organ as supreme policy-making organ and a secretariat as administrative organ. In addition a number of organizations possess a non-plenary executive organ. Furthermore some organizations have parliamentary and judicial organs, performing advisory and supervisory functions respectively (Schermers and Blokker 1995: 269 ff.).

The general congress or council of ministers is usually the main decision-making organ where all members meet at regular intervals. Decisions are taken on the basis of unanimity, majority voting or consensus (see below). In addition to the general congress, in particular when the total number of members is large, a non-plenary board may be established in order to facilitate the decision-making process. Executive boards play a secondary role under the general congress, while governing boards are equipped with independent powers (Schermers and Blokker 1995: 287).

The general purpose of commissions and committees as subsidiary organs is to support the decision-making process. Plenary commissions are usually set up to prepare the decisions of the general congress between its sessions (Schermers and Blokker 1995: 285). Non-plenary commissions and committees may have different functions (Schermers and Blokker 1995: 294-299). Functional commissions prepare decisions in a specific field. Consultative commissions assemble representatives of different interest groups. There may also be ad hoc commissions and procedural committees, such as drafting committees to formulate agreements.

The purpose of the secretariat as non-plenary administrative organ is to assist the activities of the primary organs. The tasks and influence of the secretariat varies with the tasks and influence of the organization (cp. Schermers and Blokker 1995: 300-316). However states rarely confer substantial powers to international secretariats. In most cases international secretariats do not have the powers and resources to implement decisions, but most of the implementation rests with the member states (Klabbers 2002: 194). Still on many minor issues the secretariat may have the opportunity to take action on behalf of the organization, given that it is the only permanent organ (Schermers and Blokker 1995: 310). Typical functions of the secretariat are listed in Box 3.1. While in the general congress the members represent the views of their countries, the secretariat is supposed to be neutral and impartial.

Box 3.1 Typical Functions of International Secretariats

- Administrative and clerical functions;
- Preparation of the budget;
- Dissemination of information;
- Recording of the work of the organization;
- Collection of reports and information from member states;
- Coordination between different organs of the organization;
- Representation of the organization in private and public law matters;
- Performance of instruction;
- Provision of assistance to members;
- Executive functions by the secretary-general;
- The right of initiative;
- Provision of good offices, mediation, conciliation and arbitration;
- Observation of elections;
- Depository of treaties.

Source: Schermers and Blokker (1995: 300-316)

The staff of the secretariat is usually recruited on the basis of qualification; however, often geographical considerations are taken into account. It is solely bound to the objectives of the organization. Theoretically member states may not exert influence over the staff from their country, and international officials may not favor their own country (Schermers and Blokker 1995: 334-339).

The empirical fact that an international organization may be composed of different organs is of interest for the economic analysis in the sense that whenever this is the case, an international organization has to be conceptualized as a composite interaction modus that combines different types of governance structures. The different functions these organs play can also be explained economically (see Chapter 7).

Legal status and powers

International organizations usually have the status of a legal person in both international and national law (Schermers and Blokker 1995: 976). While the majority of constitutions lack provisions on the legal status of the organizations under international law, the prevailing view maintains that international organizations are 'legal persons not *ipso facto*, but because the status is given to them, either explicitly or, if there is no constitutional attribution of this quality, *implicitly*' (Schermers and Blokker 1995: 979, i.i.o.).

As a legal person the international organization is capable of bearing rights and obligations, for instance to conclude agreements and to maintain diplomatic relations with third parties. Which rights and duties an individual organization has depends on the powers attributed to the organization (Schermers and Blokker 1995: 981). The legal personality is also the qualifying element of an organization as a whole vis-à-vis a mere organ (Schermers and Blokker 1995: 26).

From an economic perspective, the legal status of an organization, i.e. the capability to enter into contracts with third parties, is being perceived as a means to reduce transaction costs (see Chapter 7). The legal personality of an international organization may be considered as one reason for the formal set up of an international organization.

Decision-making mechanisms

Historically as a consequence of the principle of sovereignty, in most international organizations decisions were taken on the basis of unanimity (Schermers and Blokker 1995: 513-518). This is still the case for many small organizations. However in particular in large organizations unanimity may lead to stalemate in the decision-making process. After the Second World War, the United Nations introduced a majority vote for most of its organs, with the notable exception of the UN Security Council, where all permanent members have a veto. However later a number of organizations officially resorted to decision-making on the basis of consensus. According to the United Nations Office of Legal Affairs

> consensus is generally understood to mean adoption of a decision without formal objections and vote; this being possible only when no delegation formally objects to a consensus being recorded, though some delegation may have reservations to the substantive matter at issue or a part of it (in Klabbers 2002: 229).

This means that in international relations, the difference between unanimity and consensus is that in the first case all members have to consent in a formal vote, whereas in the latter a decision may be taken without a formal vote if there is no objection (see also Ipsen 1999: 109).[66] In consequence, those who are not fully satisfied with a decision are not forced to concur in a formal way.

Schermers and Blokker (1995) observe that many international organizations have faced three stages of decision-making: first unanimity, then majority voting and finally consensus. A transition from unanimity to majority voting is particularly conducive if the members of the organization have a basic feeling of belonging to a community and of the sharing of certain basic values. A majority vote may be considered a sign of an organization's relative power vis-à-vis its member states. Such a transfer of powers may be easier in domestic than international institutions, where the 'common good' may be less obvious, and overruling of a minority may be considered as contradictory to notions of sovereignty. The consensus principle can be understood as an intermediary form of decision-making, albeit it is closer to unanimity than to the majority vote. The drawbacks of consensus compared to a majority vote are lengthy negotiations and a frequent loss of substance and lack of transparency. However they are accepted for the sake of maintaining sovereignty and avoiding the overruling of a minority (see Schermers and Blokker 1995: 515). Some organizations include the provision to revert to a qualified majority vote should consensus

---

[66] In his first edition of 'International Institutional Law', Schermers (1980) pointed out that consensus is a political rather than a legal concept. Ipsen (1999) confirms that consensus is not reflected as decision-making procedure in the Vienna Convention on the Law of Treaties. This notwithstanding it appears to emerge as a distinct decision-making mechanism in state practice.

fail in order to prevent consensus from lapsing into unanimity (Klabbers 2002: 230).[67]

Thus the practice of international organizations points at a tension between the unanimity rule, the consensus principle and the majority rule. In chapter 7 this tension will be revisited from an economic perspective.[68]

Monitoring and enforcement mechanisms

As will be argued in Chapter 5, from an economic point of view monitoring and enforcement mechanisms are central institutional features to deal with collective action problems. Schermers and Blokker (1995: 971) point at the fact that the means of international organizations to monitor and enforce compliance by member states are limited and note that supervision and sovereignty are to some extent irreconcilable. However despite this basic irreconcilability, monitoring of compliance with the rules of law has become one of the most important tasks of international organizations, although the methods differ from domestic legal order.

An important instrument for monitoring are reports by member states submitted to the organization. Enforcement is largely restricted to the reaction and interaction of states. The most important sanction mechanism in this context is the sanction of non-participation, the exclusions of benefits from the organization's activities (Schermers and Blokker 1995: 973 and Barrett 2003 for an economic analysis).

The economic significance of monitoring and enforcement will be revisited in Chapter 5. Given the sovereignty of states, Barrett (1994) argues that international agreements must be self-enforcing.

3.2.3 The Relationship of Member States and International Organizations

Overall one of the key characteristics of international organizations is the tension between the sovereignty of its members and the collective purpose pursued through the organization. On the one hand, states determine whether

---

[67] While some authors are quite optimistic about the concept of consensus, Klabbers (2002: 229) and Ipsen (1999: 109) point out that consensus is often found in combination with compensation or package deals. According to Klabbers (2002: 229), such package deals may be inadequate when it comes to the codification of customary rules. These authors are more critical of package deals or issue linkage as a means towards conflict resolution than McCaffrey (2003a) (see Section 3.1.2). The potential and the limits of issue linkage will be addressed from an economic perspective in Chapter 6.

[68] The underlying economic discourse on unanimity versus majority voting goes back to Buchanan and Tullock (1962).

to establish an international organization and to a large extent also determine the fate of their creation. Sovereignty means that states are free to join or leave. On the other hand, once they have joined, sovereignty does not mean that the member states are free to do anything they wish, but as counterparts of the organization they are obligated to carry out their obligations towards the organization and other members in good faith (Schermers and Blokker 1995: 1186). This may lead to the fundamental dilemma of all organizations where collective decisions may conflict with the interests of individual members, a fact that has also been elaborated by economists: 'Just as those who belong to an organization or a group can be presumed to have a common interest, so they obviously also have purely individual interests, different from those of the others in the organization or group' (Olson 1965: 8). Klabbers points out that 'it has long be a frustration that if a theory managed to explain a lot about sovereignty, it could not cope with considerations of community; and where it could cope with community, it was invariably at the expense of considerations of sovereignty' (Klabbers 2002: 5).

In the case of international organizations, sovereignty implies that the means of international organizations to enforce compliance remain extremely limited.

Views on the fate of international organizations are divided. Some argue that increased interdependence in a globalizing world makes international cooperation including the creation of international organizations almost inevitable. They see international organizations as catalysts which demonstrate the benefits of cooperation and the costs of non-cooperation (e.g. Schermers and Blokker 1995: 1188). Others share the notion that specific transboundary problems may bring about benefits of cooperation, but do not believe that this requires the form of a formal international organization (e.g. Klabbers 2002: 338). Still others – the neo-realist school in international relations – see sovereignty as a major impediment towards meaningful international cooperation including international organizations (e.g. Waltz 1979). And yet others are more pessimistic about a state-centric perspective on international relations in general and formal intergovernmental organizations in particular, opting for decentralized transboundary solutions (Blatter and Ingram 2000 for international waters).

In this book the rationale for the set up of international organizations in the management of international waters will be revisited from an economic perspective in Chapter 7. It will be argued that while the set up of a formal organization is not necessarily required, it may help to address information problems, lower transaction costs and extend the shadow of the future. In addition Chapter 4 will provide an overview over existing state practice in international water management.

3.3 SUMMARY AND OUTLOOK

This chapter set out to examine the legal framework conditions for international water negotiations, and to present legal perspectives on the design of international water management institutions both at the level of property rights and at the level of governance structures.

Overall the above analysis shows that there is no external authority in the international system that can impose a solution, but any form of institutionalization in the management of international waters is subject to voluntary negotiations among states. However in doing so international law indicates what may be considered as equitable and as due process in view of the prevailing state practice.[69]

The law of international watercourses informs the economic analysis of the cooperation problem by specifying legal perspectives on the (initial) allocation of property rights to international waters. It rejects the theories of absolute territorial sovereignty and absolute territorial integrity (and thus both the laissez-faire and the liability rule in the Coase theorem), and instead it supports the theory of limited territorial sovereignty according to which the right to use an international watercourse is associated with an obligation to do so in a manner that takes account of the interests of other watercourse states.

The theory of limited territorial sovereignty is underpinned by the principle of equitable and reasonable utilization in the 1997 UN Watercourse Convention. At the international level, the utilization of water can be considered as equitable if it balances the uses, needs and interests of the respective riparian states. What constitutes an equitable utilization cannot be established in abstract, but has to be determined by the respective watercourse states in a process of claim and counter-claim, by balancing the factors that are relevant in a given case.[70] As such international watercourse law informs the economic analysis about due process in establishing property rights to water. However given that the list of factors to be considered also includes economic considerations, economics in turn has something to contribute towards the establishment of an equitable utilization.

With respect to the design of governance structures, international watercourse law does not come up with specific recommendations. While it argues that an institutionalization is often in the interest of the parties

---

[69] As such it can be argued that international law identifies what Ostrom (1990) refers to as 'rules in use' at the international level.

[70] While McCaffrey stresses that the theory of limited territorial sovereignty is supported by the weight of state practice, the considerations underpinning the principle of equitable utilization are of a theoretical nature – indicating how an equitable utilization should be determined.

involved and that it may be conducive towards the establishment of an equitable utilization, the set up of commissions or other mechanisms is no legal requirement. To the contrary it can be argued that the legal theory of community of interests, which posits that the physical unity created by the water creates a community of interests in the water, which may give rise to collective action, is basically an economic concept. Thus the economic analysis in Part II can be perceived as further development of the legal theory of community of interests.

Further insights into the nature and features of international organizations can be elicited from international institutional law. An international organization is established by international agreement under international law and consists of at least one organ with a will distinct from its member states. Participation in an international organization is usually determined by the need to cooperate. All member states together collectively control the powers of the organization. International organizations usually have the status of a legal person. As a legal person, they are capable to conclude agreements and to maintain diplomatic relations with third parties. Most international organizations are composed of at least two organs, a primary plenary decision-making organ and a secretariat as administrative organ. Decisions are usually taken on the basis of unanimity or consensus. An important function of international organizations is monitoring and enforcement, although the means to do so are usually limited.

While international institutional law informs the economic analysis about the nature and typical design features of existing international organizations, it can be argued that the rationale for these features can be further informed by economic considerations. This question will be taken up in Chapter 7 of this book.

Overall it can be argued that international law informs the economic analysis of the externality problem in the management of international waters about customary norms regarding the (initial) definition of property rights and design features of international organizations as reflected by state practice. Conversely, as will be shown in Part II, the economic analysis may inform international law about the incentives for interest-based cooperation and expedience considerations in the design of international organizations. As such this book can be understood to be in the 'law and economics' tradition, which was established by Coase's (1960) seminal article on 'The Problem of Social Cost'. The main findings of how international law and an economic analysis may inform each other will be synthesized in Chapter 8.

Before entering into the economic analysis in Chapter 5, Chapter 4 will provide empirical foundations for an economic analysis of international water management institutions.

4. Empirical Evidence of International Water Management Institutions

This chapter will provide empirical evidence of existing international water management institutions, both at the level of international water agreements as general form of institutionalization and at the level of organizations as more specific form of institutionalization. This will be done with respect to:

- trends in the evolution of international water management institutions and basins covered;
- the geographical and substantive scope of existing arrangements as indicators of their degree of integration; as well as
- the forms and functions of international river basin organizations.[71]

As such this chapter seeks to provide answers to the questions 'Do countries cooperate?' and 'What do existing arrangements look like?'. At this point of the analysis, the primary question is 'What is out there?' rather than 'What ought to be?'.

Overall the chapter seeks to contribute to the empirical literature on international water management institutions by providing an indication of the overall coverage with and the variety of existing institutional solutions. The chapter presents a broad range of detailed design questions negotiators face in the conclusion of international water agreements and in the set up of international river basin organizations. For the first time this chapter systematically explores the geographical and substantive scope of a large number of existing organizations. The findings of the empirical review will serve as a reference point for the economic analysis of international water management institutions in Part II.

Section 4.1 will introduce into the methodology, and Sections 4.2-4.4 will present findings. Section 4.2 will address the question whether countries do cooperate. Section 4.3 will analyze the scope of existing arrangements.

---

[71] The term 'international river basin organization' will be used for organizations pertaining to international river basins or international sections thereof and may refer to transboundary or border rivers, shared lakes or shared aquifers. It will be used as the overriding term, referring to proper organizations, commissions, committees and other forms of organization.

Section 4.4 will deal with the form and functions of existing international river basin organizations. Section 4.5 will summarize the findings and discuss research implications.

4.1   DATA AND METHODOLOGY

The following will provide an overview over relevant databases and literature (Section 4.1.1) and present the methodology chosen for the empirical analysis (Section 4.1.2).

4.1.1   Databases and Literature

There have been several attempts to collect international water treaties. The Food and Agriculture Organization of the United Nations (FAO) has collected more than 3600 treaties between 805 anno Domini (AD) and 1984 pertaining to border issues as well as navigational and non-navigation uses of international watercourses (FAO 1978; FAO 1984). More recently the Oregon State University has compiled a web-based searchable database of international water treaties as part of its Transboundary Freshwater Dispute Database (TFDD). A count on 1 April 2004, revealed a total of 506 documents including general agreements and regional conventions between 28 March 1820 and 3 December 2002.[72] Another searchable database that contains contemporary international water treaties is the FAOLEX database maintained by FAO, which assembles laws and regulations on food, agriculture and renewable natural resources.[73] A search revealed a total of 180 international water treaties.

In addition to these treaty collections a number of studies examine larger numbers of international water management institutions. In the 1970s and 1980s, the United Nations prepared a number of reports which described and compared selected existing international river basin institutions (e.g. UN 1975; UN 1983). In his review of river basin organizations Teclaff (1967) and (1996) also characterizes international organizations. Hamner and Wolf (1998) and Wolf (1998) present a preliminary analysis of selected features of 145 international water agreements. Kliot et al. (1997) undertook a literature

---

[72] See http://ocid.nacse.org/cgi-bin/qml/tfdd/treaties.qml (1 April 2004). The website's commentary explains that '[d]ocuments concerning navigation rights and tariffs, division of fishing rights, and delineation of rivers as borders or other territorial concerns are not included, unless freshwater as a resource is also mentioned in the document, or physical changes are being made that may impact the hydrology of the river system' (see http://www.transboundarywaters.orst.edu/projects/internationalDB.html (1 April 2004)).
[73] See http://faolex.fao.org/faolex/index.htm (30 September 2004).

review of 13 institutional frameworks for transboundary river management. McCaffrey (1998) provides a general overview on the range of forms and functions of international river basin organizations, drawing upon selected examples. A recent report by Burchi and Spreij (2003) lists the features of 19 international river basin organizations. Mostert (2003) reviewed the institutional arrangements and lessons on conflict resolutions based on a total of 23 cases including those analyzed by Burchi and Spreij (2003).[74]

Drawing upon the TFDD database, this chapter will consolidate and further this literature by compiling and analyzing a list of 86 international river basin organizations and by a detailed analysis of 12 organizations. In particular the question of membership and the range of issue areas covered by international agreements and organizations have never been systematically analyzed in the literature for a large number of organizations (see also Bernauer 2002: 12). But also the analysis of form and functions goes beyond McCaffrey's (1998) review. The analysis of scope can be understood as a contribution to the literature on Integrated Water Resources Management, and the question of the substantive scope will be taken up in Chapter 6. The analysis of form and functions will build the foundation for the economic analysis of the role of international organizations in the management of international waters in Chapter 7.

4.1.2 Methodology

The analysis is based on three different data sets: (1) the web-based TFDD database of 506 international water treaties; (2) an own compilation of 86 international river basin organizations; and (3) a more detailed comparative analysis of 12 organizations. These data sets were used to elicit relevant information with respect to overall coverage of basins with institutions, the geographical and substantive scope of existing arrangements and the forms and functions of existing organizations. Where appropriate, these databases were complemented by information from the literature. Table 4.1 indicates which data set provides information on which research question.

Analysis of the TFDD database of 506 treaties

In a first step the TFDD database of 506 international water treaties was used in order to identify the number of international river basins with agreements in place. The database was furthermore analyzed with respect to relevant treaty information. Treaties are searchable according to country, river basin,

---

[74] Other authors have carried out in depth comparative studies of smaller numbers of case studies (e.g. LeMarquand 1977; Durth 1996; Holtrup 1999; Verweij 2000; Marty 2001).

date, principal issue area[75] and so called non-water linkages.[76] In addition the database contains a summary sheet for each treaty including treaty basins, date, signatories, principal issue area and information on whether the treaty includes water allocations, non-water linkages as well as monitoring, enforcement and conflict resolution mechanisms (henceforth referred to as 'treaty characteristics'). This information was used to complement information on the substantive scope of agreements and on the functions of organizations (see Table 4.1).

Table 4.1   Databases and Research Questions

	Do countries cooperate?/ coverage	Geographical scope/ membership	Substantive scope/ issue areas	Form	Functions
506 treaties (TFDD) ↓	x		Principal issue areas, side-payments, issue linkage		
86 organizations ↓	x	x	x		Allocation, monitoring, enforcement, dispute settlement
12 cases		Aspect of the resource system covered		x	x

Notes: x indicates the main source of information

Source: Own presentation

---

[75] The 'principal issue area' refers to the main issue area or water use addressed by the treaty as identified by the TFDD database.

[76] In the TFDD database 'non-water linkages' refer to issue linkages on the basis of 'capital', 'land', 'political concessions' or 'other'. In the context of this book, linkages on the basis of land, political concessions or other are referred to as 'issue linkages' and linkages on the basis of capital are interpreted as 'side-payments'. In addition Chapter 6, which will study the role of issue linkages in international water negotiations in detail, will distinguish between inter-sector and intra-water sector issue linkages. While the former refer to the linkage of a water issue with a non-water issue, the latter refers to the linkage of two water-related issues.

Compilation and analysis of 86 organizations

In a second step the TFDD treaty database and other sources were used to compile a list of international river basin organizations. For this purpose all international river basins with international agreements listed in the TFDD database were reviewed for the existence of organizations. Additional organizations were added from the literature. Table A-1 in Annex 2 lists a total of 86 international river basin organizations. They are sorted by international river basin as defined by the TFDD database.[77]

The list of international river basin organizations should be comprehensive with regard to the coverage of international river basins with respective organizations in place. However it does not purport completeness with regard to the organizations covered. In particular in the case of the Rhine, the Danube and the Po Basins, it does not include all bilateral organizations. Organizations constituted by political entities that do not exist or do not have control over the respective territory any more are also excluded from this list. In particular the Soviet Union established various transboundary water commissions, which are not included. The same holds true for many colonial arrangements. The reason for excluding these cases is that this book sought to compile those organizations which can be expected to be presently in place.

The 86 organizations were analyzed with respect to the total number of river basins covered as well as with respect to their geographical and substantive scope (see Table A-1). In order to determine membership, the number of signatory states was counted. The number of signatories was furthermore compared with the number of basin states. In order to determine the substantive scope, a content analysis of the 86 underlying agreements was carried out with respect to 18 different categories of water uses or 'issue areas' (including those used by the TFDD database).[78] These 18 categories are: water quality; water quantity; hydropower; ecology; flood control; navigation; irrigation; economic development; infrastructure; fishing; river regulation; joint management; hydrological monitoring; erosion control; hazard prevention; melioration; recreation/tourism; border issues and timber floating. Content analysis means that the texts of the respective agreements were checked for the mentioning of any of the underlying search categories. The way the issue was addressed was not examined. In addition each treaty

---

[77] Basins are principally listed in alphabetical order, except for basins that are covered by boundary water commissions. In that case, all basins covered by the respective commission are grouped together.

[78] The preparation of the content analysis of international water agreements was supported by Paul Lehmann.

was reviewed for its TFDD treaty characteristics, i.e. the existence of water allocation, side-payment, issue linkage as well as monitoring, enforcement and dispute settlement mechanisms.

Comparative analysis of 12 cases

In a third step 12 organizations were selected and reviewed in greater detail (see Box 4.1). These organizations have been selected in order to reflect a broad spectrum of scope, forms, functions and contexts. They are listed in Box 4.1 in the order of their degree of organizational complexity.

Box 4.1 Twelve International River Basin Organizations Studied in Greater Detail

- Organization for the Development of the Senegal River (OMVS);
- International Commission for the Protection of the Rhine (ICPR);
- International Commission for the Protection of the Elbe (ICPE);
- Mekong River Commission (MRC);
- Nile Basin Initiative (NBI);
- International Boundary and Water Commission United States and Mexico (IBWC);
- International Joint Commission United States and Canada (IJC);
- German-Czech Commission on Boundary Waters (CBW);[79]
- Permanent Indus Commission (PIC);
- Joint Water Committee Israel and Jordan (ISR-JOR JWC);
- Joint Water Committee Israel and Palestinian Authority (ISR-PAL JWC);
- Permanent Water Commission Namibia and South Africa (PWC).

While the Organization for the Development of the Senegal River (OMVS) features a complex institutional structure and broad responsibilities and supranational authority, the Permanent Water Commission between Namibia and South Africa (PWC) consists of one organ with advisory functions only. The 12 organizations cover commissions in developed and developing countries and include long-standing institutions, such as the International Boundary and Water Commission between the USA and Mexico (IBWC) as well as very recent attempts towards institutionalization such as the Nile Basin Initiative (NBI), which represents a transitional arrangement. The organizations deal with a range of different issues,

---

[79] In German: *deutsch-tschechische Grenzgewässerkommission*, own translation and abbreviation.

including water quantity, water quality, hydropower etc. Except for the recently established organizations, many of the organizations listed have extensively been discussed in the literature and some are considered as comparatively successful examples of transboundary water cooperation. While these 12 organizations reflect a broad range of forms and functions, the number is too small in order to derive conclusions on trends in the relative frequency of certain features.[80]

These 12 organizations were analyzed for a range of issues including the analysis of the exact geographical scope, mandate, treaty organs, additional institutions, staffing of the secretariat, financing arrangements, decision-making mechanisms, legal status and powers of the organization, general functions of the organizations and the secretariat as well as specific provisions on property rights, prior notification, monitoring and enforcement and dispute settlement (see Table A-2). These categories were identified as relevant institutional design features in the content analysis of the underlying treaties. They include the features of international organizations identified by international institutional law (Section 3.2.2). In the analysis they were grouped into categories that pertain to form and those pertaining to function.

4.2   DO STATES COOPERATE? – THE QUESTION OF COVERAGE

The findings of the empirical analysis and literature review with respect to the question whether states do cooperate are divided into two parts. Section 4.2.1 will briefly touch upon the historical development of international water management institutions. Section 4.2.2 will take stock on the number of existing agreements and organizations and provide an account of the overall coverage of international river basins with agreements and organizations.

4.2.1   Historical Development of International Water Institutions

Legal scholars and sociologists point at the fact that water has always been a factor of social organization, giving rise collective action problems between individuals and groups of individuals sharing water resources (e.g. Wittfogel 1957; Teclaff 1967; McCaffrey 2003a). The earliest known transboundary

---

[80] With respect to water allocation, monitoring, enforcement and dispute settlement mechanisms, the findings of the detailed review will be supported by an analysis of the treaties pertaining to the 86 organizations listed in Table A-1 on the basis of their TFDD characterization.

water agreement is a treaty between the Mesopotamian city states of Umma and Lagash, which dates back to 3100 BC (McCaffrey 2003a: 59 f.). In the Rhine Basin the first act concerning transboundary water uses was a unilateral declaration by Charlemagne in 805 AD granting freedom of navigation to a monastery (FAO 1978). The first transboundary dam project in the Rhine Basin was agreed between Austria and Switzerland in 1588 (ibid.) and an agreement dealing with river training works dates back to 1604 (McCaffrey 2003a: 61).

Such early agreements not withstanding, international water agreements and organizations are in principle modern concepts, which have evolved with the rise of the modern nation state, the foundations of which were laid in continental Europe with the Peace of Westphalia in 1648. The Treaty of Westphalia provided for freedom of navigation and following the treaty, 13 international water agreements were concluded in the 17th century (McCaffrey 2003a: 61).

Another milestone in the evolution of international water management institutions was the Vienna Congress of 1815, which lead to the foundation of the Central Commission for Navigation on the Rhine, which was not only the first international river basin organization, but also the first international organization in general (McCaffrey 1998: 733). It is interesting to note that it was the interdependence created by the use of water that gave rise to the foundation of the first modern international organization.

In the 19th century a total of 81 international water agreements were concluded (McCaffrey 2003a: 61). The number of agreements further increased after the Second World War, during the course of decolonialization and after the end of the cold war and the breakdown of the Soviet Union. While many of the early agreements dealt with navigation, after the Second World War, growing populations, industrialization and increasing water quantity and quality problems gave rise to agreements concerning a whole range of different non-navigational uses, including water allocation for different purposes, flood control, hydropower generation, river regulation as well as pollution control and the protection of ecosystems.

4.2.2   Number of Institutions and International Basins Covered

As mentioned above, the Food and Agriculture Organization of the United Nations has listed more than 3600 treaties between 805 AD and 1984 pertaining to boundary issues as well as navigational and non-navigational uses. According to McCaffrey (2003a: 61) this collection includes more than 2000 international legal instruments concerning water resources. Together with the 506 international water treaties on non-navigational issues of the

TFDD database, these figures provide evidence of the perceived need for water-related international agreements.

A count among the 506 treaties listed in the TFDD database revealed that a total of 109 out of the 263 existing international river basins had international water agreements in place.[81] This corresponds to a coverage of international basins with treaties of 42 percent. This implies that more than half of all international river basins (58 percent) do not have transboundary management agreements in place.

At the level of international river basin organizations, as mentioned above, this book identified a total of 86 international river basin organizations, excluding a number of bilateral organizations in the Danube, Rhine and Po Basins as well as Soviet-era and colonial organizations.[82] These 86 organizations were reviewed for the total number of international river basins as well as for bipartite and multipartite basins covered. Bipartite basins are those shared by two riparian countries, and multipartite basins are those shared by three and more riparian countries.

Table 4.2 shows that out of 263 international river basins, a total of 62 – or approximately a quarter (24 percent) – have international river basin organizations in place. In some basins, such as the Rhine or Danube Basins, there are several international water organizations, each with a specific substantive and geographical scope. More than half of these organizations (or 58 percent) can be found in multipartite basins. Overall in bipartite basins, the coverage with international river basin organizations is 15 percent, while in multipartite basins it is 41 percent. This seems to indicate the likelihood that organizations are set up appears to be higher in multipartite basins than in bipartite basins.

Overall these numbers provide evidence that states do cooperate over shared waters. At the same time there is no universal coverage of international river basins, given that less than half of the existing basins have international water agreements, and approximately a quarter have international river basin organizations in place.[83] In more than half of the river basins (57 percent) in which agreements were concluded the respective riparian states also set up organizations.

---

[81] According to UNEP (2002: 7), a study authored by Aaron Wolf, the main author of the TFDD database, there were 106 river basins with agreements in place. According to Wolf et al. (2003: 45), treaties existed in 117 out of the world's 263 international river basins, corresponding to a coverage of 45 percent.

[82] According to McCaffrey (1998: 734), in 1979 the United Nations Secretariat compiled an annotated, yet unpublished, list of 90 international water bodies. It can be expected that some of these 90 organizations have ceased to exist, while new organizations have been formed, in particular after the end of the cold war (see years of foundation in Table A-1).

[83] The numbers of agreements and organizations are only minimum numbers.

This raises the question how these numbers should be interpreted. Among the basins without institutional arrangements there are certainly some, where the abundance of water obviates the need for cooperation and special institutional arrangements (e.g. between Canada and Alaska). This notwithstanding there might also be a number of cases, where prevailing conflicts may have been an obstacle towards cooperation and institutionalization (e.g. between Turkey and its co-riparian states on the Euphrates). At the same it should be noted that this section remains 'legalistic' in the review of the phenomenon of cooperation, as it only analyzes whether an agreement or an organization was put in place, but it does not say anything on their respective effectiveness (see Section 4.5).

Table 4.2   International River Basins with River Basin Organizations

	International River Basins worldwide	Basins with International River Basin Organizations (IRBOs)		
	No.	No.	Share of Total per Basin Type	Share of Basins with IRBOs
All Basins	263	62	0.24	1.00
Bipartite	176	26	0.15	0.42
Multipartite	87	36	0.41	0.58

Database: Table A-1 (Annex); Wolf et al. 1999; http://www.transboundarywaters.orst.edu/ (April 1, 2004)

4.3   THE SCOPE OF EXISTING ARRANGEMENTS – THE QUESTION OF MEMBERSHIP AND ISSUE AREAS

As mentioned in Section 1.1.3 the concept of Integrated Water Resources Management calls for an integrated management of water resources at the level of river basins. In order to analyze how integrated existing international water management institutions are, this section will review the geographical and substantive scope of international water management institutions as indicators of their degree of integration. Section 4.3.1 will address the geographical and Section 4.3.2 the substantive scope of existing arrangements. The subsequent economic analysis in Part II will address the question to what extent 'integration' is in the interest of the players involved.

4.3.1 Geographical Scope

The concept of River Basin Management often suggests that it is desirable to establish special organizational units – so called River Basin Organizations – that cover the geographical area of the river basin. However the questions are what this means in practice, whether a river basin management approach is indeed desirable and what the existing state practice looks like. Obviously one determinant of the geographical scope of an international water institution is its membership, i.e. those riparian states of a river basin that are members to a treaty or organization. In addition the empirical analysis shows that international water institutions also vary with respect to the number of basins, and the aspects of the water resource system covered.

In view of the above, the following analysis of the geographical scope of existing institutional arrangements will be broken down into the analysis of (1) membership, (2) basin versus boundary treaties and (3) the aspects of the resource system covered.

Membership

Membership addresses the question which riparian states of a river basin are members of a treaty or organization. For river basins that are shared by only two riparian countries (bipartite basins) membership of a prospective agreement is self-evident. However for those 87 international river basins with more than two riparian countries (multipartite basins) the question arises which states do and should participate in a respective agreement. While some authors have recommended basin-wide agreements, others have argued that membership should be kept as small as possible in order to enhance the respective agreement's problem-solving capacity (Section 1.1.3). From a legal perspective, affected parties should be able to participate as appropriate, but a basin-approach is no strict requirement (Section 3.1.3). From an economic perspective, it can be argued that membership is a question of the benefits of cooperation and the costs of non-cooperation and as such a question of expedience. This implies that in terms of economics basin-wide management cannot be maintained as a general policy recommendation. Instead what is expedient can only be determined on a case by case basis.[84]

---

[84] Given that Chapter 5 will largely be limited to two-person games, a systematic theoretical treatment of the question of membership will not be provided in this book. However Chapter 5 will allude to issues of membership for the case of N-person Prisoner Dilemma games. This notwithstanding the issue of membership shall be motivated as an economic problem in this chapter.

In a review of 145 treaties since 1945 Hamner and Wolf (1998) showed that 86 percent were bilateral. Using the term 'institution' synonymously with 'agreement', Wolf and his co-workers concluded in a UNEP report that 'of the 106 basins with water institutions, approximately two-thirds have three or more riparian states, yet less than 20 percent of the accompanying agreements are multilateral' (UNEP 2002: 7).

These findings are also principally reflected by the agreements relating to the 86 international river basin organizations listed in Table A-1. Table 4.3 provides a breakdown of these 86 international river basin organizations in bilateral and multilateral organizations. It furthermore identifies the number of basin-wide and boundary water organizations. In this book basin-wide organizations are multilateral organizations that include all riparian countries. Boundary water commissions are bilateral organizations that refer to several boundary and transboundary waters shared by a dyad.

Table 4.3   International River Basin Organizations by Membership

Type of Organization	Number	Share of Total Organizations
Total Organizations	86	1.00
Bilateral Organizations	57	0.66
Multilateral Organizations	29	0.34
Basin-wide Organizations (multipartite basins only)	7	0.08
Boundary Water Commissions	20	0.23

Database: Table A-1

Table 4.3 indicates that among all organizations listed in Table A-1 two thirds are bilateral, and one third is multilateral. However the actual share of existing bilateral organizations is higher, as Table A-1 does not cover all bilateral commissions in the Danube, Po and Rhine Basins. A total of 29 or a third of the 86 organizations are multilateral. These 29 organizations cover a total of 18 multipartite river basins, meaning that 20 percent of all multipartite basins have multilateral organizations in place. Several of them, such as the Rhine, Danube and La Plata Basins, feature several multilateral organizations. Among the multilateral organizations, a total of seven (or 24 percent) are basin-wide. Multipartite river basins with basin-wide organizations include the Niger Basin (nine riparians), the Amazon Basin (eight riparians), the La Plata Basin (five riparians) as well as the Gambia, the Incomati, the Scheldt and the Umbeluzi Basins (with three riparians each). In the case of the Nile, nine out of ten riparians participate in the Nile Basin Initiative, and Eritrea has announced to join.

In addition some sub-basins have sub-basin-wide organizations in place. Examples include Lake Constance, the Moselle, the Meuse or the Rio Pilcomayo Rivers.[85] However when the TFDD classification of international river basins is used as reference, the number of multipartite river basins with strictly basin-wide arrangements is small.[86]

Going beyond the list of 86 organizations, it should be noted that in a number of basins attempts are underway to establish basin-wide arrangements. As the EU Water Framework Directive calls for basin-wide management, basin-wide arrangements have recently been set up for international rivers in Europe. Efforts to established basin-wide arrangements can also be observed in Southern Africa under the Water Protocol of the Southern African Development Community (SADC). In 2000, the four riparian states of the Orange basin established the Orange-Senqu River Commission. In 2003, the Limpopo Watercourse Commission replaced the basin-wide Limpopo Basin Permanent Technical Commission of 1986. In 2004, the Zambezi Watercourse Commission was set up as a basin-wide cooperation mechanism in the Zambezi Basin (Wirkus and Böge 2005; Turton 2005).

This notwithstanding in many of the well-known multilateral river basin organizations membership has historically been limited to a subset of riparian countries. In the International Commission for the Protection of the Rhine (ICPR) only five out of nine riparians participate, however, the geographical share of the non-participating countries in the Rhine Basin is very small. The Mekong River Commission assembles the four lower riparians, while the upper riparians China and Myanmar only participate as observers. In this case China's participation appears quite critical as China pursues major river development plans (e.g. Browder and Ortolano 2000). In the case of the Organization for the Development of the Senegal River the three downstream countries Mali, Mauritania and Senegal are members, while Guinea has observer status. In the Ganges-Brahmaputra-Meghna River Basin with six riparian countries, there are only bilateral agreements in place.

Membership also appears to vary depending on the subject area covered by the respective institution. While a number of water quality agreements are multilateral (such as the International Commissions for the Protection of the Danube, Meuse, Moselle, Rhine, Saar, Scheldt or Lake Constance), the vast majority of all hydropower agreements are bilateral and focus on a particular project at a particular location (see Table A-1). One exception is the Itaipu

---

[85] In the TFDD database the Meuse River Basin is subsumed under the Rhine River Basin; in Europe it is usually treated as an independent river basin.

[86] International river basins as classified by the TFDD database differ in size by a factor of 5000. What might be expedient in one case might not be in another.

hydropower project on the Parana River, in which Argentina, Brazil and Uruguay participate.

Membership alone does not determine the geographical scope of international water agreements, as they also vary with respect to the number of basins, and the aspects of the water resource system covered.

Basin versus boundary treaties

With respect to the number of basins covered by a treaty, two broad types of agreements can be discerned: agreements in relation to a particular river basin or a sub-basin thereof and boundary water agreements among two neighboring countries. The latter type of agreements usually covers a range or all of the transboundary waters shared by the respective dyad. According to Table 4.3, approximately a quarter (23 percent) of the organizations listed in Table A-1 are boundary water commissions.

Well-known boundary water commissions include the IJC between Canada and the USA of 1909 and the IBWC between Mexico and the USA of 1944. IJC explicitly deals with all transboundary waters from coast to coast. The large European river basins, such as the Danube and the Rhine, feature both, multipartite river basin as well as bilateral boundary water commissions.

The late 1980s and 1990s have seen a surge of new boundary water commissions with a total of 13 new commissions created (see Table A-1).

Thus while it is often assumed that it is expedient to establish one organization per basin, practice shows that countries often set up one organization for all rivers along their border. This can be interpreted as a means to minimize transaction costs.

Aspects of the resource system covered

With respect to the aspects of the water resource system covered, a more thorough analysis has been carried out for the 12 river basin organizations indicated in Table A-2. A number of agreements are explicitly limited to the 'waters' or 'water resources' in the respective river basin or sub-basin (e.g. those pertaining to PIC, OMVS and NBI). Some of the more recent basin agreements also refer to 'related resources' and 'ecosystems' (e.g. those related to ICPR, ICPE and MRC). The 1999 Rhine Convention refers to the Rhine between the outlet of Lake Constance and the North Sea, groundwater and ecosystems interacting with the Rhine, and the Rhine catchment insofar as it is important for the pollution and flood control. The 1990 Elbe Convention refers to the Elbe and its drainage area.

In the case of boundary water commissions such as IJC and CBW, the geographical scope is usually more restricted, referring to border rivers, transboundary rivers in the immediate boundary area and cross-boundary water infrastructure. The 1944 IBWC agreement includes the land boundary between the two parties. The Israeli-Jordanian agreement of 1994 refers to specifically delineated parts of the Jordan River Basin and Wadi Araba.

A particular case is the Israeli-Palestinian Interim Agreement of 1995 as it covers all water and sewage resources and systems in the West Bank, but not on the Israeli side. Thus the agreement de facto provides Israel with a veto on Palestinian activities, but the Palestinians have no say on Israeli activities on the Israeli side of the shared aquifer (Dombrowsky 2003). This example shows that the exact treaty provisions matter.

4.3.2 Substantive Scope

Given that water is a multi-functional resource it goes along with a whole range of different uses. In consequence international water agreements may deal with various water uses. As argued in Section 2.2 water uses may differ with respect to the underlying economic structure of the problem (the type of externality problem) and thus with respect to the likelihood of cooperation (Chapter 5). In addition some of these uses may conflict with each other, while others may be complementary. The concept of Integrated Water Resources Management suggests that it is expedient to treat different water uses in an integrated fashion in order to avoid possible conflict and in order to make use of complementary uses. Others recommend more problem-oriented approaches. Furthermore in upstream-downstream settings economic theory argues that it might be possible to overcome unidirectional externality problems through side-payments and issue linkages (see Chapters 5 and 6). Given the multi-functionality of water, in principal, issue linkages may also be possible within the water sector. In view of these considerations, the following analysis of the substantive scope will address (1) the range of issue areas covered by international water treaties and their relative frequency, (2) the range of issue areas per treaty and (3) the application of side-payments and issue linkages.

Issue areas and their relative frequency

As mentioned above, the empirical review carried out in this book identified a total of 18 different water uses or issue areas. This section asks which issues are typically covered by international treaties, and what their relative frequency is.

Figure 4.1 presents a breakdown of all 506 TFDD treaties by 'principal issue area' as categorized within the TFDD database. It shows that in most treaties, the principal issue areas (as interpreted by the authors of the database) pertain to water quantity (27 percent), water quality (20 percent) and hydropower (18 percent). Other treaties mainly refer to border issues (16 percent), infrastructure (11 percent) and economic development (9 percent). Some treaties are classified as 'joint management'[87] (11 percent). Remarkably few agreements deal with flood control (5 percent) as principal issue area. Navigation (9 percent) is only covered when mentioned in association with other water uses or infrastructure measures.

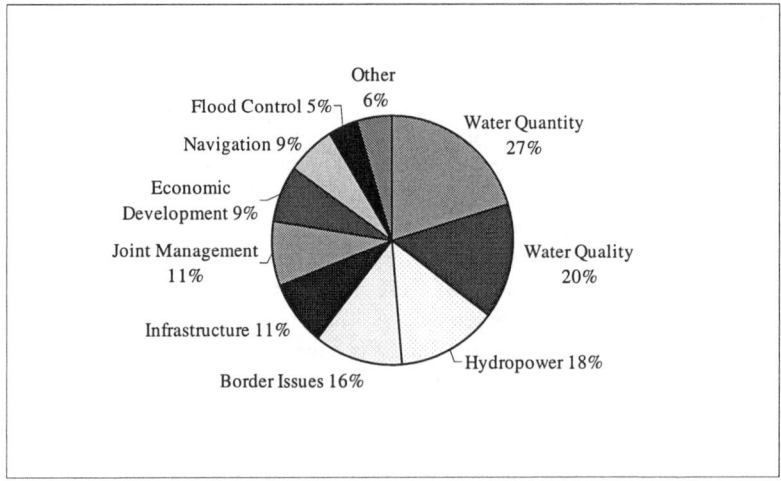

Database: Own compilation based on: http://ocid.nacse.org/cgi-bin/qml/tfdd/treaties.qml (April 1, 2004)

Figure 4.1 Breakdown of 506 International Water Treaties by Principal Issue Area

In contrast the content analysis of the treaty texts underlying the 86 international river basin organizations in Table A-1 reveals a slightly different picture. Figure 4.2 shows that when all issue areas are considered that the respective treaties refer to, the issue area most frequently mentioned is not water quantity ($N = 35$), but quality ($N = 36$), and that ecology ($N = 26$, presumably subsumed under water quality in the TFDD database)

---

[87] This term is not clearly defined on the website.

as well as flood control (N = 18) and navigation (N = 18) appear to play a more important role than for instance border issues or infrastructure. While the detailed review of the 86 treaties certainly does a higher degree of justice to the content of the treaties, the database is of course smaller than in the above analysis.[88]

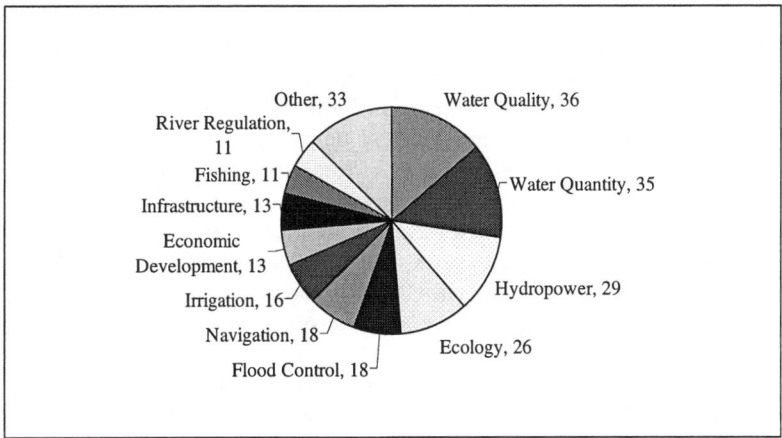

Database: Table A-1

Figure 4.2   Frequency of the Mentioning of Issue Areas in 86 International Water Treaties

It may thus be concluded that the most frequent issue areas addressed by international water treaties are water quality and quantity issues, which are in the same order of magnitude in terms of their frequency, followed by hydropower generation. At the same time the spectrum of issue areas covered is fairly broad with 18 categories identified.

This finding is maybe not surprising as water quantity and quality are obvious issues in every river and may also be considered as overriding issues. In contrast not every river will have significant potential for hydropower generation, and not every river will require flood management. However the dominance of water quality and water quantity agreements is still surprising in so far as these issues have been identified as negative

---

[88] Still the selected 86 treaties provide a relatively representative range of types of treaties, as many of the remaining treaties are precursor for follow-up treaties referring to the same set up. The structural bias of this subset is that it relates to situations in which riparian countries were ready for the set up of an organization. They thus reflect a higher degree of institutionalization.

externality problems, where cooperation – at least in the unidirectional case – is less likely than in the case of positive externality problems (see Chapter 5). This implies that riparian states do address negative externality problems in one way or the other.

Range of issue areas per treaty

The range of issue areas per treaty is an indicator of the substantive degree of integration of a river basin institution. As with membership, policy recommendations go in two directions. While the proponents of Integrated Water Resources Management argue for an integrated approach that takes account of all relevant water using sectors (e.g. to avoid negative side effects), others have recommended a problem-oriented approach that focuses on specific feasible projects. However in some cases it may even be in the interest of respective riparian states to link different water uses in order to overcome asymmetrical actor constellations. Thus the empirical analysis may show whether riparian countries find it convenient to link different water uses.

With regard to the range of issue areas covered by international water agreements, Teclaff (1996) concluded that most international water agreements were single-purpose. However the review of the treaties pertaining to the 86 organizations in Table A-1 reveals a more differentiated picture: Table 4.4 lists the number of agreements by the number of issue areas.[89] It shows that only a third (35 percent) of the agreements is strictly single-purpose. While 60 percent of the agreements include up to two issue areas, 40 percent include more than three issue areas, and 21 percent include more than five. One agreement lists a total of 12 issue areas.

Table 4.4   International Water Agreements by Number of Issue Areas Covered

No. of Issue Areas	≤ 1	≤ 2	≥ 3	≥ 5	≥ 12
No. of Agreements	30	52	34	18	1
Share of Total Agreements (N=86)	0.35	0.60	0.40	0.21	0.01

Database: Table A-1

---

[89] The identification of issue areas is a question of interpretation. In addition the number of agreements per class of issue area also depends on the degree of differentiation among the categories. The issue areas 'water quantity' and 'water quality' usually subsume a number of other issue areas (e.g. water for irrigation).

Besides single purpose treaties, a relatively high number of agreements include up to two issue areas. The obvious reason is that many water uses are related. Most treaties that pertain to water quality also consider ecological issues. Many hydropower agreements make reference to water quantity. The same holds true for the combination of water quantity and river regulation (see Table A-1). At the same time, it remains difficult to judge from these numbers whether certain issues were linked in order to overcome stalemate in asymmetrical negotiation situations, as this would require a more thorough analysis of the underlying treaties. In Chapter 6 the opportunities for intra-water sector issue linkage will be revisited from a theoretical perspective, and reference will be made to selected examples where such an intra-water issue linkage has taken place.

Treaties with side-payments and issue linkages

In particular in upstream-downstream settings, analysts tend to recommend side-payments or issue linkages as means to overcome asymmetrical interest constellations at transboundary rivers. Furthermore it is sometimes assumed that issue linkages may be more acceptable than side-payments. As side-payments and issue linkage are at the center of the economic analysis of unidirectional externality problems in Chapters 5 and 6, the following will ask for the empirical relevance of these design options.

A count among the 506 treaties in the TFDD database for side-payments (search category 'capital') and non-water issue linkage (search categories 'land', 'political concession' and 'other') revealed that in total 48 (9 percent) included a side-payment, and 27 (5 percent) of all treaties included a non-water issue-linkage.[90] In contrast 78 percent of all treaties did not have any reference to side-payments or non-water issue linkages, and the remaining 7 percent of treaties were categorized as 'not available'.[91]

The analysis of the treaties pertaining to the 86 organizations listed in Table A-1 reproduces this pattern. Among them eight treaties include side-payments (9 percent), and six treaties (7 percent) include non-water issue linkages.

In contrast to the above mentioned policy recommendations, these findings appear to indicate that explicit side-payments and non-water issue linkages are not overly common in international water treaties. Clearly these findings have to be read with some caution as they rely on the interpretation

---

[90] The database contains one treaty characterized as 'capital, other' and one treaty characterized as 'land, capital'. For the purpose of this analysis, they are subsumed under 'side-payments'.

[91] The TFDD database includes regional and international conventions. Theoretically they should have been excluded before determining the respective percentages.

of the respective search categories by the authors of the TFDD database. In particular, it is not entirely clear whether the search category 'capital' can indeed be equated with side-payments; it probably indicates that some kind of monetary transfer is being made, whether this has the character of a side-payment has to remain open at this point.

Nevertheless these findings seem to suggest that the acceptability of explicit side-payments and issue linkage is not overly high. This may be in line with the findings of international law that states tend to reject the doctrines of absolute territorial sovereignty or absolute territorial integrity and adhere to the theory of limited territorial sovereignty (Section 3.1.2). In this case there may be less room for side-payments.

A breakdown of the 506 TFDD treaties with side-payments and non-water issue linkage by 'principal issue area' furthermore reveals that whether side-payments or issue-linkage are being applied also depends on the type of treaty. Table 4.5 indicates that 29 percent of all hydropower treaties include a side-payment and 12 percent include non-water issue linkages, while only 2 percent of all water quality treaties include side-payments and only 1 percent issue-linkage. Apparently states have less hesitation to compensate for the provision of hydropower than for pollution control. A possible explanation may be that hydropower generation is being considered as a commodity, while pollution control is being considered as an obligation of all riparian states. This finding would be supported by the above legal interpretation.

Table 4.5   International Water Treaties with Side-payments and Non-water Issue Linkages

Principal Issue Area	Side-Payment ('Capital') (%)	Non-water Issue-Linkage (%)
Water Quantity	12	7
Water Quality	2	1
Flood Control	8	4
Hydropower	29	12
All Treaties (N=506)	9	5

Database: Own compilation based on http://ocid.nacse.org/cgi-bin/qml/tfdd/treaties.qml (April 1, 2004)

Still the question remains why explicit non-water issue linkages are even less common than side-payments. Theoretically issue linkage could be assumed to be more acceptable than side-payments as a pragmatic strategy of reciprocity; however, empirical evidence indicates that this is obviously not the case. One possible answer is that issue linkages are implicit (see for instance LeMarquand 1977). Another possible answer is transaction costs. Given that water negotiations are usually conducted between water agencies, these actors are not necessarily aware of options for non-water issue linkages (high search costs), or the costs of involving other sectors may be prohibitively high (high negotiation costs). Another possibility is that options for such an issue linkage simply do not exist.[92]

Yet another reason is that options for issue linkages are not sought outside, but within the water sector. In principle the water sector does offer some opportunities for internal issue linkage (see Chapter 6). The issue of side-payments and issue linkage will be taken up and analyzed from an economic perspective in Chapters 5 and 6.

While Section 4.3 addressed the geographical and substantive scope of international water management institutions, and as such two important design features of international water management institutions, Section 4.4 will further go into the details of institutional design by analyzing the forms and functions of existing organizations.

4.4 FORMS AND FUNCTIONS OF EXISTING ORGANIZATIONS

Riparian states that set up international water treaties are faced with the question whether they should also establish an international organization and if so, what exact form and which functions this organization should have. In principle there is a whole spectrum of different design options ranging from rather loose forms of cooperation to complex organizations with several organs in place and various competencies delegated from the member states to the organization (see Section 3.2.2). In order to develop a better understanding of the existing state practice, the following will analyze existing international river basin organizations with regard to form and function. As indicated above, the analysis builds upon the detailed review of 12 international river basin organizations.[93] Again the analysis will exhibit the empirical complexity of the problem. The economic rationale for the set up of organizations will be addressed in Part II in Chapter 7.

---

[92] Netanyahu (1998) discusses options for issue linkage for the resolution of the Israeli-Palestinian water problem. However in view of the asymmetry of power between the two parties, she has difficulty to find a convincing package deal. She proposes to link water and security.

[93] As mentioned above, the number is too small in order to derive conclusions on trends in the relative frequency of certain features. The following analysis will focus on the spectrum of variation as reflected by these 12 cases. For a more detailed analysis the reader is referred to Table A-2.

While form and function will be analyzed separately in the following sections, it should be noted that the two aspects are closely interrelated in the sense that ideally form follows functions. Section 4.4.1 will address the form and Section 4.4.2 the functions of international river basin organizations.

4.4.1 Form

The form of international river basin organizations is in essence a function of the powers – or functions – attributed to it. In line with the features of international organizations identified in Section 3.2.2, the following will review important form attributes of international organizations, such as (1) treaty organs including, (2) the role of secretariats, (3) legal status and formal powers, (4) decision-making mechanisms and (5) financing arrangements.

Treaty organs

The spectrum of forms of international river basin organizations is probably best reflected by the organizations' treaty organs and the existence or non-existence of formal administrative support. On the one end of the continuum there are organizations with a hierarchy of decision-making organs and international secretariats in place. On the other end are commissions and committees composed of representatives of each member state that serve as negotiation fora without any formal administrative support.[94]

Organizations with international secretariats include OMVS, ICPR, ICPE, MRC and NBI.[95] However even in these cases, the number of decision-making organs varies (see Table A-2).

Most other cases listed in Table A-2 represent commissions as joint discussion fora without formalized administrative support. In terms of form,

---

[94] The 86 organizations listed in Table A-1 are being referred to as international commissions, councils, committees, authorities and organizations. This raises the question whether name reflects form. From a legal perspective, the term 'organization' may be considered as the more general term, as an international organization may be composed of different organs, including councils, commissions and committees (see Section 3.2.2). A breakdown of the 86 organizations by their respective names in Table A-1 shows that the most common term used in international water management is commission, which is used in 63 percent of the cases; however this also seems to be the least precise term as it includes pure coordination fora as well as organizations with several organs in place. The term committee is used in 20 percent, authority in 7 percent and council and organization in 3 percent of the cases respectively. The term organization appears to be used for more complex organizations, while committees and councils appear to refer to looser forms of cooperation. In some cases the term authority is used for organizations charged with infrastructure operation. Thus the name may only be considered as a partial reflection of the form or structure of an international river basin organization.

[95] For the abbreviations see Box 4.1.

the 'simplest' organization is probably PIC, which consists of one commissioner per country, meeting at least once a year.

The boundary commissions IJC and IBWC can be understood as intermediary forms (McCaffrey 1998: 743). In these cases, each section is supported by its own permanent secretariat.

In addition to the formal treaty organs, most of the more complex basin organizations are supported by additional institutions, such as national coordination units (see Table A-2).

The role of secretariats

As discussed in Section 3.2.2, the purpose of the secretariat as non-plenary administrative organ is to assist the activities of the primary organs. In general the functions of the secretariat vary with the functions of the organizations. While states rarely confer substantial powers to the secretariat, it may still play a considerable role given that it usually represents the organization's only permanent organ. The structural advantage of the secretariat is that it is supposed to be neutral, and solely bound by the objectives of the organization. Depending on the quality of its staff, it may be in a position to play a significant role by exploring technically feasible and mutually acceptable solutions and as such serve as an agenda setter (see Section 7.2.3). Still the question remains how much powers the secretariat should have. It can be argued that if the secretariat has too much power, this may potentially create conflicts with and problems of accountability vis-à-vis the member states.

Another question is what the size of a respective secretariat should ideally have. While it may seem that a larger secretariat may be more powerful, there are still good reasons to keep secretariats small, given that the permanent staff is a significant factor in an organization's operational budget.

As mentioned above, among the 12 international river basin organizations listed in Table A-2 five have international secretariats in place (OMVS, MRC, ICPR, ICPE and NBI). Table 4.6 compares the size and the functions of these secretariats as indicated in their treaties or on their websites.

The respective secretariats differ significantly in size and in the spectrum of management functions entrusted to them. The international secretariat with the most far-reaching executive functions is the High Commission of OMVS, where the High Commission represents the organization between council sessions, followed by MRC's secretariat. These two organizations also have significantly more staff. In contrast the secretariats in the case of the Rhine, Elbe and Nile are small, and their functions are limited to administrative support to the organization. However in particular the ICPR secretariat is being considered as very efficient and effective as the substantive work is carried out in working groups composed of bureaucrats from the member states, which are coordinated by the secretariat (e.g. Holtrup 1999).

Table 4.6   Functions of the Secretariats of International River Basin Organizations

	OMVS	MRC	ICPR	ICPE	NBI
Administrative and clerical functions	x	x	x	x	x
Coordinate measuring programs			x	x	
Manage database	x	x			
Undertake studies	x	x			
Provide technical advice		x			
Propose projects	x				
Coordinate project implementation	x	x			
Monitor implementation	x		x	x	x
Executive functions	x				
Prepare budget	x	x	x	x	x
Seek financing	x				x
Public relations		x	x	x	x
Approximate staff (incl. support staff)	50	50	13	8	10

Database: Table A.2.2

Legal status and formal powers

As discussed in Section 3.2.1, international organizations usually have the status of legal persons in international and national law. For those organizations, for which the legal status is not specified, legal status under international law is often attributed implicitly (depending on the organization's rights and obligations). Closely related to the legal status of an international organization are the formal powers attributed to it, such as the power to enter into agreement, to sue and to be sued or to receive development assistance. The formal powers can be considered as a reflection of the organization's independence from its member states.

A number of the 12 organizations listed in Table A-2 explicitly have the status of international public organizations (OMVS, ICPR, MRC and

IBWC). In addition OMVS and ICPR have the status of a legal person in their respective member states.

Some of the boundary water commissions, such as IBWC and PIC, specify privileges and immunities for their commissioners as well as custom and tax exemptions on material for common works (e.g. IBWC and CBW).

Among the international river basin organizations listed in Table A-2, the organization with the broadest range of competences is OMVS which has the power to enter into contracts, acquire and dispose of property, receive grants and other financial gifts, subscribe to bonds, apply for technical assistance and go to court. According to McCaffrey (1998: 741) '[i]ts broad responsibilities and supranational authority make the OMVS unique among institutional mechanisms for the integrated development and administration of international water resources'.

MRC also has the power to enter into agreements with donors and the international community. For the other organizations listed in Table A-2 there are no specific powers specified.

Decision-making mechanisms

Another characteristic of international organizations is their decision-making mechanism. While in most international organizations decisions are taken by unanimity vote or consensus, as decision-making mechanism without formal objection or vote, a majority vote may be considered a sign of an organization's relative power vis-à-vis its member states (Section 3.2.2). Another sign of an organization's relative power is whether its decisions are binding on the respective member states. However in particular in democracies, decisions by international organizations usually have to be ratified by the parliament of the member countries.

Most of the 12 organizations listed in Table A-2 rely on unanimity or consensus as decision-making modus. In particular some of the newly established organizations without a precursor organization in place appear to show an inclination towards the consensus principle including PWC, ISR-PAL JWC and the NBI Technical Advisory Committee.

In the case of the NBI Council of Ministers, PIC and ISR-JOR JWC the decision-making modus is not explicitly specified.[96]

An exception from unanimity or consensus is IJC where decisions may be taken by majority vote. The commission consists of three commissioners on each side, and the quorum is set at a minimum of four commissioners.

---

[96] However in the two bilateral commissions, unanimity or consensus is self-evident and according to the author's personal experience, the Nile Basin Council of Ministers takes decisions on the basis of consensus.

However given that the organization has only two member states, the majority vote is practically equivalent to unanimity, unless the members within one delegation vote differently.

In OMVS decisions are binding on member states. In IBWC decisions are recorded in the form of minutes which are binding on the two members states, unless a state objects within 30 days. The ICPR's rules of procedure explicitly state that decisions are recommendations to the member states.

Financing arrangements

Another important feature of international organizations is their financing arrangements, including those pertaining to the costs of organization, and those pertaining to the costs of measures. From an economic perspective, the principle of fiscal equivalence maintains that those who benefit from a decision should also take the respective decision and carry its costs (e.g. Olson 1969; Hansjürgens 2001). While the implementation of the principle of fiscal equivalence may not be so easy in a multi-layered decision-making system, it may be considered as a riparian state's commitment towards the organization when it also carries its share in the respective operational costs.

Among the organizations listed in Table A-2, the costs of most organizations are usually born by the member states. The only exception where the operational budget is supplemented by donor contributions is MRC.[97] In the case of the boundary water commissions, each side usually covers its costs of representation. In the case of the river basin organizations with international secretariats in place, the costs are usually divided by a certain key. Often they are divided on an equal basis. In ICPR Germany, France and the Netherlands each pay a share of 32.5 percent, Switzerland pays 12 percent, and Luxembourg and the European Union each pay 2.5 percent (ICPR 2003: 7).[98]

In those cases, in which the member states are responsible for implementation, the costs of measures are usually carried by the member states (e.g. ICPR). The costs of joint measures and projects are often shared in the proportion of benefits (e.g. OMVS, IBWC and CBW). In the case of international river basin organizations in developing countries, the costs of studies are often covered by technical assistance, and infrastructure measures are frequently funded by financial assistance.

---

[97] Some argue that a number of international river basin organizations in developing countries have mainly been established because there appears to be a relatively high willingness among donors to provide funds for regional cooperation projects (e.g. Mostert 2003: 30).

[98] The numbers are quoted from the ICPR Rules of Procedure. They do, however, not add up to 100 percent.

Apart from form, the specific powers of an organization are reflected by its functions.

4.4.2   Functions

An international organization may be vested with a range of competences pertaining to the achievement of its substantive objectives. In principle international organizations are competent to act as far as powers have been attributed to them. Important functions of international river basin organizations include:

1. the planning and implementation of measures;
2. the definition of property rights;
3. the exchange and management of data;
4. monitoring and enforcement and
5. dispute settlement.

These different functions will be addressed in the following. They will also be at the heart of the economic analysis in Part II. Chapter 5 will address the issue of property rights and enforcement mechanisms. In Chapter 7 it will be argued that it is the performance of these functions which may justify the set up of an organization. Thus they are of particular interest from an economic point of view.

Planning and implementation of measures

The main substantive function of many international river basin organizations is the identification of measures and projects related to the development, management and protection of international water resources. In addition some organizations are also vested with powers to implement these measures.

Virtually all of the 12 organizations listed in Table A-2 are vested with broad project planning powers. The only exception is IJC, whose authority to make plans and recommendations is limited to situations in which it is formally requested by the parties to do so.

In a number of river basins, strategic action programs have been or are being prepared for this purpose (e.g. ICPR, ICPE, NBI and MRC). In some cases such as OMVS and MRC the international secretariat plays an important role in the project identification process. In contrast in the case of the ICPR, ICPE and NBI working groups composed of bureaucrats from the member states have been set up for this purpose, and the respective secretariats only provide logistical support to the working groups. This ensures that those who are close to the problem and responsible for implementation are directly involved in the planning process.

In most cases, the responsibility for project implementation is with the member states. In the case of ICPR and ICPE the action programs define certain target values, time lines and lists with potential measures; however the responsibility for the selection of specific measures is with the member states. This takes account of sovereignty and of different legal frameworks for the implementation of measures. In contrast OMVS, IBWC and CBW have the powers to plan, construct, operate and maintain agreed works. The power to implement measures can be considered as a reflection of an organization's independence vis-à-vis its member states.

The specification of property rights

Closely related to the identification of measures for the development and protection of international water resources is the definition of property rights to water, understood as the rules regulating the use of water. As indicated in Section 3.1.3, the rights and obligations of states towards international watercourses have to be defined in a process of negotiation among the respective states. The issue of property rights is often considered as sensitive, as it is generally perceived as a zero-sum game, in which the gain by one party is equivalent to the loss of another party. In the case of water quantity conflicts, political declarations recommend focusing on the sharing of benefits from water instead of the sharing of water (Section 1.1.3). Economists point at the fact that incentives for the definition of (private) property rights are the creation of assets, e.g. by maintaining the resource against depletion or pollution and by establishment of the preconditions for potential gains from the trade in property rights (e.g. Libecap 1989). However the clear-cut definition of private property rights to water is exacerbated by the fluidity and multi-functionality of the resource, and their enforcement has often the structure of a social dilemma (Chapter 5).

The way states deal with this issue varies greatly. In some cases states explicitly negotiate property rights, quantify them and fix them in the form of an international agreement. Examples for agreements with water allocations include the 1944 Treaty between Mexico and the USA, the 1959 Nile waters agreement between Egypt and Sudan or the 1994 water agreement between Israel and Jordan. The Indus waters treaty of 1960 divided the eastern and the western tributaries of the river among the two parties, and thus 'nationalized' the river. According to the TFDD treaty classification, among the treaties pertaining to the 86 international river basin organizations listed in Table A-1, a total of 31 (or 40 percent) feature water allocation mechanisms.

Other agreements entrust the organization or one of its organs with the specification of property rights, sometimes on an ongoing basis (IJC, OMVS and MRC).[99]

In the case of the PWC, the function of the commission is limited to advice on the criteria to be adopted in the allocation and utilization of common resources.

In the Rhine Basin, the attempt to define legally binding threshold values on chemical pollutants proofed difficult and was abandoned with the adoption of the 1987 Rhine Action Program (e.g. Durth 1996). While the Rhine Action Program still defines target values, these are not legally binding, but rather perceived as political targets.

Closely related to the rights and obligations of the member states is the obligation of prior notification on planned measures (Section 3.1.3). Most organizations listed in Table A-2 that deal with water quantity issues have explicit prior notification requirements in place (OMVS, MRC, PIC, IJC, both JWCs and CBW). In the case of the water quality agreements, prior notification appears to be less relevant. ICPR however includes requirements to notify promptly in the case of accidents and extreme events such as floods.

What is interesting is the relative importance of the planning of measures vis-à-vis the definition of property rights. Unless water is very scarce, the planning of specific infrastructure measures that realize specific benefits can be perceived as a more constructive negotiation strategy than distributional bargaining on (often abstract) property rights.[100]

Exchange of information and data

Usually a precondition for the identification of measures and for property rights negotiations is the exchange of information and data. Given that data are usually collected and processed at national and sub-national level, data are rarely readily available at the river basin level. This may present a major obstacle towards cooperation. Thus an important sub-ordinate function of

---

[99] Possible reasons may be that negotiations on specific values (e.g. water quantities) have proofed difficult. Also some agreements that fix certain values have been found not to be flexible enough (see for instance problems in the implementation of the Israeli-Jordanian water agreement of 1994 (Dombrowsky 2003)).

[100] This strategy is currently being pursued in the Nile Basin where the realization of property rights to water in Ethiopia largely hinges on infrastructure measures for hydropower production and irrigation. In contrast in the Jordan River Basin, where water is even more scarce and the issue is access to absolute quantities of water, it can be argued that the concentration on specific infrastructure measures in the 1994 agreement with Jordan and the 1995 interim agreement with the Palestinian Authority helped Israel to avoid a reallocation of property rights to water (e.g. Dombrowsky 2003).

international river basin organizations is the exchange and sometimes also the measurement and management of data.

In some cases one explicit function of the commission is the exchange of information and data provided for in the treaty or requested by the parties (e.g. IBWC, PIC and ISR-JOR JWC).

ICPR and ICPE are responsible for the preparation of an international measuring program on water quality. One function of CWB is the monitoring of water quality and quantity and the exchange of data.

In some cases the international secretariat is entrusted with the management of databases (OMVS and MRC). In the case of the NBI, the secretariat has no separate data management function, but data are dealt with in the context of specific projects.

The lack of mentioning of data exchange mechanisms may also be telling. The Israeli-Palestinian Interim Agreement of 1995 only refers to the exchange of information relating to water laws and regulation, but not to data.

Sometimes it is being proposed that in the evolution of international water management institutions, the exchange of data could be a first step in order to build trust and confidence among the parties involved. However other authors have emphasized that the exchange of data for its own sake may also be used strategically, for instance in order to prevent specific action.[101] The question of exchange of information may also be sensitive in the case of unilateral dependencies and asymmetries of power (Sharma et al. 1995; Chenoweth and Feitelson 2001). Still the exchange of data becomes a critical function of an international river basin organization when specific planning and projects are involved. The agreements pertaining to the 12 organizations reviewed show that countries tend to be careful in designing their data exchange mechanisms.

Monitoring and enforcement

One important function of international organizations is the monitoring of compliance and, possibly also the enforcement of agreements. In particular in the case of cooperation dilemmata, where parties have incentives to free-ride on the cooperative behavior of others, monitoring and enforcement is critical towards the realization of benefits of cooperation (Chapter 5). However in the international system, there is no external authority that may enforce agreements. Therefore monitoring and enforcement must be provided by the parties involved. This is why Barrett (1994a) has called for

---

[101] In the context of the so called Hydromet Project (1967-1982) in the White Nile Basin, cooperation never went beyond the collection of data (e.g. Waterbury 1997).

self-enforcing agreements for the management of international environmental problems so that participation is in the interests of the players involved.

According to the TFDD treaty characterization, a total of 48 (or 56 percent) of the 86 international river basin organizations listed in Table A-1 have monitoring, but only 9 (or 10 percent) have enforcement mechanisms in place. These numbers point at the difficulties states face with enforcement. At least three of the organizations with enforcement mechanisms are operational authorities.

Among the 12 organizations listed in Table A-2, five neither contain any provisions on monitoring nor on enforcement (MRC, IJC, NBI, ISR-JOR JWC and PIC).

Others have monitoring mechanisms in place: In the case of IBWC, PIC and OMVS the commission or secretariat regularly reports on implementation. In the Rhine Basin, the parties regularly report on measures, results and problems. The Commission submits an annual activity report and informs the public about the state of the Rhine and the results of its work (Holtrup 1999). As such ICPR ensures a certain level of public accountability. In the case of ICPR, ICPE and CBW one explicit function of the respective commissions is to evaluate the effectiveness of their programs.

Going beyond reporting, some treaties provide for inspections by the commission (PIC, OMVS and ISR-PAL JWC).[102]

However the only treaty which contains provisions on actions if the treaty provisions are not fulfilled is the 1999 Convention on the Protection of the Rhine. In the case of non-compliance, ICPR may assist the member states in implementation. This provision can be understood as a positive sanction mechanism (Holtrup 1999: 159).

None of the 12 treaties contains negative sanctions. Contrary to the TFDD classification, according to which the PIC, ISR-PAL JWC and CBW should contain enforcement mechanisms, it can be concluded that the only agreement with an explicit enforcement mechanism is ICPR. This is an interesting finding in view of the importance attached to enforcement by economic theory.

Dispute settlement

A further function of international river basin organizations is the settlement of disputes. A general purpose of the establishment of a commission or another coordination mechanism is the creation of a forum for the discussion

---

[102] In the case of ISR-PAL JWC inspections are only carried out in the West Bank but not inside Israel.

of issues that may arise among the respective parties and as such to institutionalize the interaction between the parties. For those organizations with international secretariats in place, the secretariat may also serve as an agenda setter and mediator among the parties. Dispute settlement can be understood as a typical 'regime' function, i.e. the provision of fair procedures if no agreement can be reached (but it can also be interpreted economically as a threat point).

According to the TFDD treaty characterization, a total of 36 (or 42 percent) of the 86 international river basin organizations listed in Table A-1 have conflict resolution mechanisms in place.

Eight of the 12 agreements pertaining to the organizations listed in Table A-2 explicitly list the settlement of differences as one function of the organization. In the majority of cases (OMVS, ICPR, PIC, IJC), the matter of dispute is referred to formal arbitration. In the case of IJC, in the first instance the matter is referred to the technical level within IJC. In the case of MRC, IBWC and PWC the respective governments are supposed to seek agreement through diplomatic channels.

The remaining four organizations (NBI, ISR-JOR JWC, ICPR and CBW) do not contain any specific provisions on the settlement of disputes.

4.5   SUMMARY AND RESEARCH IMPLICATIONS

This chapter took stock of the global coverage of international river basins with international water management institutions and sought to provide empirical evidence of the way states design international water agreements and organizations. The following will first summarize the findings and then discuss research implications.

- In terms of coverage the findings show that many countries do cooperate over transboundary waters. At the same time, the coverage is by no means universal given that agreements exist in less than 50 percent of all international river basins worldwide. In about one quarter of all basins cooperation is institutionalized in form of an organization. A number of basins have several organizations in place.
- In terms of design, the analysis demonstrates that the 86 identified organizations vary greatly in geographical and substantive scope, form and function.
- With regard to geographical scope, the findings show that the majority of the identified organizations are bilateral. Approximately 20 percent of all multipartite basins feature multilateral organizations, but only seven of

them are basin-wide. A fifth of the 86 organizations are boundary water commissions referring to various boundary waters shared by a dyad.

- The identified organizations cover a wide spectrum of water uses and issue areas and thus of substantive scope. The issue areas most frequently addressed are water quality, water quantity and hydropower production. While the majority of treaties are comparatively narrow in scope, some agreements cover a whole range of different water uses. Despite the asymmetries of interests in transboundary rivers, explicit side-payments and non-water issue linkages are comparatively rare. Interestingly, side-payments are more prevalent than non-water issue linkages.
- The majority of international river basin organizations are called commissions; however the term may cover a whole range of different forms. The continuum of forms ranges from bilateral commissions composed of one commissioner per country without any formal administrative support, over boundary commissions composed of two sections each with a secretariat, to river basin organizations with a hierarchy of decision-making organs and an international secretariat in place. Decisions are usually taken on the basis of unanimity or by consensus. Some of those international secretariats are fairly large and entrusted with a whole range of functions, while others have very few staff and are limited to support functions.
- Important functions of international river basin organizations include the planning and sometimes also the implementation of projects, the specification of property rights to water, the exchange of data, monitoring and enforcement and the settlement of disputes. While most of the 12 organizations that were reviewed in greater detail have project planning functions, fewer organizations have the power to implement projects. Some agreements explicitly quantify property rights. In other cases the organization or one of its organs is entrusted with the specification of property rights, often on an ongoing basis. While the majority of the analyzed organizations have explicit monitoring functions, only one of them contains an enforcement mechanism.
- Overall the powers of international river basin organizations tend to be limited, which, however, is quite common in international relations.

The question is how these findings should be interpreted and evaluated. Is the existing state practice satisfactory or is there scope for change? Can some designs be considered as more expedient than others? What, if any, are the implications of these findings for prevailing policy recommendations?

There are no easy answers to these questions. One possibility to address them is to assess the effectiveness of these institutions. However a comparative study of effectiveness would be a major research effort in its own (e.g. Young and Marc 1999; Bernauer 2002).[103] Another possibility may be to compare how well theoretical explanations and predictions and empirical findings match. This will be pursued in the following: On the one hand, theory might be in a position to explain outcomes and to show room for improvement. On the other hand, the comparison with empirical outcomes will serve as a test whether actors behave according to the assumptions and predictions of theory and whether theory asks relevant questions.

In the following, the empirical findings will be used as reference point to guide the examination of the explanatory power of economic theories for the design of international water management institutions. This will include the following questions:

- What is the role of problem structure for cooperation and institutional design (Chapter 5)?
- What is the role of issue linkage for resolving asymmetrical actor constellations (Chapter 6)?
- What is the role of international organizations for cooperation (Chapter 7)?

All three subsequent chapters deal with the phenomenon of cooperation and as such seek to make an economic contribution to the question under which conditions states cooperate. Depending on the alignment of hydrological and political boundaries and the underlying uses Chapter 5 seeks to explore under which conditions it is in the interest of players to cooperate and how must institutions be designed in order to realize cooperation. In doing so, the focus of Chapter 5 is on the problem of undefined property rights and enforcement (and thus on functions). Chapter 6 will address the substantive scope of international water management institutions by exploring the role of issue linkage and by asking for the

---

[103] First it is often not easy to measure effectiveness. A regime may be considered effective if it meets its objective. However given that implementation processes in water resources management usually take significant time, this can usually only be done for agreements that have been long enough in place. Second even if an institution is found to be effective, this does not yet imply that the findings are transferable to a different setting. Neither does it imply that another institutional form may not be effective. Nor does it necessarily imply that all conflict has been eliminated, since the objectives of an agreement may also stimulate new dispute, for instance with affected third parties. Another fundamental problem is that the effectiveness of a transboundary agreement is not only a function of the respective institutional arrangement, but also of external factors, such as the political and economic environment. If an institution is found not to be effective, this may not necessarily be due to institutional design, but due to external factors. Thus if the aim is to generalize conclusions, it is necessary to control the respective variables by comparing a relatively high number of cases. This, however, would be a major research effort on its own.

potential for issue linkage within the water sector. Chapter 7 will address the form of institutional arrangement by asking whether it is expedient to go beyond pure agreements and to further institutionalize cooperation. A synthesis of the study's theoretical and empirical findings will be presented in Chapter 8.

PART II

Economic Analysis of the Cooperation Problem and Institutions

5. The Role of the Problem Structure for Institutional Design and Cooperation

Chapter 5 will examine the role of the structure of different international water management problems for the prospects of cooperation as well as the implications of the underlying problem structure for institutional design. In order to do so it will take up the four types of externality problems in the management of international waters identified in Section 2.2 and will reconstruct them in a game-theoretic manner. Non-cooperative game theory analyzes the interests and incentives of the actors involved in a situation and the implications of strategic interaction under the assumption that no binding commitments can be made. As such non-cooperative game theory is particularly conducive for the analysis of international water management problems as in the international system there is no external authority which could impose a solution and any cooperation relies on voluntary negotiations.

Non-cooperative game theory allows the differentiation of different problem structures that are represented by various game types, including different types of collective action problems or social dilemmata. Social dilemmata refer to situations in which individual rationality leads to collectively undesirable outcomes. They are of special interest in the context of this book, as they imply that under certain circumstances joint decision-making may lead to Pareto improvements for the players involved. Institutions can be understood as rules that restructure incentives in order to realize gains of cooperation in such social dilemma situations. The way such institutions must be designed depends on the structure of the problem. Therefore, it is necessary to understand (1) the relationship of problem structure and institutional design, and (2) the structure of a situation if recommendations on institutional design shall be made.

In a first step this chapter will analyze the theoretical interrelationship between the structure of a problem and institutional design (Section 5.1). In doing so, it will draw upon the Coase theorem and non-cooperative game theory.

In a second step the chapter will reconstruct the different types of externality problems identified in Section 2.2 – negative and positive reciprocal as well as negative and positive unidirectional externality problems – in a game-theoretic manner (Sections 5.2 and 5.3). This game-theoretic reconstruction serves a number of purposes:

- First it seeks to identify the underlying game structure of these different types of problems. As such it tests under which conditions cooperation on international waters has the potential to realize benefits of cooperation.
- Second depending on the structure of the problem, it allows predictions on whether cooperation can be expected if rational self-interested behavior is assumed.
- Third it identifies impediments towards cooperation and options for the reconstruction of incentives through institutions. As such it contributes to the debate on institutional design, by analyzing how institutions must be shaped in order to achieve cooperation.

In the analysis, particular attention will be given to the fact that without further action on the part of the riparian states, the underlying property rights are de jure not specified (Section 3.1).

The theory and the models used in this chapter rely on a number of assumptions. First it will be assumed that the respective actors (states) behave rationally and that they pursue their self-interest, i.e. that they choose the outcome that makes them individually better off irrespectively of the outcome of the other players involved.[104] Second for the purpose of the analysis it will be assumed that the players involved have perfect information, i.e. that they do not only know their own cost and benefit functions, but also those of the other players involved. This assumption will be questioned in Chapter 7.

Section 5.1 will analyze the interrelationship of problem structure and institutional implications. Section 5.2 will address negative and positive reciprocal and Section 5.3 negative and positive unidirectional externality problems. Section 5.4 will present conclusions.

---

[104] The purpose of this assumption is not to say that states always behave this way, but to make conditional statements if they behaved this way. This assumption may be questioned in two respects. First the question is whether states always pursue their self-interest. For instance Chayes and Chayes (1993: 175-205) argue that states tend to comply with their treaty obligations irrespectively of whether they are in their narrow self-interest or not. Second it may be questioned whether they always behave rationally. For instance international relations theory argues that under certain conditions states do not pursue absolute, but relative gains (e.g. Grieco 1988).

5.1 PROBLEM STRUCTURE AND INSTITUTIONAL IMPLICATIONS: THEORETICAL FOUNDATIONS

This section will provide the theoretical foundations for the following analyses by examining the interrelationship of problem structure and institutional design. Section 5.1.1 will introduce into theories of external effects and the Coase theorem. The Coase theorem may be considered as the starting point for the analysis of unidirectional externality problems. However it will be shown that only its game-theoretic analysis reveals the different types of interaction problems involved in Coasian negotiations, and spells out the institutional preconditions for an internalization of external effects through negotiations in a systematic fashion. Section 5.1.2 will then introduce into different game structures that are potentially relevant for the analysis of international water management problems, including social dilemmata, and will analyze their institutional implications in a static and a dynamic context. Section 5.1.3 will summarize the findings.

5.1.1 External Effects and the Coase Theorem

The theory of external effects deals with situations in which the economic activity of one economic agent entails positive or negative effects on another economic agent that are not mediated by the price mechanism:

> An externality is present whenever the well-being of a consumer or the production possibilities of a firm are directly affected by the actions of another agent in the economy... When we say 'directly,' we mean to exclude any effects that are mediated by prices (Mas-Colell et al. 1995: 352).

The standard definition of externalities refers to non-pecuniary or 'technological' effects that are not reflected by relative prices, as opposed to the effects of production and consumption decisions which are reflected by market prices (e.g. Sohmen 1992). From a welfare economic point of view, the former are perceived as problematic since they lead to inefficiencies (see below), while the latter are considered as socially desirable as they lead to efficient allocation of scarce resources.

Famous examples of production externalities include a rancher's cattle roaming onto a farmer's land leading to the destruction of crops or a pulp mill discharging pollutants into a river diminishing the income of a fish farm downstream. An early case which dealt with transboundary externalities is the Trail Smelter arbitration on sulfur dioxide emissions from British Columbia to Washington State in 1938 (Section 3.1.2). While some economic activities go along with negative external effects, others entail positive external effects, effectively providing a public good.[105] An example of positive external effects would be the flowers planted in a front garden enhancing the utility of passengers.

Whenever externalities occur, this entails inefficiencies in the allocation of resources, since the party causing the external effect does not take the external costs or benefits of its decision into account. In the case of negative externalities this leads to the over-production, in the case of positive external effects to the under-provision of a good. Externalities are thus one reason for market failure. From the perspective of welfare economics, the problem of externalities is not so much the harm per se or possible ensuing conflict between different actors, but the misallocation of scarce resources and the resulting inefficiencies.

The problem of externalities has given rise to an extensive debate with regard to policies and appropriate institutional arrangements that allow for a correction of a respective market failure by 'internalizing' external effects into the respective agent's decision-making calculus. In his seminal work 'The Economics of Welfare', Pigou (1920) argued that external effects justified government intervention, and proposed the imposition of a tax on those causing negative external effects or subsidies for those creating positive external effects. In 'The Problem of Social Cost', Coase (1960) rejected the notion that externalities constituted a prima facie cause for government intervention, and proposed to compare the capacity of different institutional arrangements such as negotiations, markets or different forms of government intervention to increase efficiency in a given case, taking all costs including transaction costs into account. For that purpose he analyzed under which conditions voluntary negotiations would lead to a Pareto efficient internalization of external effects (the so called Coase theorem).

'The Problem of Social Cost', one of the most frequently cited articles in economics, has given rise to an extensive debate on the capacity of voluntary negotiations to deal with negative external effects. The reason is that if voluntary negotiations were capable to lead to an internalization of externalities, this would obviate the need for government intervention. In the context of this book the question whether voluntary negotiations are able to internalize external effects is of great interest in so far, as the use of international rivers entails pervasive externalities (see Section 2.2), however, in the international system there is no external authority in place that could impose a solution; hence in the international system, an internalization of externalities has to rely on voluntary approaches and negotiations.

---

[105] The theory of public goods can be considered as part of the theory of externalities (e.g. Feess 1998: 43).

In a first step the Coase theorem will be presented. In a second step the implications of the Coase theorem on the capacity of negotiations to deal with unidirectional negative effects in a bilateral setting will be addressed.[106]

The Coase theorem

In 'The Problem of Social Cost' Coase (1960) argues that from an economic perspective the problem of externalities is one of a reciprocal nature: while the actor causing a negative external effect on another actor incurs costs on the latter, preventing the negative effect would incur costs on the former. Therefore from an economic perspective the question is under which conditions the total harm is minimized or to put it positively, the total value of production is maximized:

> We are dealing with a problem of a reciprocal nature. To avoid the harm to B would be to inflict harm on A. The real question that has to be decided is, Should A be allowed to harm B or should B be allowed to harm A? The problem is to avoid the more serious harm (Coase 1960: 2).

Coase illustrates the externality problem by using the case of a farmer and a cattle raiser operating on neighboring land without a fence in place. As the cattle strays onto the farmer's land it incurs costs to the farmer by damaging his crop with the total damage depending on the number of cows. While Coase (1960) uses a numerical example, the presentation does at this point divert from the original and represent the underlying interrelationships in the usual diagrammatic form (see Figure 5.1).[107] In Figure 5.1:

- q refers to A's level of externality causing economic activity (e.g. the number of cows raised causing crop destruction);
- MB refers to A's marginal benefit of an additional unit of externality causing economic activity (e.g. income to the rancher generated from one additional animal). The maximum level of externality causing activity (q_{max}) is reached, when the marginal benefit of an additional unit of the externality causing economic activity is zero;

---

[106] The consideration of standard economic instruments for the internalization of externalities that are used by national governments, such as taxes, tradable emission permits or liability rules, would go beyond the scope of this book. In any case, in the international area, they are no structural alternative to negotiations, as any agreement on the set up of such instruments would have to rely on international negotiations. To my knowledge taxes and tradable emission permits have so far not been employed in international river management. However in the European Union an international liability rule is in place, and the European Court of Justice confirmed the right of victims to sue polluters in victim or polluter countries (Bernauer 1997: 186).

[107] A similar presentation can be found in Feess (1998: 133).

- MC refers to B's marginal damage costs generated by an additional unit of externality causing economic activity (e.g. the damage to the farmer from one additional cow destroying his crop).

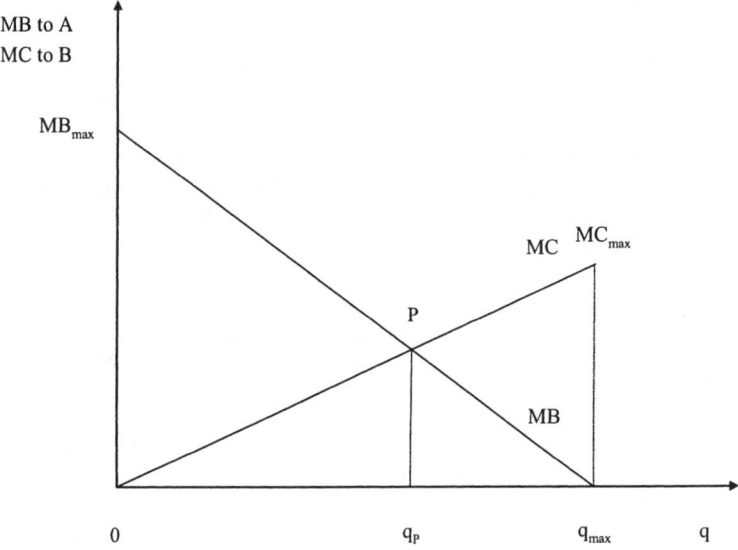

Figure 5.1   Pareto Efficient Internalization of Externalities

Coase first considers the case where the rancher is liable for any damage incurred on the farmer, i.e. should he inflict any damage on the farmer, he is obliged to compensate the farmer for the damage incurred (so called 'liability rule'). In this case all rights are with the farmer, and the rancher does not have any right to raise cattle (0 in the diagram). However rather than not to raise any cattle it would be worthwhile for the farmer to raise some cattle and to compensate the rancher for the damage incurred. This is equivalent to buying the right to carry out an externality causing economic activity. The reason for entering into such negotiations is that at least initially the marginal benefits for the rancher can be expected to exceed the marginal damage costs incurred on the farmer. This allows for the generation of a net benefit corresponding to the vertical distance between the MB and MC curve. The cattle raiser can be expected to buy so many rights so that the income generated from the last additional cow equals the compensation paid to the farmer for the additional damage incurred. This is represented by q_p in the diagram. Level q_p is equivalent to an internalization of external effects. The minimum compensation offered to the farmer corresponds to the area under the MC curve between 0 and q_p. The total net benefit of these negotiations corresponds to the area between the MB and MC curve left to q_p. If the rancher was already raising q_{max} cows in the status quo, he would reduce his production to q_p and compensate the farmer for the remaining damage.

In a second step Coase considers the opposite distribution of property rights. In this case all rights are with the rancher, and the status quo is represented by q_{max} (so called 'laissez-faire rule'). The rancher raises so many cows so that the marginal benefit from one additional cow is zero. In this case given that in the status quo the marginal damage costs to the farmer exceed the marginal benefits to the rancher, the farmer may realize a net benefit if he offers a side-payment in order to induce the farmer to reduce his level of externality causing activity. The farmer maximizes his net benefit if the side-payment corresponds to the area $q_p q_{max} P$, thus compensating the rancher's income loss, and realizing a benefit of the area $q_{max} MC_{max} P$. Again the Pareto optimal level of the externality is reached when marginal benefits equal marginal damage costs.

If the externality is in the form of pollutants, it may not be necessary to reduce the respective externality causing economic activity per se, but it may suffice to install a respective abatement technology. In this case the optimal level of pollution is reached when marginal abatement costs equal marginal damage costs.

If the status quo is characterized by q_{max}, under the liability rule, the harming party covers the abatement costs and compensates the harmed person for the residual damage. Under the laissez-faire rule, the harmed party covers the abatement costs and bears the residual damage costs.

These considerations suggest that under the assumptions that property rights are fully specified and enforced, and that transaction costs can be neglected, negotiations lead to a Pareto efficient level of external effects irrespective of the initial allocation of property rights:[108]

> It is necessary to know whether the damaging business is liable or not for damage caused, since without the establishment of this initial delimitation of rights there can be no market transactions to transfer and recombine them. But the ultimate result (which maximizes the value of production) is independent of the legal position if the pricing system is assumed to work without cost (Coase 1960: 8).

---

[108] 'Property rights of individuals over assets consist of the rights or the powers, to consume, obtain income from and alienate these assets' (Barzel 1989: 2).

This passage reflects what Stigler (1966: 113) referred to as the 'Coase theorem'. The Coase theorem contains two hypotheses, first that under certain conditions negotiations on externalities lead to their internalization (efficiency hypothesis), and second that this is irrespective of the initial allocation of property rights (invariance hypothesis, see Endres 1977: 639).

Negotiations as a means towards the internalization of externalities?

As mentioned above, the Coase theorem has raised the question whether negotiations can be understood as a means towards the internalization of external effects, as this would obviate the need for government intervention. This question has created a wealth of literature the comprehensive review of which would go beyond the purpose of this section. However several points are important.

First Coase himself points at the significance of transaction costs defined as search, negotiation, contracting, monitoring and enforcement costs in real world situations, and at the fact that whenever transaction costs exceed the potential gains from negotiation, it will not be in the interest of the parties involved to negotiate:[109]

> Once the costs of carrying out market transactions are taken into account, it is clear that such a rearrangement of rights will only be undertaken when the increase in the value of production consequent upon the rearrangement is greater than the costs which would be involved in bringing it about (Coase 1960: 15 f.).[110]

For Coase the implication is that transaction costs need to be taken into account in the making of economic policy. He argues for a different analytical approach to deal with externalities, namely to start with the analysis of the status quo and to analyze alternative institutional arrangements taking all costs, including transaction costs, into account. Alternatives to deal with externalities may include negotiations, the firm, different forms of government regulation or the zero alternative to do

---

[109] It is unclear whether Coase's definition of transaction costs includes information costs.

[110] As Coase points out, one implication of taking transaction costs into account is that the initial delimitation of property rights may indeed have an effect on the efficiency of the economic system (Coase 1960: 15 f.). He uses this argument to advocate the economic analysis of law.

nothing. This line of argumentation, in particular the potential role of organizations ('the firm') will be taken up in Chapter 7.[111]

Second while the specification of property rights is assumed to be without effects on allocative efficiency (invariance hypothesis), it of course has significant effects on the distribution of income. Endres (1977: 639 ff.) demonstrates that when these income effects are taken into account, it can be shown that the initial allocation of property rights also has repercussions on allocative efficiency.

Third a debate has emerged whether the Coase theorem in fact has the status of a theorem, as Coase does not strictly show that negotiations lead to a Pareto efficient level of externalities, but Coase implicitly assumes that the actors involved negotiate until they reach a Pareto efficient outcome. In order to analyze whether the actors have an incentive to negotiate a respective agreement, Schweizer (1988) has sought to reconstruct the Coase theorem on the basis of non-cooperative game theory. He assumes a game in three steps. Under the laissez-faire rule in a first step the harmed party B offers a contract to A, offering a side-payment for reducing the level of externality causing activity to the optimal level. Under the assumption that B does not make a counter-proposal, the compensation offered can be assumed to equal A's income loss due to the reduction of the externality causing activity. In a second step A may accept or decline the contract. If A accepts the side-payment, he is assumed to adjust his level of externality causing activity respectively. In a third step B adjusts its level of activity according to A's new level of activity. Under the assumption of perfectly rational actors, this game can be solved by backward induction. An analogous game can be constructed for the liability rule.[112] Thus it can be argued that the Coase theorem has indeed the status of a theorem (see also Weimann 1995: 50).

Fourth the 'Schweizer game' illustrates that next to the two assumptions explicitly mentioned by Coase, i.e. specified and enforced property rights and sufficiently low transaction costs, the Coase theorem contains a number of further implicit assumptions:[113]

---

[111] The article's policy recommendations with regard to transaction costs are often neglected in the literature. Coase (1988a: 159) himself felt that many criticisms of his article were 'for the most part, either invalid, unimportant or irrelevant. Even those sympathetic to my point of view have often misunderstood my argument, a result which I ascribe to the extraordinary hold which Pigou's approach had had on the minds of modern economists' (see also Hansjürgens 2000).

[112] Given that the Schweizer game assumes perfect information and no bargaining, transaction costs can be assumed to be low.

[113] It may be argued that some of these implicit assumptions are part of the transaction cost assumption.

- The actors are assumed to be able to communicate freely which may not always be the case under real world conditions or which may involve transaction costs.
- The actors involved are assumed to have perfect information, i.e. they know not only their own but also the other party's production or abatement cost function as well as the damage function involved as a function of both parties' levels of activity. However in contrast to competitive markets, in a bilateral monopoly situation there is no inherent incentive for the players involved to reveal their true preferences. Under the laissez-faire rule the harming party may claim higher abatement costs in order to extract a higher side-payment. Under the liability rule, the victim has an incentive to overstate the damage costs. The problem of incomplete information has given rise to the so called 'theory of incentives', which examines whether it is possible to design negotiations mechanisms that may lead to efficient outcomes under incomplete information (for a review see Weimann 1995: 51-56). Myerson and Satterthwaite (1983) show for a bilateral trade game that an incentive compatible, individually rational negotiation mechanism cannot be ex post efficient. A mechanism is incentive compatible if each player has the incentive to reveal his true preferences. It is individually rational if each actor expects ex ante a positive utility from participation in the negotiations. The criterion of ex post efficiency is context dependent. In Myerson and Satterthwaite's case, a mechanism is ex post efficient if the bargain is only realized if the buyer attaches a higher utility to the good than the seller (in Weimann 1995: 52 f.). In addition Rob (1989) shows for a pollution game with N victims that the likelihood that an efficient result is achieved decreases with the number of victims (in Weimann 1995: 55). Hence even if transaction costs are assumed to be zero, the theory of incentive shows that under incomplete information it remains uncertain whether an agreement will be reached even if benefits from negotiation exist, and not every agreement reached will be efficient. The reason is that parties behave strategically under private information.
- In the Schweizer game it is assumed that the parties involved reach an agreement on the sharing of the benefits of cooperation. A is assumed to accept B's initial compensation offer, so that B accrues the net benefits of cooperation. However the likelihood that A agrees to B's offer is very small. Instead it can be assumed that A will wish to participate in the gains of cooperation. He is thus likely to make a counter-proposal. A process of proposal and counter-proposal could lead to a never-ending 'Rubinstein game' (Rubinstein 1982; in Requate N.d.: 31).
- The Schweizer game assumes that if A accepts the contract, the specifications of the contract will be implemented accordingly. In other

words, the assumption is that the contract will be enforced at no costs. However it will later be argued that a 'side-payment game' has the structure of a Prisoner's Dilemma game in which the cooperative solution cannot be maintained as an equilibrium outcome in the one-shot game. This raises the question how enforcement can be assured.

- The theorem applies to bilateral negotiations. If there are several sources or several victims, additional problems of free-riding behavior occur.

Overall the Coase theorem shows that under highly specific conditions, bilateral negotiations may indeed lead to an internalization of external effects. The explicit and implicit assumptions include (see also Mäler 1990: 84):

- Property rights are fully specified and enforced at no costs;
- Total transaction costs are smaller than the net benefits of negotiations; in particular
  o the parties involved reveal the relevant information;
  o the parties reach agreement on the sharing of the net benefits of cooperation and
  o the agreement is being enforced at sufficiently low costs.
- Changes in distribution of rights will not change the respective cost functions;
- The issue at hand is seen in isolation from other issues.

Given that these assumptions are rather restrictive, the implication is that the power of voluntary negotiations to resolve externality problems is extremely limited. As Weimann (1995) aptly put, it cannot be expected that missing markets will be substituted by voluntary negotiations:

> Zusammenfassend können wir damit feststellen, daß das Coase-Theorem nicht dazu führt, dass wir uns über externe Effekte keine Gedanken mehr zu machen brauchen. Mit ihm läßt sich die Unvollständigkeit des Marktsystems nicht heilen, wir können nicht hoffen, daß die fehlenden Märkte durch freiwilllige Verhandlungen ersetzt werden. Allerdings bedeutet dies nicht automatisch, daß der Staat aufgerufen ist, aktiv zu werden. Die Privaten verfehlen zwar das Effizienzziel, aber woher sollen wir wissen, ob der Staat es besser macht? (Weimann 1995: 57 f.)

The Coase theorem and its game-theoretic reconstruction will provide the starting point for the analysis of negative unidirectional externality problems in the management of international waters in Section 5.2.2. It will be argued that in international water management the problem is particularly pronounced, as we do not only have to handle transaction costs, but we are dealing with situations in which in the absence of agreement among the parties the property rights are not defined in the first place. However before resorting to the analysis of international water management problems, first the ground will be prepared for the analysis of all four externality problems identified in Section 2.2. For instance in the case of reciprocal externality problems, both parties impose external effects on each other. The ensuing strategic interaction leads to a symmetric actor constellation where both players have the choice either to impose or reduce the externality. Game theory is particularly conducive towards the analysis of these types of interaction. However in view of the different types of externality problems identified, Section 5.1.2 will look at both, reciprocal or symmetric and unidirectional or asymmetric problem structures and will present them in a unified manner in the form of 2x2 games.

5.1.2   Game-theoretic Analysis of Different Problem Structures

The purpose of this section is to differentiate between different game types that are potentially relevant for the analysis of international water management problems including different types of social dilemmata and to gain an understanding of the prospects for cooperation and the institutional ramifications of the various game types. As such this section will serve two functions. First it will provide the foundations for a game-theoretic reconstruction of international water management problems. Second it will develop the institutional implications of these different types of games at a theoretical level. As such this section provides a further important theoretical basis for the following analyses.

In a first step basic game-theoretic concepts will be introduced and a number of 2x2 games that are potentially relevant for the analysis of international water management problems will be identified. In a second step different definitions of social dilemmata will be presented in order to identify those 2x2 games that may be considered as social dilemmata. In a third step the 2x2 game identified will analyzed for their institutional implications in a static context, i.e. for situations in which the game is only played once, and in which both players move simultaneously. In a fourth step it will be asked, how the prospects of cooperation change if a Prisoner's Dilemma game is infinitely repeated and hence for institutional implications in a dynamic context.

Games and game-theoretic solution concepts

Game theory can be understood as a general meta-language to analyze problems of strategic interaction, where the outcome of one actor's decision also depends on the decisions of all other actors involved. Non-cooperative game theory analyzes the incentives for cooperation under the assumption that no binding commitments can be made, whereas cooperative game theory assumes that agreements will be binding (e.g. Rasmusen 2001). Therefore non-cooperative game theory is particularly useful to analyze the structure of a problem and the conditions under which cooperation can be expected to come about if self-interested rational behavior is assumed, i.e. under the assumption that each actor maximizes his utility irrespectively of the other actors' utility. In contrast cooperative game theory primarily analyzes the negotiation process in situations where gains of cooperation exist, including the formation of coalitions and the analysis of mechanisms for the sharing of the gains of cooperation. Given the absence of an external authority in international water management, the main focus of this chapter is on conditions under which cooperation can be expected and thus on non-cooperative game theory.

The simplest and most general form of a game is described by a 2x2 matrix, representing two players, each of which has two choices, leading to four possible outcomes (see Figure 5.2 for a selection of 2x2 games).[114] In the analysis of collective action problems these alternative choices are usually described as cooperate (C) or defect (D), depending on whether the choice maximizes the outcome of both players or whether ego maximizes his outcome irrespectively of what alter does. In Figure 5.2, it is assumed that the players have strictly ordered preferences over the four possible outcomes, whereby outcome 4 is a player's best outcome and 1 his worst outcome. The first number in the cells refers to player A's and the second to player B's outcome. Each player's preference orders associated with a game are indicated below the name of the game. While the numbers 1 through 4 usually depict ordinal preference orders, sometimes it is assumed that outcomes 1 through 4 represent cardinal payoffs that may be aggregated and are interpersonally comparable.[115]

Given that each player's four outcomes can be distributed differently over the four cells, in ordinal payoffs there are theoretically 4! x 4! = 576 different combinations (Rapoport and Guyer 1966). Out of these, Rapoport and Guyer (1966) have identified 78 strategically distinct games, 12 of which are symmetric and 66 are asymmetric. In symmetric games, both players have the same (only mirrored) preference orders, whereas in asymmetric games

---

[114] A 2x2 game is usually interpreted as bilateral negotiation; however it may also be interpreted as a game of one party against all other parties.

[115] The advantage of the use of interpersonally comparable cardinal payoffs is that they allow the identification of those outcomes that maximize welfare for society as a whole (the aggregated welfare optimum). However the determination of interpersonally comparable payoffs may entail methodological difficulties.

the preference orders differ among the players. In asymmetric games each players plays a different 'basic' game.

Figure 5.2 presents nine 2x2 games which are frequently quoted in the literature, six symmetric games (Pure Coordination, Assurance, Prisoner's Dilemma, Chicken, Battle of the Sexes and Deadlock) and three asymmetric games (Rambo I, Rambo II and Constant Sum).[116] These games are presented here as they were found to be potentially relevant for the reconstruction of international water management problems.

If we assume rational self-interested players with perfect information that maximize their individual utility irrespectively of the other actor's utility, for each game the outcome can be predicted on the basis of various game-theoretic solution concepts. Solutions to games are analyzed in terms of possible equilibria that may result from the combination of each player's strategy in a game. A player's strategy is a rule that tells him which action to choose at each instant of the game given his information set. The information set is defined as each player's knowledge at a particular time of the values of different variables and the payoffs each player receives if the game is being played out (e.g. Rasmusen 2001). An equilibrium is a strategy combination consisting of a best strategy for each player of the game. A player's best response to the strategies chosen by the other players is the strategy that yields him the greatest payoff. A strategy is a dominant strategy if it is a player's strictly best response irrespectively of which strategy the other players might choose. A dominant strategy equilibrium is a strategy combination consisting of each player's dominant strategy. A strategy combination is a Nash equilibrium if no player has an incentive to deviate from his strategy given that the other players do not deviate. Therefore a dominant strategy equilibrium is always a Nash equilibrium, but a Nash equilibrium must not necessarily be a dominant strategy equilibrium. A Maximin equilibrium is the combination of each player's maximin strategy which maximizes each player's minimum outcome. The dominant strategy equilibrium, the Nash equilibrium, and the Maximin equilibrium are defined for ordinal and cardinal preference orders. Figure 5.2 indicates any Nash equilibrium (N) as well as any Maximin equilibrium (M) for each game.

These equilibrium outcomes can be evaluated on the basis of different criteria. An outcome is a Pareto optimum (P) if there is no other outcome for which at least one player can be made better off without making any other

---

[116] According to Holzinger (2003) the term Rambo game was introduced by Zürn (1992: 209 ff.). This notwithstanding the game has been described before in the context of social dilemmata, for instance by Stein (1982). The terminology Rambo I and Rambo II is based on Zürn (1992: 209ff.). Rambo I is a combination of a Deadlock and a Pure Coordination game. Rambo II is a combination of a Chicken and a Prisoner's Dilemma game. The Constant Sum game combines a Prisoner's Dilemma and a Deadlock game.

player worse off. An advantage of the Pareto optimum is that it is defined for ordinal and cardinal preference orders. However given the fact that a game may have several Pareto optima, this raises the question whether any of these is preferred from a social point of view.

If cardinal preference orders are assumed, two more evaluation criteria can be introduced, the welfare or Kaldor-Hicks criterion and an equality criterion. The aggregated welfare optimum (P+) is defined as the outcome that maximizes the sum of individual payoffs. Assuming that potential losers are compensated by winners the aggregated welfare optimum can be perceived as the socially desirable outcome among all Pareto outcomes in a game. The socially desirable outcome can be further qualified in form of the qualified Pareto Optimum (P+*) (Zürn 1992: 154). The qualified Pareto optimum (P+*) is defined as the outcome which maximizes the product of the individual payoffs.[117] As such it indicates the aggregated welfare optimum with the greatest equality of payoffs. The assumption is that (political) actors are ceteris paribus more interested in a fair than an unfair solution (Zürn 1992: 155).

The outcome of a game may furthermore differ depending on whether the game is only played once (one-shot game) or whether it is finitely or infinitely repeated. Furthermore it makes a difference whether both players move simultaneously or whether they move sequentially. Therefore game theory distinguishes between static games, which refer to simultaneously played one-shot games and dynamic games, which includes sequential games and repeated games. Static games are usually presented in strategic form and represented in the matrix form presented in Figure 5.2. Dynamic games are usually presented in extensive form in form of a game tree. Both will be addressed below.

		Player B					Player B	
		C	D				C	D
Player A	C	4,4 N,M,P+*	2,3		Player A	C	4,4 N,P+*	1,3
	D	3,2	1,1			D	3,1	2,2 N,M

a. Pure Coordination (PC)/	b. Assurance/Stag Hunt
Game without Conflict	**Ranked Coordination**
A,B: CC>DC>CD>DD	A,B: CC>DC>DD>CD

---

[117] The qualified Pareto optimum is only defined for payoffs > 1. It is being introduced here in order to test Zürn's 'Rambo-Hypothesis' (see below).

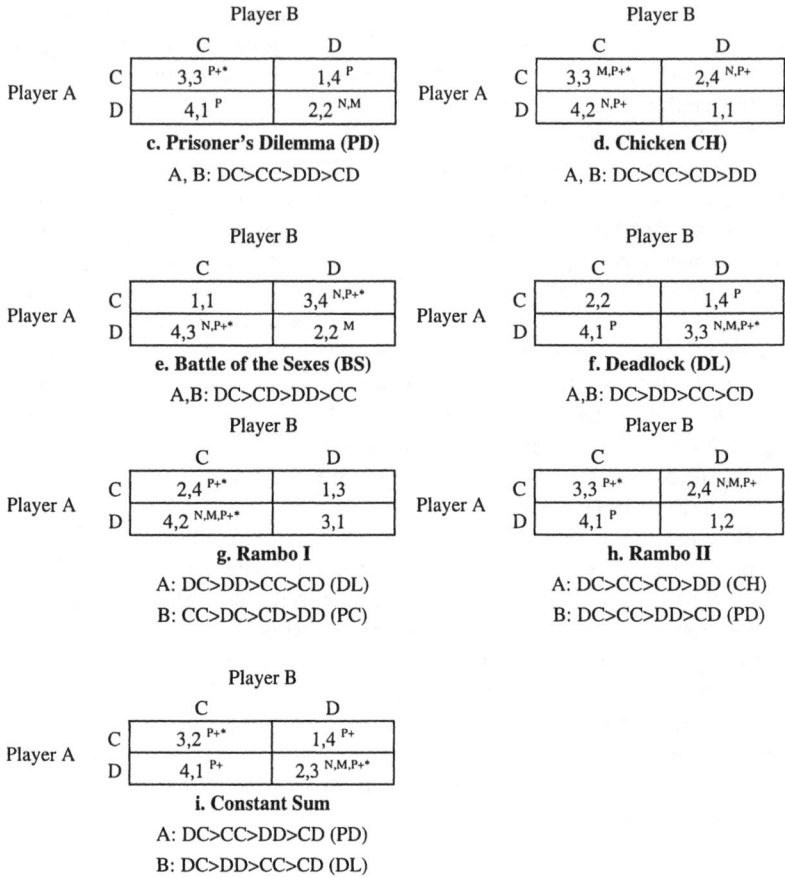

Legend:

C: cooperate
D: defect
N: Nash equilibrium
M: Maximin equilibrium
P: Pareto optimum
P+:   aggregated welfare optimum, maximizes the sum of utilities (for cardinal payoffs only)
P+*:   qualified Pareto optimum, maximizes the product of utilities (for cardinal payoffs only)

Source: Own presentation

Figure 5.2   Selected 2x2 Games Relevant for International Water Management

Typologies of collective action problems

Drawing upon these game-theoretic solution concepts and evaluation criteria, there have been different attempts to identify those games that may be considered as collective action problems or social dilemma situations. The concept of social dilemmata shall be introduced here in order to identify those games in Figure 5.2 that represent a social dilemma as they principally offer room for cooperation and coordination. Stein (1982: 312) distinguishes between 'dilemmata of common interests' or 'collaboration (or cooperation) problems' on the one hand and 'dilemmata of common aversions' or 'coordination problems' on the other.[118] Cooperation problems occur when 'independent decision making leads to equilibrium outcomes that are Pareto-deficient' (Stein 1982: 304). The paradigmatic form of a cooperation problem is the Prisoner's Dilemma game. Coordination problems are situations where actors 'have a common interest in avoiding a particular outcome' (Stein 1982: 309). They include the Assurance, the Battle of the Sexes and the Chicken game. Cooperation and coordination problems differ with respect to their need for the enforcement: while in the case of cooperation problems agreements rely on the set up of an enforcement mechanism, in the case of coordination problems agreements that endorse an equilibrium outcome are self-enforcing, as any player who departs from the agreed outcome hurts himself (Stein 1982: 312 ff.; Barrett 2003: 92; and see below).[119]

Liebrand (1983: 124) defines a 'social dilemma' as 'a situation in which (1) there is a strategy that yields the person the best payoff in at least one configuration of strategy choices and that has a negative impact on the interests of the other persons involved, and (2) the choice of that particular strategy by all persons results in a deficient outcome'. Among the symmetric games, based on this definition, in addition to the Prisoner's Dilemma the Assurance and the Chicken games are considered as social dilemmata (Liebrand 1983: 127). Among the asymmetric games in Figure 5.2 theses conditions also apply to the Rambo II game.[120]

---

[118] The notion 'dilemma of common aversion' goes back to Rapoport and Chammah (1969).

[119] In the cases of the Chicken or the Battle of the Sexes games it may, however, be difficult to reach agreement on one of the two equilibria.

[120] Condition 1 refers to games in which a player has a 'most threatening' strategy (Liebrand 1983: 125 f.). A strategy is most threatening if player A prefers player B not to play Defect irrespectively what A does and vice versa. In Figure 5.2 this refers to all games except the Battle of the Sexes game. Condition 2 states that both players are better off if both choose Cooperate than if both choose Defect. In Figure 5.2 this applies to the Prisoner's Dilemma, Chicken, Assurance and Rambo II game. Hence according to this definition the latter four games may be considered as social dilemmata.

Zürn (1992: 154) considers a 2x2 game as 'socially problematic' if at least one qualified Pareto optimum exists which is not simultaneously a Nash equilibrium and a Maximin equilibrium. He introduced the notion of the qualified Pareto optimum in order to be able to choose the Pareto optimum that may be considered as socially most desirable, as it maximizes welfare and it entails the greatest equality of payoffs. Based on the concept of the qualified Pareto optimum Zürn considers certain asymmetric games as socially problematic situations. The Maximin equilibrium is included in the above definition in order to account for behavior under uncertainty (Zürn 1992: 155). Based on his definition, Zürn identifies four classes of games which may be considered as socially problematic, (1) coordination games without distributional conflict (e.g. Assurance), (2) coordination games with distributional conflict (e.g. Battle of the Sexes, Chicken and games without equilibria), (3) dilemma games (e.g. Prisoner's Dilemma) and (4) Rambo games as asymmetric games (see below).[121]

According to Pies (2000: 42) a social dilemma refers to a situation in which conflicting individual interests at the action level constitute a collective interest at the constitutional or 'rule' level to set up rules that help the actors to realize gains of cooperation.

In the context of international negotiations on climate change, Ohl (2003: 50) restricts her analysis to symmetric games in which the cooperative outcome (CC) is the best possible outcome for the society as a whole (aggregated welfare optimum). These include the Prisoner's Dilemma, the Chicken and the Assurance as social dilemmata and the Game without Conflict (Pure Coordination) as unproblematic situation.

Thus different authors use different criteria and terminology. Broadly spoken social dilemmata may be defined as situations where individual rationality leads to collectively undesirable outcomes. This definition includes the Prisoner's Dilemma, Assurance and Chicken games. Another definition differentiates between cooperation problems where the mutual choice of the cooperative strategy may lead to a Pareto improvement vis-à-vis the equilibrium outcome (Prisoner's Dilemma) and coordination problems that avoid an undesirable outcome (Assurance, Chicken, Battle of the Sexes). The broadest definition is presented by Zürn who also considers Rambo games as 'socially problematic'. Whenever a situation has the structure of a social dilemma, joint decision-making is principally in the interest of the players involved. Among the games presented in Figure 5.2 Pure Coordination, Deadlock, and Constant Sum are not 'socially

---

[121] The question is why Zürn did not include Constant Sum Games in the list of socially problematic situations, as they also feature a qualified Pareto optimum which is not simultaneously a Nash and a Maximin equilibrium.

problematic'. They are nevertheless included, as they represent situations where mutual cooperation is either endogenous or not desired.

As mentioned before in the following these games will be analyzed for their institutional implications. First a static analysis of the nine games represented in Figure 5.2 will be carried out. In this context, static analysis means that it will be assumed that the game will be a one-shot game and that both players move simultaneously. Thereafter it will be asked how the institutional implications change if a game is infinitely repeated. This dynamic analysis will be carried out for the case of the Prisoner's Dilemma game. In both sections the institutional ramifications of the respective game structures will be developed at a theoretical level. Section 5.2-5.4 will then analyze under which conditions these games may become relevant in the management of international rivers.

Static analysis: selected 2x2 games and their institutional implications

In the following the nine games indicated in Figure 5.2 will be analyzed for their institutional implications. The game matrix per se only describes the incentives for the actors involved or the 'logic of the situation' (Zürn 1992). The game-theoretic solution concepts predict outcomes on the basis of unilateral action, however, the matrix per se does not yet indicate which mode of interaction – unilateral action, negotiation, voting or hierarchical coordination of interaction – will be applied in a real world situation (Scharpf 1997: 72). Real-world actors usually have the opportunity to select a mode of interaction, for instance to enter into negotiations or, in cases which involve multiple actors, to introduce a majority vote or even hierarchical decision-making. Actors may furthermore seek to alter the incentives of the situation for instance by concluding agreements. The conclusion of an agreement is equivalent to the creation of an institution, and to a change of the rules of the game. If this is done at the international level, theories of International Relations tend to speak of the formation of a 'regime'. As noted in Section 1.3.2, a widely accepted definition in international relations defines international regimes as: 'implicit and explicit principles, norms, rules, and decision-making procedures around which actors' expectations converge in a given area of international relations' (Krasner 1983: 2). In this definition the term regime is used synonymously with the set up of issue-area specific institutions. In other cases it is defined more broadly as all international interactions within a given issue area.[122]

---

[122] A broader regime definition is provided by Stein (1982: 301), according to whom a regime exists 'when the interaction between the parties is not unconstrained or is not based on independent decision making'.

The following analysis of each game will proceed as follows. First the logic of the situation will be described for a one shot-game, i.e. a game that is played only once and in which both players move simultaneously. The assumption is that in a one-shot game, players are unable to make binding commitments.[123] Second the incentives for the negotiation of an international agreement and for the implementation of this agreement in a one-shot game will be analyzed. Third at the end of each analysis the static perspective will briefly be abandoned and an outlook will be provided onto what happens if the game is played sequentially or if it is infinitely repeated.

Game without Conflict
In the Game without Conflict (Pure Coordination, Figure 5.2a) both players prefer joint cooperation over unilateral defection over unilateral cooperation over joint defection. Thus the preference order is CC > DC > CD > DD. In this case the cooperative outcome (CC) is the dominant strategy equilibrium (and hence the only Nash equilibrium and Maximin equilibrium) and the only (qualified) Pareto optimum. In a game of perfect information, cooperation is the equilibrium outcome even without communication. Whenever there is uncertainty as to the choice of alter, the cooperative outcome is self-enforcing when the players have the opportunity to communicate. In this case pre-play communication conveys real information about each player's intentions.

Assurance
The Assurance Game (also Ranked Coordination or Stag Hunt after a parable by Rousseau,[124] Figure 5.2b) differs from the Game without Conflict in that joint defection is preferred over unilateral cooperation. Hence the preference order is CC > DC > DD > CD. Both joint cooperation (CC) and joint defection (DD) are Nash equilibria, however, only the cooperative outcome is a (qualified) Pareto optimum. Therefore it is principally in the interest of both players to cooperate, and joint cooperation is a focal point.[125] Joint

---

[123] It will furthermore be assumed that the players have common knowledge. Information is common knowledge if it is known to all the players, and if each player knows that all the players know it.

[124] The Stag Hunt parable tells the story of a hunting society. For the society as whole, food security can be secured if all members participate in a stag hunt where they jointly circle the stag. However given the uncertainty of the other hunter's behavior, when the opportunity arises, a single player has an incentive to break out of the circle and hunt a rabbit individually, which, however, only secures his own minimum food requirements. If one player leaves the circle, the stag may escape. If all hunt individually, they are worse off than if they had all participated in the stag hunt (see Ohl 2003: 58).

[125] A focal point is a Nash equilibrium which for psychological reasons is particularly compelling (Rasmusen 2001: 32).

defection on the other hand is the Maximin equilibrium. This implies that unilateral action may lead to the socially desirable outcome (CC), but will not necessarily do so. In particular, whenever there is uncertainty whether alter behaves rationally, be it that any of the players has incomplete information or be it that there are doubts whether alter has analyzed the structure of the problem correctly or whether he may be trusted to behave solely according to his rational self-interest, it may be rational to choose the maximin strategy. If both players select maximin strategies, the outcome is joint defection, which makes both players worse off than the cooperative outcome. The uncertainty whether the socially desirable outcome will be achieved may give rise to negotiations and possibly regulation. Stein (1982: 303) believes that in an Assurance game, no regime is needed, since both actors agree on a most preferred outcome. Zürn (1992: 180) argues that in international relations, most Assurance problems may not necessarily require issue-area specific regimes, but may be solved through the diplomatic channels. However as Barrett (2003: 93) argues, pre-play communication leaves the players' calculus and the incentive problem unchanged. If one player intended to defect, he would still prefer the other player to cooperate. However in contrast to the Prisoner's Dilemma (see below) each player would cooperate if he believed that the other player cooperated. This means that ego needs an assurance that alter cooperates. Cooperation is conditional on the other player's cooperation (Ohl 2003: 59). Barrett (2003: 93) argues that in international relations, such an assurance may be provided by a treaty. If one state was party to a treaty requiring cooperative behavior, other states have an incentive to join. Once a treaty is ratified, international customary law requires states to hold their promises. In contrast to a Prisoner's Dilemma or a game of Chicken, in an Assurance game states have an incentive to do so. The uncertainty problem is avoided if the game is played sequentially: if the first player cooperates, the second will cooperate too. Hence in the sequential game, joint cooperation is a unique equilibrium.

Prisoner's Dilemma

The cover story of the Prisoner's Dilemma Game (Figure 5.2c) is rooted in the chief witness rule of the American legal system (Luce and Raiffa 1957: 95). Two suspects are taken into custody and held separately. The district attorney is convinced of their guilt, but has no clear evidence to convict them on a trial. He provides them with two alternatives: to confess or to deny. If both deny, they will be charged of illegal possession of weaponry and get a minor punishment. If both confess, they will be convicted, but they will get less than the most severe sentence. However if one confesses and the other denies, the confessor will receive indulgent treatment for providing evidence of the deed, whereas the denying suspect will get the most severe sentence possible. In this case confession is equivalent to defection and denial to cooperation. Both players prefer joint denial (CC) over joint confession (DD), but prefer unilateral confession (DC) over joint denial (CC). The resulting preference order is DC > CC > DD > CD. Whatever alter does, ego will be better off to confess. The consequence is that both will confess (DD) – which is a deficient outcome for the culprits, but the most desirable result for society as a whole as the two are convicted.[126] Joint defection (DD) is the dominant strategy equilibrium and hence the only Nash equilibrium as well as the Maximin equilibrium. At the same time, it is the only outcome that is no Pareto optimum. Both players would be better off if they cooperated; hence joint cooperation is Pareto superior vis-à-vis the Nash equilibrium. Under cardinal payoffs, the cooperative outcome is also the only aggregated welfare optimum as well as the only qualified Pareto optimum. However the cooperative outcome is no equilibrium in the one-shot game, since each player has the incentive to defect unilaterally. Ego has the incentive to free-ride on the cooperative behavior of alter. Thus in a Prisoner's Dilemma situation the players have theoretically an incentive to negotiate an agreement, given that cooperation could make them better off, but even if they communicated before the play of the game and concluded an agreement to cooperate, they would not have an incentive to implement this agreement. In other words agreements are not self-enforcing in the one shot game (Barrett 2003: 61-64).[127] In a static context the prospects for cooperation in a Prisoner's Dilemma situation are bleak if self-interested rational actors are assumed.

The Prisoner's Dilemma is a foundation of the contractarian model of the modern state (e.g. Stein 1982: 306). According to this understanding states are coercive institutions that allow individuals to eschew their dominant strategies. Analogously regimes in international relations can be understood to deal with suboptimal outcomes that emerge from unilateral action in specific issue areas. However if self-interested rational behavior is assumed, this still raises the question under which conditions states are willing to participate in such regimes and to ensure their enforcement. The game-theoretic answer to this question is that cooperation will not occur in a static context; however if the game is repeated infinitely, cooperation may under certain conditions emerge (see below).

---

[126] In the equilibrium, the effect of the chief witness rule is neutralized: the culprits convict each other.

[127] They may, of course, be enforced if an external enforcement entity exists. However also external enforcement comes at a cost.

Chicken

The Chicken Game (Figure 5.2d) tells the story of two car drivers who drive straight at each other on a narrow road. If they continue on course they will collide. The driver who swerves first avoids the worst case scenario, but he is the 'chicken' and the other driver wins the game. If they both veer off simultaneously, the worst case is prevented, but there is no winner. The Chicken game resembles the Prisoner's Dilemma, but unilateral cooperation is preferred over joint defection (given that in the latter case according to the cover story both could be dead). Hence the preference order is $DC > CC > CD > DD$. There are two Nash equilibria neither of which is Pareto dominated, DC and CD. The cooperative outcome (CC) on the other hand is the Maximin equilibrium and a Pareto and welfare optimum too, and if the numbers in Figure 5.2 are interpreted as cardinal payoffs it is the only qualified Pareto optimum.[128] It therefore may be considered as the socially desirable outcome. The structure of the game implies that for distributional reasons it is unlikely that negotiations would lead to an agreement on any of the two Nash equilibria (however if agreement on any of the Nash equilibria was reached, it would be self-enforcing). Instead an agreement could fix the cooperative outcome as socially desirable solution; however this solution cannot be sustained as an equilibrium in the single-shot game (at least not in pure strategies).[129] Similar to the Prisoner's Dilemma, agreement on the cooperative outcome is not incentive compatible and not self-enforcing in the one-shot game. However in contrast to the Prisoner's Dilemma game, the players share a common aversion against joint defection. If one player makes a credible commitment to defect, the other will cooperate (maximin strategy). In a sequentially played game, the player who moves first has a first-mover advantage: if the first player defects, the second will cooperate and the outcome is a unique equilibrium. Which equilibrium will be reached depends on who moves first. This is why one player may try to preempt the other, and the game of Chicken gives rise to strategic behavior. The unilateral provision of a public good can be described as a Chicken game (Lipnowski and Maital

---

[128] According to Rapoport and Chammah (1969: 151) in the Chicken game the aggregate value of the cooperative outcome (CC) needs to be greater as the aggregate value of the respective Nash equilibria (DC or CD). This strict inequality is not satisfied if the numbers in Figure 5.2 are interpreted as cardinal payoffs. Where this inequality applies, the cooperative outcome is the aggregated welfare optimum.

[129] A pure strategy is a rule that tells the player which action to choose. In contrast in a mixed strategy an action is played with a certain probability. In the Chicken game the cooperative outcome (CC) is an equilibrium outcome in mixed strategies (Rapoport and Chammah 1969: 153). Given that both players get less payoff by choosing CC in mixed strategies, which is an equilibrium outcome, than in pure strategies, which is not, this is another reason why the chicken game may be perceived as a social dilemma (ibid.).

1983), but in equilibrium the provision of the good is likely to be sub-optimal.

Battle of the Sexes

The cover story of the Battle of the Sexes Game (Figure 5.2e) describes a situation in which a male and a female have an interest in doing something together, but they differ in the preferred choice. While the female prefers to go to the theater, the male would rather play football. Therefore for the female (A) going to the theater is equivalent to defection, while playing football corresponds to cooperation. For the male (B) it is just the other way around. For both players, the preference order is DC > CD > DD > CC. This means that there are two Nash equilibria each of which is also a (qualified) Pareto optimum, however, the first equilibrium makes A better off and the second B. In that sense Battle of the Sexes can be characterized as a coordination game with distributional conflict. If both apply the maximin strategy, each partner does what he or she does want to do, but they do it without the partner, a Pareto inferior result. The cooperative outcome, where both do what the other person prefers to do, is the least desirable outcome. This is also the reason, why the Battle of the Sexes is no cooperation problem. Still it obviously is a coordination problem as it is a dilemma of common aversion with divergent interests (Stein 1982: 309). Given the potential costs of non-coordination, there are incentives for negotiation and regulation, but an agreement on any of the two qualified Pareto-optimal Nash equilibria may be difficult to reach as each equilibrium outcome will prefer one party over the other.[130] This situation changes in a sequentially played game, where one player moves first and the other follows. In this case the first mover will defect and the second cooperate, resulting in a unique equilibrium. In a (infinitely) repeated setting, an agreement could foresee that both equilibria are chosen interchangeably (so called correlated strategies).

Deadlock

The Deadlock Game (Figure 5.2f) also resembles the Prisoner's Dilemma, but in this case both players prefer joint defection over cooperation. The preference order is DC > DD > CC > CD. Joint defection is the dominant strategy equilibrium (and hence the Nash and the Maximin equilibrium) as well as the (qualified) Pareto optimum. The cooperative outcome (CC) is a

---

[130] Zürn (1992: 192) argues that in the Battle of the Sexes both equilibria satisfy the qualified Pareto criterion as well as Rawls' difference principle as criterion for distributive justice. Hence in contrast to the game of Chicken, any of these two equilibria may be considered as socially desirable.

Pareto inferior outcome. Thus Deadlock is neither a collaboration nor a coordination problem and in that sense not socially problematic.[131]

These six games are symmetric games, where both players have the same (only mirrored) preference orders. In contrast in the following asymmetric games the preference orders differ among the players.

Rambo I

In the Rambo I game (Figure 5.2g), A plays a game of Deadlock and B a game of Pure Coordination. Unilateral defection by player A is the dominant strategy equilibrium (the only Nash and the Maximin equilibrium) as well as a (qualified) Pareto optimum. However the cooperative outcome is a (qualified) Pareto optimum too. While A prefers unilateral defection, B prefers joint cooperation. Hence the equilibrium outcome leaves one player aggrieved (Stein 1982: 305). Zürn (1992) considers this game as socially problematic, given that there are two qualified Pareto optima, only one of which is an equilibrium.

Rambo II

In the Rambo II Game (Figure 5.2h) player A plays a game of Chicken and player B a game of Deadlock. Unilateral defection by player B is a Nash and the Maximin equilibrium as well as a Pareto optimum. However Rambo II has the interesting feature that the cooperative outcome is the only qualified Pareto optimum and may thus be considered as the socially desirable outcome. The Rambo II game may also be considered as a social dilemma according to Liebrand's (1983) definition. However in contrast to the Prisoner's Dilemma, the Nash equilibrium (CD) is also a Pareto optimum, and transition from the equilibrium to the cooperative outcome makes one player worse off, and at least with the payoff structure in Figure 5.2 the players cannot collectively improve through transition to the cooperative outcome.

When cardinal payoffs apply and distributive effects are taken into account, the existence of one qualified Pareto optimum for the cooperative outcome such as in Rambo II or the coexistence of two qualified Pareto optima with unequal payoffs such as in Rambo I indicate distributional conflict.

Stein (1982: 304) maintains that in a Rambo I situation no regime will evolve, since the satisfied player has no reason to forego his advantaged position. In contrast Zürn (1992: 213 ff.) argues that the disadvantaged actor

---

[131] This notwithstanding in an asymmetric game, the player who is not playing a game of Deadlock may find it problematic that the other player plays a game of Deadlock (see below).

has an incentive to seek to alter the structure of the situation. Given that there is no option for Pareto improvements within the game – even not with side-payments – one option may be the linkage of two inversed Rambo games. According to Zürn, a linkage strategy may result in a dilemma or a deadlock situation. This linkage hypothesis will be further pursued in Chapter 6. Another possibility, according to Zürn is the evolution of institutions which legitimize the equilibrium outcome. However it remains difficult to see that the aggrieved party will accept the status quo.

Constant Sum

In a Constant Sum Game (Figure 5.2i), player A plays a Prisoner's Dilemma and player B a Deadlock game.[132] Joint defection is the dominant strategy equilibrium and a (qualified) Pareto optimum. However all other outcomes are Pareto optima too, and the cooperative outcome is a qualified Pareto optimum. Similar to a Rambo game, while the equilibrium outcome (joint defection) makes player B better off, the cooperative outcome would make player A better off. There may therefore be distributional conflict over the preferred outcome, but given that the game is constant sum, there is no negotiation space for a transition to the cooperative outcome.

The next section will examine how the outcome of a game changes if we move from a static to a dynamic context. In particular in international relations, it can be argued that a dynamic perspective is more realistic, as most transboundary problems are of a dynamic nature and even possess structural time dependence. In doing so, the section will focus on the Prisoner's Dilemma game as the proto-type of a social dilemma. Given that this book is interested in the expedient membership of international water management institutions, consideration will also be given to N-player games.

Dynamic analysis: the infinitely repeated Prisoner's Dilemma game

If a Prisoner's Dilemma game is repeated infinitely, the cooperative outcome can under certain conditions be sustained as an equilibrium. According to the Folk theorem, in an infinitely repeated N-person game each feasible pair of Pareto-improving pay-offs can be sustained as a subgame-perfect Nash equilibrium if discount rates are sufficiently small and if the actors use trigger strategies (Fudenberg and Tirole 1991: 150 ff.; Missfeldt 1999:

---

[132] The game is Constant Sum for cardinal payoffs.

308).[133] The assumption is that in the infinitely repeated game the other players have an option to punish the defector, and while punishment comes at a cost, a player is willing to punish for a better future. The Folk theorem does not only apply to the Prisoner's Dilemma game, but at least for the two-person case also to other social dilemmata, such as the Chicken or the Rambo II game, as the cooperating players will be willing to punish the defector for the sake of a better future.[134]

In the following three different punishment strategies – Grim, Tit-for-tat and Getting-even – will be assessed for the capacity to overcome enforcement problems in the case of the infinitely repeated Prisoner's Dilemma game. This will be done for two-person and in view of international waters with three and more riparian states also for N-person games. The last paragraph will address the question to what extent the assumption of indefinite repetition applies to interaction between states.

Grim strategy

One possibility to sustain cooperation in an infinitely repeated Prisoner's Dilemma game is that both players adopt the Grim strategy. The Grim strategy says to start by choosing Cooperate and to continue to play Cooperate unless some other player chooses Defect, in which case one should choose Defect forever.[135] A 'Grim treaty' is an agreement in which all parties agree to play the Grim strategy (Barrett 2003: 276). It can be shown that if all players agree to playing Grim, the full cooperative outcome can be sustained as a subgame-perfect equilibrium of the infinitely repeated N-person Prisoner's Dilemma game provided that the discount factor is sufficiently close to one (i.e. that the players are sufficiently patient) (Barrett 2003: 277). The reason is that if all players play the Grim strategy, the benefit stream from defection, which yields a one time higher pay-off than cooperation, but lower payoffs than cooperation (or none) thereafter, will be lower than from cooperating forever. The Grim strategy is sub-game perfect

---

[133] The theorem is referred to as Folk theorem as its origins are hazy (Rasmusen 2001: 112). One problem with the Folk theorem is that, under certain assumptions, any feasible outcome can be sustained as an equilibrium outcome (see Barrett 2003: 272). However if pre-play communication is permitted, it can be expected that the players select the full cooperative outcome as the socially desirable outcome.

[134] The Folk theorem does not only apply to the Prisoner's Dilemma, but to any game in which the discount rate is zero or sufficiently small, the probability that the game ends is zero or sufficiently small, and the set of payoff combinations that strictly Pareto dominate the minimax payoff combinations in the mixed extension of the one-shot game is n-dimensional (Rasmusen 2001: 112 f.). The last condition only applies to games with three or more players. The applicability of Folk theorem to Chicken and Rambo II games with more than two players would have to be examined.

[135] Also the player who defected first will choose Defect forever.

or individually rational given that no player has an incentive to deviate from the cooperation phase if no other player deviates.[136] In this context, individual rationality means that no party can gain from failing to comply with the treaty (Barrett 2003: xiii).

However this is only the case for infinitely repeated games. As soon as there is common knowledge that the game will end at some point, it is rational to defect in the last game as there won't be any punishment thereafter. However if it is rational to defect in the endgame, it can be shown by backward induction that it is rational to defect in the entire game as it is rational to defect in the game before the endgame and so on. This phenomenon has been described by Selten (1978) as the Chainstore Paradox (in Rasmusen 2001: 110). However if a game is played infinitely, or even if there is a certain probability that it will be played infinitely, the prospect of cooperation increases significantly. In fact in this case the Folk theorem raises the question why full cooperation is not always sustained.

According to Barrett (2003: 272), this is not the case as the Grim strategy satisfies individual, but not collective rationality. In this context, collective rationality means that the parties cannot gain collectively by changing their treaty (Barrett 2003: xiii). The Grim strategy is a severe punishment as it calls for the complete dissolution of an agreement should any of its parties defect.[137] In a two-person game it is rational for ego to punish alter, given that if alter defects forever, ego's payoff will be higher from joint defection than from unilateral cooperation (although it could be argued that both players have an incentive to renegotiate and revert to the Getting-even strategy, see below). However in a multiparty game the parties that enforce the agreement may harm themselves more by punishing (complying with the Grim strategy) than by not punishing (Barrett 2003: 279). This means that collectively, the players have an incentive to deviate from the punishment phase and instead to renegotiate the agreement (Barrett 2003: 279). The Grim strategy is not collectively rational – and hence not credible – because it is not renegotiation-proof. From the perspective of all players, playing Grim would only be credible if the parties could commit not to renegotiate the agreement. Hence while Grim is credible from the perspective of each player (sub-game perfect), in a multiparty game, it may not be credible from

---

[136] For dynamic games, the concept of the Nash equilibrium needs to be further refined by the idea of perfectness that takes account of the order of moves. A strategy combination is a sub-game perfect (Nash) equilibrium if it is a Nash equilibrium for the entire game and if its relevant action rules are a Nash equilibrium for every sub-game (Rasmusen 2001: 91).

[137] In the case of defection, the dissolution of a treaty is allowed according to the Vienna Convention on the Law of Treaties. It is a typical provision for bilateral treaties, but it is also used in the 1957 and 1976 Conventions on the Conservation of North Pacific Fur Seals (Barrett 2003: 277).

the perspective of all players (not renegotiation-proof). This is the reason why it may be difficult to sustain cooperation in a multi-player game using the Grim strategy.

Tit-for-tat strategy

An alternative punishment strategy is Tit-for-tat. The Tit-for-tat strategy became famous after Anatol Raporport won a series of Prisoner's Dilemma computer tournaments by using this strategy (Axelrod 1984). The Tit-for-tat strategy starts by cooperating on the first move and then by doing whatever the other player did in the previous period. This implies, if both players play Tit-for-tat, a single defection will result in an infinite alternation of cooperation and defection.[138] While Tit-for-tat won the compute tournament, Tit-for-tat, unlike the Grim strategy, is not credible. The first question is whether ego, given that alter plays Tit-for-tat, has an incentive to defect once. The answer is no, given that for sufficiently high discount factors, the benefit stream from defecting once will be lower than from cooperating forever. The second question is whether alter's threat to punish is credible. This, however, is not the case given that for sufficiently high discount factors, the benefit stream from not punishing a single defection will be higher than the benefit stream from punishing (playing Tit-for-tat) (Barrett 2003: 278; Rasmusen 2001: 112). Therefore, Tit-for-tat cannot enforce cooperation.

Getting-even strategy

Another 'forgiving' strategy of reciprocity is Getting-even (Barrett 2003: 278).[139] The Getting-even strategy requires that ego cooperates unless ego has played Defect less often than the other players in the past. Unlike in Tit-for-tat, the punishing players will resort to cooperation, once the defecting player cooperates, and the defecting player will not punish the punishment. It can be shown that for sufficiently high discount factors, in a two-person game the threat to carry out the punishment is credible for Getting-even (Barrett 2003: 278). Therefore, for the 2 person game, cooperation should not be a problem. However whether Getting-even is renegotiation-proof for a greater number of players depends on the underlying benefit and cost functions. Barrett (2003: 280 f.) shows for a N-person Prisoner's Dilemma with $b, c > 0$ and $N > c/b$ and a discount factor near to one that playing Getting-even is individually rational if $N > c/b$ (which applies by

---

[138] If the defector does not return to cooperation in the game after the defection, both will defect forever. Thus Tit-for-tat does not restore cooperation.

[139] According to Folmer and von Mouche (2000: 242) this strategy is based on Abreu's (1986) 'stick and carrot' approach.

assumption) and collectively rational if $c/b + 1 \geq N$.[140] Thus game theory predicts that cooperation is likely to be restricted to few players; the exact number depends on the underlying cost and benefit functions with $c/b < N \leq (c/b) + 1$.[141] While cooperation is individually rational in infinitely repeated Prisoner's Dilemma games, it is collective rationality that limits cooperation.

The above assumes that actions can be monitored at no costs. If actions cannot be observed at all, an agreement on the cooperative outcome cannot be enforced. Monitoring, however, need not be perfect. With perfect monitoring, no country would ever defect in equilibrium, given that the threat of punishment is credible. With imperfect monitoring, punishment will be needed in equilibrium (Barrett 2003: 284).

The implication is that in international relations, cooperation is likely to be limited to few countries in a Prisoner's Dilemma-type situation. The critical number of countries which can sustain a cooperative outcome depends on the problem at hand. While cooperation can be sustained by two countries if the countries are sufficiently patient, in some cases, cooperation may even not be sustained by three countries. The reason is that it may pay for two of these three countries to cooperate, even if the third country does not cooperate (Barrett 2003: 283). In the three country case defection by one country may not have severe consequences. However cooperation will be more difficult to sustain as the number of countries which may free-ride on the cooperative behavior of other countries increase.

Given that the theory of infinitely repeated games has originally been developed for problems of strategic interaction among individuals, the question is whether the above considerations in fact apply to states.

Applicability to states?

The above argumentation rests on the assumption that the respective games are played infinitely. This raises the question whether the assumption of infinite repetition applies to states in general and to international water negotiations in particular. It can be argued that infinite repetition does not apply in the international system since states can disappear. In addition Ohl (2003: 54) questions the existence of infinitely repeated games between states, given that the time horizon of the individual decision-maker which makes a decision on behalf of the state is limited. Barrett (2003: 273) on the other hand argues that the possibility that states may disappear is not important to the theory of repeated games. It would only be a problem if a

---

[140] Whereby N = number of players, b = benefits and c = costs.

[141] This is in line with Olson's (1965: 33 ff. and 50) argument that on a voluntary basis collective goods will only be provided by sufficiently small groups.

state's dissolution was common knowledge. Furthermore international law requires successor states to obey the international obligations entered into by their predecessor. With respect to international water negotiations, it can be argued that they rarely correspond to a one-shot game. Instead in the case of water, physical interdependence implies a certain degree of compulsiveness of the relationship. In most instances, interaction on water issues will take place over extended time periods, both in the planning and in the operation of water-related infrastructure. Water abstraction or wastewater discharge tends to take place on a continuous basis. Thus international water management can generally be assumed to be repeated infinitely in the sense that nobody knows whether the game will end at some point.

Furthermore the question is whether the assumption of rational self-interested behavior applies to states. As mentioned above, Chayes and Chayes (1993) argue that most states comply with most agreements most of the time. If that is true enforcement may not be as important as assumed by economic theory. However Downs et al. (1996) point at the fact that in many cases it may be easy for countries to comply, as many treaties do not ask their signatories to play Cooperate, but confirm the non-cooperative outcome. If that is true, Chayes and Chayes argument carries less weight. Barrett (2003) also believes that enforcement mechanisms are needed to sustain international cooperation in a Prisoner's Dilemma situation. However he argues that the problem of compliance has been overemphasized in the literature. The reason is that a country that intends not to comply will not accede to the respective agreement in the first place or withdraw from the treaty (Barrett 2003: 291). This means that irrespectively of whether the behavioral assumptions of economic theory indeed apply to states in each and every case, according to Barrett (2003) an economic analysis may inform international negotiations by (1) supporting the design treaties that improve over the non-cooperative outcome, (2) by deterring free-riding by non-participation in multiparty games and (3) by ensuring enforcement.[142]

5.1.3 Results

This section analyzed the interrelationship of problem structure and institutional design. For unidirectional externality problems, the Coase theorem spells out the institutional preconditions, namely well defined

---

[142] In international water management the participation problem can be expected to be less pronounced as in negotiations on global public goods given that the majority of international watercourses are bipartite. However in contrast to the provision of global public goods, we are often faced with negative unidirectional externality problems and thus with asymmetric incentive structures.

property rights and sufficiently low transaction costs, under which voluntary negotiations lead to an internalization of external effects. The problem is that in the international system there is no supranational authority which could define and enforce property rights. Therefore, it may be useful to analyze different types of cooperation and coordination problems in terms of non-cooperative game theory.

Non-cooperative game theory allows the differentiation of game types, including games of pure harmony, games that represent conflict and those that signify social dilemmata. The static analysis of selected 2x2 games shows that whether cooperation (both players choose Cooperate) and coordination (both players coordinate in order to avoid an undesirable outcome) can be expected depends on the structure of the game. In a Game without Conflict cooperation is endogenous in the sense that both players independently choose Cooperate. In an Assurance game, cooperation will only occur with certainty if the players coordinate and provide themselves adequate assurances that the other player will cooperate. In international relations, this may be achieved through an agreement which, in the case of an Assurance game, is self-enforcing. In a game of Chicken we can expect unilateral, but not full cooperation in pure strategies. If one player makes a credible threat to defect, the other will cooperate. Unilateral cooperation can also be expected in the game Battle of the Sexes. In this case the players have an incentive to coordinate in order to avoid joint defection. In the Prisoner's Dilemma game no cooperation can be expected in the one-shot game. Both players could be better off if they cooperated, but even if the players communicate pre-play and agree on cooperation, an agreement is not self-enforcing. In a number of asymmetric games, such as Rambo I, Rambo II and the Constant Sum game, joint cooperation is collectively equivalent to the equilibrium outcome. However given that transition to the cooperative outcome makes one player worse off, cooperation cannot be expected to occur. In the Deadlock game, joint defection is an equilibrium outcome, and cooperation is not desired.

In contrast to the static analysis, the dynamic analysis of the infinitely repeated Prisoner's Dilemma game shows that the cooperative outcome can be sustained as a equilibrium if (1) the parties conclude an agreement in which they agree to cooperate and to punish defective behavior through the Grim or Getting-even strategy, (2) the discount rate is sufficiently small and (3) the number of players is sufficiently small. While the cooperative outcome can be sustained in a two-person game, the exact number of participants that may sustain the cooperative outcome in a multi-person game on the basis of the Getting-even strategy depends on the game's underlying cost and benefit functions where $c/b < N \leq (c/b) + 1$. This means that for a N-party Prisoner's Dilemma game, the expedient level of participation can only be determined for a specific case. Given that we are usually dealing with infinitely repeated games in international relations, we may assume that the above also applies to international water negotiations if they have the structure of a Prisoner's Dilemma game. In particular for 2x2 games, the Folk theorem also applies to other game structures.

In essence, this section argues that if we know the structure of the game, we may say something about adequate institutional design. In the case of the Assurance game, coordination can be achieved in a one-shot game, and an agreement is self-enforcing. In many other situations in a one-shot game the prospects of cooperation are low. However under certain conditions well designed agreements with enforcement mechanisms (and for that matter institutions) may be able to restructure incentives and to sustain cooperation in an infinitely repeated game. This applies to the Prisoner's Dilemma, but for instance also to bilateral Chicken or Rambo II games.

This section has identified different problem structures or game types and has analyzed their institutional implications at a theoretical level. As such it has created the basis for the identification of possible problem structures in the management of international water resources and for the deduction of policy recommendations on institutional design. In view of the above, the central question now is under which conditions are we dealing with which problem structure in the management of international waters. This shall be analyzed in the following sections. Section 5.2 will address negative and positive reciprocal and Section 5.3 negative and positive unidirectional externality problems. Section 5.4 will present conclusions.

5.2 NEGATIVE AND POSITIVE RECIPROCAL EXTERNALITY PROBLEMS

This section will analyze reciprocal externality problems at symmetric common pool resources. As argued in Section 2.2.2 in the case of common pool resources, such as contiguous rivers and aquifers, shared lakes or regional seas, external effects are reciprocal in the sense that every actor imposes externalities on himself as well as on all other actors that share the resource. Whether these effects are positive or negative depends on the use. Therefore, the following will discuss three different uses as examples for pure negative externalities, combined negative and positive externalities and pure positive externalities. Section 5.2.1 will address water quantity problems as a resource appropriation problem that may entail negative externalities. Section 5.2.2 will deal with water quality problems as a combined resource appropriation and provision problem where a negative externality may be mitigated by the provision of a positive externality.

Section 5.2.3 will analyze the provision of retention area at a border river as a 'pure' positive externality problem. Section 5.2.4 will present conclusions.

5.2.1   Water Withdrawal from a Common Pool Resource

Water withdrawal from a symmetric common pool resource (CPR), such as a shared lake or a shared aquifer, can be characterized as a resource appropriation problem. Whenever a symmetric common pool resource is used by a group of users, rivalry of consumption and problems of exclusion come into play, and individually rational decision-making is likely to lead to collectively undesirable outcomes. Individual appropriation decisions may go along with negative appropriation externalities, impacting other users' appropriation opportunities. An externality is present whenever increased appropriation by one user reduces the average return other users receive for a given level of investment in appropriation and vice versa. The appropriation externality thus reflects the production relationship between users. In the case of water withdrawal, increased water withdrawal by one user reduces the water other users obtain from a given level of investment in pumping equipment. A race on the resource may begin that may lead to the exploitation of the resource.

In a first step a generic appropriation model will be presented building upon Ostrom et al. (1994: 57 f.). The purpose of the generic model is to show that resource appropriation, such as water withdrawal, does not necessarily have the structure of a social dilemma, but to indicate the conditions under which it does so and under which it does not. In a second step a slightly different numeric model will be presented where water withdrawal from a common lake or aquifer has the structure of a Prisoner's Dilemma. The numeric model will be used in order to discuss the relationship of externalities, property rights and institutional design. In a third step the findings will be contrasted with empirical evidence.

A generic appropriation model

Let us assume two players, each with two strategies. Each player has one unit of productive input (token) to invest. He could either invest in an outside opportunity, strategy $x_i = 0$, resulting in a fixed return (wealth) w. The alternative strategy $x_i = 1$ is to appropriate the resource. The output from appropriation is a function of total appropriation by both players $F(\Sigma x_i)$. If one player appropriates one unit, the output is $F(1)$, if both appropriate one unit, each players' output is $F(2)/2$.

The outcome of the game depends on the relationship of w, $F(1)$ and $F(2)/2$ as well as on the functional shape of F and the value of w. F may principally have diminishing ($F' > 0$, $F'' < 0$) or increasing ($F' > 0$, $F'' > 0$) returns. Given that this model deals with appropriation problems with rivalry of consumption, in the following it will be assumed that F has diminishing returns (concave function), meaning the first unit invested in the resource diminishes the return of a second unit of investment.[143] In this case $F(2)/2 < F(1)$ applies, and depending on the values of w, $F(1)$ and $F(2)/2$ three cases can be differentiated (Figure 5.3).

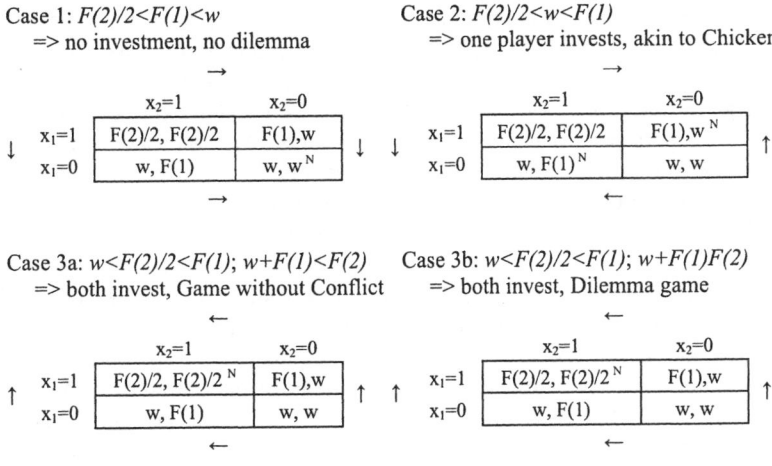

Case 1: $F(2)/2<F(1)<w$
=> no investment, no dilemma

Case 2: $F(2)/2<w<F(1)$
=> one player invests, akin to Chicken

Case 3a: $w<F(2)/2<F(1)$; $w+F(1)<F(2)$
=> both invest, Game without Conflict

Case 3b: $w<F(2)/2<F(1)$; $w+F(1)F(2)$
=> both invest, Dilemma game

N: Nash equilibrium

Source: Own development based on Ostrom et al. (1994: 57 f.)

Figure 5.3   Generic Resource Appropriation Model

The arrows in Figure 5.3 indicate a player's best choice given the choice of the other player. The arrow to the left indicates the choice of player 1 if player 2 chooses 1 ($x_2 = 1$). The arrow to the right indicates the choice of player 1 if player 2 chooses 0. The arrow to the top indicates the choice of player 2 if player 1 chooses 1. And the arrow to the bottom indicates the choice of player 2 if player 1 chooses 0. If two arrows point at the same cell,

---

[143] A situation of increasing returns (convex function) is conceivable if both players pool their resources and apply an appropriation technology, e.g. by drilling a deeper well, which yields a higher return per unit invested than individual investment. However in this case it is assumed that there are no resource constraints, therefore this problem will not be considered in this section. The problem of joint infrastructure provision will, however, be addressed in the next section.

the respective outcome is a Nash equilibrium. If all four arrows point at the same cell, the respective outcome is a dominant strategy equilibrium.

In Case 1 ($F(2)/2 < F(1) < w$), given that $F(1) < w$ and $F(2)/2 < w$, investment in the resource is neither individually nor collectively rational. This means that playing w is the dominant strategy equilibrium and no resource appropriation can be expected.

In Case 2 ($F(2)/2 < w < F(1)$), we assume sharply diminishing returns so that $F(2)/2 < w$. In this case it is individually rational ($w < F(1)$), but not collectively rational to appropriate the resource. In this case the game has two equilibria, each with one player appropriating the resource, and the other staying out. Ostrom et al. (1994: 57) argue that this situation has the structure of a game of Chicken. However strictly spoken, it is only akin to Chicken, as the 'cooperative outcome' (w, w) is no Pareto optimum and $w + w < w + F(1)$.[144] Basically, in this situation, only one party is able to appropriate the resource, and there is no opportunity for cooperation.

In a static game, this is a quite unrealistic result for the case of water resources, since it would be possible to decrease the size of the unit appropriated. However in the real world it may be quite relevant, as resource appropriation processes have to be seen in a dynamic context. Often one riparian appropriates first, preempting the opportunities for appropriation by his co-riparians. An example may be the usage of the shared groundwater resources between Israelis and Palestinians (see below). Furthermore Waterbury and Whittington (1998) raise the question whether Ethiopia and Egypt are currently engaged in a game of Chicken on the Nile River, as Egypt is pursuing the 'New Valley Project' and Ethiopia considers the development of dams upstream, two endeavors that appear to exclude each other.

In Case 3 ($w < F(2)/2 < F(1)$), it is individually rational to appropriate ($w < F(1)$), and the returns do not diminish as fast so that $F(2)/2 > w$. In this case appropriating the resource (playing $x_i = 1$) is a dominant strategy for each player, and the game has one dominant strategy equilibrium with both player appropriating the resource. However whether this is a dilemma or not depends on the relationship of $F(1)$, $F(2)/2$ and w:

1. If w is very small so that $F(1) + w < 2F(2)/2$, the equilibrium outcome is the aggregated welfare optimum and the best outcome for all players involved. The situation corresponds to a Game without Conflict (Case 3a).

---

[144] As noted above, according to Rapoport and Chammah (1969: 151) in the Chicken game the aggregate value of the cooperative outcome (CC) needs to be greater as the aggregate value of the respective Nash equilibria (DC or CD).

2. However if $F(1) + w > 2F(2)/2$, the equilibrium outcome is collectively inefficient. In this case the players would be collectively better off if only one player appropriated the resource. Thus this situation may be considered as a social dilemma situation (Case 3b). It is, however, no Prisoner's Dilemma, as in the Prisoner's Dilemma the players are collectively best off if both cooperate.

Thus the above analysis serves as a reminder that it would be wrong to assume that collective appropriation of water from a shared aquifer necessarily results in a Prisoner's Dilemma situation. Instead the structure of the game depends on the resource and appropriation characteristics and the ensuing cost and benefit functions. Depending on the parameters involved, appropriation from a symmetric common pool resource may be unproblematic (no investment at all or Game without Conflict), may take the structure of a game akin to Chicken or of a Dilemma game. The situation is unproblematic whenever the parties are not interested in appropriating the resource or whenever the safe yield exceeds the total amount appropriated. It takes the structure akin to the Chicken game if basically only one player appropriates the entire resource. It takes the structure of a Dilemma game if total appropriation exceeds the safe yield leading to a 'race' on the resource by the players involved.

The question is what this implies for the game-theoretic reconstruction of negative reciprocal externality problems. Given that Cases 1 and 3a are unproblematic, these cases are no negative externality problems. Externality problems do, however, exist in Cases 2 and 3b. This implies that negative reciprocal externality problems may either take the structure of a Dilemma game or a game akin to the Chicken game.

The problem with the above model is that the choice is framed as alternative investment opportunities, but not in terms of cooperation and defection. In order to show that water withdrawal from a shared lake or aquifer may, under certain conditions, also have the structure of a regular Prisoner's Dilemma game, the next section will frame the problem in terms of cooperation and defection, and a numeric model will be introduced which will result in a Prisoner's Dilemma game.

Water withdrawal from a CPR as a Prisoner's Dilemma

In contrast to the above generic model, in the following model, each player's choice is not to either invest in the water resource or in an outside opportunity, but to extract at a high or a low rate. High extraction implies defection and low extraction cooperation.

Let us assume two homogenous countries A and B which may choose between a high and a low rate of extraction from a shared aquifer. It shall furthermore be assumed that as soon as at least one country extracts at a high rate, total extraction exceeds the safe yield, leading to dropping groundwater tables, and a respective increase in pumping costs for both countries (and eventually to the destruction of the resource). If both extract at a high rate, these costs increase further.

The following payoffs shall be assumed: High extraction yields a gross benefit of 6 and low extraction of 3. If both extract at a low rate, there are no costs due to falling groundwater tables involved. If one party plays High and the other Low, the costs of falling groundwater are 2 for each. If both play High, the costs of falling groundwater tables are 4 for each. The payoffs of the different strategies are presented in Table 5.1 and Figure 5.4.

Table 5.1   The Water Extraction Game: Assumed Payoffs

Strategy combination	Benefits of extraction	Costs of falling groundwater table	Net Benefits
Low, Low	3,3	0,0	3,3
High, High	6,6	4,4	2,2
High, Low	6,3	2,2	4,1
Low, High	3,6	2,2	1,4

Source: Own presentation

Under these conditions, the game has the structure of a Prisoner's Dilemma game, and for each player high extraction (Defect) is a dominant strategy. While the players would be better off if both extracted at a low rate (Cooperate), each player has the incentive to free-ride on the potential cooperative behavior of the other player.

		Country B	
		Low extraction (C)	High extraction (D)
Country A	Low extraction (C)	3,3	1,4
	High extraction (D)	4,1	2,2 [N]

N: Nash equilibrium

Source: Own presentation

Figure 5.4   Water Extraction from a Shared Aquifer as Prisoner's Dilemma Game

In such a situation, the players principally have an incentive to conclude an agreement in which they would agree to cooperate by extracting at a low rate. However if rational self-interested behavior is assumed, an agreement alone will not be sufficient to sustain the cooperative outcome as an equilibrium outcome, but the agreement would have to contain an enforcement mechanism. If we assume that the water extraction game is repeated, and we do not know whether there will be an end-game, the cooperative outcome (Low-Low) can be sustained as an equilibrium outcome if the parties' discount rates are sufficiently low, and if the two parties agree to play Low and to punish playing High through the Grim or Getting-even strategy. This, of course, presumes that each party's pumping regime can be observed, which may be difficult to achieve in practice. Hence a respective agreement also needs to contain provisions on monitoring.

An agreement to cooperate would be tantamount with a mutual delimitation of property rights to water. Hence in the case of an ideal symmetric reciprocal externality situation, the mutual delimitation of property rights is in the self-interests of the players involved and only depends on effective enforcement.

Empirical evidence

An example of the simultaneous water extraction from shared groundwater resources under conditions of water scarcity is the Mountain Aquifer shared between Israelis and Palestinians. In this case it can be argued that Israel 'moved first', and when the two parties started to negotiate a pumping regime following the Oslo Declaration of Principles in 1993, absolute and relative per capita water extractions were highly unequal in favor of Israel. Thus in this case the problem was not only to limit total withdrawal to the safe yield, but the Palestinians demanded an equitable share in the use of the resource. The 1995 interim agreement (so called Oslo B agreement) confirms the Israeli uses and aims at the 'joint' development of additional water for the Palestinians, which however proved difficult given the resource constraints (e.g. Dombrowsky 2003). The agreement seeks to limit total abstraction (although some critics have argued that the assumed safe yields exceeds the long-term average), but, it hardly reallocates the resource. Thus the efficiency problem is superimposed by an equity problem. While it is the interest of the parties to limit total abstraction, they do not agree on the distribution of the rights to abstract.

Thus in this case the situation is rather asymmetric, and it appears to be more akin to a Chicken than a Prisoner's Dilemma game. If the cooperative outcome where both extract at a rate that is compatible with the safe yield and where the opportunities for extraction are more equally distributed among the two parties was a Pareto, or even a welfare, optimum a transition to the cooperative outcome would be collectively desirable. However this entails distributional implications and it is unclear how to get there. If the cooperative outcome was a welfare optimum, the Palestinians could make a side-payment to the Israelis if they accepted the status quo as starting point for negotiations. If agreement on the cooperative outcome can be reached, it may be maintained as an equilibrium outcome in a repeated game through the set up of an enforcement mechanism. This empirical example shows that the numeric example of the Prisoner's Dilemma game presented above refers to an 'ideal' case where both parties have similar starting conditions.

5.2.2 Pollution of a Common Pool Resource

Whenever a water resource is being polluted, this may be another reason for the occurrence of negative externalities. The act of pollution may entail a negative externality and is equivalent to the appropriation of property rights to water quality. This case is reflected by the generic appropriation model presented in Figure 5.3. However if pollution is abated by the application of a wastewater treatment technology, the negative externality is mitigated by the provision of a positive externality. The act of wastewater treatment therefore is a provision problem, providing a positive externality or a public good.[145] Hence water quality problems may be considered as combined appropriation and provision problems.

In order to model the provision of wastewater treatment, in a first step a generic model for the provision of a public good will be introduced. In a second step a numeric example will be provided. Given that the structure of a provision problem furthermore depends on whether we are dealing with a continuous or a discrete public good, both the provision of a continuous and of a discrete public good will be addressed (see Ostrom et al. 1994: 61f.). In the case of a continuous public good each actor's contribution benefits all actors involved. In the case of a discrete public good, the good will only be provided if all players contribute. This applies to larger infrastructure measures which rely on more than one contribution. At the end of the section some empirical evidence will be provided.

---

[145] Other combined appropriation and provision problems are conceivable in transboundary water management, such as humanly caused siltation remedied through watershed management or humanly caused flood risks remedied through the rehabilitation of flood plains.

A generic provision model

Continuous public goods

Let us again assume two players, each of which has one unit of input (measured in tokens) to invest. For instance two neighboring companies located at a shared lake have to decide whether or not to invest in wastewater treatment. Each player (company) could invest in an outside opportunity, strategy $x_i = 0$, resulting in a return of w (e.g. investment in R&D). The alternative strategy $x_i = 1$ is to invest in the public good (e.g. wastewater treatment). Given that the benefits from the investment in wastewater are non-excludable, for each token contributed to the provision of the public good each player receives a value of v (e.g. improved water quality in the lake). Thus if one player invests, the return is v for each player ($F(1) = v$), if both invest, it is $2v$ for each ($F(2) = 2v$). In this case the structure of the game depends on the relation of w, v and $2v$, and again three different cases can be differentiated (Figure 5.5).

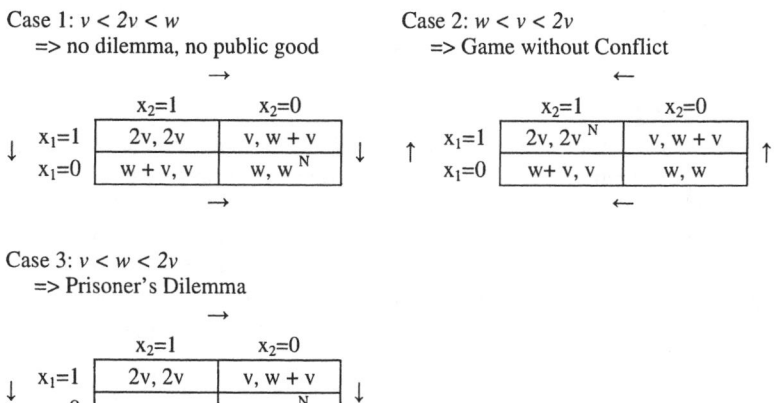

Case 1: $v < 2v < w$
 => no dilemma, no public good

Case 2: $w < v < 2v$
 => Game without Conflict

Case 3: $v < w < 2v$
 => Prisoner's Dilemma

N: Nash equilibrium

Source: Own development based on Ostrom et al. (1994: 61 f.)

Figure 5.5   Generic Provision Model for a Continuous Public Good

In Case 1 ($v < 2v < w$), no player will have an incentive to invest in the public good, and the equilibrium outcome is (w, w). However this is no dilemma as both are individually and collectively better off if they invest in the outside opportunity. The public good will not be provided.

In Case 2 ($w < v < 2v$) both are better off if they invest in the public good. Providing the public good is the dominant strategy equilibrium and the only Pareto optimum. The game has the structure of a Game without Conflict.

In Case 3 ($v < w < 2v$), $2v$ is smaller than $w + v$ and v is smaller than w. Hence it is rational for each player to play w. However (w, w) is inferior to the result where both played v. Thus this constellation has the structure of a Prisoner's Dilemma (e.g. nobody invests in wastewater treatment).

Hence three cases can be distinguished in the provision of a continuous public good. First the provision of the public good is not in the interest of the players; this situation is unproblematic. Second the provision of the public good is in the interest of both players and unproblematic as it is individually rational for each player to provide the good (Game without Conflict). Third the provision is in the interest of the players involved, but individual costs exceed individual benefits, and each player seeks to free-ride on the other's players provision (Prisoner's Dilemma).

Similar to the case of negative reciprocal externalities, positive reciprocal externalities do not necessarily imply a Prisoner's Dilemma situation, but they may also be unproblematic (Game without Conflict) if each player has an incentive to provide the good unilaterally.

Discrete public goods

The situation changes if the public good is discrete meaning that both players' contributions are required for its provision. In this case if only one player contributes to the good, this involves costs, but has no utility, hence $F(1) = -1$. If both invest, the payoff remains $F(2) = 2v$. In the above example, this could be the case if the objective of wastewater treatment is to reach bathing water quality, and if that can only be achieved if both treat the wastewater. For positive v and w, we may distinguish between two cases, $2v < w$ and $w < 2v$ (Figure 5.6).

For Case 1 ($2v < w$), the players have no incentive to invest in the public good, and the outcome (w, w) is a dominant strategy equilibrium. There is no dilemma, and the public good will not be provided. In the above example, for all players involved, the value of investment in F&E is assumed to be higher than the value of bathing water quality.

For Case 2 ($w < 2v$), the game has two equilibria ($2v, 2v$) and (w, w). This game has the structure of the Assurance game. In principle the outcome ($2v, 2v$), in which both contribute to the public good, is preferred to the outcome (w, w). However as long as ego is not sure how alter will behave, contributing to the public good becomes a 'dangerous' strategy, and it will be safer to play w (maximin strategy).

Case 1: $2v < w$

=> no dilemma, no public good

Case 2: $w < 2v$

=> Assurance game

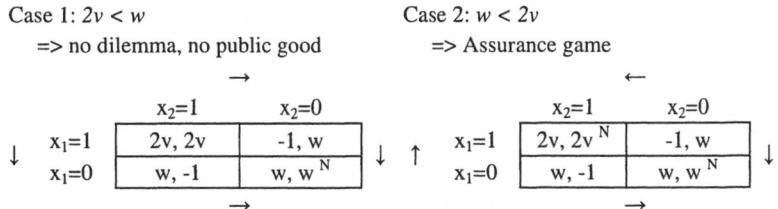

N: Nash equilibrium

Source: Own development based on Ostrom et al. (1994: 61 ff.)

Figure 5.6   Generic Provision Model for a Discrete Public Good

Thus if the provision of a discrete public good is principally in the interest of the players involved, each player's contribution is needed for the provision of the good. In this case the game has the structure of an Assurance game.

Wastewater treatment at a shared lake

As Prisoner's Dilemma

In the following, a numeric example will be presented where the separate provision of wastewater treatment at a shared lake has the structure of a Prisoner's Dilemma game. Let us assume two homogenous countries A and B sharing a symmetric lake. In the status quo, each country produces one unit of pollution, creating a cost of 2.5. Each unit of pollution avoided thus creates a benefit of 2.5. Let us further assume that treatment costs 3 per unit. If both treat one unit, each party pays 3 and receives a benefit of 5, resulting in a net benefit of 2 for each. If only one country treats, it pays 3 and receives a benefit of 2.5, leading to a net loss of 0.5. However the other party receives a benefit of 2.5. The assumed payoffs are presented in Table 5.2 and Figure 5.7.

In this situation, contribution to wastewater treatment has the structure of a Prisoner's Dilemma game. The solution to this game is very much akin to the water extraction game discussed above: If the provision of wastewater treatment can be considered as an infinitely repeated game, the two parties can be assumed to be able to maintain the cooperative outcome as an equilibrium if their interest rate is sufficiently low, and if they conclude an agreement to abate and set up a monitoring and an enforcement mechanism to punish defective behavior. However the question is how effective the punishment of pollution through defection of the other party, i.e. through pollution, would be, and whether the cooperating party, if it has carried out investments in treatment plants, would be willing to forego the benefits from treatment.

Table 5.2   The Wastewater Treatment Game: Assumed Payoffs

Strategy combination	Benefit of treatment	Cost of treatment	Net benefits
Pollute, Pollute	0, 0	0, 0	0, 0
Pollute, Abate	2.5, 2.5	0, -3	2.5, -0.5
Abate, Pollute	2.5, 2.5	-3, 0	-0.5, 2.5
Abate, Abate	5, 5	-3, -3	2, 2

Source: Own presentation

Given that in the case of pollution, a negative externality is mitigated by the provision of a positive externality, the agreement to cooperate can again be understood as a mutual delimitation of property rights to water (in this case to pollution rights). Similar to the case of reciprocal water withdrawal, in the case of symmetric reciprocal pollution problems a mutual delimitation of property rights is in the interest of the parties involved and can be achieved if an adequate enforcement mechanism is being put in place.

		Country B	
		Abate (C)	Pollute (D)
Country A	Abate (C)	2, 2	-0.5, 2.5
	Pollute (D)	2.5, -0.5	0, 0 ^{N}

N: Nash equilibrium

Source: Own presentation

Figure 5.7   Wastewater Treatment at a Shared Lake as Prisoner's Dilemma Game

As an Assurance Game
The structure of the above game changes if the possibility of economies of scale from joint treatment is added. Let us assume that pollution mainly stems from two cities, located close to each other at the border separating the two countries (Figure 5.8).

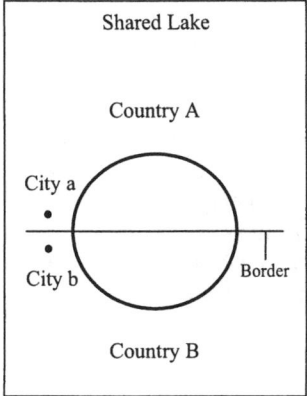

Source: Own presentation

Figure 5.8 Actor Constellation of Joint Wastewater Treatment

In addition to the above assumptions let us assume that joint treatment costs only 2 per unit. Thus if the countries treat 2 units jointly, each country pays 2 and receives a gross benefit of 5, resulting in a net benefit of 3 for each. Under these conditions, each country may choose among three strategies as indicated in Figure 5.9. If one country chooses joint treatment and the other individual treatment, only one unit will be treated. The payoff of the party choosing joint treatment is: $-2 + 2.5 = 0.5$. The payoff for the party choosing individual treatment is: $-3 + 2.5 = -0.5$. If one party chooses joint treatment, but the other does not treat, the payoffs are -2 and 0 respectively.

		Country B		
		Joint treatment	Individual treatment	No treatment
	Joint treatment	3, 3	0.5, -0.5	-2, 0
Country A	Individual treatment	-0.5, 0.5	2, 2	-0.5, 2.5
	No treatment	0, -2	2.5, -0.5	$0, 0^N$

N: Nash equilibrium

Source: Own presentation

Figure 5.9 Joint Wastewater Treatment with Economies of Scale as Assurance Game

The overall game has the structure of an Assurance game. Each party maximizes its outcome by choosing joint treatment, but will resort to no treatment if there is uncertainty as to the behavior of the other party (maximin strategy). Hence under this scenario, achieving the cooperative outcome relies on the mutual provision of assurances. This may be done in the form of an agreement on the construction of a joint treatment plant. Once an agreement is reached, implementation is self-enforcing, in the sense that it is in the interest of each actor to abide by the agreement.

Again the agreement to cooperate can be understood as a mutual delimitation of pollution rights, which is in the interest of the parties involved, and in this case even self-enforcing.

Empirical evidence

There are many examples of pollution control efforts at internationally shared lakes and closed seas, including the regimes for the Great Lakes region in North America, Lake Constance, Lake Geneva and the Baltic Sea in Europe or Lake Victoria in Africa. In 1960, Switzerland, Austria and the German States (Länder) of Baden-Württemberg and Bavaria established the International Commission for the Protection of Lake Constance. The agreement obliges the member states to cooperate in the protection of the lake against pollution, to enforce applicable water protection regulations and to mutually notify on planned measures relevant to water protection. A first joint investment program was agreed in 1967, followed by programs in 1973, 1981, 1985 and 2004. Since the establishment of the Commission, the riparian countries invested about Euro 4 billion in wastewater collection and treatment around the lake leading to a significant improvement of the water quality and a decline in phosphorous concentrations (IKGB 2005). Obviously, provision of wastewater treatment at Lake Constance has the structure of a Prisoner's Dilemma game. Apparently in this case the enforcement problem was primarily solved through repeated mutual commitments and monitoring of joint investment programs in the context of the International Commission for the Protection of Lake Constance. Whether the parties also undertook joint investments in order to realize economies of scale would have to be scrutinized.

5.2.3 Provision of Flood Control at a Border River

As a last example of a reciprocal externality problem, an example of a 'pure' positive reciprocal externality shall be given, namely the provision of retention areas for flood control at border rivers, where retention areas on either side of the river benefit both parties.[146]

Let us assume that for each riparian country the provision of one unit of retention area costs 3 and provides a benefit of 2 for each of the two parties. In this case the problem has the structure of a Prisoner's Dilemma game as indicated in Figure 5.10 with the same institutional implications with regard to enforcement as discussed above.

		Country B	
		Retention area (C)	No retention area (D)
Country A	Retention area (C)	1,1	-1,2
	No retention area (D)	2,-1	$0,0^{N}$

N: Nash equilibrium

Source: Own presentation

Figure 5.10 Provision of Retention Area at a Border River as Prisoner's Dilemma Game

This implies that positive reciprocal externality problems are faced with the same cooperation problems as negative reciprocal externality problems, i.e. interested-based cooperation can only be sustained with a monitoring and enforcement mechanism in place.

However in contrast to negative externalities such as water abstraction or water pollution this 'pure' positive reciprocal externality does not involve contested property rights to water. Thus positive reciprocal externality problems differ from negative reciprocal externality problems in the sense that they are not confronted with contested property rights to water (they may, however, involve contested land rights within each state). However compared to negative externality problems, this does not change the prospects of cooperation, given that in the case of negative reciprocal externality problems the conclusion of an agreement to cooperate that delimits property rights to water is principally in the interest of the parties involved.[147]

---

[146] If the issue is the rehabilitation of flood plains, it can be argued again that a negative externality, the destruction of flood plains, is mitigated by a positive externality, the rehabilitation of flood plains.

[147] They may, however, involve other property rights issues, such as land use rights.

Empirical evidence

An example of a border river which has recently been affected by severe floods is the Oder River shared by the Czech Republic, Poland and Germany. In 1996, the three countries and the European Union established the International Commission for the Protection of the Oder against Pollution (ICPO). However in contrast to other commissions the ICPO does not maintain a website, and the author is not aware whether they have put an action program on flood control in place. Such action programs exist for the Rhine (ICPR 1998) and the Elbe (IKSE 2003), which have also been affected by severe floods, but these rivers are mainly transboundary rivers. These examples show that an agreement is not only a function of the immediate interests of the parties involved, but also of other factors.

5.2.4 Results

Whenever reciprocal externalities occur in the use of water resources, the actions of the respective actors involved are characterized by a high degree of interdependence. This may result in a dilemma situation, however it would be wrong to assume that simultaneous resource appropriation or infrastructure provision necessarily creates a social dilemma. Instead whether the situation has the structure of a social dilemma depends on the underlying cost and benefit functions.

Negative reciprocal externalities, such as those stemming from simultaneous water withdrawal at a shared lake or aquifer, result in a Prisoner's Dilemma situation if the combined rate of extraction exceeds the safe yield of the resource, so that each player's extraction imposes a cost on all players involved. In contrast if one player moves first and appropriates the 'entire' resource, we are dealing with a situation akin to a Chicken game.

Positive reciprocal externalities such as those stemming from the provision of retention areas or wastewater treatment at border rivers lead to a Prisoner's Dilemma situation if individual costs exceed individual benefits, and if the benefits of collective provision exceed individual costs. They may also be unproblematic (Game without Conflict) if each player has an incentive to provide the public good unilaterally. If we are dealing with the provision of a discrete instead of a continuous public good (such as joint wastewater treatment that realizes economies of scale), the game has the structure of an Assurance game.

In principal, water quality problems represent combined resource appropriation and provision problems. While the problem may be characterized as a negative externality problem, the 'solution' has the character of a positive externality problem.

Whenever a social dilemma occurs, it will be in the interest of the parties involved to conclude an agreement in which they agree to pursue the respective cooperative action. In the case of an Assurance game such an agreement to cooperate will be self-enforcing. In contrast in a Prisoner's Dilemma or a Chicken situation, an agreement to cooperate per se will not be self-enforcing, but will rely on the set up of an adequate enforcement mechanism. If it can be assumed that the respective 'game' is infinitely repeated, such an enforcement mechanism may be the threat to dissolve the contract if any player defects (Grim strategy) or to punish defective behavior by defection until all players get even (Getting-even strategy). However the above examples, such as water extraction from a shared lake or the provision of wastewater treatment at a shared lake, raises the question of how effective enforcement strategies such as the Grim or the Getting-even strategy would be in practice, and how monitoring can be realized.

The difference between negative externality problems and 'pure' positive externality problems is that while the former involve disputed property rights to water, the latter do not. An agreement on the restriction of extractions to the safe yield or on the provision of adequate wastewater treatment is tantamount to the mutual definition of property rights vis-à-vis the resource. In an ideal symmetric setting, the delimitation of property rights is in the interest of the players involved as it allows them to realize gains of cooperation and only hinges on the set up of adequate enforcement mechanisms. Thus while negative and positive reciprocal externality problems differ with respect to the need to agree on property rights, they do not differ with respect to the prospects of cooperation.

In particular in the case of pollution, empirical evidence supports the notion that in the case of reciprocal externality problems, states tend to delimit pollution rights and conclude cooperative agreements. The example of the Mountain Aquifer shared by Israelis and Palestinians illustrates that often real world cases are not as symmetric as the idealized cases developed by theory may suggest. Also in reciprocal settings, the first-mover has an advantage.

5.3 NEGATIVE AND POSITIVE UNIDIRECTIONAL EXTERNALITY PROBLEMS

The previous section has dealt with reciprocal externality problems at border rivers, shared lakes or shared aquifers. However as argued in Section 2.2.2 given the flow of water, in the use of transboundary rivers, externalities are usually unidirectional leading to the typical upstream-downstream constellation. Unidirectional externality rules out reciprocal effects in the same use.

The starting point for the economic analysis of unidirectional externalities is the Coase theorem (see Section 5.1.1). The Coase theorem shows that if property rights are well defined, and transaction costs are sufficiently small, negotiations may internalize external effects and thus realize efficiency gains through side-payments (efficiency hypothesis). In the case of the laissez-faire rule, downstream would make a side-payment to upstream to compensate upstream for any losses upstream incurs by moving to the efficient allocation. In the case of the liability rule, upstream would compensate downstream for the right to use the water up to the efficient level. In the absence of income effects, both rules will result in the same allocation (invariance hypothesis). These results contain the implicit assumptions that the players have perfect information, that they reach agreement on the sharing of the respective efficiency gains and that monitoring and enforcement mechanisms are in place.

In the case of negative unidirectional externality problems on international rivers, we are not only faced with the problem of transaction costs, but also with the fact that there is no external authority that defines property rights to water among riparian states. Hence states may either accept the de facto allocation as the starting point for negotiation or not. In the latter case, downstream may or may not morally persuade upstream to negotiate the underlying property rights as a precondition for the realization of benefits of cooperation.

Going beyond the Coase theorem, a few authors have explicitly sought to express upstream-downstream constellations in terms of non-cooperative game theory. Bennett et al. (1998) model upstream water withdrawal with side-payments as a Prisoner's Dilemma game. Zürn (1992: 211) characterizes upstream water pollution problems as a Rambo game. Bernauer (2002: 6) refers to upstream-downstream pollution as a Deadlock game. Folmer et al. (1993) and Folmer and de Zeeuw (2000) introduce an asymmetric game that resembles the Prisoner's Dilemma. Others allude to zero-sum constellations.

Given that there appears to be some uncertainty as to which conditions we are faced with under each game constellation (in the sense of the respective logic of the situation), this section will revisit typical negative and positive unidirectional externality problems at transboundary rivers in terms of non-cooperative game theory. In particular Zürn's (1992) notion of 'Rambo games' appears to be used in the literature on transboundary river management without specifying the conditions under which one may speak of a Rambo game (e.g. Haftendorn 2000: 62).[148]

Similar to Section 5.2, Section 5.3 will again address the three cases, water abstraction, water pollution and flood control as examples for pure negative, combined negative and positive and pure positive externality problems. Section 5.3.1 will address upstream water withdrawal as an appropriation problem that may entail negative externalities. Section 5.3.2 will address upstream pollution as an example of a combined appropriation and provision problem where negative externalities are mitigated by the provision of a positive externality. Section 5.3.3 will address the upstream provision of flood control as example of the provision of a 'pure' positive unidirectional externality. Section 5.3.4 will present conclusions, and Section 5.3.5 will provide an outlook on how the simultaneous bargaining of property rights and efficiency gains can be conceptualized in terms of cooperative game theory, indicating how an agreement under the principle of equitable utilization could be conceived.

5.3.1   Upstream Water Withdrawal

Upstream water withdrawal is a typical appropriation problem that may entail negative unidirectional externalities. Let us assume an upstream country A and a downstream country B. Upstream country A diverts water from the river for consumptive uses (generating a certain level of welfare), thus reducing the natural inflow into downstream country B. Given that water is scarce in downstream country B, B requests a higher share of river water from A for its economic activities.

If we assume that both countries pursue their self-interest irrespectively of the other country's interests, A is in a position to reject B's request for a share of water and may instead ask for a side-payment for any additional releases. The reason is that in the absence of specified property rights on international rivers, A has the power to exclude the downstream user from the water.[149] De facto, the principle of absolute territorial sovereignty (the laissez-faire rule of the Coase theorem) applies. The following will consider four cases. In all four cases it will be assumed that A insists on the doctrine of absolute territorial sovereignty, but they will differ depending on whether downstream party B does or does not accept the doctrine of absolute territorial sovereignty (and hence a side-payment) as starting point of

---

[148] While she does not refer to water, Holzinger (2003: 13) claims that Rambo games are probably very common and have not received enough attention in the literature.

[149] Complete exclusion remains technically difficult to achieve unless the entire river was transferred into another river basin.

negotiations, and whether upstream party A does or does not accept a side-payment. The end of the section will ask for empirical evidence.

B accepts A's absolute territorial sovereignty – A accepts side-payment

If A insists of absolute territorial sovereignty and asks for a side-payment, and if these terms are acceptable to B, we may assume in accordance with the Coase theorem that side-payment and sharing is preferred over no side-payment and no sharing for both players. In this case both players' preference order may be assumed to be DC > CC > DD > CD and the game has the structure of a Prisoner's Dilemma game. A potential pay-off structure is presented in Figure 5.11 (see also Bennett et al. 1998).[150]

		Downstream country B	
		Side-payment (C)	No side-payment (D)
Upstream	Shares (C)	3,3	1,4
country A	Does not share (D)	4,1	2,2 ^{N}

N: Nash equilibrium

Source: Own presentation

Figure 5.11 Upstream Water Withdrawal with Side-payment as Prisoner's Dilemma Game

In the one-shot game, joint defection (no sharing – no side-payment) is the dominant strategy equilibrium, and while the players would be better off if they cooperated, full cooperation is no equilibrium outcome. In the absence of an enforcement mechanism, both players have the incentive to defect unilaterally from the cooperative outcome: A does not release the water, speculating on B's payment irrespectively of A's release, and B does not pay speculating on A's release of the water irrespectively of a payment. In this case it is likely that the two parties would not conclude the agreement in the first place. Thus this game-theoretic reconstruction of the 'side-payment game' shows that while a side-payment could realize efficiency gains, a pure side-payment agreement is not yet self-enforcing.

However given that water is usually not shared once, but on a continuous basis, we may assume that the water sharing game is being played repeatedly. In this case the two states may design the agreement in a way that

---

[150] Despite the apparent symmetry, the game is asymmetric, as the two players have two different action sets, given that the strategy 'sharing – no sharing' is not available to player B.

it is self-enforcing. Next to the above mentioned punishment strategies, one possibility is a 'policy of small steps' (*Politik der Trippelschritte*). In a first step a partial payment is made for a partial water release, and payments and releases are gradually increased over time on the condition that both sides cooperate. In this case a water sharing agreement on the basis of a side-payment from downstream to upstream could be sustained as an equilibrium outcome.

B accepts A's absolute territorial sovereignty – A rejects side-payment

Alternatively under certain conditions the upstream country A may not be willing to share, even if B is willing to pay for the water. A reason may be that A believes that it cannot do without the water because there is no substitute for water, even if the value of the water was compensated (A's abstraction level is efficient). This may for instance be the case for a landlocked upstream country under conditions of extreme water scarcity without access to alternative water sources or seawater desalination. In this case A's preference order is DC > DD > CC > CD,[151] thus A plays a game of Deadlock, while B's remains the same as in the Prisoner's Dilemma game above. The resulting hybrid game has the structure of Constant Sum Game I, where B prefers joint cooperation over joint defection, but joint defection is the dominant strategy equilibrium (Figure 5.12).[152]

		Downstream country B	
		Side-payment (C)	No side-payment (D)
Upstream	Shares (C)	2,3	1,4
country A	Does not share (D)	4,1	$3,2^N$

N: Nash equilibrium

Source: Own presentation

Figure 5.12 Upstream Water Withdrawal where A rejects a Side-payment as Constant Sum Game I

---

[151] DC is preferred over DD as A would prefer reception of the 'side-payment without sharing' over 'no side-payment – no sharing'.

[152] The Constant Sum game is sometimes also referred to as Zero Sum game. While in the Constant Sum game the payoffs in each cell of the payoff matrix add up to the same number, in the Zero Sum game they all add up to zero.

In this case no agreement can be expected, as the transition to the cooperative outcome would make A worse off, and B would not be able to compensate A adequately.

B rejects A's absolute territorial sovereignty – A accepts side-payment

The structure of the game furthermore changes if B rejects the doctrine of absolute territorial sovereignty and, by implication, side-payments on the basis that the doctrine of absolute territorial sovereignty contradicts the principle of equitable and reasonable utilization in international customary law and for distributional reasons. B could for instance argue that it has a right to an equitable share of the natural inflow of water into its country. In this case B's preference order may be assumed to be DC > DD > CC > CD (no sharing and no side-payment is preferred over sharing and side-payment) which corresponds to a game of Deadlock. If A continues to insist on absolute territorial sovereignty and a side-payment, A still plays a Prisoner's Dilemma game, and the ensuing hybrid game has the structure of Constant Sum Game II (Figure 5.13). Again no agreement can be expected.

In this case the downstream riparian may appear to be the 'bad' guy who does not cooperate. However the reason why B may reject a side-payment to A is that B does not accept the implied property rights regime, although it could realize gains of cooperation if it accepted the status quo as a staring point for negotiations. As such B rejects an implied 'victim pays principle' (Mäler 1990: 83; Bennett et al. 1998: 63).

		Downstream country B	
		Side-payment (C)	No side-payment (D)
Upstream	Shares (C)	3,2	1,4
country A	Does not share (D)	4,1	$2,3^{\text{N}}$

N: Nash equilibrium

Source: Own presentation

Figure 5.13 Upstream Water Withdrawal where B rejects a Side-payment as Constant Sum Game II

B rejects A's absolute territorial sovereignty – A rejects side-payment

A further option is that both countries – albeit for different reasons – do not accept side-payments in which case both have a preference order of DC > DD > CC > CD, resulting in a game of Deadlock. In this case joint defection is not only the dominant strategy equilibrium, but also the only (qualified) Pareto optimum, and therefore a stable outcome, which appears to indicate that cooperation is not desired (Figure 5.14).[153]

In conclusion, the above analysis shows how the structure of the game and the likelihood of cooperation depend on the underlying assumptions on property rights and on the acceptability of side-payments. Cooperation can only be expected if both parties implicitly or explicitly agree on the underlying allocation of property rights to water. If both accept the status quo and hence a de facto doctrine of absolute territorial sovereignty as a starting point for negotiations and if side-payments are acceptable to both, the game can be described as a Prisoner's Dilemma 'side-payment' game. However if downstream – for moral or strategic reasons – does not accept the doctrine of absolute territorial sovereignty as a starting point for negotiations and if upstream country A insists of absolute territorial sovereignty, no cooperation can be expected. Cooperation will also not come about if upstream party A rejects a side-payment because it feels that water is not substitutable.

		Downstream country B	
		Side-payment (C)	No side-payment (D)
Upstream	Shares (C)	2,2	1,4
country A	Does not share (D)	4,1	$3,3^{N}$

N: Nash equilibrium

Source: Own presentation

Figure 5.14 Upstream Water Withdrawal where A and B reject a Side-payment as Deadlock Game

In terms of the structure of the game the analysis shows if only one party accepts side-payments, the resulting game has the structure of a Constant Sum game. If both parties reject a side-payment, the game has the structure of a Deadlock game. As such the analysis also demonstrates that it would be wrong to characterize upstream water withdrawal as a Rambo game, as sometimes suggested on the basis of Zürn (1992) (e.g. Haftendorn 2000: 62). The problem with all three non-cooperative outcomes is that – despite their stability – B may still suffer from insufficient water supplies.

---

[153] Note that the seeming symmetry of the Deadlock game conceals the asymmetry of the strategies available to the two parties and the unequal distribution of power between the upstream and the downstream party.

Empirical evidence

Despite the problems involved in upstream-downstream water quantity issues, a number of international water sharing agreements have been negotiated in water scarce areas, including those pertaining to the Colorado-Rio Grande between Mexico and the USA (1944), the Nile between Egypt and Sudan (1959), the Indus between India and Pakistan (1960), the Lesotho Highlands project between Lesotho and South Africa (1986) and the Jordan River between Israel and Jordan (1994). At the same time, in other water scarce basins, such as the Euphrates-Tigris, no permanent agreement has been reached so far.

Among the above mentioned treaties, the only agreement that contains a 'side-payment' for water is the agreement pertaining to the Lesotho Highlands project, however, the Lesotho Highlands project is different from a usual water sharing problem, as the payment is made for water that is transferred out of the Orange Basin. Thus in this case water is 'sold' from one river basin to another. The 1959 Nile agreement divides the natural flow of the Nile between the two most downstream countries Sudan and Egypt, allocating 55.5 billion cubic meters to Egypt and 15.5 billion cubic meters to Sudan (e.g. Waterbury 1979). The other eight Nile riparian countries which are not party to this agreement also assert rights to the Nile. In the case of the Colorado and Rio Grande a water sharing agreement was reached by linking the two river basins (e.g. Fischhendler et al. 2004). In the case of the Jordan River, Israel as the upstream riparian was by and large able to maintain its use level vis-à-vis the downstream riparian Jordan, however, the agreement seeks to implement projects that mobilize additional water for Jordan (e.g. Dombrowsky 2003).

These examples indicate that in order to judge how states dealt with the property rights issue in water quantity conflicts, a more thorough analysis would be required. At the same time, this initial review does not support the notion that downstream countries easily accept the principle of absolute territorial sovereignty and make side-payments in order to pay for water from upstream. Instead either the situation corresponds to a Constant Sum or Deadlock game, or the parties resort to some interpretation of the doctrine of limited territorial sovereignty and the principle of equitable utilization. This observation is supported by international law which argues that the weight of existing treaties reflects the doctrine of limited territorial sovereignty (Section 3.1.2). This does not necessarily imply that all existing treaties may necessarily be considered as equitable or fair; instead the above appears to indicate that they often rather reflect the balance of powers between the respective states. Still those countries that conclude agreements tend to make at least some concessions.

5.3.2   Upstream Water Pollution

Upstream water pollution is another use that may lead to negative unidirectional externalities. As mentioned above in the case of pollution a negative externality may be remedied by the provision of a positive externality. In principle upstream water pollution can be modeled analogously to the upstream water withdrawal game, however in contrast to water abstraction problems upstream party A can always be expected to accept a side-payment by downstream party B. The reason is that it is not rational for A to reject a side-payment given that it would be compensated for its costs of pollution control, and given that it could potentially participate in the gains of cooperation.

Hence if A insists on the doctrine of absolute territorial sovereignty, B may either accept or reject this doctrine. However instead of making a side-payment to A – in the case of pollution – there is a further option that B cleans up the polluted water itself, e.g. by applying additional treatment to the water pumped from the river. Hence overall three cases can be distinguished.

B accepts A's absolute territorial sovereignty and a side-payment

If B accepts A's absolute territorial sovereignty and a side-payment, the game has the structure of a Prisoner's Dilemma side-payment game analogously to Figure 5.11 above.

B rejects A's absolute territorial sovereignty and a side-payment

If B rejects A's absolute territorial sovereignty and hence a side-payment, the game has the structure of a Constant Sum Game II analogously to Figure 5.13 above.

B rejects a side-payment and abates A's pollution

If B rejects a side-payment, B may decide to clean up A's polluted water itself.[154] In that case B's preference order can be assumed to be DC > CC > CD > DD, meaning that B prefers unilateral pollution control by A (CD) over joint pollution control (CC) over one-sided pollution control by B (DC) over no pollution control at all (DD). In this case B plays a game of

---

[154] This however implies that B, at least implicitly, accepts that A maintains absolute territorial sovereignty.

Chicken. If we assume that A continues to play a Prisoner's Dilemma game, the resulting game has the structure of a Rambo II game (Figure 5.15).[155]

In the Rambo II game unilateral defection by A (DC) is the only Nash equilibrium and a Pareto optimum, but the cooperative outcome is the only qualified Pareto optimum. Thus the game has the interesting feature that for society as a whole the cooperative outcome (CC) is the preferred outcome. Still an agreement cannot be expected as the transition from the Nash equilibrium to the cooperative outcome makes A worse off. However if an agreement on the cooperative outcome could be reached, it could be maintained as an equilibrium outcome in an infinitely repeated game with an enforcement mechanism in place.

		Downstream country B	
		Abates A's pollution (C)	Does not abate A's pollution (D)
Upstream	Abates (C)	3,3	1,4
country A	Pollutes (D)	4,2 ^{N}	2,1

N: Nash equilibrium

Source: Own presentation

Figure 5.15 Upstream Pollution where B treats A's Pollution as Rambo II Game

The problem with this reconstruction is that it is questionable whether B really prefers joint treatment over its unilateral treatment. The question is how joint treatment (CC) should be interpreted. If it means that the water would be treated twice, it does not make sense. However if it means that the two countries share the burden of treatment, the above assumption may be

---

[155] Zürn (1992: 333) reconstructs the problem of upstream-downstream pollution as Rambo I game. He assumes that A's preference order is DC > DD > CC > CD which means that A plays a game of Deadlock. This implies that A rejects a side-payment and prefers that B unilaterally reduces pollution (DC) over joint defection (DD). Zürn furthermore assumes that B's preference order is CC > DC > CD > DD, which corresponds to a game of Pure Coordination. This implies that B prefers joint pollution reduction (CC) over one-sided pollution reduction by A. However there are a number of problems with Zürn's Rambo I game. First, as argued above, it is unclear why A should reject abatement on the basis of a side-payment given that it would be compensated for its costs. Second it is unclear why B should prefer joint over one-sided pollution reduction. Instead B may rather be assumed to prefer unilateral pollution reduction by A (DC) over joint pollution reduction (CC). Third Zürn assumes that pollution control on B's part refers to his own wastewater. However this does not solve B's problem that the water it receives from A is not suitable for consumption in the first place. For these reasons the reconstruction of upstream water pollution problems as Rambo I games has to be rejected.

reasonable. Still it is unlikely that an agreement would be reached, unless A reverts from a position of absolute territorial sovereignty. A solution in which both countries contribute towards treatment may in fact be perceived as a more equitable solution, which provides some right to pollute to the upstream party and a limited right to water of a good quality to the downstream party.[156]

While in an upstream-downstream pollution situation the upstream party can be assumed to play a Prisoner's Dilemma game, the downstream party B has principally three options: First to offer a side-payment so that A abates upstream (resulting in a Prisoner's Dilemma side-payment game); second to reject a side-payment and to do nothing (resulting in a Constant Sum I game); and third to treat the polluted water itself (resulting in a Rambo II game). From B's perspective, the question whether it should rather offer the side-payment or treat the water itself is a function of the respective costs, including transaction costs, involved. For society as a whole, one argument for treatment at the source is that it is likely to entail additional benefits for other users of the river, providing a positive externality for all downstream users. But irrespectively of whether B reduces A's pollution or offers a side-payment, as long as A persists on a position of absolute territorial sovereignty, B is in the disadvantaged position.

Empirical evidence

In practice a great number of water quality agreements at international rivers have been concluded, many of them in Europe, including the agreements for the protection of the Rivers Rhine (1963 and 1999), Elbe (1990), Danube (1994) and Oder (1996). In the Rhine Basin, the negotiation of specific pollution thresholds in the 1970s and 1980s proved difficult, and an international contribution towards pollution control was first realized through the Rhine Action Program of 1987 (e.g. Bernauer and Moser 1996; Durth 1996; Holtrup 1999). In all these agreements both upstream and downstream parties agreed to carry out abatement measures. The only agreement that includes some form of side-payments is the 1976 Chloride Convention on the Rhine, however even in this case it cannot be argued that France as the upstream country maintained a strict position of absolute territorial sovereignty (see Section 5.3.5). Thus where water quality agreements have been concluded, it seems that the doctrine of absolute territorial sovereignty has not been maintained. This would correspond to the findings of international law (Section 3.1.3) and the finding in Section 4.3.2 that side-

---

[156] International law argues that the no harm rule is more strictly applied in the case of pollution than in water quantity conflicts (Section 3.1.3).

payments are most rarely applied in the case of water quality agreements. Thus empirical evidence does not appear to support the assumption that upstream and downstream riparians play Prisoner's Dilemma side-payment games in the case of negative unidirectional externality problems.

5.3.3 Upstream Provision of Flood Control

In some cases upstream infrastructure measures change the natural conditions of a river system and thereby provide 'pure' positive externalities downstream. For instance the Blue Nile is characterized by the annual Blue Nile floods that are caused by the region's specific meteorological conditions and that carry a high degree of silt loads caused by natural erosion processes. In this case measures in Ethiopia which contribute towards retaining these natural floods and silt flows would have positive external effects for Sudan and Egypt downstream (e.g. Guariso and Whittington 1987). A simplified case along these lines shall be examined in the following model.[157]

Joint construction of a multipurpose dam upstream as a coordination game

Let us assume that a mountainous upstream country A and a flat downstream country B share a river. Downstream country B is affected by severe floods and considers options for the construction of a reservoir to regulate the river. However, given its flatness, the best location for a reservoir would be inside the territory of A, requiring an agreement with A. Upstream country A is considering options for a hydropower development. There are several potential dam sites as indicated in Figure 5.16.

Furthermore the assumed hydropower and flood control benefits of these dams are presented in Table 5.3.[158] Due to the head in the river, the best dam for hydropower generation is assumed to be dam a. Due to the storage capacity of the river valley, the best site for river regulation is dam b. In this situation, a joint dam may yield benefits for both parties. For upstream country A, a joint dam has the advantage that it lowers the costs per unit of hydropower produced, but has the disadvantage that it will have to coordinate dam operation with downstream country B. For B, a joint dam has the advantage that it allows for greater water storage at lower unit costs than a unilateral project. It has the disadvantage that it creates unilateral dependence on the upstream country.

---

[157] An earlier German version of this model has been presented in Dombrowsky (2005a).
[158] For the time being, we neglect potential negative externalities of the dam.

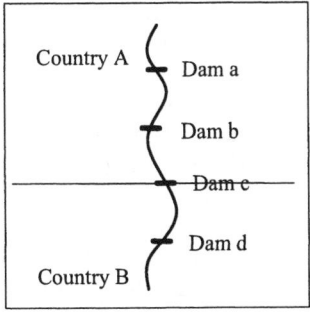

Source: Own presentation

Figure 5.16 The Dam Game: Assumed Actor Constellation

Under the given constellation it can be assumed that B has an interest to enter into negotiation with A as it will be able to realize higher flood control benefits if project b is realized instead of project a or d. (Project a would be preferred by A and project d might be realized by B unilaterally.) Hence if downstream country B is interested in participating in the dam's design and operation, both countries have an incentive to enter into negotiation on the construction of a joint dam.[159] In this case B compensates A for the provision of a positive externality.

Table 5.3   The Dam Game: Assumed Payoffs

Dam	Net Hydropower Benefits	Net Flood Protection Benefits	Net Aggregated Benefits
a	4	1	5
b	2.5	3.5	6
c	2	2	4
d	0	1	1

Source: Own presentation

---

[159] If B's interest to participate in project design and operation is less pronounced, the behavior of B depends on the assumed behavior of A, namely, whether A is likely to go ahead with the construction of a project anyway or not. If there is a high likelihood that A builds the project unilaterally, B may be tempted to do nothing and to free-ride on the positive externality provided by A. In this case B plays a game of Poker. A Poker game is a Constant Sum game where the gains by one party equal the losses of the other party. Upstream riparian A may either go ahead with the project or not, or it may approach downstream riparian B and enter into negotiations as described below.

The two countries may then choose among discrete project alternatives a, b, c or d. Assuming that B is primarily interested in regulation (e.g. because it has alternative energy resources, such as oil reserves), in a first approximation we shall assume that A would tap the hydropower and B the flood protection benefits. Figure 5.17 displays the four projects' benefits for A and B graphically, assuming that all hydropower benefits will go to A, and that all flood protection benefits will go to B. The status quo (SQ) is represented by the origin of the diagram. All values to the right of the y-axis represent an improvement in A's welfare, while all values above the x-axis improve the position of B. The aggregated welfare of A and B is enhanced by any project above the northwest-southeast diagonal through the origin of the diagram. Projects within the north-east quadrant represent Pareto improvements for both.

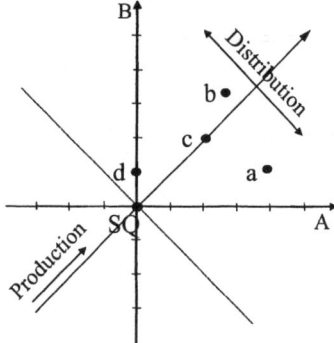

Source: Own presentation

Figure 5.17 The Dam Game: Negotiation Space

Given the payoffs of the respective projects, A would prefer project a, while B would prefer project b. In the absence of side-payments it might be difficult to reach agreement on either project. For instance given that downstream country B is interested in flood control and not necessarily in cash, agreement on project a plus a side-payment may not be an acceptable solution for B.[160] If side-payments are not acceptable, in the above case the two parties might still consider to forego the aggregated benefits of projects a or b and to go for project c with equal benefits for both parties. However if

---

[160] The question is whether the side-payment would be sufficient to cover potential flood damage costs.

side-payments are acceptable, the party receiving higher benefits could compensate the other party. In this case the combined welfare-level of both parties would be maximized if they agreed on project b, with B compensating A.

The situation has the structure of a coordination game, however, with distributional conflict. It involves a 'production problem', i.e. to identify the measure which maximizes welfare and a 'distribution problem', i.e. agreement on the sharing of the net benefits among the actors involved (see Figure 5.17). While the identification of welfare increasing measures has the structure of a game of Pure Coordination (Game without Conflict), bargaining on the sharing of the gains of cooperation has the characteristics of a Constant Sum Game, in which gains to one party imply a loss to the other party. Once agreement on a welfare enhancing project is reached, it is in the interest of both players to implement the agreement. The agreement to a coordination problem is self-enforcing (Barrett 2003: 93). Again this positive externality problem does not involve property rights to water.

Thus if downstream has an interest to participate in the design and operation of upstream measures that provide positive unidirectional externalities, the problem can be conceptualized as a coordination problem. In that case, the downstream party compensates the upstream party for a positive externality provided. If the downstream party is less inclined to participate in project design and operation, it may also play a game of poker, whether upstream will unilaterally go ahead with the project and seek to free-ride on the positive externality provided.[161] Thus whether cooperation can be expected depends on the interests of the downstream party.[162]

The problem revisited as 2x2 game

If the parties' choices are reduced to two projects (e.g. a and b), which may either be pursued jointly or separately by either party, the structure of the game can be expressed as a 2x2 game. Joint action is preferred over unilateral action, but the actors differ with respect to their preferred choices. The countries furthermore share a common aversion for separate action. In terms of their ordinal preference orders, upstream country A prefers joint construction of dam a over joint construction of dam b over separate action

---

[161] The question is what international law has to say about this problem. Would it require the downstream country to compensate the upstream country for positive externalities provided?

[162] A further option is that upstream has no immediate interest in the project, and that downstream asks upstream to carry out a measure that is being paid for by the downstream country. In this situation, upstream provides a service for downstream. Depending on downstream alternatives it entails a certain danger that upstream may behave strategically in order to extract a high side-payment, and enforcement is an issue.

where A pursues a and B pursues b, over separate action where A pursues b and B pursues a. Hence for both players the preference order is $DC > CD > DD > CC$.[163] Thus the situation has the structure of the game Battle of the Sexes (Figure 5.18).[164]

		Downstream country B	
		Project a (C)	Project b (D)
Upstream country A	Project b (C)	1,1	3,4 [N]
	Project a (D)	4,3 [N]	2,2

Note: The numbers refer to ordinal preference orders
N: Nash equilibrium

Source: Own presentation

Figure 5.18 Joint Construction of a Dam as Battle of the Sexes Game

The Battle of the Sexes game is a coordination game with distributional conflict. If only ordinal preference orders are considered, it may be difficult to reach agreement on any outcome. Given that the construction of a dam has to be considered as a one-shot rather than an infinitely repeated game, correlated strategies are not an option either. However it is possible to conceive that one country moves first and the other joins in, in which case the first country would have a first-mover advantage. However if cardinal payoffs are considered, as discussed above the game offers the possibility to implement the outcome that maximizes aggregated welfare and to make a side-payment to the player that will be worse off.

Empirical evidence

Examples for the joint construction of hydropower dams upstream with flood control benefits downstream include the Manantali dam on the Senegal River, shared by Mali, Senegal and Mauritania and dams on the Columbia River shared by Canada and the USA (for the latter example see Chapter 6). The Manantali is located in the upstream country Mali, but it is jointly owned and operated by Mali, Senegal and Mauritania within the framework of the Senegal River Development Organization (OMVS). The dam is being used

---

[163] Given that country A prefers project a it 'cooperates' if it agrees on project b and vice versa for country B.

[164] This reconstruction contains the somewhat unlikely assumption that downstream country B may unilaterally act in upstream country A. This is also the reason for the more elaborate presentation in the previous section.

for hydropower generation and river regulation and costs and benefits are supposed to be shared equitably among the parties (e.g. Godana 1985). Thus empirical evidence in principal supports the notion that downstream countries at times participate in the provision of upstream projects that provide positive externalities downstream.

5.3.4   Results

In the case of unidirectional externality problems the prospects for cooperation are less obvious than in the case of reciprocal externality problems.

In the case of negative unidirectional externality problems, for instance caused by upstream water withdrawal or upstream water pollution, cooperation can only be expected if both parties implicitly or explicitly agree on the underlying allocation of property rights to water. If both accept the status quo as a starting point for negotiations, in accordance with the Coase theorem an agreement can be reached on the basis of a side-payment, and the game can be described as a Prisoner's Dilemma side-payment game. In this case successful cooperation furthermore relies on the set up of an enforcement mechanism. If only one party accepts side-payments, the resulting game has the structure of a Constant Sum game. If both parties reject side-payments, the game has the structure of a Deadlock game. The reason why the downstream party B may reject a side-payment is that it may seek to convince upstream to pursue an equitable solution, thus rejecting a victim pays principle. Thus in the case of negative unidirectional externality problems three different outcomes are conceivable: (1) cooperation accepting the status quo (doctrine of absolute territorial sovereignty) as a starting point, (2) no cooperation or (3) transition to the simultaneous bargaining of an equitable allocation of property rights and of efficiency gains (see Section 5.3.5). However the latter step would be morally induced and may prima facie not be explained by non-cooperative game theory.

Furthermore in the case of upstream pollution, the downstream party has an additional option, namely to treat the water polluted by A itself. Such a situation can be described as Rambo II game. While transition to the cooperative outcome where both treat a portion of the water might be socially desirable, this requires a concession by A and may thus not be expected if strictly self-interested behavior is assumed.

In contrast to negative unidirectional externality problems, positive unidirectional externality problems do not (directly) involve disputed property rights to water. In principal positive unidirectional externality problems are more amenable to cooperation. Cooperation can be expected if the downstream party has an interest to participate in the design and operation of upstream infrastructure that provides positive externalities downstream. In the case of a multipurpose project, the problem can be characterized as a coordination problem, either a game of Pure Coordination if no distributional conflict is involved or as Battle of the Sexes game if it involves distributional conflict. Once agreement on a welfare enhancing project is reached, the agreement to a coordination problem is self-enforcing. However if downstream has no immediate interest to participate in upstream infrastructure design and operation, cooperation may be more difficult to achieve.

Thus negative and (pure) positive unidirectional externality problems differ in two respects: First while the former involve disputed property rights to water, the latter do not. Second while an agreement in the case of negative externality problems relies on the set up of an enforcement mechanism, a coordination problem in the case of positive externality problems is self-enforcing. This is why positive unidirectional externality problems are more conducive towards cooperation than negative unidirectional externality problems.

Empirical evidence indicates that countries conclude agreements both in the case of negative and of positive unidirectional externality problems. However contrary to what may be expected on the basis of the Coase theorem, in the case of negative externality problems these agreements usually do not tend to rely on side-payments. Instead they reflect the application of the doctrine of limited territorial sovereignty. This raises the question of how this outcome can be explained. Therefore the next section will provide an outlook of how the simultaneous bargaining on property rights and efficiency gains can be conceptualized in terms of cooperative game theory.

5.3.5 Outlook: Simultaneous Bargaining on Property Rights and Efficiency Gains

The above considerations have illustrated that an agreement on negative unidirectional externalities relies on an implicit or explicit agreement on property rights to water. While the Coase theorem shows that a side-payment may realize gains of cooperation if the status quo is inefficient, it requires that either the doctrine of absolute territorial sovereignty (laissez-faire rule) or the doctrine of absolute territorial integrity (liability rule) applies. Given that international customary law endorses neither of the two rules, it can be argued that the preconditions for the application of the Coase theorem do not exist in the case of international upstream-downstream problems. Instead of accepting upstream's factual power, in the case of water quantity problems downstream is likely to invoke the opposite doctrine of absolute territorial integrity.[165] In the case of upstream pollution downstream may reject a side-payment with reference to the polluter pays principle.[166]

A middle ground can be reached if both upstream and downstream concede, by accepting the principle of equitable utilization under the doctrine of limited territorial sovereignty (Section 3.1.2). The conventional interpretation is that the move towards the principle of equitable utilization is morally induced and thus cannot be explained by the self-interest of the upstream player (and hence not by non-cooperative game theory). However Barrett (1996) offers yet another interpretation, arguing that the move towards an equitable allocation is motivated by customary law and that the wish of countries to adhere to custom can be explained as equilibrium behavior that is in their self-interest. The reason is that a particular upstream-downstream constellation cannot be looked at in isolation from other matters. If a country adopts an extreme doctrine in one situation, this may set a precedent which can be held against it in another (see also Barrett 1994a: 18):

> Customary law serves to coordinate expectations about how other states will behave, and it also prescribes how each state would behave itself. Custom is therefore an equilibrium behavior: when other countries consent to the custom, it is in each state's own interest to consent to the custom as well. . . . States wish to agree to an allocation and consent to a custom because there is some penalty for failing to agree and consent. The penalty could be armed aggression, but it could just as well be a threat to reciprocate in the case of another issue where the tables are turned, to reciprocate in the management of the same resource at some future time (Barrett 1996: 268).

As argued in Section 3.1.2, and indicated in the above examples, existing international water agreements do reflect the fact that both upstream and downstream countries accept the doctrine of limited territorial sovereignty. Under the doctrine of limited territorial sovereignty all riparians recognize that every riparian on a river has rights and obligations and that the rights of one party are limited by the rights of the other, irrespectively of the fact that the upstream riparian has the power to control the river. The problem is that it is not clear what exactly the principle of equitable utilization implies, except that it shall balance the interests, needs and uses of the countries

---

[165] If the doctrine of absolute territorial integrity applied, the game structures of the games presented in Sections 5.2.1 and 5.2.2 would be reversed.

[166] The question is whether the polluter pays principle is equivalent to the liability rule and the doctrine of absolute territorial integrity in international law. As argued in Section 3.1.3 international lawyers maintain that Paragraph 21 of the 1972 Stockholm Declaration, which has been interpreted as a defense of the polluter pays principle (e.g. Mäler 1990: 82), constitutes a due diligence obligation not to cause damage to the environment of other States. If it is a due diligence obligation, it may be weaker than the doctrine of absolute territorial integrity.

involved. We know that it is neither absolute territorial sovereignty nor absolute territorial integrity, but what constitutes an equitable utilization in a given case has to be negotiated on the basis of a bargaining process of claim and counter-claim.[167]

In doing so the challenge, and the opportunity, is to resolve questions of equity and efficiency at the same time. As Barrett (1996: 271) argues: 'We can, however, expect that the final allocation will be efficient; otherwise, by definition, one party could be made better off without any other party being made worse off.' In a 2-party case, the efficient allocation is determined by the intersection of the marginal cost and the marginal benefit curve (see Section 5.1.1). Depending on the circumstances, the allocation of property rights according to the Pareto optimum may also be considered as an equitable solution. In a multiparty case, the set of efficient allocations can be defined by the concept of the core.[168]

In this context Barrett (1996: 271-274) presents a three country negotiation model on river pollution drawing upon cooperative game theory, i.e. under the assumption that binding commitments and an agreement of the distribution of the benefits of cooperation can be made. In order to determine an equitable and efficient allocation, he proposes a three step procedure: In a first step the parties determine an allocation that maximizes the gains of cooperation vis-à-vis the non-cooperative (equilibrium) outcome under the doctrine of absolute territorial sovereignty and share the gains equitably. In a second step the actors settle on an allocation that maximizes the gains of cooperation under the doctrine of absolute territorial integrity and again share the gains of cooperation. In a last step they determine the average outcome for each player under both rules. If an equitable and efficient solution is reached, the challenge still remains to enforce the agreement. This model assumes that the move towards the equitable allocation of property rights is based on the interest of states to adhere to custom.

Whatever agreement is reached on the allocation of the underlying property rights, from an economic perspective, it is recommendable that the respective property rights be tradable in order to be able to maintain an efficient solution under changing conditions.[169]

---

[167] A theory which conceptualizes distributive bargaining as process of claim and counter-claim under bounded rationality is proposed by Ahlert (2004).

[168] 'An allocation is in the core of the cost-sharing game if no participant or group of participants, pays more than its stand-alone cost. In other words, a cost allocation is in the core if the cost-savings of every subgroup of participants is nonnegative' (Young 1994: 85). Roger (1997) explores the potential for benefit-sharing in transboundary water management between Bangladesh, India and Nepal, using the core approach.

[169] In other words, the riparians do not need to adopt one of the extreme rules in order to achieve an efficient result, but an efficient result can be achieved from whatever property rights allocation as long as these rights are tradable.

Empirical evidence

Barrett (1996: 274) mentions the 1976 Chloride Convention on the Rhine as an example of the simultaneous bargaining of property rights and efficiency gains. The agreement sought to realize efficiency gains by reducing Chloride emissions where this could be done at least cost, namely at a potash mine in France and agreed on a cost-sharing formula whereby the Netherlands carried 34 percent of the costs, Germany and France each 30 percent and Switzerland 6 percent. While the Potash mine was the single largest emitter of Chlorides in the basin, the other riparians also contributed to the problem. As such the agreement neither endorsed the doctrine of absolute territorial sovereignty nor of absolute territorial integrity. However not only the negotiation, but also the implementation process proved to be extremely difficult. Bernauer (1996: 220) concludes that too little was achieved too late, and the Rhine riparian countries themselves were cautious that the Chloride agreement did not serve as a precedent for other negotiations. One reason for objecting the Chloride agreements is that it is often being perceived as contradictory to the polluter pays principle as the Netherlands, as the main victim of Chloride pollution, carried the greatest share of the burden (Schulte-Wülwer-Leidig 2003).

While it is debatable whether the Chloride agreement is an example of efficient and equitable sharing or for a side-payment game that contradicts the polluter pays principle, the underlying discourse shows that the acceptability of monetary side-payments in the case of upstream-downstream pollution tends to be low.

5.4   CONCLUSIONS

Drawing upon the theory of externalities and non-cooperative game theory, this chapter analyzed the role of the problem structure for cooperation at international waters and asked for institutional implications. It was argued that if we know the structure of a game, we can say something about adequate institutional design. It was furthermore argued that whether cooperation and coordination can be expected, depends on the underlying structure of the game. In general cooperation and coordination are more likely in reciprocal than in unidirectional externality problems and more likely in positive than in negative unidirectional externality problems. As such this book confirms Marty's (2001: 33-38) hypotheses regarding the likelihood of cooperation in international water management and underpins them theoretically.

In the case of negative reciprocal externality problems the actions of the respective actors involved are characterized by a high degree of interdependence. Negative reciprocal externality problems, such as simultaneous water abstraction or pollution at a border river, shared lake or shared aquifer may under certain conditions create a Prisoner's Dilemma situation in which all parties defect, however in which they would be better off if they cooperated (e.g. by limiting abstraction or pollution respectively). The implication is that it is in the self-interest of the actors involved to negotiate an agreement in which they agree to cooperate. The agreement to cooperate can be understood as the mutual delimitation of property rights in order to achieve a sustainable resource use. However given that all parties have incentives to free-ride on the cooperative behavior of the other parties, they will only be able to sustain the cooperative solution as an equilibrium outcome if they are able to overcome monitoring and enforcement problems. Theoretically they will be able to do so in an infinitely repeated game if the number of players and the discount rate are sufficiently small, and if they agree on an adequate punishment strategy (e.g. to play Grim or Getting-even). A cooperative solution is less likely if the status quo is characterized by significant differences in the level of resource appropriation.

Pure positive reciprocal externality problems, such as the provision of flood control at a border river, differ from negative reciprocal externality problem in the sense that they do not involve disputed property rights to water. This notwithstanding they may also take the structure of a Prisoner's Dilemma with the same implications for enforcement as above. At least under ideal symmetric conditions, positive and negative reciprocal externality problems do not differ with respect to the prospects for cooperation. The provision of a discrete public good, such as joint wastewater treatment with economies of scale at a shared lake, may take the structure an Assurance game. In this case an agreement is self-enforcing.

In the case of negative unidirectional externality problems the upstream country has no immediate interest in voluntarily reducing his externality causing economic activity; it would only do so on the basis of a side-payment. The downstream country has also an interest to realize gains of cooperation; however due to the distributional implication it may reject the status quo as a starting point for negotiation arguing that it has a right to water of reasonable quantity and quality in the river. Such a stand is principally supported by international water law. Thus in the case of negative unidirectional externalities three different outcomes are conceivable. First the upstream country is able to blackmail the downstream country into a side-payment scheme (factually applying the doctrine of absolute territorial sovereignty). This outcome is efficient – and thus has the potential to make both players better off vis-à-vis the status quo – but not necessarily equitable.

Second no agreement is reached. The outcome is likely to be inefficient and inequitable. Third the downstream country is able to persuade the upstream country morally to pursue an equitable solution (doctrine of limited territorial sovereignty). This has the potential to lead to an efficient and equitable outcome; however this outcome cannot be explained on the basis of narrowly interpreted self-interested behavior alone. One way to determine an equitable and efficient allocation is to determine an efficient allocation under each of the two extreme doctrines and to average the outcome for each player under both rules. If an equitable and efficient solution is reached, the challenge remains to enforce the agreement.

The provision of a positive unidirectional externality is usually a by-product of an infrastructure measure upstream. Given the multi-functionality of water measures often generate different streams of benefits and disbenefits (so called multi-purpose projects). Whether the upstream country is able to entice the downstream country into a side-payment for the benefit provided depends on the readiness of the upstream country to go ahead with the project irrespectively of downstream's contribution and on the interest of the downstream country to have a say in the design and operation of the upstream project. If downstream is interested in participating in an upstream project that provides benefits upstream and downstream, the problem has the structure of a coordination problems in which case an agreement is self-enforcing. Positive unidirectional externality problems are no property rights problems in a narrow sense, since they are concerned with the provision of a service, but not with water resource appropriation in terms of quantity or quality.

Thus in terms of interests, there are significant differences between reciprocal as well as negative and positive unidirectional externality problems. While in the case of border rivers, shared lakes and shared aquifers reciprocity in use means that it is in the players' mutual interest to reach an efficient outcome through a mutual delimitation of property rights, in the case of transboundary rivers, an efficient outcome depends on an implicit or explicit agreement on the underlying property rights regime which might be difficult to reach given the distributional repercussions. Positive unidirectional externality problems yet differ from negative unidirectional externality problems in that they are less affected by the issue of property rights to water quantity and quality and enforcement.

Empirical evidence indicates that states tend to conclude agreements even in negative unidirectional externality problems. The desire of countries to reach an equitable utilization can also be explained by their desire to conform to custom. This can even be interpreted as equilibrium behavior which is in the self-interest of the players involved.

Chapter 6 will revisit the problem of negative unidirectional externality problems and ask what happens if the unidirectional externality problem is not looked at in isolation, but if opportunities for issue linkage both outside and inside the water sector are taken into account.

6. The Role of Issue Linkage for the Resolution of Unidirectional Externality Problems

Issue linkage has often been mentioned as a strategy to overcome upstream-downstream problems (LeMarquand 1977; Wolf 1997; Bernauer 1997; Bennett et al. 1998; Marty 2001; Mostert 2003). Issues are linked when they are simultaneously discussed for joint settlement. If countries are engaged in several areas of negotiation, they may reach an agreement by exchanging concessions in areas of relative strength.

In the case of unidirectional externalities, issue linkage has been proposed to solve some of the problems associated with side-payments. As discussed previously side-payments are problematic in international water negotiations as long as the underlying property rights regime is disputed. Affected states may reject a side-payment as this appears to endorse a victim pays principle. Offering a side-payment may be associated with the reputation as a weak negotiator. Furthermore the anticipation of side-payments may provide incentives for strategic behavior by the party advantaged by the status quo in order to extract larger side-payments (e.g. Mäler 1990: 85 f.).

In the context of water resources management, issue linkage is of particular interest, given that water is a multi-functional resource that goes along with a whole array of different uses which may, at least partly, take effect into different directions. One of the tenets of the concept of Integrated Water Resources Management (IWRM) is that an integrated management which takes different water using sectors into account has the potential to minimize conflict in the long run (see Section 1.1.3). A systematic analysis of opportunities for issue linkage within the water sector would thus be able to show under which conditions the integration of different uses is in the interest of the players involved.

This chapter will revisit the role of issue linkage for the resolution of asymmetric water problems in general and of unidirectional externality problems in particular. Section 6.1 will introduce into the concept of issue linkage and into the theory of interconnected games and apply the theory to reciprocal externality problems with asymmetric payoffs as well as to unidirectional externality problems. As such Section 6.1 will revisit the hypothesis that unidirectional externality problems are more easily solved through issue linkage than through side-payments. Section 6.2 will ask to what extent there are opportunities for issue linkage among different uses within the water sector, both at a conceptual level and empirically.

6.1 ISSUE LINKAGE AND THE THEORY OF INTERCONNECTED GAMES

Issue linkage, package deals or interconnection have long been known as negotiation strategies. More recently, a number of authors have started to analyze issue linkage in a more formal way. Tollison and Willet (1979) discuss issue linkage as a negotiation strategy to overcome distributional issues and to avoid side-payment in international relations. In his comprehensive review, Sebenius (1983) shows how adding or subtracting issues and parties in negotiations can enhance as well as reduce a possible 'zone of agreement'. He points at the fact that issue linkage is not uncontested in politics: while it can be used to overcome distributional conflict, the more powerful party may also use issue linkage as a leverage to impose its solution on other issues as well. McGinnis (1986) models the linkage of repeated Prisoner Dilemma games in international relations and shows how linkage may create new opportunities for cooperative outcomes. Folmer et al. (1993) analyze interconnected games for international environmental problems using direct sum and tensor games,[170] and show that interconnection may sustain more cooperation. Bennett et al. (1998) and Netanyahu (1998) apply the theory of interconnected games to international water management problems.

The following will first illustrate the principles behind interconnection for the linkage of two reciprocal externalities games with asymmetric payoffs, drawing upon Folmer and de Zeeuw (2000: 463-466) (Section 6.1.1) and then discuss interconnection for unidirectional externality problems (Section 6.1.2).

6.1.1 Reciprocal Externality Games with Asymmetric Payoffs

Folmer and de Zeeuw (2000: 463-466) assume a two-country setting with an asymmetric pollution problem where B suffers more from A's pollution than A from B's. An example may be the pollution of a shared lake with asymmetric payoffs. The costs associated with reducing one unit of pollution

---

[170] Direct sum games are composed of games in strategic form; tensor games are composed of repeated games (Folmer et al. 1993: 316).

(cooperation) are assumed to be 5 for country A and 6 for country B. The benefits of reducing one unit of pollution are assumed to be 2 for A and 5 for B, regardless of which country carries out the reduction. The payoff of not reducing a unit of pollution (defection) is assumed to be zero. The resulting payoffs are represented in Figure 6.1a. In this case agreement on the cooperative outcome would rely on a side-payment from B to A, and the cooperative outcome could only be sustained as an equilibrium outcome in an infinitely repeated game with an enforcement mechanism in place.

a. International Pollution Game

B

		Abate C	Pollute D
A	Abate C	-1,4	-3,5
	Pollute D	2,-1	$0,0^N$

b. International Trade Game

B

		Trade C	No trade D
A	Pay C	4,-1	-1,2
	No pay D	5,-3	$0,0^N$

c. The Interconnected Game

B

		C,C	C,D	D,C	D,D
A	C,C	3,3	-2,6	1,4	-4,7
	C,D	4,1	-1,4	2,2	-3,5
	D,C	6,-2	1,1	4,-1	-1,2
	D,D	7,-4	2,-1	5,-3	$0,0^N$

N: Nash equilibrium

Source: Folmer and de Zeeuw 2000: 464 f., adapted

Figure 6.1   Interconnecting an International Pollution and an International Trade Game

It is furthermore assumed that at the same time the two countries are involved in a second set of negotiations on trade issue. The background of these trade negotiations is that country B restricts imports from country A, a practice which A would like to see discontinued. For the sake of illustration it is assumed that the payoffs in the trade game are reversed compared to the pollution problem as presented in Figure 6.1b.[171] It is furthermore assumed that the constituting games are strategy and payoff independent, meaning that

---

[171] It is unclear whether this is a reasonable assumption. However for the time being it shall be maintained for the sake of illustration. Hauer and Runge (1999) model the granting of mutual concessions to expand areas of non-discrimination in bilateral trade as a symmetrical Assurance game. However the above game is meant to be asymmetrical.

a choice in one game does not influence the strategies available or the payoffs in the other game (Folmer et al. 1993: 316).

In this situation, the two countries could base an agreement on an exchange of concessions by linking these two issues, with country A reducing pollution and country B in exchange lifting its import restrictions. Interconnection yields a game matrix as presented in Figure 6.1c.

The interconnected game presents all possible action combinations of the action choices in the pollution game (game a) and the trade game (game b). In the action cell, the first letter refers to a player's action in game a and the second letter to a player's action in game b. For instance for A (C,D) means that A cooperates in game a and defects in game b. A player's payoff in the interconnected game is obtained by adding the player's payoffs in both games. For instance the payoff (4,1) for the action combination ((C,D), (C,C)) is obtained by adding the payoffs (-1,4) for the action combination (C,C) in game a and the payoff (5,-3) for the action combination (D,C) in game b.

The analysis of the interconnected game yields a Nash equilibrium for joint defection in both games ((D,D), (D,D)).[172] At the same time, the two players would be best off if they cooperated in both games, as cooperation in both games ((C,C), (C,C)) represents the welfare optimum and a (qualified) Pareto optimum vis-à-vis the Nash equilibrium.[173] Thus the interconnected game has the structure of a Prisoner's Dilemma game. While the cooperative outcome is no equilibrium in the one-shot game, in an infinitely repeated game, the two parties will be able to maintain the cooperative outcome as an equilibrium outcome if an enforcement mechanism is put in place.

Linking these two games has a number of advantages. First linkage provides an opportunity to create a zone of agreement and as such an alternative to monetary side-payments. In the linked game, A's concession to cooperate in game a is based on B's concession to cooperate in game b. Effectively, B pays for A's pollution abatement by lifting the trade restrictions, and A pays for B's lifting of trade restrictions by abating pollution. If the concessions in both games are in the same order of magnitude, they equalize each other, and no monetary transfer is necessary.

As Folmer et al. (1993) show, a further advantage of issue linkage is that in infinitely repeated games, interconnection offers an additional option for punishment, as B may punish defection by player A in game a by defection in game b and vice versa. In other words, A makes cooperation in game a

---

[172] The Nash equilibrium is determined by determining the highest payoff for A in each column and the highest payoff for B in each row.
[173] There are several Pareto optima, but the cooperative outcome ((C,C), (C,C)) is the game's welfare optimum and the qualified Pareto optimum.

conditional on B's cooperation in game b. Given that A has a preference for defection in game a and B has a preference for defection in game b the threat of punishment is credible.[174]

Linkage also has disadvantages. First it is likely to increase transaction costs. This includes the search costs of finding an appropriate option for linkage and increased negotiation costs as the number of participants in the negotiations increase (e.g. Tollison and Willet 1979: 446). Second while the above example represents an ideal case where two perfectly mirrored games are interconnected, in the real world, it is unlikely to find cases in which payoffs are exactly reversed. However even roughly off-setting distributional patterns may increase the likelihood of reaching an agreement. Third while trade issues are often mentioned as an option for linkage with environmental issues, the most favored nation clause of the World Trade Organization (WTO) may undermine interconnection of environmental and trade games.[175]

The above analysis makes clear that as in the case of side-payments issue linkage requires the recognition of a certain property rights allocation as a starting point for negotiations. Usually this will be the status quo – and thus the de facto property rights regime (absolute territorial sovereignty) will be taken as a given. This implies that issue linkage does not 'resolve' disputed property rights to water. From an economic point of view, it does not make a difference whether a problem is solved by monetary side-payment or linkage. In other words, issue linkage can be understood as a side-payment in kind. But psychologically, it may be easier to agree to an issue linkage as this may not entail the image of being a weak negotiator. In that sense issue linkage represents a pragmatic solution to simultaneous asymmetric interdependencies. It may 'help' countries to 'live' with disputed property rights to water, but it does not change the status quo allocation of property rights.

---

[174] Kroll et al. (1998) tested whether or not interconnection influences cooperation using an experimental laboratory approach finding that interconnection does lead to more cooperation. In addition they explored the difference between interconnecting games through an informal and a formal institution. A formal institution implies a joint institutional framework that integrates distinct actions into a single payoff before any decisions are made on how to play the game. An informal institution involves two parallel institutions where the players make the interconnection themselves during the play. They found that institutional setting matters as efficient outcomes were more common under the formal institution. Obviously, once a formal institution is in place it has the potential to decrease transaction costs.

[175] The most favored nation clause says that a party which grants an advantage with respect to trade conditions to a country must extend this advantage to all WTO countries (Folmer and de Zeeuw 2000: 466).

6.1.2 Unidirectional Externality Games

While the above example shows that linkage of two inversed reciprocal externality games with asymmetric payoffs may sustain cooperation without side-payments, the question is whether linkage is also a feasible solution in the case of unidirectional externality problems. As mentioned above a number of authors have proposed that upstream-downstream problems could be overcome by issue linkage. Bennett et al. (1998) discuss the linkage of two side-payment games. Zürn (1992: 211 and 216) argues that the interconnection of two Rambo games may yield a dilemma (or a deadlock) situation and thus enhance the likelihood of cooperation.

If it is assumed that the doctrine of absolute territorial sovereignty de facto applies, upstream-downstream water quantity and quality problems can be reconstructed as a Prisoner's Dilemma side-payment game if a side-payment is acceptable to both parties (see Section 5.3.1). In addition it was argued upstream-downstream pollution may possibly have the structure of a Rambo II game if downstream considers to clean up the polluted water itself (Section 5.3.2).[176] The following will therefore first address the linking of two inversed Prisoner's Dilemma side-payment games and then of two inversed Rambo II games. Empirical evidence will be discussed thereafter.

Linkage of two inversed Prisoner's Dilemma side-payment games

This linkage is presented in Figure 6.2. The interconnected game is presented in Figure 6.2c. The analysis shows that the interconnected game has the structure of a regular Prisoner's Dilemma game.

Thus under ideal circumstances, the side-payments equalize each other and obviate the need for a monetary transfer. As in each single game, in the interconnected game the cooperative outcome can be maintained as an equilibrium outcome in an infinitely repeated game if an enforcement mechanism is put in place. However in doing so interconnection offers an additional punishment option. Hence interconnection of two inversed side-payment games has the advantage that in an ideal situation the cooperative outcome can be sustained in an infinitely repeated game without side-payments, and interconnection offers additional punishment options. While the above numerical example may represent a very ideal situation as the payoffs of the two games are exactly mirrored this idealized case nicely shows the mechanisms of linkage.

---

[176] Zürn's (1992) reconstruction of upstream pollution problems as Rambo I game was rejected (Section 5.3.2).

a. Prisoner's Dilemma Game

		B	
		Pay C	No pay D
A	Abate C	3,3	1,4
	Pollute D	4,1	$2,2^N$

b. Inversed Prisoner's Dilemma Game

		B	
		Trade C	No trade D
A	Pay C	3,3	1,4
	No pay D	4,1	$2,2^N$

c. The Interconnected Game

		B			
		C,C	C,D	D,C	D,D
	C,C	6,6	4,7	4,7	2,8
A	C,D	7,4	5,5	5,5	3,6
	D,C	7,4	5,5	5,5	3,6
	D,D	8,2	6,3	6,3	$4,4^N$

N: Nash equilibrium

Source: Own presentation

Figure 6.2   Interconnecting Two Inversed Prisoner's Dilemma Games with Side-Payments

Linkage of two inversed Rambo II games

This linkage is shown in Figure 6.3. Interconnection yields an interconnected game in which unilateral cooperation by B in game a and by A in game b ((D,C), (C,D)) is a Nash equilibrium and a qualified Pareto optimum. The cooperative outcome ((C,C), (C,C)), on the other hand, is a qualified Pareto optimum too, but no Nash equilibrium. While it might be possible to sustain the cooperative outcome in an infinitely repeated game, the cooperative outcome does not improve the players' position vis-à-vis the Nash equilibrium. Thus in terms of payoffs it does not matter which of the two outcomes are chosen.[177] Interconnection yields the same outcome as if each game was played in isolation with A defecting in game a and cooperating in game b, and B cooperating in game a and defecting in game b.

The above analysis comes to the somewhat unexpected result that interconnection of two reversed Rambo games (in this case Rambo II games) does not yield a dilemma situation as Zürn (1992: 211 and 216) claims. As such this book does not only reject Zürn's (1992) reconstruction of upstream

---

[177] The countries may, however, in an infinitely repeated game choose the cooperative outcome in order to improve their relations.

pollution as a Rambo I game, but also his hypothesis that the linkage of two Rambo games may yield a dilemma game.[178]

Instead this book argues that if the status quo (and the use of side-payments) is accepted as a starting point for negotiations, negative unidirectional externalities are more appropriately represented as Prisoner's Dilemma game with side-payments, and that the interconnection of two inversed Prisoner's Dilemma games with side-payments may under ideal conditions sustain the cooperative outcome without monetary transfer.

a. Rambo II Game

		B	
		C	D
A	C	3,3	1,4
	D	$4,2^N$	2,1

b. Inversed Rambo II Game

		B	
		C	D
A	C	3,3	$2,4^N$
	D	4,1	1,2

c. The Interconnected Game

		B			
		C,C	C,D	D,C	D,D
	C,C	6,6	5,7	4,7	3,8
A	C,D	7,4	4,5	5,5	2,6
	D,C	7,5	$6,6^N$	5,4	4,5
	D,D	8,3	5,4	6,2	3,3

N: Nash equilibrium

Source: Own presentation

Figure 6.3   Interconnecting Two Inversed Rambo II Games

Thus if the status quo is accepted as starting point for negotiations, issue linkage may serve to overcome distributional issues in asymmetrical actor constellations and obviate the need for monetary transfers, and a possible loss of face that is associated with the victim pays principle. Furthermore it has been argued that issue linkage may strengthen cooperation in infinitely repeated games. Still whether issue linkage increases or decreases the zone of agreement depends on the situation at hand. In some cases it may also be used as leverage in the exercise of power to yield one-sided gains. At the same time, it should be emphasized that issue linkage is no panacea against disputed property rights in an upstream-downstream setting. Issue linkage is

---

[178] It can be shown that an analogous result can be reached if two inversed Rambo I games are interconnected.

basically a means for the downstream riparian to accept the de facto power of the upstream riparian, implying that downstream at least implicitly recognizes the doctrine of absolute territorial sovereignty, knowing that in another area of cooperation this asymmetry is reversed.

Empirical evidence

Two frequently mentioned examples for an inter-sector issue linkage between transboundary river management problems and non-water issues are the Columbia River Treaty between Canada and the USA in 1961 and the International Boundary and Water Commission (IBWC) Minute 242 on the Colorado between the USA and Mexico in 1973.

- The Columbia treaty aimed at integrated development of hydropower and flood control in the Columbia River Basin. Despite the wish to share the benefits from joint development, in his analysis of the treaty, Krutilla (1967) found a relative loss of US\$ 250 to 375 million for the USA compared to other alternatives (in LeMarquand 1977: 68). Obviously the reason for the USA to accept the treaty was that there were other interests at stake, including defense issues and the will to strengthen the strategic partnership with Canada in the context of the Cold War. Thus this case included an intra-water sector issue linkage of hydropower and flood protection issues and an inter-sector issue linkage by implicitly linking water issues and security issues.
- In the Colorado case, the USA as upstream country responded to Mexican complaints about high salinity levels in the river by several measures including the construction of a desalination plant. According to LeMarquand (1977: 46) President Nixon was willing to go ahead with the agreement because of the desire to be seen by the world as a responsible nation, for legal reasons and in order to maintain good relations with Mexico for the resolution of other important bilateral issues. Thus in this case water issues were implicitly linked to image concerns.

While these examples do not reflect an explicit 'formal' issue linkage where side-payments were avoided by linking two inversed issues, they illustrate that in international relations the implications of a particular issue are usually seen in the overall context of the respective bilateral relations.

The analysis of 506 international water treaties in Section 4.3.2 showed that states rarely apply explicit inter-sector issue linkages, and that issue linkage is least common in the case of water quality and water quantity problems. As mentioned in Section 4.3.2, there may be different explanations for these findings. One is that issue linkage is rather sought within than outside the water sector. This hypothesis will be pursued in the next section.

6.2   OPPORTUNITIES FOR ISSUE LINKAGE WITHIN THE WATER SECTOR?

Given the multi-functionality of water, the question is to what extent there are opportunities for issue linkage within the water sector. As argued earlier water uses may take effect in different directions and may go along with positive and negative effects (see Table 2.1). Furthermore a country's negotiation position may change if it is simultaneously involved in negotiations in different river basins in which it holds different riparian positions. Thus different types of intra-water sector issue linkage are prima facie conceivable and shall be explored in the following, including the linkage of:

* water uses controlled by downstream with uses controlled by upstream (Section 6.2.1);
* effects directed upstream with effects directed downstream (Section 6.2.2);
* positive and negative externalities (Section 6.2.3); and
* river basins with reversed riparian positions (Section 6.2.4).

All things equal, it can be assumed that intra-water issue linkage will be easier to implement than inter-sector issue linkage. The reason is that in the case of inter-sector issue linkage, representatives from different sectors will have to negotiate for whom it will be difficult to appreciate the reciprocity within the arrangement. Therefore, unless a higher level government entity with a particular interest in such an arrangement is involved in the negotiations, inter-sector negotiations are less likely to materialize than intra-water sector negotiations. In other words, inter-sector negotiations are likely to involve higher transaction costs than intra-water sector negotiations. A possible drawback of intra-water issue linkage is that the strategies in each single game may not be independent from each other.

In the following sections, the above types of linkage will be explored conceptually and empirically.[179]

---

[179] An earlier version of Sections 6.2.1 to 6.2.4 has been presented in Dombrowsky (2005b).

6.2.1 Linking Uses Controlled by Downstream with Uses Controlled by Upstream

Conceptual considerations

While many river uses are controlled by the upstream riparian, some uses are controlled by the downstream riparian. These include navigational uses or the upstream movement of migratory fish (fish patency). The downstream user could therefore theoretically make measures to improve the movement of vessels or migratory fish conditional on upstream water releases or pollution control.

Let us assume that downstream suffers from upstream pollution. Accepting that the de facto rights are with the upstream party (absolute territorial sovereignty), the downstream riparian considers offering a side-payment so that upstream reduces pollution to an efficient level and both parties are able to realize gains from reduced pollution. At the same time, upstream places a value on the return of migratory fish which requires that downstream demolishes a number of weirs or installs fish ladders.

Let us furthermore assume that downstream does not care for migratory fish. In this case upstream may consider a side-payment to downstream that would cover the costs of fish ladders. If the two issues were linked, and the respective side-payments were in the same order of magnitude (which, however, is rather unlikely), the reduction of upstream pollution could be carried out in exchange for the installation of fish ladders downstream, obviating the need for mutual side-payments.[180]

Empirical evidence

In the Rhine Basin, the interconnection of pollution control and the reintroduction of migratory fish under the header 'Salmon 2000' in the context of the Rhine Action Program of 1987 led to a breakthrough in the work of the International Commission for the Protection of the Rhine. Durth (1996: 202) argues that in this case the upstream-downstream problem was transformed into a public good problem where the provision of good water quality and the reintroduction of the salmon were in everybody's interest. Connecting pollution control with fish patency certainly transformed the

---

[180] One problem with this particular reconstruction is that upstream needs to reduce pollution anyway for the fish to return, so that the threat to pollute in the absence of a side-payment may not be credible. Furthermore it is also doubtful whether it can be assumed that downstream does not have any interest in migratory fish. Thus the two games are not strategy independent. These concerns not withstanding it can be argued that in the Rhine basin pollution control was linked with the return of migratory fish (see below).

incentives for the upstream riparian, as the upstream riparians now had an interest to abate themselves. But according to Durth (1996: 202) also the Netherlands as the most downstream country had an interest in the return of the salmon if only for public relation reasons. This means that through linkage both upstream and downstream parties became interested in both issues. Hence in this case linkage did not imply a mutual exchange of concessions obviating monetary transfers, but transformed the perception of the issues from an upstream-downstream into a public good problem.[181] However in principle the example supports the hypothesis that the linkage of uses controlled by downstream with uses controlled by upstream may contribute towards conflict resolution.

An example of the linkage of navigational uses with water quality and water quantity issues is the 1994 agreements pertaining to the Scheldt and Meuse Rivers. In 1994 Belgium and the Netherlands linked dredging works to improve the navigability of the Scheldt River, water quality issues in both basins, water quantity issues in the Meuse as well as the alignment of a railway line to a package deal – although in the end four separate treaties were concluded (Meijerink 1999; Mostert N.d.). Thus this case included various water and non-water issue linkages, including the linkage of navigation with water quantity and quality and the linkage of different river basins.

6.2.2   Balancing Upstream and Downstream Effects

Conceptual considerations

While most of the time, upstream measures create negative external effects downstream, in some – albeit rare – cases downstream measures may also create physically mediated negative external effects upstream. An example is the construction of a downstream dam that floods upstream. If at the same time the upstream riparian imposes a negative effect on the downstream riparian, e.g. by pollution, the two parties could conclude an agreement which foresees the reduction of their respective economic activities to an

---

[181] The transformation of the upstream-downstream problem in the Rhine into a public good problem raises the question how the second-order problem of free-riding was resolved. It appears that this was mainly achieved through a high degree of public accountability rather than playing a Grim or Getting-even strategy. Given that ICPR had publicly declared the reintroduction of the salmon until the year 2000, it created a target that was easy to communicate and monitor, increasing the pressure on the respective governments to achieve these objectives vis-à-vis their constituencies (e.g. Holtrup 1999: 135). It may thus be argued that international commitment was created through internal accountability mechanisms rather than international enforcement mechanisms. This was reinforced through international reporting and the publication of progress reports by ICPR.

efficient level. Under the doctrine of absolute territorial sovereignty downstream will offer a side-payment to upstream in order to reduce pollution to the efficient level, and upstream will offer a side-payment to downstream in order to downsize the dam. If the side-payments are equal in size, cooperation can be achieved without monetary transfers.[182]

Empirical evidence

An example of a reservoir flooding upstream is Lake Nasser behind the Aswan High Dam in Egypt. The lake has a total length of 500 km (Waterbury 1979: 112), approximately a quarter of which floods into Sudan. The 1959 agreement between Egypt and Sudan foresaw the payment of 15 million Egyptian pounds for the resettlement of 50,000 Nubians in Wadi Halfa and for the flooding of 20,000 feddans (c. 8,400 ha) of their land (Waterbury 1979: 73). When both countries negotiated the project in the 1950s, Egypt's Nile quota was already significantly above Sudan's on the basis of an agreement dating back to 1929 (48 versus 4 billion cubic meters per year). This means that in this situation Sudan could theoretically have extracted more water rights from Egypt – and not the other way around – for Egypt's right to flood. While the 1959 Nile agreement increased both countries' Nile quota vis-à-vis the 1929 agreement (55.5 versus 16.5 billion cubic meters per year), this was based on the additional storage provided by the reservoir (Waterbury 1979: 68-73). There is no indication that Sudan tried to link the water rights and the resettlement question, and Egypt presumably paid a one-time compensation (if this payment has taken place), instead of lowering its Nile quota forever. Thus in this case the issues were not linked.

6.2.3 Balancing Negative and Positive Effects

Conceptual considerations

Theoretically, another option for an issue linkage might be to balance negative and positive external effects in an upstream-downstream situation. As discussed in Section 5.3.3, in some cases, infrastructure measures change the natural conditions on a river and thus provide 'pure' positive externalities downstream, e.g. by buffering extreme high and low flows or by trapping silt caused by natural erosion.

---

[182] The problem with this scenario is while pollution can be abated at reasonable costs, downstream would probably not be ready to forego the dam's benefits.

Let us assume that downstream suffers from anthropogenic upstream pollution as well as naturally caused flooding. Under the principle of absolute territorial sovereignty, downstream would offer a side-payment to upstream to reduce negative externalities (pollution) to an efficient level, and upstream would ask for a side-payment for the provision of flood control as positive externality. However this would mean that in both cases the payment would be made from downstream to upstream. Thus this reconstruction illustrates that under the doctrine of absolute territorial sovereignty, there are no opportunities for the linkage of negative and positive downstream effects. Linkage would only be possible under the doctrine of absolute territorial integrity (liability rule), in which case downstream would ask for compensation from upstream for bearing the (remaining) level of the negative externality, and upstream would ask for a side-payment from downstream for the provision of a positive externality. Thus if the status quo (doctrine of absolute territorial sovereignty) is accepted as a starting point for negotiations, there are no opportunities to balance negative and positive downstream effects. Also, the author is not aware of an empirical case in which positive and negative effects were linked.

6.2.4 Taking Account of Different Riparian Positions (Spatial Linkage)

Conceptual considerations

A country's negotiation position may also change if it simultaneously holds different riparian positions in various river basins. For instance Germany is an upstream riparian on the Danube River, a midstream riparian on the Rhine River and a downstream riparian on the Elbe and Oder Rivers. The USA and Mexico share three river basins along their border, the Rio Grande/Rio Bravo, the Colorado and the Tijuana River Basins. While on the Colorado the USA is an upstream riparian and Mexico the downstream riparian, on the Rio Grande both Mexico and the USA are upstream riparians and the US State of Texas is the downstream riparian. On the Tijuana River, Mexico is the upstream and the USA the downstream riparian. If negotiations on various river basins of a dyad are conducted simultaneously, one may speak of 'spatial linkage' (Fischhendler et al. 2004: 634). The relatively high number of bilateral border commissions identified in Table A-1 indicates that countries do consider different shared river basins simultaneously (although they may not necessarily involve reversed riparian positions).

Let us assume a dyad of countries A and B which share two river basins, where country A is upstream in river 1 and downstream in river 2 and vice versa. In both cases, the respective downstream country suffers from upstream pollution. If the status quo is accepted as a starting point for negotiations (doctrine of absolute territorial sovereignty), country B can be expected to offer a side-payment to A on river 1, and country A will offer a side-payment to B on river 2 in order to reduce pollution to the efficient level. If the two side-payments are in the same order of magnitude, and if the cooperative outcome where both abate to the efficient level can be sustained without monetary transfers, the game can be transformed into a Prisoner's Dilemma game without side-payments.

Alternatively, the simultaneous consideration of these two negotiation settings may motivate the two countries to adopt the principle of equitable utilization as property rights doctrine. In this case an agreement could be reached according to which on each river the upstream country carries the costs of abatement to the efficient level, and the downstream country does not insist on compensation for the remaining damage. Interestingly, this would factually result in the same outcome as the linkage above. Hence from a theoretical point of view, there appears to be a particular potential for looking beyond single river basins in order to overcome upstream-downstream problems. This supports Barrett's (1996: 268) argument that in international relations the implications of single negotiations are usually not looked at in isolation and that countries are careful not to set a precedent in one issue area which may be held up against it in another area of international relations (Section 5.3.5).

These considerations imply that the linkage of river basins with reversed riparian positions may not only be conducive towards cooperation, but also towards a mutual delimitation of property rights to water. At the same time it must be clearly said that the opportunity to look at different river basins primarily applies to federal governments, but is limited for local stakeholders and lower levels of government.

Empirical evidence

In the US-Mexican case, it was decided in the 1920s to negotiate all three river basins simultaneously, and since 1944 the three basins are covered by one treaty and one organization, the International Boundary and Water Commission.[183] While in the beginning the two countries in fact invoked contradictory legal doctrines on the Rio Grande and Colorado Rivers, in the end the spatial linkage led both states to abandon the extreme doctrines

---

[183] Besides these long-term spatial linkages, different sub-agreements were based on additional short-term linkages (e.g. the 1944 treaty was based on Mexico's support for the establishment of the United Nations).

(Fischhendler et al. 2004: 638 f.). Proponents of the agreement argue that spatial linkage was a prerequisite towards reaching an agreement in the first place and has allowed sustaining cooperation over 60 years. In contrast Fischhendler et al. (2004) maintain that spatial linkage did not only lead to short-term complications, such as delays in negotiations due to lack of data, inconsistencies in the legal doctrines held by the different parties (which, however, were resolved in the end) and resistance at the local level, but also had long-term ramifications, as it currently impedes renegotiation of the treaty and adaptation to recurrent droughts and demographic growth in the Mexican part of the upper Rio Grande basin. Even though it would go beyond this section to evaluate this case, it is an interesting example of the short-term and long-term effects of different linkage strategies. It does, however, support the notion that the linkage of river basins with reversed riparian positions is conducive the abandonment of extreme property rights doctrines and a mutual delimitation of property rights to water.

6.3   CONCLUSIONS

The above analysis asked which role issue linkage may play in the resolution of unidirectional externality problems and whether opportunities exist for issue linkage within the water sector. The section showed that if two Prisoner's Dilemma side-payment games with inversed payoffs are linked, the resulting game has the structure of a Prisoner's Dilemma game without side-payments. In the case of infinitely repeated games the cooperative outcome can be maintained as an equilibrium outcome if an enforcement mechanism is in place. It was furthermore shown that contrary to assumptions in the literature, the linkage of two Rambo games does not increase the likelihood of cooperation.

Issue linkage can be understood as a side-payment in kind. From an economic perspective, the main advantage of issue linkage is that in a Prisoner's Dilemma-like situation it provides an additional punishment strategy in the attempt to sustain cooperation as an equilibrium outcome. The main disadvantage vis-à-vis a side-payment is that it is likely to increase transaction costs. However as side-payments, issue linkage requires the recognition of a certain property rights allocation (usually the status quo) as a starting point for negotiations. Thus it presupposes the explicit or implicit definition of property rights and does not contribute towards resolving contested property rights to water. However when property rights are contested and no equitable settlement appears to be feasible, from a psychological point of view it may be easier for the disadvantaged party to conclude an agreement in which issues with different distributional implications are interconnected than to offer a side-payment. In that sense issue linkage may be perceived as a pragmatic solution to overcome stalemate, and it can be argued that issue linkage increases the likelihood to reach an agreement. Once an agreement is concluded the additional punishment option provided by the linkage increases the likelihood of cooperation.

Given the multi-functionality of water, issue linkage is not only possible between different economic sectors and issue areas, but there are principally also opportunities for issue linkage within the water sector. One potential advantage of issue linkage within the water sector is that it is more likely to involve lower transaction costs than issue linkage between different economic sectors. While the analysis confirms that such opportunities exist, they also appear to remain limited. Within a river basin, there may be some opportunities for balancing uses controlled by downstream with uses controlled by upstream as well as downstream and upstream effects. In contrast balancing negative and positive downstream effects proves to be difficult if the status quo (doctrine of absolute territorial sovereignty) is taken as the starting point for negotiations. In particular if river basins with reversed riparian positions are linked (spatial linkage), this may create a higher level of reciprocity, which is conducive towards cooperation and the mutual delimitation of property rights to water. Thus not issue linkage in general, but looking beyond the particular constellation in a single river basin may be conducive towards the mutual delimitation of property rights.

The conclusions that can be drawn from this chapter may even be taken a step further. Where opportunities for intra-water sector issue linkage exist, the 'integration' of different water uses, as called for by the concept of Integrated Water Resources Management, is in the interest of the actors involved. As such intra-water issue linkage may explain the substantive scope of international water management institutions. Given that intra-water issue linkage may enhance or reduce the zone of agreement, 'integration' as promoted by the concept of Integrated Water Resources Management may or may not be in the self-interest of the riparian countries involved. Furthermore as mentioned above, sometimes it may be worthwhile to look beyond the scope of a single river basin, which hints at the limits of a narrow river basin management approach. However whether integration is in the self-interest of the actors involved does not say anything yet about what is normatively desirable.

In principle the examples mentioned in this chapter provide evidence that riparian countries do apply both (implicit) inter-sector and explicit intra-water issue linkages. Thus in practice riparian states are likely to take all opportunities at hand, and it may be difficult to test the hypothesis that intra-issue sector linkage is more likely than inter-sector issue linkage.

While Chapters 5 and 6 have dealt with the conclusions of cooperative agreements in the management of international waters, Chapter 7 will address the economic rationale for the set up of organizations. In doing so, Chapter 7 will leave the game-theoretic framework and will draw upon transaction costs economics.

7. The Role of Organizations for Cooperation

Chapters 5 and 6 have analyzed the role of the structure of a problem and of issue linkage as negotiation strategy for cooperation and for the set up of institutions at international rivers. By and large this was done under the assumption of perfect information. It was argued that depending on the structure of the problem riparian states can be expected to conclude agreements in order to realize gains of cooperation. It was highlighted that in negative unidirectional externality problems any substantial agreement that seeks to realize gains of cooperation also has to tackle the question of property rights, either explicitly or implicitly. It was furthermore argued that in Prisoner's Dilemma-type situations, cooperation can only be expected if agreements are self-enforcing. As such Chapter 5 was able to reconstruct the rationale for the conclusion of international agreements, the definition of property rights and the set up of enforcement mechanisms. However in contrast to Chapter 1, which argued that there is often an assumption in the policy discourse that it is desirable to establish special river basin organizations, and Chapter 4, which showed that riparian states do not only conclude water-related agreements, but that they also establish international organizations, organizations did not play any role in Chapters 5 and 6. This raises the question whether the establishment of international organizations can also be explained economically.

The expediency of international organizations has rarely been addressed in the literature on international water management. As argued in Section 3.1.4 international watercourse law suggests that the set up of commissions and other arrangements is conducive towards the negotiation of rights and obligations on international waters. Marty (2001: 45 f.) posits that institutional arrangements are more effective if they are endowed with an effective organization. He distinguishes between a centralized and a decentralized type of organization but does not suggest that one type is more effective than the other, arguing that while the set up of centralized organizations entails higher costs than decentralized organizations, they may effect cost savings in running the organization. In terms of an economic treatment of the topic, one rare exception is Durth (1996: 104 ff.), who at a very abstract level discusses the cost-benefit calculus of respective riparian governments with regard to the establishment of an international water commission.

This chapter will build upon transaction cost economics in the New Institutional Economics in order to address the rationale for organizations. In a first step it will explore the explanatory power of transaction cost economics, which was initiated by Coase (1937; 1960) and further developed by Williamson (1985) (Section 7.1).[184] In a second step it will present Scharpf's (1997) actor-centered institutionalism, which also builds upon transaction cost economics, but incorporates other theories within the New Institutional Economics, such as public choice and principal agent theories as well as theories within the political sciences (Section 7.2). Even though neither Williamson nor Scharpf present a theory of international organizations, these two authors have been selected as starting points for the movement towards an economic theory of international organizations in general and international river basin organizations in particular. Section 7.3 will draw conclusions with respect to the problem of international water management.

In the following, the assumption of full rationality will be released, and it will be assumed that we are dealing with boundedly rational actors whose access to information and whose information processing capabilities are limited. In contrast to Chapters 5 and 6 the emphasis is not on the question of how institutions may emerge from voluntary interaction, but how different institutional settings can be expected to influence the problem-solving capacity of actors if bounded rationality is assumed.

7.1 TRANSACTION COST ECONOMICS AND ITS IMPLICATIONS FOR INTERNATIONAL WATER MANAGEMENT INSTITUTIONS

The problem of transaction costs led Coase (1960) to advance a different analytical approach to deal with externalities, namely to start with the analysis of the status quo and to analyze alternative institutional arrangements taking all costs, including transaction costs, into account. He

---

[184] This means that the study by and large abandons the game-theoretic framework at this point. An alternative approach would have been to approach problems of information asymmetry in terms of non-cooperative game theory. However given the focus on the role of organizations, the idea was to use transaction cost economics as 'classic' economic theory of organization as a starting point of the analysis.

mentions negotiations, the firm, different forms of government regulation or the zero option to do nothing as alternative arrangements:[185]

> A better approach would seem to be to start our analysis with a situation approximating that which actually exists, to examine the effects of a proposed policy change, and to attempt to decide whether the new situation would be, in total, better or worse than the original one (Coase 1960: 43).

He later added:

> Without the concept of transaction costs... it is my contention that it is impossible to understand the working of the economic system, to analyze many of its problems in a useful way, or to have a basis for determining policy (Coase 1988b: 6).

Already in 1937, Coase had argued that transaction costs – in particular the costs of 'using the price mechanism' and the costs of contracting – are the main reasons for the existence of the firm. The firm can be understood as a special long-term contractual relationship where the entrepreneur is able to direct resources in order to allow for adaptation to changing circumstances (Coase 1937: 38 f.). Hence within the firm, individual bargains are substituted by an administrative decision (Coase 1960: 16). However as Coase (1960: 17) contends, in the case of environmental pollution, adjusting the boundaries of private firms to the geographical scope of the problem will often be infeasible.[186] In this case some form of government regulation may be necessary. However while the government may impose and enforce an optimal solution, this will also always go along with administrative costs. Furthermore governments may take 'bad' decisions due to mistakes or pressures and lack of competitive control. Therefore in situations in which the gain from regulation will be less than the costs involved, the preferred solution might even be the zero alternative to do nothing.[187] According to Coase (1988b: 28), the purpose of economic policy is to identify those institutional arrangements that maximize the total value of production. This cannot be made in abstract, but needs to consider a given case, taking all effects into account: 'In devising and choosing among social arrangements

---

[185] In the absence of externalities, markets may be considered as a further transaction cost-reducing mechanism: 'Markets are institutions that exist to facilitate exchange, that is, they exist in order to reduce the cost of carrying out exchange transactions' (Coase 1988b: 7).

[186] Following Coase's (1960) considerations with respect to the adjustment of environmental problems to the boundary of the firm, Kneese and Bower (1968: 184 ff.) have used the concept of the 'basin-wide firm' as a starting point for the introduction of the concept of river basin organizations.

[187] Critics argue that this approach tends to cement the status quo (e.g. Weimann 1995: 42).

we should have regard for the total effect. This, above all, is the change in approach which I am advocating' (Coase 1960: 44).

Williamson (1971; 1985) has taken up Coase's (1937) question regarding the rationale for the existence of the firm. The question is if markets represent efficient coordination mechanisms, why are there firms? The following will present Williamson's transaction cost economics (TCE) and ask to what extent TCE may inform the choice and design of institutional arrangements for the management of international waters if bounded rationality and the possibility of opportunistic behavior are taken into consideration. Section 7.1.1 will introduce into the problem of vertical integration in industrial organization, which Williamson used as a starting point for the development of his theory. Section 7.1.2 will compare the governance structures of industrial organization, and Section 7.1.3 will present the extension of TCE to the public sector. Each section will first present Williamson's contribution, and then ask for possible implications of the theory for international water management institutions. Section 7.1.4 will summarize the results.

7.1.1　The Problem of Vertical Integration in Industrial Organization

Williamson's contribution

Taking the problem of vertical integration – or make-or-buy decisions – in industrial organization as a starting point, Williamson examines under which conditions it is expedient for a firm to make a product or service, i.e. to integrate a supplier of products or services in his firm, and under which conditions it is expedient to buy, i.e. to buy the respective product or service on the market.[188] This make-or-buy question corresponds to a choice between markets and hierarchies.

Williamson finds that the question whether a firm acquires products or services on the market or whether it employs the supplier of the respective products and services within its own firm largely hinges on the costs of contracting – or transaction costs. Unlike transactions on spot markets where the exchange is a singular and instant event (so called classical or spot

---

[188] So called mundane vertical integration involves integration of successive stages within the core technology. Backward integration refers to integration into basic materials, lateral into components and forward integration into distribution (Williamson 1985: 105).

contract),[189] in industrial organization and other areas, such as public policy, transactions are usually repeated and based on longer-term relationships. The time dimension, however, brings a new quality into the contracting process and may create transaction costs due to necessary adaptations that cannot be neglected in the economic decision-making process. Williamson posits which transaction costs occur and their temporal development depends on the attributes of the transaction.

In the context of industrial organization, Williamson (1985: 52-61) identifies three important attributes of transactions, (1) the frequency with which transactions occur, (2) the uncertainty (disturbances) to which they are subject and, most importantly, (3) the condition of asset specificity. Frequency of transaction implies that contracts are long-term. The consequence of uncertainty is that not all eventualities, including the moves of the contractual partner, can be anticipated. Asset specificity occurs if one contractual partner (e.g. the supplier) has to make specific investments in order to fulfill the contractual obligations and if this investment cannot (easily) be redeployed for other purposes should the contract be terminated prematurely:

> (1) [A]sset specificity refers to durable investments that are undertaken in support of particular transactions, the opportunity cost of which investments is much lower in best alternative uses or by alternative users should the original transaction prematurely be terminated, and (2) the specific identity of the parties to a transaction plainly matters (Williamson 1985: 55).

Specific investments may take place at the level of physical assets, human assets, site specificity and dedicated assets. Williamson argues that asset specificity gives rise to a condition of bilateral dependency, 'whereupon what may have been a large numbers supply condition at the outset gets transformed into a small numbers exchange relation thereafter' (Williamson 1998: 36). Hence what used to be a situation of full competition is transformed into a bilateral monopoly. However, in a bilateral monopoly, adaptation is usually connected with strategic bargaining on how potential efficiency gains from adaptation are shared and thus gives rise to bargaining costs which may even be prohibitively high. The prospect of strategic bargaining may give rise to opportunistic behavior, both ex ante in the negotiation leading up to a contract and ex post in a renegotiation of the

---

[189] In reference to Mcneil (1978), Williamson (1985: 68-72) distinguishes classical, neo-classical and relational contracts. The classical contract refers to the ideal transaction-cost free transaction in law and economics. The neo-classical contract refers to long-term contracts under conditions of uncertainty. In the case of relational contracts, there does not need to be an explicit agreement, but obligations are based on the relation between the parties.

contract.[190] Opportunistic behavior means that actors are willing to use guile in the pursuit of their self-interest (Williamson 1985: 30). According to Williamson (1985: 61 ff.) in the course of the transaction, asset specificity in combination with opportunism leads to a 'fundamental transformation' from market to bilateral monopoly conditions, where the attributes of the transaction give rise to hazards that reduce the efficiency of the outcome. This reduced efficiency is the reason why spot contracts may not be an expedient form of contract in each and every case.

Any of the three transaction attributes imply that contracts become longer-term and more complex. However complex contracts are incomplete in the sense that they cannot anticipate all eventualities. Contracts are incomplete because actors are not omniscient, but only boundedly rational, and because actors are prone to behave opportunistically.

In terms of its behavioral assumptions, transaction cost economics assumes self-interested behavior, but it follows Simon (1957) that actors are boundedly rational. Bounded rationality assumes that individuals behave intendedly rational, but only limitedly so, given that they usually do not have all relevant information and given that their cognitive abilities are constrained. In addition as indicated above, transaction cost economics also posits that actors may behave opportunistically. The theory does not purport that opportunism is the rule, but it takes account of the fact that opportunism may occur if the opportunity arises. One implication is that mere promises without credible commitments cannot be expected to be self-enforcing (Williamson 1998: 31).

However even if actors are boundedly rational and may behave opportunistically, this does not imply that they cannot look ahead, anticipate hazards and design contracts in a way to mitigate foreseeable harzards. Thus the design of contracts is a critical step and there are different contractual options – or governance structures – to manage transactions. According to this understanding, the very purpose of governance is to anticipate potential hazards and to design contracts in a way that maximizes the effective gains of cooperation: '[G]overance is the means by which order is accomplished in a relation in which potential conflict threatens to undo or upset opportunities to realize mutual gains' (Williamson 1998: 37, i.i.o. with reference to Commons 1932).

---

[190] The latter is sometimes referred to as holdup situation. In a holdup the quasi rent of the party with the greater specific investment is captured by the other party. An example would be a steel mill located close to a power station in order to buy electricity cheaply. Once the steel mill has been set up, the power company may renegotiate the contract and demand higher prices (Furubotn and Richter 1997: 131).

The purpose of the choice of the most expedient governance structure is to reduce opportunism: 'Attenuating the ex post hazards of opportunism through the ex ante choice of governance is central to the transaction cost economics exercise' (Williamson 1998: 31).

In industrial organization these different governance structures include markets (spot contracts) and hierarchies (private firms) as extreme forms, representing the market-hierarchy dichotomy, and hybrids (incomplete contracts) as intermediary form. With reference to Alchian and Demsetz (1972), the firm is perceived as a 'nexus of contracts' (Williamson 1991: 106).

Implications for international water management

For international water management the analysis of transaction costs in the contractual relations in industrial organization is of interest as the three transaction attributes identified by Williamson that give rise to increased transaction costs, namely uncertainty, frequency of transaction and asset specificity, are highly relevant in international water negotiations. This applies both to the negotiation of property rights and of infrastructure measures. In the case of property rights, the negotiations are usually characterized by uncertainty with regard to exact interests, needs and requirements of the states involved, and the distributional implications of the allocation of property rights gives rise to strategic and opportunistic behavior. Once an agreement is reached, they usually tend to have long-term ramifications, as prior agreements greatly influence future negotiations.[191]

Water infrastructure is usually heavy, capital intensive and relative immobile, and investments in the water sector tend to be long-term. These characteristics give rise both to asset specificity as investments cannot be easily redeployed as well as to frequent transactions. Often, the planning horizon for water infrastructure is 20 years and more. This also means that decisions have to be made under uncertainty with regard to economic and societal developments. They also have to deal with hydrological uncertainty and the potential implications of climate change. Once investments are made, the possibilities to adapt to changing circumstances are usually limited.

---

[191] Many river basins with agreements in place experience what can be referred to as path dependency. In the Nile Basin, the current property rights situation is shaped by the 1959 agreement between Egypt and Sudan the design of which again was influenced by an agreement between Egypt and Great Britain on behalf of the Sudan in 1929. As argued in Section 6.2.4 in the Rio Grande River Basin, at present adaptation to demographic and climatic change is hindered by the linkages of the 1944 agreement, which made water releases in the Rio Grande Basin conditional on water releases in the Colorado Basin and vice versa. This is why McCaffrey (2003b) calls for a flexible design of international water treaties.

Given these transaction attributes, negotiations in international water management are likely to give rise to strategic and opportunistic behavior and thus to contractual hazards and ex ante and ex post transaction costs. Thus once the assumption of perfect information is abandoned, TCE contributes towards the analysis of the negotiation problem in international water management.

In contrast to industrial organization, in international water management markets are not the starting point of transactions, but the condition of bilateral monopoly or oligopoly exists from the beginning.[192] Thus international water management does not experience the phenomenon of a 'fundamental transformation' from a market to a bilateral monopoly situation.[193]

After the analysis of typical problems that give rise to transaction costs, the next section will address institutional responses to the problem of transaction costs, namely the three governance structures of industrial organization markets, hybrids and hierarchies and the way in which they remedy contractual hazards.

7.1.2 The Governance Structures of Industrial Organization

Williamson's contribution

Williamson (1991: 271-281) argues that the three governance structures, i.e. markets, hybrids and hierarchies, that can be found in industrial organization differ in three respects, namely:

1. in their performance attributes or adaptation mechanisms;
2. in their (control) instruments or enforcement mechanisms and
3. in the underlying contract law or dispute resolution mechanisms (Table 7.1).

1. The overriding distinguishing feature of different governance structures are what Williamson refers to as performance attributes or adaptation mechanisms, i.e. the ability of alternative governance structures to adapt when unanticipated disturbances occur. Following Hayek (1945), in the

---

[192] This applies at least if governments are assumed to be the primary actors at the international level. International water markets in which individual right holders trade rights are theoretically conceivable, but to the knowledge of the author there is no empirical evidence for international water markets so far. As indicated in Section 1.2, Fisher (1995) and other authors propose their set up in the Jordan River Basin but they are institutionally demanding.

[193] This does not imply that specific infrastructure measures may not create specific 'fundamental transformations' between the respective riparian countries.

(neoclassical) market, adaptation occurs autonomously through the price mechanism when consumers and producers respond independently to parametric price changes so as to maximize their utility and their profits, respectively (Williamson 1991: 277 f.). Under ideal market conditions, adaptation is costless and the outcome is efficient. Williamson refers to this mechanism as autonomous adaptation or adaptation A. In contrast, in line with Barnard (1938), in hierarchies, adaptation is based on deliberate and intended cooperation or fiat within the hierarchy. This is being referred to as cooperative adaptation or adaptation C. Unlike autonomous adaptation, cooperative adaptation entails transaction costs. This means whenever changes are reflected in relative prices, the market will be the most efficient adaptation mechanism. However when this is not the case, intentional and coordinated responses may be required. While markets and hierarchies rely on distinct adaptation mechanisms, hybrids contain elements of both autonomous and cooperative adaptation in the sense that incentives for autonomous adaptation exist (e.g. to change the contract partner in the case of inefficiency). At the same time contracts contain safeguards such as information disclosure, enforcement and dispute settlement mechanisms in order to mitigate contractual hazards. According to Williamson (1991: 278) adaptation can be understood as the central problem of economic organization. Adaptation is required to resort to efficiency when contractual hazards occur. The respective adaptation mechanisms are also closely related to enforcement (control instruments) and dispute settlement mechanisms.

2. The term control instruments can be understood to refer to the mechanisms of alternative governance structures to induce compliance or, in the terminology of this book, enforcement mechanisms. Alternative control instruments are what Williamson refers to as incentive intensity and administrative controls. In markets, incentive intensity is high, and there is no need for administrative controls. In the case of hierarchies incentive intensity tends to be low, but transactions may be enforced by administrative controls, such as monitoring and accounting, awards and penalties and other forms of informal organization. Hierarchies use flat incentives (such as a flat salary structure) deliberately because these elicit greater cooperation. In the case of hybrids, incentives still persist, albeit in an attenuated fashion and control is partly realized through administrative controls.

3. In addition each governance structure is supported by a different kind of contract law. This is of particular relevance for the settlement of disputes. The contract law of markets is legalistic and relies on court orderings. In contrast in hierarchies disputes are settled by fiat or private ordering within the hierarchy. In that sense the firm is its own court of ultimate

appeal. With reference to the so called 'business judgment rule', Williamson (1991: 274) argues that the implicit law of hierarchy is that of forbearance. The business judgment rule holds that in the absence of bad faith, or corrupt motive, directors are usually not liable to the corporation for mistakes of judgment. This means that courts will refuse to hear internal disputes within the firm. The underlying rationale is that parties to an internal dispute have better access to information and potential solutions than external courts, thus internal solutions will be less costly. Hybrids usually feature special dispute settlement mechanisms, but conflicts are ultimately referred to courts if the matter cannot be settled internally.

Table 7.1   Distinguishing Attributes of Governance Structures in Industrial Organization

	Governance structure		
Attributes	Market	Hybrid	Hierarchy
Performance attributes			
Autonomous adaptation (A)	++	+	0
Cooperative adaptation (C)	0	+	++
Control instruments			
Incentive intensity	++	+	0
Administrative controls	0	+	++
Contract law	++	+	0

++ = strong; + = semi-strong; 0 = weak

Source: Williamson 1991: 281, adapted

Thus while markets and hierarchies possess distinct adaptation, enforcement and dispute resolution mechanisms, hybrids feature all of the governance attributes listed in Table 7.1, however in an attenuated form. While they preserve ownership autonomy (high incentives, adaptation A), long-term contracts contain contractual safeguards, such as information disclosure or dispute settlement mechanisms, which attenuate incentives and introduce elements of adaptation C. One advantage of hierarchies over hybrids is that internal contracts can be more incomplete. In addition adaptations to disturbances are least costly within hierarchies.

These interrelationships between the attributes and costs of a transaction and governance structures are summarized by the discriminating alignment hypothesis, which says that:

[T]ransactions, which differ in their attributes, are aligned with governance structures, which differ in their costs and competencies, in a discriminating (mainly transaction-cost-economizing) way (Williamson 1991: 277).

The discriminating alignment hypothesis reflects the predictive content of Williamson's transaction cost economics. Using the case of asset specificity as transaction attribute, the interrelationships between governance structures, varying transaction attributes, and transaction (or governance) costs are presented in Figure 7.1.

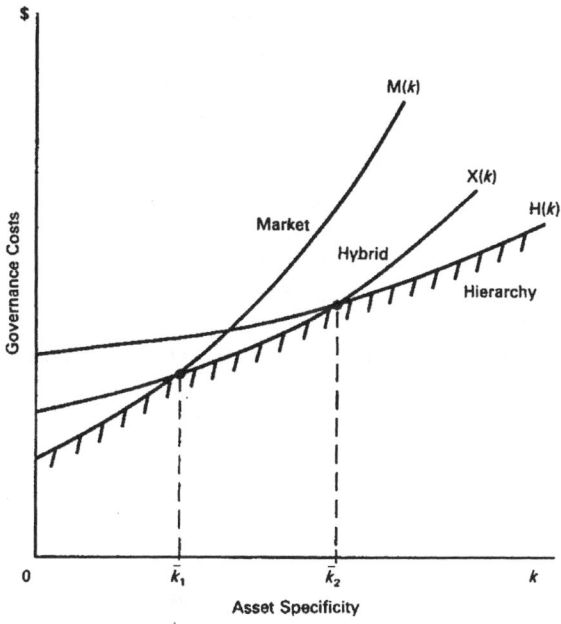

Source: Reprinted from Williamson, Oliver E. (1991), 'Comparative Economic Organization: The Analysis of Discrete Structural Alternatives', *Administrative Science Quarterly*, **36** (2), 284 by permission of Johnson Graduate School of Management, Cornell University. © Johnson Graduate School of Management, Cornell University.

Figure 7.1   Governance Costs as a Function of Asset Specificity

In Figure 7.1, the horizontal axis depicts asset specificity and the vertical axis governance costs. Production costs are assumed to be the same for all governance structures. If asset specificity is low (e.g. a product is produced by a general purpose technology), the transaction can be carried out on the market at comparatively low governance costs. In the absence of contractual hazards, markets feature the most efficient governance structure, i.e. the governance costs of markets are lower than those of hybrids and those of hybrids lower than those of hierarchies.

In contrast if asset specificity is high (e.g. a product relies on a special purpose technology that is not readily available on the market), the order is reversed, as market transactions might entail hazards that significantly increase transaction costs. In this case internal transactions within hierarchies may involve comparatively less governance costs, as they can rely on comparatively cheap internal adaptation mechanisms. Hence in the case of high asset specificity, hierarchies can be considered as the most efficient governance structure, comparatively spoken. Of course absolute governance costs are still higher than in the case of markets in the absence of contractual hazards. These efficiency considerations are reflected by the remediableness criterion which says that 'an extant mode of organization for which no superior feasible alternative can be described and implemented with expected net gains is presumed to be efficient' (Williamson 1998: 43).

For an intermediate asset specificity, hybrids feature lower governance costs than markets and hierarchies. This implies that there are critical values of asset specificity k_1 and k_2 (with $k_1 < k_2$), at which a transition from markets to hybrids and from hybrids to hierarchies is warranted in order to minimize governance costs.

In summary the discriminating alignment hypothesis predicts that (at least in industrial organization) boundedly rational actors will (usually) choose the most efficient governance structure for the given situation.

Implications for international water management

The question is what the implications of the above are for the choice of the most expedient governance structures in international water management. In principle international water management relies on voluntary negotiations; there is neither a price mechanism nor the possibility of fiat readily in place. Indeed, the institutional prerequisites for the set up of international water markets are very high, requiring the unambiguous definition of tradable water rights and supporting mechanisms that facilitate the exchange and pricing of water units. Hence markets cannot be considered as a starting point of the process of institutionalization. Hierarchies at the other end of the spectrum, which rely on fiat or hierarchical direction as ultimate decision-making mechanism, would require the transfer of sovereign powers from the member states to the hierarchy. Given that states tend to be reluctant to infringe on sovereignty, hierarchies are not a very obvious option either. Instead in principal international water agreements can be conceptualized as hybrids, understood as long-term incomplete contracts:

- In terms of adaptation, international water management relies on voluntary negotiations. In the absence of a price mechanism or the possibility of fiat, adaptation is located somewhere between Williamson's adaptation A and C, but closer to adaptation C.
- In terms of control instruments or enforcement, it has been argued that whenever the problem has the structure of a Prisoner's Dilemma, cooperation relies on the set up of incentive intensive enforcement mechanisms (self-enforcing agreements) (Chapter 5). Administrative controls play a certain role once the riparian states set up an organization that monitors implementation. However in contrast to hierarchies, the possibilities of the organization to provide awards and penalties are limited to punishments carried out by the members of the organization themselves (Section 5.1.2). Hence the predominant control instrument is incentive intensity, which however, relies on conscious design, added by administrative controls. Thus in terms of control instruments, international water agreements can also be characterized as hybrids.
- In terms of contract law or dispute settlement, as argued in Section 4.4.2 international water agreements and organizations often contain provisions to refer the matter of dispute to the International Court of Justice for arbitration should it not be possible to reach an agreement. However this requires that all parties agree to this procedure, and it has rarely been applied.[194] Thus while in principle dispute settlement to a large extent relies on negotiations among the members as in hierarchies, there is an option of last resort which is characteristic of markets. Hence also in that respect international water agreements can be understood as hybrids.
- According to Williamson hybrids tend to contain contractual safeguards such as information disclosure, enforcement and dispute settlement mechanisms. All these mechanisms have been identified as 'functions' of international river basin organizations in Section 4.4.2.

Thus one finding is that in terms of the governance structures Williamson identified, in the context of industrial organization, international water agreements can be understood as 'hybrids'. Given uncertainty, frequency of interaction and asset specificity, riparian states tend to set up agreements with respective contractual safeguards. Thus Williamson's analysis significantly contributes towards the understanding of the design of water agreements in view of the transaction costs involved in international water management.

---

[194] Examples are the 1929 decision of the Permanent Court of Justice on the jurisdiction of the International Commission for the River Oder and the 1997 judgment of the International Court of Justice on the Gabčikovo-Nagymaros case on the Danube (see Section 3.1.2).

However the question is under which category international river basin organizations would fall. Given the absence of fiat in existing international river basin organizations, it appears that international river basin organizations can also be conceptualized as 'hybrids'. However this would imply that Williamson's distinction of governance structures in industrial organization remains too coarse for a differentiated understanding of the rationale for the set up of mere agreements vis-à-vis formal organizations. While international river basin organizations can be understood as hybrids that are closer to hierarchies, mere agreements without organizations are hybrids that are closer to markets. However the question is whether this already does justice to the concept of international river basin organizations. According to international law, international organizations are established by international agreement under international law and consist of at least one organ with a will distinct of its member states (Section 3.2.1). How is the nature of such an organ reflected by Williamson's distinction of markets, hybrids and hierarchies?

Given that in his later work Williamson went beyond the analysis of industrial organization and also asked for the rationale public sector organizations, this further development of Williamson's theory shall be presented in the next section in order to examine whether this does contribute towards a further understanding of the rationale for the set up international river basin organizations.

7.1.3   Moving from Industrial to Public Sector Organization

Williamson's contribution

Besides the problem of vertical integration, transaction cost economics has been applied to other problems of industrial organization, such as the organization of labor, the oligopoly problem, technical and organization innovation, the organization of work, the modern corporation, problems of contracting for natural monopoly (esp. franchise bidding), various non-standard forms of contracting and corporate governance (Williamson 1998: 45). More recently, Williamson has moved beyond industrial organization and examined public sector governance structures such as regulation and public agencies (Williamson 1998; Williamson 1999). Typical public sector transactions include procurement, redistributional, regulatory, sovereign, judicial and infrastructure, such as the provision of roads etc. (Williamson 1999: 319). The questions are what the economic rationale is for the existence of public agencies and which activities should be carried out by public sector institutions, and which should be privatized or managed by public regulation?

Williamson (1999) explores the rationale for public agencies, using an extreme case, namely so called sovereign transaction carried out by the foreign service. The question is why is a privatization of the foreign service comparatively unsuited? Similar to industrial organization, he approaches the problem by asking for the attributes of the respective transaction and by exploring potential hazards associated with a privatization.

In terms of the transaction attributes identified in the context of industrial organization, one issue is human asset specificity. Career staff in the foreign service usually require specific training with regard to issues, procedures and protocols. This means that for government it is costly to invest in its staff and for the staff the service goes along with considerable specialization, both of which is not conducive towards a hire and fire policy. Furthermore uncertainty also plays a significant role in terms of external events that must be reacted to flexibly. In addition to these private sector transactions attributes, Williamson identifies probity as key attribute of sovereign transactions, understood as the loyalty and rectitude with which the transaction is carried out.

Probity has three dimensions, vertical, horizontal and internal. The vertical dimension calls for reliable responsiveness of the agency to the president (or government); the horizontal dimension requires accurate communication to counterparts; and the internal calls for commitment to the agency's mission. Hazards to probity would be posed if the president or counterparts lacked confidence in information and assessments provided by the agency, or if the integrity of the mission would be at stake. Lack of probity in foreign affairs, however, is not only undesirable, but puts the entire system at risk. Therefore it does not suffice to deter defection through pecuniary penalties, but insufficient probity may be treated as treason.

This reliance of transactions on probity is reflected in the special employment contracts of the public agency, including those of politically appointed executives, and those of the civil service or career staff. The focus of the appointed leadership staff is on vertical probity through responsiveness to the president, while the career staff mainly focuses on the integrity of the mission (internal probity). Remuneration is comparatively flat, hence incentive intensity is low, but there are complex rules and procedures promoting horizontal coordination in the management of operational affairs and vertical coordination in response to extraordinary events. This implies that probity is mainly supported by cooperative adaptation mechanisms, both horizontally and vertically. While these entail bureaucratic costs, the operating cost savings from privatization can be assumed to be small. This means that cooperative adaptation is the preferred adaptation mechanism, and there is no strong cost argument against this.

This notwithstanding Williamson explores what would happen if the foreign service would be fully privatized or managed through regulation. In the case of full privatization, a contract would have to be drawn up with a private firm. However in view of the contingencies involved with foreign affairs, this contract would have to be highly incomplete. A competitive bid would be meaningless as it would be extremely difficult to come up with a list of contingent events and virtually impossible to cost them. However even if these obstacles were overcome, there would be additional problems. A cost-saving oriented leadership would be wary to take on unexpected assignments and hence less responsive. Instead there would be greater emphasis on cost control, and the career staff would be less protected and hence less committed. The credibility of the agency vis-à-vis counterpart bureaus in other nations might decline.

In contrast a regulatory arrangement that involved a regulatory agency would allow for a greater replication of the public bureaucracy by embedding the agency in a complex regulatory apparatus, by executive appointments and by providing the staff with greater employment security and greater social conditioning. Regulation would be conceivable as a very long-term incomplete contract of a cost-plus reimbursement structure. However compared with the public agency, this option also poses additional problems. The regulatory agency would add an additional level of bureaucracy. Differences of control might occur between the political leadership and the regulatory agency, both in terms of substance and of cost control. In addition given that the regulatory agency is not directly involved in operational activities, it may lack the required first-hand knowledge for accurate judgments. Who would take responsibility if things went wrong? All this implies that rules, regulations and procedures of the public agency are not fully replicated. Instead regulation resembles the hybrid mode in industrial organization, featuring a syndrome of attributes located between the polar modes of private firms and public agencies (Williamson 1999: 321-336).

In analogy to Table 7.1, the attributes of the three public sector governance structures privatization, regulation and the public agency are listed in Table 7.2. In Table 7.2 the attribute 'contract law' is further differentiated into the employment relation, i.e. the autonomy of executives and staff security and the presence or absence of legislative dispute settlement. Furthermore Williamson partly uses slightly different terminology compared with Table 7.1.

While private firms feature high incentive intensity, adaptive autonomy, strong executive autonomy, little staff security and a legalistic dispute settlement mechanism, the public agency relies on bureaucratic controls, cooperative adaptation (or 'adaptive integrity'), little executive autonomy, high staff security and internal dispute settlement mechanisms. Regulation features aspects of all attributes, but in more attenuated form. Williamson (1999: 338 f.) argues this scheme may also be used to determine the most expedient governance structure of other public sector transactions.

By moving from industrial to public sector organization, the list of governance structures can be extended by regulation and public agencies. This means that the initial choice between markets and hierarchies has been reformulated as a choice of the most expedient governance structure, where spot markets and public agencies present extreme and hybrids, private firms and regulation represent intermediary forms in a spectrum of five discrete structural alternatives. In terms of efficiency, markets are principally assumed to be the preferred and public agencies are the least preferred choice. However depending on the attributes of a particular transaction, markets or for that purpose other intermediate governance structures may entail hazards giving raise to transaction costs that make the market-oriented variant less efficient than the next more hierarchy-oriented governance structure. According to the remediableness criterion, in certain situations, public agencies may be considered the most efficient governance structure, given the absence of other feasible alternatives. This rationale is reflected by Figure 7.2.

Table 7.2 Comparative Public Sector Organization

	Governance structure		
Attributes	Privatization	Regulation	Public Agency
Performance attributes			
Adaptive autonomy	++	+	0
Adaptive integrity	0	+	++
Control instruments			
Incentive intensity	++	+	0
Bureaucratization	0	+?	++
Contract law			
Employment relation			
Executive autonomy	++	+	0
Staff security	0	+	++
Legalistic dispute settlement	++	+	0

++ = strong; + = semi-strong; 0 = weak

Source: Williamson 1999: 336, adapted

The end nodes in Figure 7.2, labeled with the letters A through F, represent the alternative governance structures in the order of their preferred choice in terms of efficiency if transaction costs due to potential hazards are neglected. In addition to the five governance structures represented by points A and C through F, point B represents a markets situation with 'unrelieved hazard'.

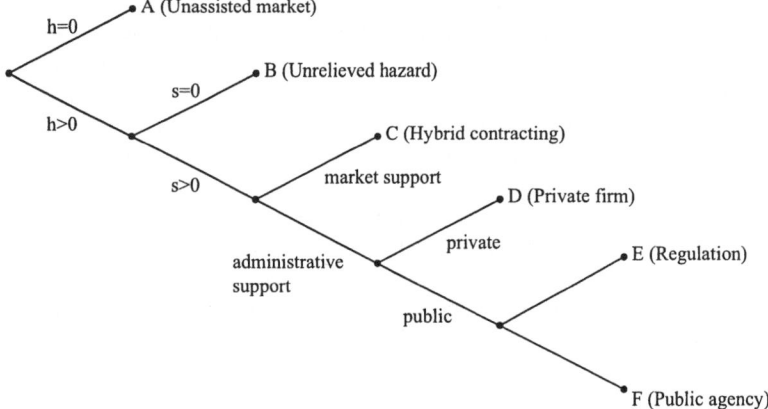

Source: Reprinted from Williamson, Oliver E. (1999), 'Public and Private Bureaucracies: A Transaction Cost Economics Perspective', *The Journal of Law, Economics, & Organization*, **15** (1), 337 by permission of Oxford University Press.

Figure 7.2   Williamson's Extended Contracting Scheme

In a first step the decision maker asks whether the respective transaction goes along with contractual hazards (h) due to asset specificity, uncertainty, the frequency of transaction or probity concerns. If not, the unassisted market (A) is the most expedient governance structure (h = 0). If contractual hazards may occur (h > 0), the question rises whether they can be mitigated by contractual safeguards (s > 0). If not, unrelieved hazard (B) prevails (s = 0). Two types of safeguards can be distinguished, market and administrative safeguards. If the hazard can be managed by market support, the preferred governance structure in terms of efficiency is hybrid contracting (C). In this case it is expedient to design the contract in a way that it contains specific safeguards, e.g. in the form of provisions on information disclosure, penalties for non-compliance and specific dispute settlement mechanisms, such as arbitration (Williamson 1998: 38). If the transaction costs for monitoring, enforcement and dispute settlement are prone to be high, or if frequent renegotiation can be expected, a hierarchical solution under unified ownership with administrative support may be more expedient. A hierarchy has the advantage that management may react flexibly to changing conditions and advise their staff respectively.[195] A hierarchical solution is conceivable within the private or public sector. In terms of efficiency, a private sector solution, namely integration into a private firm (D), is preferred to a public sector solution. However if a private sector solution is not possible or if it involves hazards that may be mitigated by a public solution, the question is whether sub-contracting through regulation (E) is feasible, or whether the transaction should be directly carried out by a public agency (F). A public agency is warranted if the transaction poses issues of probity. The underlying heuristic of Figure 7.2 is 'try markets, try hybrids, try firms, try regulation, and resort to public bureaus only when all else fails (comparatively)' (Williamson 1998: 47).

In contrast to the theory of bureaucracy (e.g. Niskanen 1971; Moe 1997), according to which bureaucrats do not necessarily pursue the public interest but seek to maximize their budget leading to inefficient results, Williamson (1999) maintains that for certain transactions the public agency can be considered the most efficient mode of organization, comparatively spoken. As such Williamson's contribution has been to explain the economic rationale for the set up hierarchies, both within the private and the public sector.

While Williamson's transaction cost economics has long been primarily concerned with efficient private sector organization, more recently, TCE has been used to ask for the rationale for public versus private sector provision. This extension can be understood as a contribution towards the debate on privatization in which Williamson reinforces certain public sector functions.

Implications for international water management

By moving from a private sector to a public sector organization, Williamson has expanded the initial choice between markets and hierarchies to a choice between five discrete structural alternatives, namely markets, hybrids, private firm, regulation and public agency. As mentioned above, this further differentiation can primarily be understood as contribution to the debate on deregulation and privatization. However the question is whether it may also explain the rationale for the set up of international river basin organizations.

Clearly for the case of water management, Williamson's extended theory can be used to revisit the role of the government on the one hand and the private sector on the other in water resources management within states. As such it may inform the ongoing discourse on water governance including the

---

[195] The employment contract is a special contract where the employee agrees to follow the orders of management and thus accepts the delimitation of his or her autonomy for the sake of contractual security.

discourse on the privatization of water services (Section 2.1.3). It may furthermore contribute towards the ongoing discussion to what extent transboundary water management should be seen as a pure government affair, and what role private and non-governmental actors might play (see Durth 1996 and Blatter and Ingram 2000). It is likely that an analysis in terms of TCE would reinforce certain roles of governmental actors. If we assume that international water negotiations are primarily carried out by representatives of public agencies, Williamson's public sector theory explains the basic actor unit. However with respect to the question whether the respective riparian states should go beyond the conclusion of agreements and establish an international river basin organization or commission Williamson's extended theory does not necessarily provide what this book was looking for.

It has been argued that the transition from hybrids to hierarchies is expedient if the transaction costs for monitoring, enforcement and dispute settlement are prone to be high, or if frequent renegotiation can be expected. Clearly an international organization with a secretariat in place adds support to these functions by facilitating the exchange of information and by collecting, and possibly publishing, implementation reports from member states. By serving as an agenda setter it may propose ideas that are acceptable to all involved. However a secretariat does not support its member states by fiat or hierarchical direction. Thus the question is whether an international organization with secretariat in place can be understood as 'hierarchy' in Williamson's sense.

As mentioned above, according to international law the distinguishing feature between mere international agreements and international organizations is the presence of an organ with a distinct will; however this is different from the notion of hierarchical direction as distinctive criterion between hybrids and hierarchies. Instead of introducing the possibility of fiat, the highest decision-making organ in an international organization continues to rely on negotiations, given that decisions are taken on the basis of a unanimity vote or the consensus principle, and often decisions are not binding on the member states (see Section 4.4.1). In addition international organizations may be hierarchically organized in the sense that the ultimate decision-making organ may be supported by technical and administrative bodies. But the establishment of an international organization does not imply that the decision-making power is transferred to one ultimate decision-maker.

This implies that in Williamson's terminology even an international organization that is composed of different organs remains a 'hybrid' that relies on negotiated decision-making, but a hybrid that contains elements of hierarchies.

7.1.4   Results

This section explored in what way Williamson's transaction cost economics is able to inform the choice and design of institutional arrangements for international water management. Given that in the water policy discourse there is often an implicit or explicit assumption that it is desirable to establish international river basin organizations or commissions, and as many international water agreements foresee the set up of a commission, the section in particular asked whether TCE can explain the economic rationale for the set up of international river basin organizations beyond mere agreements.

Williamson has contributed towards economic theory by emphasizing the role of transaction costs for private and public sector organization and by distinguishing and comparing different types of governance structures, namely markets, hybrids, private firms, regulation and public agencies. He shows that when we are dealing with long-term contracts under conditions of bounded rationality, the transaction cost that occur ex ante in their negotiation and ex post in their implementation imply that markets, and sometimes even mere contracts ('hybrids'), may not be the most efficient governance structure. Four transaction attributes are particularly prone to give rise to transaction costs: uncertainty, frequency of transaction, asset specificity and probity. The respective governance structures differ in their performance attributes or adaptation mechanisms, in their control instruments or enforcement mechanisms and in the contract law, including their dispute settlement mechanisms and employment contracts (the latter only applies to hierarchies).

Transaction cost economics is principally relevant for the analysis of international water management problems as we are dealing with transactions in a bilateral monopoly or oligopoly situation, in which strategic and opportunistic behavior under incomplete information does play a role. However in contrast to industrial organization this monopoly situation exists from the beginning and is not the result of a fundamental transformation due to specific investments.

Once agreements are concluded they are usually long-term. In Williamson's terminology, these agreements correspond to hybrids. Thus the starting point for an institutionalization of international water negotiations are hybrids, but the question is whether it is expedient to go beyond hybrids.

It can be argued that three of the four transaction attributes identified by Williamson that may give rise to a more 'integrated' governance structure, i.e. uncertainty, frequency of transaction and asset specificity, are highly relevant in international water management. Both at the level of property rights and at the level of infrastructure measures decisions have usually long-term implications. These transaction attributes therefore give rise to contractual hazards, which may motivate the move towards a more 'integrated' governance structure.

However the question is what such more integrated governance structures may look like in international water management. It is immediately clear that the 'hierarchical' governance structures identified by Williamson, i.e. the private firm, public sector regulation and the public agency, are no direct structural alternatives. In contrast to industrial organization, where negotiations are under ideal circumstances carried out between owners of firms, in the case of international waters, negotiations are usually conducted by government representatives. This means that the actors are members of governments and representatives of public agencies. In that sense public agencies are not a solution, but the 'basic' actor unit. Instead in international water management the question is whether the respective riparian states go beyond the conclusion of agreements and establish an international river basin organization or commission. However the concept of an international organization is not (yet) included in Williamson's extended contracting scheme.

According to international law the distinguishing feature between agreements and organizations is the presence of an organ with a distinct will; however this is a different distinguishing feature than the notion of hierarchical direction. While international organizations may be hierarchically organized in the sense that the ultimate decision-making organ may be supported by technical and administrative bodies, the establishment of an international organization does not imply that the decision-making power is transferred to one ultimate decision-maker. Instead the highest decision-making organ in an international organization continues to rely on negotiations, given that decisions are taken on the basis of a unanimity vote or the consensus principle.

This, however, means that international organizations do not 'solve' the negotiation problem by hierarchical direction or fiat. Instead it can be argued that in Williamson's terminology even an international organization remains a 'hybrid' that relies on negotiated decision-making. At the same time, the organization adds structure that is not included in the concept of the hybrid. While the phenomena at hand cannot fully be categorized in terms of Williamson's typology of governance structures, the functions of international organizations can be understood as safeguards in Williamson's sense.

In order to pursue the question of the role of hybrids versus hierarchies further, Section 7.2 will introduce Scharpf's (1997) 'actor-centered institutionalism', which also builds upon transaction cost economics, but incorporates other theories within the New Institutional Economics. A further theoretical advantage of Scharpf's approach is that it explicitly distinguishes between different procedural and structural elements of coordination. While Scharpf does not provide an explicit theory of international organizations either, this distinction of procedural and structural elements will further contribute towards the understanding of their nature.

7.2 ACTOR-CENTERED INSTITUTIONALISM AND ITS IMPLICATIONS FOR INTERNATIONAL WATER MANAGEMENT INSTITUTIONS

Actor-centered institutionalism is a theoretical framework developed by Fritz Scharpf and Renate Mayntz (Mayntz and Scharpf 1995), which builds upon a range of theories in the New Institutional Economics, including transaction cost economics, public choice, principal agent theory, game theory as well as on theories of democracy. It assumes that social phenomena are structured by the interaction of intentional actors, but that these interactions are shaped by the characteristics of the institutional settings within which they occur. As such it combines actor-centered and institution-centered approaches and thus rational-choice (economic) and structuralist (sociologic) paradigms (Scharpf 1997: 36). Policy is assumed to be the outcome of 'the interactions of resourceful and boundedly rational actors whose capabilities, preferences, and perceptions are largely, but not completely, shaped by the institutionalized norms within which they interact' (Scharpf 1997: 195). The reason for combining different theories is to get into a better position to explain empirical phenomena. The disadvantage is that the resulting 'theoretical framework' lacks the parsimony of a single theory. In this theoretical framework, the central category is 'interaction' instead of 'transaction'.

This section will present a typology of coordination mechanisms developed within the framework of actor-centered institutionalism. It will be argued that this typology takes Williamson's typology of governance structures a step further by distinguishing structural and procedural elements of coordination or governance and by identifying 'intermediate' forms between hybrids and hierarchies, such as associations. The focus is on the 'problem-solving capacity' of alternative coordination mechanisms, understood as the capacity of these mechanisms to enhance efficiency, to solve problems of distribution and to ensure the legitimacy of policy outcomes. Thus next to efficiency two additional evaluative criteria, distributive justice and legitimacy, are taken into account. Again the question in this section will be to what extent the framework is able to explain the rationale for the set up of international river basin organizations or of other institutional arrangements in international water management.

Section 7.2.1 will introduce Scharpf's (1997) typology of coordination mechanisms. Section 7.2.2 will compare the problem-solving capacity of two extreme coordination mechanisms, namely negotiations under quasi anarchical conditions and hierarchical direction within hierarchical organizations and discuss their relevance for international water management. The analysis will reinforce the significance of negotiations for international water management, but it will be argued that the problem-solving capacity of freestanding negotiations under conditions of anarchy remains limited. Therefore, Section 7.2.3 will analyze how the problem-solving capacity of negotiations change if they take place under more 'integrated' institutional settings, such as networks, regimes, joint-decision systems, associations or organizations. Section 7.2.4 will present results.[196]

7.2.1 A Typology of Coordination Mechanisms

In the analysis of coordination and cooperation problems, Scharpf (1997: 47) discerns four types of interaction modes and four classes of institutional settings (Table 7.3). The four interaction modes comprise 'unilateral action', 'negotiated agreement', 'majority vote' and 'hierarchical direction', representing different procedural forms of coordination or decision-making.[197] The four classes of institutional settings, namely (1) anarchic fields and minimal institutions, (2) networks, regimes and joint-decision systems, (3) associations, constituencies and representative assemblies and (4) hierarchical organizations and the state signify different structural forms of coordination. Interaction modes pertain to different empirically possible forms of human interaction by which certain actor constellations are converted into policy outcomes (Scharpf 1997: 97). As such they represent different forms of individual and collective decision-making. Unilateral action means that ego takes a decision without interacting with alter. Negotiated agreement implies that a decision is a result of a negotiation process. Negotiated agreements require consent by all negotiation partners. In the case of a majority vote, a rule exists that a collectively binding decision may be taken on the basis of the majority of the existing votes. In the case of hierarchical direction, ego is able to specify some of alter's

---

[196] An earlier German version of Sections 7.2.1 to 7.2.3 has been presented in Dombrowsky (2005a).

[197] In the following the cells of Table 7.3 will be referred to as different coordination mechanisms.

decision premises. This may be on the basis of superiority or legitimacy (Scharpf 1997: 172).

Table 7.3   Modes of Interactions and Institutional Settings

	Institutional Settings			
Modes of Interaction	Anarchic fields, minimal institutions	Networks, regimes, joint-decision systems	Association, representative assemblies, constituencies	Hierarchical organizations, the state
Unilateral action	X	X	X	X
Negotiated agreement	(X)	X	X	X
Majority vote	-	-	X	X
Hierarchical direction	-	-	-	X

Source: Based on Scharpf 1997: 47[198]

Interaction furthermore takes place under various structural conditions or institutional settings. The assumption is that interaction modes are shaped both by the presence or absence of specific institutional rules and by the broader institutional setting within which they take place.[199] Anarchic fields refer to an institution-free context in which the actions of one actor are only constrained by physical limitations and the countermoves of other actors (Scharpf 1997: 98). The international system is often considered as a typical example of anarchic fields.[200] Minimal institutions refer to a minimal state which enforces property rights and contracts, as such providing the preconditions for the existence of markets. In the case of anarchic fields and minimal institutions the predominant interaction mode is unilateral action. Negotiations are possible, but the outcome of negotiations remains uncertain.[201] Networks, regimes and joint-decision systems have in common that they allow for unilateral action and negotiated agreements on the basis of unanimity. The structural difference between them and associations, constituencies or representative assemblies is that in these cases decisions

---

[198] The cells with a bold X will be analyzed in greater depth in this sub-chapter.

[199] Scharpf follows a narrow notion of 'institution' as 'sanctioned rules that effectively change the costs and benefits that an actor can expect when following a certain course of action' (Scharpf 1997: 38).

[200] This is one reason why anarchic fields will be analyzed in more detail in the following section.

[201] As argued in Chapter 5 it makes a huge difference for negotiations on transboundary externalities whether property rights are defined or not. Therefore, the fact that Scharpf grouped anarchic fields and minimal institutions together can only be understood as a first approximation.

may also be taken on the basis of a majority vote. Hierarchical organizations or the state allow for decisions by hierarchical direction. In the case of associations or organizations, a number of individual actors constitute a composite actor who is capable of intentional action.

If unilateral action is excluded as coordination mechanism, the above 4x4 matrix results in seven alternative coordination mechanisms: negotiated agreements under four different institutional settings, majority vote within associations or organizations and hierarchical direction within organizations.

Scharpf puts forward three major hypotheses with regard to the relationship of interaction modes and institutional settings.

1. The institutional setting constraints the interaction modes which may be employed (Scharpf 1997: 47). This is immediately clear from Table 7.3. For instance hierarchical direction is only possible within a hierarchical setting. Unilateral action is always an option, and hierarchical organizations do not only allow for hierarchical direction, but for all four interaction modes. Each class of institutional setting can be considered a 'possibility frontier' in the sense that it cannot support a more demanding mode of interaction (ibid.). In international water management without further institutionalization, interaction takes place under quasi anarchical conditions. In this case the only 'cooperative' mode of interaction is negotiated decision-making. This would change if an institution was created that allowed for a different mode of interaction.
2. Second the interaction modes differ with respect to their capacity to solve policy problems, understood as the capacity to increase welfare, to solve distributive conflicts and to ensure the legitimacy of policy outcomes. This will be illustrated by comparing the problem-solving capacity of freestanding negotiations and hierarchical direction in Section 7.2.1.
3. Third a specific mode of interaction will change its problem-solving character from one institutional setting to another. This will be pursued in Section 7.2.2 for the case of negotiations.

Scharpf (1997) analyzes the 'problem-solving capacity' of these various coordination mechanisms with respect to their capacity to enhance efficiency, to solve problems of distribution and to ensure legitimate outcomes:

- In this context, an increase in efficiency is understood as an increase in aggregated welfare, taking transaction costs into account.
- With respect to distributional issues, the emphasis is on the capacity of a coordination mechanism to address issues of distributive justice or fairness. Given the spectrum of competing (and partly complementary)

concepts of distributive justice, such as equality, equity or need, no a priori criterion is provided as to what a just distribution could look like in a given case.[202] This not withstanding, the problem of distributive justice is included, given that in many negotiations solving problems of distribution becomes a necessary condition for the factual realization of gains of cooperation.

- Legitimacy may have different sources, such as tradition, charisma, formal legality or democratic accountability (Scharpf 1997: 172; with reference to Weber 1947). Democratic theory distinguishes between two types of democratic legitimacy, input- and output-oriented legitimacy (Scharpf 1997: 153). Input-oriented arguments ask whether those who are asked to comply with a decision can agree to it. As such input-oriented legitimacy is a process-based criterion, and legitimacy is generated by consensual decision-making. Output-oriented arguments ask for substantive criteria according to which the legitimacy of a policy decision can be evaluated. Under this perspective, policy choices can be considered as legitimate if they increase welfare (thus serving the 'public interest') and are in accordance with notions of distributive justice.[203] Thus output-oriented legitimacy becomes particularly relevant when decisions are made on behalf of other individuals.

In analyzing the explanatory power of Scharpf's (1997) approach for the study of international water management institutions, the following will first compare the problem-solving capacity of negotiations under quasi anarchical conditions on the one hand and of hierarchical direction within hierarchical organizations on the other as two extreme coordination mechanisms in international water management (Section 7.2.2). Section 7.2.3 will then analyze how the problem-solving capacity of negotiations changes if we move from anarchical conditions to more 'integrated' institutional settings.

---

[202] Theories of distributive justice usually distinguish three criteria for distribution, equality, equity and need (e.g. Tugendhat 1993: 373 f.). Equality means that all parties receive equal shares of a good. If there are no good reasons why every party should not receive an equal share, an equal distribution may be considered as just or fair. However in some situations, an equal distribution may not necessarily be considered as just, given that some parties are particularly needy or given that some parties have undertaken particular efforts to contribute towards the provision of the good. Thus need or equity may be reasons to divert from an equal distribution. According to a principle of equity, a good or benefits are distributed in proportion to each individual's contribution. If a good or benefits are distributed according to need, those who need more of a good will receive more.

[203] Thus output-oriented legitimacy refers back to the previous two criteria, efficiency and distributive justice.

7.2.2   Voluntary Negotiations versus Hierarchical Direction

This section will analyze and compare the problem-solving capacity of two extreme and idealized forms of coordination mechanisms, namely voluntary negotiations under quasi anarchical conditions on the one hand and hierarchical direction within a hierarchical organization on the other. Voluntary negotiations under quasi anarchical conditions apply to situations in which no institutional arrangements are in place. The assumption is that the parties have not dealt with each other before, and that it is uncertain whether they will do so in the future. In game-theoretic terms this corresponds to a one-shot game. Hierarchical direction within hierarchical organizations on the other hand would become relevant if an international river basin organization with an ultimate decision-maker was established. The ultimate decision-maker could be an individual or a board, but it would have the power to impose binding decisions on member states and their constituencies within the basin.

Given that the international system is often considered as anarchical, the reason for analyzing the problem-solving of negotiations under quasi anarchical conditions is to explore how far one can get with negotiations in international water management without any further institutionalization.

In view of proposals in the literature to set up international river basin organizations, the reason for analyzing the problem-solving capacity of hierarchical direction is to explore if hierarchical river basin organization with the possibility of hierarchical direction would theoretically be desirable.[204] As such this section also explores the desirability of Williamson's 'hierarchy' for the case of international water management.[205]

While one-shot encounters are conceivable in international water management, it has been argued in Chapter 5 that they are not the norm. Furthermore as argued in Section 4.4 the literature is not aware of the existence of a hierarchical international river basin organization as conceived in this section. In that sense this section may also be thought of as a thought experiment that explores if these extreme forms are theoretically desirable. The analysis of the extreme forms will furthermore serve as a heuristic that will facilitate the analysis of the intermediate forms.

---

[204] Usually respective policy recommendations do not specify what is meant by 'river basin organization' – so we do not know whether they have the possibility of hierarchical direction in mind.

[205] Given that markets have no readily available alternative in international water management, this section does not compare markets and hierarchies, but freestanding negotiations and hierarchies as polar coordination mechanisms.

Voluntary negotiations under anarchical conditions

In order to assess the problem-solving capacity of voluntary negotiations under quasi anarchical conditions, the question is under which conditions negotiations on external effects lead to efficient, fair and legitimate outcomes.

Efficiency

As argued in Section 5.1.1 the Coase theorem indicates the efficiency conditions for negotiations on unidirectional externalities. It states that negotiations on external effects lead to efficient outcomes if property rights are fully defined, and if there are no transaction costs involved, including search, information, negotiation, bargaining, monitoring and enforcement costs. As argued before in the case of international water negotiation, none of these efficiency conditions can be expected to hold. Instead negotiations are prone to go along with relatively high transaction costs. In the following, these costs will be briefly revisited:

- Search costs pertain to the often self-organized process of determining who the relevant negotiation partners are. This largely depends on the perceptions of what the negotiation problem is and who is considered to have a stake in these negotiations. The exclusion of affected parties may lead to conflict in the implementation of negotiated agreements. The identification of the respective negotiation partners has impacts on the (input-oriented) legitimacy of the negotiation outcomes (see below).
- With respect to information costs, it is useful to distinguish between information costs concerning substantive issues related to water resources on the one hand and the preferences and potential strategies of the respective actors on the other. Substantive information about water resources and their behavior requires scientific monitoring and analysis. Thus the compilation of respective information entails considerable transaction costs. In the case of international water resources, each actor usually only has access to information within his jurisdiction, and in the absence of further arrangements there are no mechanisms in place to analyze this information and to develop management measures at the river basin level. This might present a major obstacle towards identifying mutually advantageous solutions. With respect to information about the preferences and potential strategies of the respective participants, negotiations have the distinct advantage that all participants may articulate their preferences. However as argued in Section 5.1.1 in doing so the question is whether the negotiators have incentives to reveal their 'true' preferences. Lax and Sebenius (1986: 39) argue that negotiators are often

faced with the so called Negotiator's Dilemma. Negotiators must solve two problems. They have to identify potential welfare-enhancing solutions (problems of production), and they have to agree on the sharing of the net gains of cooperation (problems of distribution). However simultaneous problem-solving and distributive bargaining requires contradictory negotiation attitudes. While the solution of production problems requires creativity, effective communication and trust, the success of distributive bargaining depends on strategic and opportunistic behavior and the withholding of information (Scharpf 1997: 139 f.). The implication is that those who seek to contribute in good faith to problem-solving make themselves vulnerable to exploitation should negotiations fail or when it comes to the sharing of the benefits of cooperation. In other words, regardless of how alter will behave, ego is better off to withhold information. This implies that the Negotiator's Dilemma has the structure of a Prisoner's Dilemma game.[206]

- Negotiation costs pertain to costs of bringing negotiators together and to the time required to reach an agreement. Both can be relatively high in an international context. Transaction costs usually increase with the number of players involved. From an analytical point of view if each actor has to negotiate with each other actor, the number of negotiations increases exponentially with the number of actors.
- Bargaining costs apply to costs of reaching an agreement on the sharing of the gains of cooperation (see also information costs above and distributional issues below).
- Additional transaction costs occur with respect to the monitoring and enforcement of agreements, as any monitoring and sanctioning mechanism involves extra costs for the member states. In Section 5.1.2 it was argued that in the case of Assurance games, agreements are self-enforcing. However in the case of Prisoner's Dilemma games, cooperation relies on credible enforcement mechanisms.

Thus voluntary negotiations under anarchical conditions are prone to entail high search, information, negotiation, bargaining, monitoring and enforcement costs – thus reducing the efficiency of the outcome. Or negotiation may even fail due prohibitively high transaction costs.

In addition to these transaction costs, property rights to water are often disputed. The issue of property rights is often being perceived as zero-sum

---

[206] This implies that under imperfect information a Prisoner's Dilemma game with respect to the appropriation of the resource may be superimposed by a second order information-related Prisoner's Dilemma. This second order dilemma did not appear in Sections 5.2-5.4, as they assumed perfect information.

bargaining. However as discussed in Section 5.3.1, in the case of negative unidirectional externality problems the mutual recognition of property rights has welfare enhancing effects in the sense that it allows the capture of gains of cooperation. While in the case of ideal negative reciprocal externality problems the mutual delimitation of property rights is principally in the interest of the players involved, in the case of negative unidirectional externalities, the specification of property rights has distributional implications.

Distributive justice
Distributional bargaining has the structure of a Zero (or Constant) Sum game. Negotiations are usually able to reach agreement on the sharing of the gains of cooperation (e.g. through splitting the difference) if the status quo is accepted as a starting point for negotiations and if side-payments are acceptable. In this case distributional bargaining can be conceptualized as a process of offer and counter-offer (or claim and counter-claim). However when the status quo is put into question, such as in the case of negative unidirectional externalities in international water management, it will usually also be extremely difficult to reach an agreement on the standard for the sharing of benefits from cooperation. In this case property rights and efficiency gains have to be negotiated simultaneously, and the gains of cooperation may or may not present an incentive to reach an agreement on the underlying property rights regime (Section 5.3.1) Scharpf (1997: 146) argues if redistribution is the central policy issue, negotiations are not a very powerful mode of interaction.

Legitimacy
In principle negotiations present a mechanism which allows for the consideration of the legitimate interests of those who have a seat at the negotiation table (input-oriented legitimacy). Reversely the legitimacy of the negotiation process may thus be reduced by not involving affected parties. The (often self-organized) process of determining the relevant negotiation partners is therefore a crucial first step in any pre-negotiations. In contrast output-oriented notions of legitimacy become particularly relevant when certain representatives (governments or non governmental organizations) negotiate on behalf of greater constituencies, as in the case of intergovernmental water negotiations. In this case a negotiation outcome can be considered legitimate if it takes account of the reasonable interests of these constituencies. There might be different mechanisms to ensure the accountability of the representative vis-à-vis the respective constituencies, with particular importance attached to democratic mechanisms. Under such an output-oriented form of legitimacy, outcomes will usually be measured by

their capacity to enhance overall welfare and to solve issues of distribution. This implies that once negotiations are carried out by representatives of different groups, the overall legitimacy of a negotiated outcome depends on the mechanisms ensuring the accountability of the representative vis-à-vis his constituency and the inclusiveness of the negotiation process itself.

In conclusion, well-designed negotiations are generally a powerful mechanism to identify efficient and legitimate policy outcomes, and they are clearly indispensable in international water management. However negotiations tend to go along with transaction costs and various social dilemmata, both at the resource level (see Chapter 5) and at the informational level (Negotiator's Dilemma).[207] If these dilemmata are not well managed, negotiations may lead to stalemate despite potential gains of cooperation. Also, the capacity of negotiations to deal with distributional issues tends to be limited and they are not well-suited to redistribute initial endowments. Legitimacy concerns come into play if not all affected parties have a seat at the negotiation table, or if the accountability of representatives who negotiate on behalf of their constituencies is not ensured. Given these limitations of freestanding negotiations, the next section will ask what the advantages and disadvantages of the set up of an organization with the possibility of hierarchical direction as interaction mode would be.

Hierarchical direction within organizations

While negotiations require each negotiation partner's consent in order to reach a decision, in the case of hierarchical direction, a decision-maker exists who can impose a solution on other actors. In order to understand the position of a hierarchical decision-maker, it is useful to have a theory of 'hierarchies' or 'organizations'. In the economic theory of the firm, there are two main arguments: As discussed in Section 7.1, internally, the firm can be described as a special contractual relationship between its members which allows for the adaptive management of longer-term contracts. The employer offers a longer-term contract and in return the employee accepts directions of the employer within the terms of the contract. The main aim is to lower transaction costs in the management of contractual relationships. Externally, the firm constitutes a composite actor who has the character of a legal person and may enter into contracts with third parties. While the set up of organizations usually involves transaction costs, it is assumed that this investment will pay by lowering the long-term transaction costs internally among the members of an organization and externally between the

---

[207] These social dilemmata can be understood as explanations why transaction costs occur.

organization and third parties (e.g. Homann and Suchanek 2000: 333-349). Similarly, in the public sector, contract theories building upon Hobbes and Locke conceptualize the state as a contractual relationship between a governor and those governed, in which the state taxes citizens and in return provides internal and external security and other public goods (e.g. Locke 1983).

In the case of international rivers, the set up of a hierarchical international river basin organization would require that sovereign countries transfer powers and competencies to the river basin organization. However as indicated above, states will usually be unwilling to give up sovereignty. Still the possibility of such a transfer of competencies should not be entirely excluded, especially if such a step enables the parties to capture gains of cooperation which cannot be captured otherwise.[208]

The remainder of this section assumes that a hierarchical international river basin organization with an ultimate decision-maker and the possibility of hierarchical direction is in place. Then the question is under which conditions hierarchical direction leads to efficient, fair and legitimate outcomes. It can be argued that this will be the case if the decision-maker has all relevant information and uses them, and if he or she acts in the interest of all members of the organization and their constituencies. The first condition points at the position of the omniscient and the second at that of the benevolent dictator. Reversely, this implies that the efficiency, equity and legitimacy of decisions may be decreased by information and motivation problems (Scharpf 1997: 174-183).

Information problems

In general, hierarchical organizations face the problem of transmitting information from lower to higher levels of organization, which may often either lead to information overload or impoverishment at the decision center. The result may be ill-informed or unresponsive decisions. In the case of private firms, transaction cost economics tends to be rather optimistic about the possibility of a relatively frictionless transfer of information within private organizations if the 'principle of selective intervention' is applied, which says that superiors should strictly limit their interventions to matters that must be handled at their own organizational level (Williamson 1985:

---

[208] For a literature review on the problem of delegation of power, see Voigt and Salzberger (2002). If one considers, for example, the water negotiations between Israelis and Palestinians, the thought of an independent hierarchical decision-maker may be tempting. For instance Becker and Loehman (2004) propose the establishment of a non-profit regional water utility that would establish limits on water use, determine water prices and make investments from system revenues.

133-135). In contrast principal-agent theory assumes that fundamental information asymmetries exist between principal and agent, leading to moral hazard and opportunistic behavior (Grossman and Hart 1983). For public bureaucracies, Hayek (1945) has pointed out that hierarchies tend to lack mechanisms to mobilize information in the form of local knowledge, both concerning production opportunities or management options and concerning demand. While these issues can only be touched upon at this point, it becomes clear that hierarchies are principally faced with the problem of the transmission of information from affected people and lower levels of administration to the decision-making center. How severe these problems are, depends on how successfully organizations realize the principles of subsidiarity and participation.[209]

Motivation problems

Motivation problems pertain to principal-agent problems and the problem of government failure. They are at the heart of the principal-agent and the public choice literature. The motivation problem in the public sector may be illustrated by contrasting it with decision-making in the private sector: When it is assumed that the owner and the manager of a firm coincide in the same person, and that the owner-manager is also the residual claimant of profits and losses, motivation problems can be largely neglected. In this case the pursuit of the self-interest of the owner-manager can be expected to coincide with the overall interest of the firm. If, however, the company is owned by shareholders and the firm is managed by an employed executive manager, this relationship between the shareholders and the executive manager can be characterized as a principal-agent problem, in which the executive manager's interest does not necessarily coincide with the shareholders' interest. Similarly in the public sector, if we drop the assumption that politicians and bureaucrats solely act in the public interest, but if it is assumed that they represent rational, self-interested individuals, then there may be many situations in which decision-makers do not decide in the public interest even

---

[209] The purpose of participation is to ensure that the legitimate interests of people affected by a decision have the opportunity to 'participate' in the decision-making process (it would have to be clarified what 'participation' means in a given case). Participation contributes towards the mobilization of local knowledge, thus alleviating information problems and strengthens the link between principal and agent, thus alleviating motivation problems. The subsidiarity principle calls for decisions at the lowest possible decision-making level. If applied to organizations, it corresponds to Williamson's principle of selective intervention. If the subsidiarity principle is adhered to, the decisions of international river basin organizations are strictly limited to issues that can only be resolved at the international level, thus limiting information and motivation problems.

if they know what the public interest is.[210] In the public sector, the motivation problem can to a certain extent be alleviated once mechanisms ensuring democratic accountability are in place. This requires the set-up of a circular relationship between the governor and those governed. Elections then provide the opportunity to elect the candidate who best represents the interest of the voter and to deselect politicians who did not act in the voter's interest.

At the same time, it should also be acknowledged that even in democratic societies, some decisions continue to rely on 'non-democratic' forms of legitimacy, in particular when the resolution of problems is highly dependent on expert knowledge that is neither generally available nor easily acquired (Scharpf 1997: 153 f.). Examples are central banks entrusted with far-reaching competencies for monetary policy or the politically independent judiciary. In these cases, the public-interest orientation and as such the output-oriented legitimacy of policy decisions, relies on formal and informal forms of professional discourse and peer review. Hierarchical authority is considered acceptable as long as individual decisions are sustained by the mainstream of the professional discourse.

What would be the implications of hierarchical international river basin organizations equipped with far reaching decision-making competencies with respect to information and motivation problems? With respect to information problems, it can be argued that international river basin organizations would have a distinct advantage to generate and process relevant information at the river basin level by setting up special basin-wide data and decision-support systems. However at the same time it must be acknowledged that river basin organizations are not a necessary condition for the establishment of such systems, though they might certainly facilitate their set up. Also the information processed by the organization will only be as good as the information the organization receives from its member states and its subsidiary organizations.

With respect to motivation problems, the problem is how to maintain accountability once decision-making competencies are transferred from (democratically or otherwise) accountable governments to an international river basin organization. Two options are conceivable.

---

[210] Strictly speaking, in the public sector there are two principal-agent problems, one between citizen (principal) and politician (agent) and one between politician (principal) and bureaucrat (agent). Similarly, it can be argued that in international water management there is a principal agent problem between citizen and government representative and one between government representative and the international river basin organization (see below).

- First assuming that adequate accountability mechanisms between the respective member states and their constituencies are in place (which may not always be the case), a procedure would have to be set up that ensures the accountability of the organization vis-à-vis the member states. While it is assumed that the organization could make binding decisions for the member states and their constituencies within the basin, the representatives of the member states in the plenary organ can be expected to ensure that the organization only takes decisions that are acceptable to the member states.[211] This would effectively mean that the member states maintain their sovereignty as principals and that the powers of the organization as agent remain limited. In this case ensuring accountability results in the model of an international organization which is able to make decisions that are binding on member states, but which still relies on negotiated decision-making among its member states. This, however, still corresponds to a negotiation model, possibly with hierarchically organized administrative support, but not to a model of hierarchical direction.
- A second possibility would be to establish a direct link between the international organization and the population within the basin. However even if the member states were willing to delegate powers to the organization, what could this accountability mechanism look like? Obviously, consultation and participation in the planning process would be a first step. However participation alone would not yet create a circular relationship between the organization and its constituency. Would the basin population be able to deselect the river basin organization in case the organization does not act in the public interest? (And how would the 'public interest' be defined at a river basin level given upstream and downstream interests?).

These considerations show that the concept of an independent hierarchical river basin organization does not only fail due to unwillingness of national states to relinquish sovereignty, but also in terms of accountability it is difficult to conceive. It seems that in the case of international water management, the need for expert knowledge does not justify a curtailment of

---

[211] While it makes a formal difference whether or not the decisions of international organizations are binding on its member states, the question is whether the two forms effectively lead to different outcomes. If the international organization has the power to make binding decisions, this is likely to complicate the international negotiation process as representatives will be careful which decisions they consent to. However once a decision is reached it can be expected to be implemented, and under ideal circumstances the organization may be able to impose an efficient and fair solution on member states. If the decisions are only recommendations to the member states, it may be easier to reach an agreement at the international level, but there is less certainty whether or in what way it will be implemented.

accountability associated with a transfer of powers from member states to international organizations. This notwithstanding participation mechanisms that ensure that the legitimate interests of affected parties are taken into consideration are desirable regardless of the exact organizational form.

In conclusion, the above 'thought experiment' shows that neither voluntary negotiations under quasi anarchical conditions, nor hierarchical direction within a hierarchical international river basin organization present ideal coordination mechanisms. It can be argued that hierarchical river basin organizations are neither realistic – given the unwillingness of states to infringe on sovereignty – nor particularly desirable, given the difficulty to limit motivation problems and to ensure accountability of the organization vis-à-vis the population in the basin. Therefore, in the case of international water management, negotiations are not only the starting point for an institutionalization, but also remain unavoidable to problem solving. However due to transaction costs and possible problems of distribution, it remains uncertain whether voluntary negotiations under quasi anarchical conditions will lead to cooperation, even if gains of cooperation exist. This, however, again raises the question what role institutions can play in the resolution of negotiation problems. Therefore the next section will analyze the role of different institutional settings for the problem-capacity of negotiations, and as such how the institutional framework conditions influence the outcome of negotiations.

7.2.3 The Role of Different Institutional Settings for the Problem-solving Capacity of Negotiations

Negotiations under anarchic fields and hierarchical direction within hierarchical organizations represent extreme coordination mechanisms. In particular, the notion of a hierarchical coordinator remains an unrealistic assumption for water negotiations between sovereign states. However as argued in Section 5.1.2 international water negotiations rarely correspond to a one-shot game. Instead in the case of water, physical interdependence implies a certain degree of compulsiveness of the relationship. In most instances, interaction on water issues will take place over extended time periods and can be assumed to be repeated infinitely in the sense that nobody knows whether the game will end at some point. This raises the question of to what extent (infinitely) repeated interaction is conducive towards an institutionalization, and what the implications of a respective institutionalization are for the negotiation process?

In contrast to Chapter 5, which asked for a game-theoretic solution to the cooperation problem in infinitely repeated games though punishment strategies, the following will ask for the effects of different institutional settings on the negotiation process (see Figure 1.2). In this context Scharpf's typology of institutional settings can be understood as a range of different degrees of institutionalization. The following will therefore discuss the potential role of networks and trust, regimes, joint-decision systems, associations and organizations in international water negotiations. While Chapter 5 asked under which conditions cooperation emerges, treating institutions quasi as a by-product, this section argues the other way around, asking how different institutional settings influence the negotiation behavior. It will be maintained that the main effect of these different institutional settings is to reduce transaction costs and thus in terms of efficiency.

Networks and trust

Once actors interact regularly on a voluntary basis, this may lead to the emergence of network-like structures and the build up of trust. Networks can be defined as 'informal and self-organizing structures that evolve from the frequency of voluntary dyadic interactions' (Scharpf 1997: 141). They arise and are maintained because of the benefits they incur in comparison to one-shot encounters. The assumption is that the members of the network remember past encounters and have an expectation to deal with each other again in the future. Networks can thus be expected to reduce opportunistic behavior by casting ahead a 'shadow of the future' and by increasing the visibility of interactions to other networks members. By casting ahead a 'shadow of the future', networks lower the parties' discount rate, which according to the Folk theorem is conducive towards cooperation (see Section 5.1.2).

Repeated interaction also leads to the build up of *trust*. Building trust can be understood as an investment in the sense that individuals may have to forego certain short-term advantages in order to capture long-term gains of cooperation, implying the transition from a 'myopic' to an 'enlightened' self-interest. Trusting behavior implies reduced opportunistic behavior, which may, for instance, help to overcome the Negotiator's Dilemma. It may also contribute towards the resolution of distributional conflict. However trusting behavior remains a voluntary mode and trust can be broken once actors resort to unilateralism and non-cooperative behavior. The downside of trusting behavior is that the trusting person becomes vulnerable to exploitation. Network structures may also lead to asymmetrical dependence if one partner has access to other sources and the other has not (which might be quite relevant for asymmetrical water problems).

Despite these potential problems, it can be argued that in general the build up of network-like structures and trust is conducive towards the problem-solving capacity of negotiations, irrespectively of the degree of formal institutionalization. For instance repeated interaction in the technical working groups of the International Commission for the Protection of the Rhine has reportedly lead to a situation in which bureaucrats from the different member states resolve smaller problems by direct telephone communication (Holtrup 1999: 152).

Regimes

Actors might also more explicitly agree on rules of interaction by the set up of regimes. Scharpf (1997: 141) defines regimes as

> purposefully created normative frameworks governing negotiations among a formally specified set of actors that have explicitly undertaken to respect certain interest positions of other parties, to pursue certain substantive goals and to follow certain procedures in their future interactions.

In contrast, as mentioned in Section 1.3.2, a widely accepted definition in international relations defines international regimes as: 'implicit and explicit principles, norms, rules, and decision-making procedures around which actors' expectations converge in a given area of international relations' (Krasner 1983: 2). Thus while Scharpf limits his definition to explicit rules systems, Krasner's definition includes implicit arrangements. Given the ambiguity in definition, it is also not definitely settled to what extent regimes are tantamount with the underlying legal rules, such as framework conventions or other treaties. What is constitutive of Scharpf's notion of a regime is that the detailed substance of the interaction it not specified by the regime itself, but by subsequent interaction under the regime's rules. According to this understanding, a regime may for instance be reflected by a framework convention. The framework convention would then be specified by substantive protocols. The negotiations of the protocol are expected to be facilitated by the fact that agreement exists on principal goals, that certain damaging unilateral strategies that could be used as threat strategies are ruled out, and that fair procedures are available for the settlement of future disputes.

In the language of game theory, a regime promotes binding commitments. These voluntary commitments can be expected to promote a 'cooperative' attitude and may thus again reduce opportunistic behavior. Whether such formal commitments in the form of regimes or informally built trust are more conducive towards promoting cooperation depends on the situation at hand. In some cases formal regimes may also remain 'lip service'.[212]

Irrespectively of the exact definition, regimes certainly play a significant role in the case of international waters. For instance the 1999 Rhine Convention[213] can be understood as such a framework agreement with regime character: It defines the scope, aims and guiding principles (including the polluter pays principle and the precautionary principle) of the International Commission for the Protection of the Rhine (ICPR) and broadly outlines the undertakings of the member states (e.g. to cooperate, to inform each other, to carry out analyses and to initiate actions in order to achieve the goals of the organization). It furthermore specifies the manner in which the member states collaborate within the Commission and defines dispute settlement mechanisms (see also Table A-2). While these provisions certainly promote a cooperative attitude, the question is to what extent they rule out damaging unilateral strategies in a strict sense.

Joint-decision systems

Joint-decision systems refer to situations in which 'parties are either physically or legally unable to reach their purposes through unilateral action and in which joint action depends on the (nearly) unanimous agreement of all parties involved' (Scharpf 1997: 143). In these situations, all parties have a veto right and agreement can only be reached by unanimity. Examples of physically motivated joint-decision systems include infrastructure or environmental projects of neighboring states that rely on the contributions of both parties. A specific case might be a joint wastewater treatment plant (Section 5.2.2) or a joint multi-purpose dam, such as the Manantali dam on the Senegal River (Section 5.3.3). Examples of legally motivated joint-decision systems are international negotiations in which states are unwilling to forego sovereignty. As such international regimes that rely on unanimity or the consensus principle have the character of joint-decision systems.

The advantage of all three institutional settings discussed so far, networks, regimes and joint-decision systems, is that they confer a high degree of (input-oriented) legitimacy to decisions, since all parties involved have a de facto veto. The disadvantage is that the situation might turn into a 'joint-decision trap', in which those who benefit from the status quo can block reforms or at least demand inappropriately high compensation (Scharpf

---

[212] In the end adherence to the regime depends on the self-interest of the parties involved as well as on the willingness of the member states to enforce these rules by sanctioning breaches of regime obligations.

[213] Convention on the Protection of the Rhine, Bern, April 12, 1999.

1997: 144). Thus while the unanimity rule is recommended for the set up of collective decision-making mechanisms and thus for constitutional questions, it may significantly increase the transaction costs of operational decisions (Buchanan and Tullock 1962). In order to alleviate these problems, in some situations, it may be possible to resort to an association ruled by a majority vote (see below).

Where this is not possible, the limitations of the unanimity rule can be enhanced by the involvement of an agenda setter. An agenda setter supports the negotiating parties in the discovery of technically feasible and mutually acceptable solutions. Given that the agenda setter has no stake in the negotiations, it is usually easier for the agenda setter to explore the limits of acceptability of each of the parties involved and thus to identify an acceptable solution. As such the agenda setter might help to overcome the Negotiator's Dilemma. Examples of agenda setters may be secretariats of international organizations or other facilitators. In the negotiation of the Indus Water Treaty (1960) between India and Pakistan, the World Bank played the role of an agenda setter (Kirmani and Rangeley 1990), and since 1997 the World Bank has facilitated international water management in the Nile Basin.[214]

Associations

Once the negotiating parties set up a formal association, decisions may be taken on the basis of a majority vote. A majority rule might be more conducive towards avoiding joint decision traps, and in particular in the case of choices by large numbers of actors it may lower transaction costs significantly. The disadvantage of a majority rule is that it cannot be ruled out that the majority decides at the expense of the excluded minority. A majority rule, thus, raises concerns with regard to the legitimacy of respective decisions, and there is no reason to believe that majority votes will systematically increase (productive) efficiency and distributive justice (Scharpf 1997: 161).[215] Decisions in associations may also be supported by an agenda setter.

With respect to the problem-solving capacity of negotiations, the formal introduction of a majority vote may serve as a 'threat' of how to proceed if no consensual agreement can be reached. This may be conducive towards overcoming a joint decision trap through consensual decision-making. Experiences with committees show that even if a formal majority vote is in

---

[214] See http://www.worldbank.org/afr/nilebasin/faq.htm (October 20, 2005).

[215] However if a majority vote is set up by a constitutional decision on the basis of unanimity, it may nevertheless, from a procedural point of view, be considered as legitimate.

place, decisions will often be endorsed by consensus (Schermers 1980: 393). Members may prefer to avoid overriding the interests of a minority, knowing that they themselves could be in the same position at some point.

Examples of domestic water associations that work on the basis of a majority vote are the *Wasserverbände* in the German State of North-Rhine Westphalia and the *Agences de Bassin* in France. In the case of the German *Wasserverbände*, the highest decision-making organ is the general assembly, in which different user groups as well as municipalities are represented (Holm 1988: 61). In the case of the French *Agences de Bassin*, the highest decision-making organ is the *Comite de Bassin* with 40 to 60 members, including private users, municipalities and representatives of the bureaucracy (Bower et al. 1981: 105). Given that the *Verbände* and the *Agences* assemble a comparatively high number of individual actors from the public and the private sector at the local level, the majority vote represents a means to lower transaction costs.

In international negotiations, states usually insist on the application of the unanimity rule or the consensus principle in order to maintain their sovereignty (Section 4.4.1). International water commissions that allow for a majority vote include the US-Canadian International Joint Commission and the Salto Grande Commission, but both consist of only two delegations so that the majority vote only becomes effective if members within one delegation differ in their vote (see also Mostert 2003: 28 f.) Thus the option of associations is mainly relevant for domestic water negotiations.

Organizations

Hierarchical organizations or the state allow for decisions to be taken on the basis of hierarchical direction. However even within a hierarchical organization hierarchical direction is by no means the only interaction and decision-making mode, but hierarchies to a great extent also rely on negotiations (Scharpf 1997: 197 ff.). In particular within the ministerial bureaucracy, lower-level negotiations between different ministries are a widespread phenomenon. Policy proposals are usually prepared by various 'horizontal negotiations' among lower-level units within and across ministries as well as with third parties within the parliament and lobby groups. Besides these horizontal negotiations, each of the participating units is also involved in a 'vertical dialogue' with its respective political leadership. Reference to the superior's position allows for the introduction of credible threats on both sides of the negotiation table. Thus negotiations take place under the expectation to reach agreement, but each side has the option to appeal to higher authority if it is confronted with unfair bargaining strategies. For such negotiations within bureaucratic hierarchies as well as for self-organization processes that take place in the shadow of the state Scharpf has coined the term 'negotiations in the shadow of hierarchy'. Again the effect is that transaction costs are reduced, and it is likely that the fairness of the outcome is increased. Given that usually different policy sectors deal with water, the concept of negotiations in the shadow of hierarchy is highly relevant for an inter-sectoral coordination of water issues. However it may also apply to the negotiation of inter-country working groups within international organizations.

As mentioned above in the case of international organizations, we are usually confronted with an ultimate decision-making plenary organ. This plenary organ usually takes decisions on the basis of unanimity or consensus, and the power to exert hierarchical direction vis-à-vis the member states tends to be limited. For instance in the case of International Commission for the Protection of the Rhine (ICPR), decisions only have the character of recommendations to their members.[216] However the internal organization of international organizations remains hierarchical with the respective highest decision-making organ being able to direct its secretariat and lower-level committees and working groups. In the case of ICPR, substantive negotiations are carried out by lower-level technocrats in thematic working groups. Experience shows that the success of these working groups greatly depends on high level commitment at the ministerial level (e.g. Holtrup 1999: 153).

As already indicated in Section 7.1, international organizations thus tend to combine different governance structure or interaction modes. In the terminology of actor-centered institutionalism they combine elements of horizontal regimes or joint-decision systems and vertical hierarchies. Still as long as the primary decision-making organ is a plenary organ in which all member states are represented, the primary interaction mode is negotiated or consensual decision making, even if decisions are binding on member states. Negotiated decision-making may be supported by elements of hierarchical decision-making. As the experience of ICPR in the context of the Rhine Action Program of 1987 demonstrates, within the organization, lower level negotiations benefit from vertical political commitment. In that context, the concept of negotiations in the shadow of hierarchy is highly relevant.

---

[216] Rare exceptions are the Organization for the Development of the Senegal River (OMVS), in which case decisions by the organization are binding on member states and the International Boundary and Water Commission (IBWC) between Mexico and the USA, in which case minutes are binding unless the parties object within 30 days (Section 4.4.1).

Summary

The discussion in this section shows that the problem-solving capacity of negotiations depends on the institutional setting under which they take place. Informal and formal institutional settings such as networks and trust, regimes, joint-decision systems, associations and organizations can be expected to reduce the opportunism of negotiations under anarchical conditions and as such to lower transaction costs. In doing so, the respective institutional setting vary in their effects as summarized in Table 7.4.

Table 7.4   Effects of Different Institutional Settings on Negotiations

Institutional Setting	Effects on Problem-Solving Capacity of Negotiations
Anarchic fields	• Opportunism prevails.
Networks/ Regimes/ Joint-decision systems	• Repeated interaction may create trust and reduce opportunism and transaction costs. • Trust increases the shadow of the future. • Regimes support binding commitments through joint objectives, the out-ruling credible threats and fair procedures. • By identifying agreeable solutions, an agenda setter may help to overcome the Negotiator's Dilemma.
Associations	• The threat of a majority vote may avoid a joint-decision trap.
Organizations	• The power of superiors to adopt or reject horizontal negotiation outcomes reduces opportunism ('negotiations in the shadow of hierarchy').

Source: Own presentation

Overall the main effect of these institutional settings is to reduce transaction costs and therefore in terms of efficiency. As long as negotiated (consensual) decision-making is the underlying interaction modus, the institutional setting does not change the legitimacy of outcomes, and distributive justice is only indirectly affected in the sense that the renouncement of opportunistic behavior may also be conducive towards overcoming distributional conflict.

7.2.4   Results

This section analyzed the relevance of actor-centered institutionalism for explaining international water management institutions. Actor-centered institutionalism distinguishes four types of interaction modes, representing procedural elements of coordination and four classes of institutional settings, representing structural elements of coordination. If unilateral action is excluded, this results in seven distinct coordination mechanisms: negotiated decision-making under four different institutional settings, majority vote within associations or organizations and hierarchical direction within organizations.

In order to analyze the problem-solving capacity of these different coordination mechanisms, in a first step the study analyzed two extreme forms of coordination, namely voluntary negotiations under quasi hierarchical conditions and hierarchical direction in hierarchical organizations. Negotiations were found to be theoretically desirable from an efficiency and legitimacy point of view, however transaction costs may be high and the capacity of freestanding negotiations to solve social dilemmata and to overcome problems of distribution tends to remain limited. In contrast in a hierarchical organization an omniscient and benevolent hierarchical decision-maker could theoretically impose an optimal and fair solution. However once the sovereignty of riparian countries in international water management is recognized, it is difficult to conceive under which conditions decision-making powers would be transferred to a hierarchical decision-maker. Moreover, even if such a transfer took place, information and motivation problems remain an issue. It is also difficult to conceive how the accountability of an 'independent' hierarchical international river basin organization vis-à-vis the population in the river basin could be ensured. The implication is that negotiations represent the most important interaction mode in international water management, and an 'independent' hierarchical river basin organization remains difficult to conceive.

However actor-centered institutionalism argues that the problem-solving capacity of negotiations may, at least partly, be facilitated by a greater degree of institutionalization, be it through the build up of networks and trust, the set up of regimes or joint-decision system, the involvement of an agenda setter or even through the creation of a formal association or organization. The building of trust and thus taking a longer-term view in interactions, is certainly conducive towards collective problem-solving, but it is a 'soft' instrument that hinges on the continued nurturing of the parties involved. The set up of formal negotiation regimes that agree on common goals and procedures may support negotiated decision-making. It remains open whether international regimes would go as far as to constrain unilateral actions. An agenda setter may specifically address problems of asymmetric information and the Negotiator's Dilemma by identifying mutually acceptable solutions. An international organization with several organs combines negotiated horizontal decision-making among the member states and hierarchical decision-making within the organization. In such an international organization, the secretariat may play the role of an agenda setter.

The implication of this analysis is that (1) negotiated decision-making at the level of member states appears to remain the most expedient form of decision-making – despite the limitations of negotiations to deal with social dilemmata and issues of distribution. (2) Members states may manage some of the social dilemmata they may encounter by shaping the institutional setting under which the negotiations take place. This may involve the set up of informal and formal institutions and may include the set up of a formal international organization with different organs. The main effect of these institutional settings is to lower transaction costs. (3) While the analysis points at the specific effects of these different institutional settings, it remains difficult to come up with generic policy recommendations how much 'institutionalization' may be considered as desirable.

7.3 IMPLICATIONS FOR THE INSTITUTIONALIZATION OF INTERNATIONAL WATER NEGOTIATIONS

7.3.1 Insights from Transaction Cost Economics and Actor-centered Institutionalism

Drawing upon Williamson's transaction cost economics and Scharpf's actor-centered institutionalism this chapter addresses the role of organizations and other institutional settings in the resolution of international water conflicts. In contrast to Chapters 5 and 6 the emphasis was not on the question of how institutions may emerge from voluntary interaction, but of how different institutional settings influence the interaction and the problem-solving capacity between actors if bounded rationality is taken as a given. Thus the main question was under which conditions it would be economically expedient to move to more 'integrated' governance structures beyond negotiated agreements. The gist of both approaches was that under certain conditions hierarchies may represent a means towards overcoming negotiation problems, thus realizing gains of cooperation that could not be realized otherwise and representing the most efficient mode of organization comparatively spoken.

According to Williamson's approach the choice of the most expedient governance structure depends on the attributes of the transaction. Asset specificity, uncertainty, frequency of interaction and transactions requiring probity may be reasons to move to more 'integrated' governance structures including hierarchies. Scharpf's approach remains more critical of hierarchies, in view of possible information and motivation problems, and instead highlights the role of different institutional settings, such as networks and trust, regimes, joint-decision systems and also of associations and hierarchical organizations for the problem-solving capacity of negotiations.[217] By distinguishing structural and procedural elements of coordination, actor-centered institutionalism adds 'intermediate' forms of coordination mechanisms between 'hybrids' and 'hierarchies', such as the possibility of a majority vote within associations as well as negotiated decision-making within associations and organizations.

One problem with regard to the applicability of these theories to international water management is that neither Williamson nor Scharpf present a theory of international organizations. This notwithstanding, in particular, Scharpf's analytical categories were found useful to develop an understanding of international organizations that combine different interaction modes and institutional settings, including negotiated horizontal decision-making among the member states in the form of a regime or joint-decision system as primary mechanism (in Williamson's terminology: 'hybrids') and hierarchical decision-making within the organization (allowing inter alia for coordination within the 'shadow of hierarchy'). Hence the primary interaction modus in international organizations remains negotiated decision-making, and international organizations are no hierarchical organizations in a narrow sense, which would be able to exert hierarchical direction over member states or their constituencies. The reason is that sovereign states tend to be unwilling to relinquish sovereignty. The analysis furthermore showed that even if they did, this would raise the question of how the accountability of the organization vis-à-vis its constituencies could be assured.

7.3.2 Is the formal set-up of an international organization economically expedient?

Still the question remains whether the set up of a formal international organization is economically expedient in international water management. On the one hand, it may be argued that the building of trust, the involvement of an agenda setter, public participation processes and possibly the set up of decision support systems represent more direct means to address negotiation problems, obviating the set up of a formal organization. On the other hand, it can be argued that an international organization establishes a negotiation

---

[217] In the latter two cases, the possibility of a majority vote or hierarchical direction respectively is introduced, but not necessarily used.

forum and as such lowers transaction costs by facilitating search, information, bargaining, monitoring and enforcement problems. It facilitates information problems by organizing the exchange of information; bargaining problems by serving as an agenda setter (e.g. through an international secretariat); monitoring problems by collecting (and publishing) reports on implementation by the member states; and enforcement problems by creating an expectation of future interaction, thus decreasing the states' discount rate. As such it forms the basis for repeated interaction and a long-term relationship and the creation of trust. In this case a formal institution may foster the creation of informal institutions.

As long as the international organization does not possess a secretariat and permanent staff, the organization may be perceived as an expression of a higher level of commitment, but does not lead to significant changes in the cost structure vis-à-vis more spontaneously organized negotiations. In this case the operational costs basically depend on the number of meetings and the number of actors involved. While the set up of a formal organization without secretariat involves some costs, it lowers transaction costs in the long run by predefining who is supposed to interact on which range of matters. The disadvantage is that a formally established international organization may not be flexible enough to adjust to a given problem which would benefit from more spontaneous forms of organization.

The cost implications of an international organization will change if the organization includes the set up of an international secretariat, which involves costs for permanent staff and offices. However at the same time the secretariat can be expected to lower transaction costs by performing administrative and clerical functions, by disseminating information, by recording the work of the organization, by collecting reports and information from member states and possibly by providing good offices, mediation, conciliation and arbitration.[218] In international water negotiations, the secretariat may in addition support the establishment of a transboundary data bank and possibly a decision-support system. Overall a secretariat may at least partially substitute an external facilitator. Thus from an economic point of view the question is whether the gains of cooperation that may be realized through the set up of the secretariat outweigh the costs of the secretariat.

This discussion shows that the question whether it is expedient to set up an international organization in international water management is difficult to answer in abstract. The experience of the International Commission for the Protection of the Rhine (ICPR) certainly demonstrates how decision support may be organized through flexible working groups and how the functions of

---

[218] See also the detailed description of the tasks and functions of international secretariats in Section 3.2.2 and Section 4.4.1.

the secretariat can be limited to coordinative functions (e.g. Holtrup 1999: 152-162).

Overall it may be concluded that the choice of adequate institutional arrangements for international water management thus is not or at least not alone a question of markets versus hierarchies, but the challenge is to complement negotiations with carefully crafted informal and formal institutions that contain opportunism and reduce transaction costs. This chapter has shown that a number of institutional settings exist which may perform these functions.

8. Synthesis and Conclusions

This book set out to make an economic contribution to two ongoing, partly interrelated discourses on international water management, (1) the discourse on conflict and cooperation and (2) the discourse on Integrated Water Resources Management. The discourse on conflict and cooperation raised the central research question addressed by this book, namely under which conditions cooperation is in the interest of riparian states, and how institutions must be shaped in order to realize gains of cooperation. The discourse on Integrated Water Resources Management raised more detailed design questions about the membership, scope and form of international water management institutions asking how much integration can be considered as economically expedient. It was argued that economics contributes to the understanding of the conditions under which cooperation and the set up of institutions can be expected as well as to the analysis of the economic effects of alternative institutional arrangements.

The economic analysis of conflict, cooperation and institutions was built upon an economic conceptualization of the underlying hydrological phenomena and was embedded in an analysis of legal perspectives on the institutional design. It was furthermore complemented by an empirical analysis of international water management institutions in form of a cross-country review of agreements and organizations. As such this book is located at the interface of hydrology, law and economics, and it is driven by both theoretical and empirical insights.

It turned out that the term 'institution' is a multifaceted concept that has to be further specified. In line with the economic understanding of institutions as the rules of the game (North 1990), the term institution may refer to property rights and enforcement mechanisms or the 'institutional environment' on the one hand and the rules pertaining to the set up of organizations or 'governance structures' on the other. International water management institutions are based on voluntary agreements to cooperate among riparian states, which may contain provisions on any of the above. In the terminology of the New Institutional Economics (Section 1.3.1), the study addressed both the level of the institutional environment (property rights economics) and the level of governance structures (transaction cost economics), as neither of them can be considered as given in the international system. Furthermore in view of the fact that there is no external authority (no omniscient and benevolent dictator) in the international system which could enforce an optimal solution, the study primarily took an actor-oriented game-theoretic perspective analyzing the interests and incentives of the different actors involved and predicting outcomes which can be expected under voluntary action.

This chapter will summarize the study's findings and draw together different lines of argumentation within the study. Section 8.1 will summarize and synthesize the main theoretical and empirical insights of the study into the nexus of conflict, cooperation and institutions. In doing so, it will contrast the findings of the economic chapters (Chapters 2, 5, 6 and 7) with the empirical findings in Chapter 4. Section 8.2 will address the relationship of international law and economics with respect to the design of institutions for international water management, contrasting the economic chapters with Chapter 3. Section 8.3 will ask for implications of the economic analysis for the discourse on Integrated Water Resources Management, as such addressing an important topic raised in Chapter 1. Section 8.4 will present some concluding remarks.

8.1   SYNTHESIS OF THEORETICAL AND EMPIRICAL FINDINGS

This section summarizes and synthesizes the main theoretical and empirical findings of the study, providing answers to the question under which conditions it is in the interest of riparian states to cooperate, and how institutions must be designed in order realize and sustain cooperation. These findings are meant to inform the ongoing discourse on conflict and cooperation in international water management (Section 1.1.2). Given that the economic analysis is mainly presented in Chapters 2, 5, 6 and 7, and that the empirical findings are to a large extent presented in Chapter 4, this section synthesizes the respective findings and examines to what extent theoretical arguments and empirical findings match and identifies gaps and further research needs. In order to do so, this section is organized according to the headings of the economic chapters (Chapters 2, 5, 6 and 7).

8.1.1 Economic Conceptualization of International Water Management Problems

Overall considerations on conflict and cooperation

Theoretical considerations

While some predict that water may increasingly become a cause of conflict and possibly war, others stress that water may also serve as a catalyst for cooperation (Section 1.1.2). This book showed that an economic analysis of the incentives of the actors involved can shed light on this tension between conflict and cooperation by indicating potential gains of cooperation, but also by identifying the factors that inhibit cooperation in the management of international waters: In principle international water problems can be interpreted as transboundary externality problems (Section 2.2). The presence of an externality points at inefficiencies in the use of scarce resources. In turn this implies that there are potential gains of cooperation if transaction costs are sufficiently low. At a general level, major obstacles towards cooperation are the absence of an authority that could define property rights in the international system, information uncertainties and asymmetries and the lack of an external enforcement authority. However these obstacles may at least to a certain extent be remedied through the set up of adequate institutions by the respective riparian states (Part II).

Empirical evidence

The empirical analysis in Section 4.2.2 shows that many, but by no means all riparian states at international waters cooperate as expressed by the conclusion of international water agreements and the set up of related organizations: agreements exist in 42 percent of all international river basins and approximately a quarter of all basins have some form of international river basin organization in place. These numbers can be understood as a reflection of the tension between conflict and cooperation. This notwithstanding they show that in a significant number of cases states do set up institutions to deal with international water management problems. At the same time these figures do not say anything yet about their effectiveness.

An economic typology of international water management problems

Theoretical considerations

The study argues that the likelihood of cooperation and the exact institutional requirements to bring cooperation about depend on the type of the underlying externality problem and its 'problem structure'. Therefore, in order to identify typical externality problems in international water management, in a first step the physical process of the appropriation of water resources and the provision of water-related infrastructure had to be conceptualized in economic terms (Section 2.1). Water is a multifunctional resource which is extracted for domestic, agricultural and industrial uses, and which is used for transport, hydropower generation and the discharge of wastewater. In addition water resources are habitats for fish and water-related ecosystems and these ecosystems buffer water flows and perform important functions for human health, nutrition and recreation. The appropriation of resource units for different purposes creates a value for their respective users. It usually also goes along with costs that are associated with the provision of infrastructure for resource appropriation. While some uses are non-consumptive (such as navigation), many uses are characterized by rivalry in consumption, which may lead to competing claims on the resource. From a welfare economic perspective this competition can be expressed in form of the concept of externalities, understood as the direct effects of one economic agent's production or consumption activity on the production or consumption opportunities for another economic agent.

As argued in Section 2.2 depending on the water use, one may distinguish negative and positive externalities. While the appropriation of resource units often entails negative externalities (such as water abstraction or wastewater discharge), sometimes the provision of water-related infrastructure also entails positive externalities (such as wastewater treatment or the regulatory effects of a dam). Furthermore depending on the alignment of hydrological and political boundaries and on the behavior of water in its respective geophysical environment, one may distinguish unidirectional or reciprocal externality problems. In transboundary rivers water uses usually entail unidirectional externalities which exclude reciprocal effects in the same use. In border rivers, shared lakes or shared aquifers externalities are more reciprocal, meaning that the users affect each other. The combination of positive and negative and unidirectional and reciprocal externality problems leads to a typology of four different types of externality problems (Table 8.1). While different authors have alluded to different dimensions of international water management problems before, this book sought to describe them in a systematic manner in economic terms.

Empirical evidence

The empirical review confirms that next to water quality and water quantity problems, international water agreements deal with many other issues, including hydropower, ecology and flood control. This supports the initial working hypothesis that we are dealing with multiple issues in international water management. A contribution of this book has been to translate these different problems into an economic typology of problem structures.

Table 8.1   A Typology of International Water Management Problems

Type of externality	Reciprocal	Unidirectional
Negative	Type 1 E.g. Water abstraction from a border river/shared lake or aquifer Wastewater discharge into a border river/shared lake	Type 3 E.g. Upstream water abstraction Upstream water pollution
Positive	Type 2 E.g. Wastewater treatment at a border river/shared lake Provision of retention area at a border river	Type 4 E.g. Upstream wastewater treatment Upstream provision of retention area

Source: Own presentation

8.1.2   The Role of the Problem Structure for Institutional Design and Cooperation

Game-theoretic reconstruction of different types of externality problems

In order to analyze the likelihood of cooperation and how institutions must be designed to bring cooperation about, the four types of externality problems were analyzed in game-theoretic terms (Chapter 5). A one-to-one translation of an externality problem into a specific game structure is not possible, but the structure of an externality problem depends on the underlying circumstances:

- Negative reciprocal externality problems (Type 1) typically have the structure of a Prisoner's Dilemma game where the resource appropriation by both parties incurs costs on each other. Alternatively, if one player moves first and appropriates the entire resource, the situation can be described as a game of Chicken (Section 5.2.1).
- If the parties provide a continuous public good, positive reciprocal externality problems (Type 2) also have the structure of a Prisoner's Dilemma game. If the parties provide a discrete public good, the situation may take the structure of an Assurance game. If each player has the incentive to provide the good unilaterally, we are faced with a Game without Conflict (Sections 5.2.2 and 5.2.3).

- Negative unidirectional externality problems (Type 3) may be analyzed on the basis of the Coase theorem. If side-payments are acceptable to both players, the problem can be described as a Prisoner's Dilemma side-payment game. If a side-payment is rejected by one party, the game has the structure of a Constant Sum game. If both reject a side-payment, the game can be described as a Deadlock game (Section 5.3.1). In the case of upstream water pollution, the game can be described as a Rambo II game if downstream rejects a side-payment and treats the polluted water itself (Section 5.3.2). Zürn's (1992) characterization of upstream water pollution as Rambo I game was rejected as inadequate (Section 5.3.2).
- In the case of positive unidirectional externality problems (Type 4) the structure of the game depends on the incentives of the downstream party. If downstream has an interest to participate in the design and operation of infrastructure measures upstream that provide positive externalities downstream, the problem has the structure of a coordination game. A coordination game with distributional conflict can also be described as Battle of the Sexes game. If downstream has no immediate interest it may play a Poker (Constant Sum) game (Section 5.3.3).

The possible game structures identified in Chapter 5 are summarized in Table 8.2. While different authors have alluded to different game types in international water management, this book sought to spell out the conditions under which a certain game structure can be expected in a systematic manner.

Table 8.2   Possible Game Structures of Different Externality Problems

Type of externality	Reciprocal	Unidirectional
Negative	Type 1 • Prisoner's Dilemma game • Chicken game	Type 3 • Prisoner's Dilemma side-payment game • Constant Sum game • Deadlock game • Rambo II game
Positive	Type 2 • Prisoner's Dilemma game • Assurance game • Game without Conflict	Type 4 • Coordination/Battle of the Sexes game • Poker (Constant Sum) game

Source: Own presentation

Problem structure and institutional implications

The study furthermore found that the different externality problems vary (1) in terms of the need to define property rights and (2) with respect to the need to set up enforcement mechanisms as summarized in Table 8.3 and explained below.

Property rights – theoretical considerations
Negative and positive externality problems differ in the sense that while the former are water rights problems in a narrow sense, the latter are not: Negative externalities result from the appropriation of the water resource in terms of quantity or quality, raising the question who has the right to appropriate the resource. In contrast positive externality problems are generated by infrastructure measures (e.g. the regulatory effects of a dam). Sometimes these infrastructure measures are supposed to remedy negative externalities (such as in the case of wastewater treatment), but the provision of the positive externality per se does not involve property rights to water. Hence property rights to water have only to be settled in the case of negative externality problems. Furthermore in an ideal reciprocal externality situation, which takes the structure of a Prisoner's Dilemma, at least in infinitely repeated games, cooperation is principally in the interest of the parties involved. In this case the transition from defection to cooperation can be interpreted as a mutual delimitation of property rights to water. Hence in the case of negative reciprocal externality problems a mutual delimitation of property rights to water is in the interest of the players involved (and only hinges on enforcement). This implies that in terms of property rights to water the problematic case are negative unidirectional externality problems (Sections 5.2 and 5.3). To the knowledge of the author this property right implication of negative versus positive externality problems in international water management has so far not been described in the literature.

Thus in the case of negative unidirectional externality problems the realization of gains of cooperation relies on an implicit or explicit agreement on property rights to water. The Coase theorem shows that gains of cooperation may be realized through a side-payment if either the laissez-faire rule or the liability rule applies (Section 5.1.1). However, as was shown in Section 3.1.2, both the doctrines of absolute territorial sovereignty and of absolute territorial integrity, which correspond to the Coasean rules are disputed among riparian states, and international law rejects both of them and instead supports the principle of equitable and reasonable utilization (Section 3.1.3). Such an equitable utilization can only be established in a process of negotiations on the basis of claim and counter-claim by taking all relevant factors into account. Hence riparian states have to negotiate property rights and efficiency gains simultaneously. In this context, economic theory can show what gains could be realized if the parties agreed on property rights, but it has no 'recipe' to offer how the property rights issue should be settled – the bargaining problem persists despite potential gains of cooperation. Whether agreement on the underlying property rights will be reached and what such an agreement would look like depends on a number of factors, including (1) bargaining power, (2) the question to what extent the party disadvantaged by the status quo can morally persuade the advantaged party and (3) the interest of states to adhere to customary norms (Sections 5.3.1 and 5.3.4).

Property rights – empirical evidence
The empirical evidence shows that states adopt different approaches to deal with disputed property rights:

- The review of the application of side-payments and issue linkages in 506 international water treaties in Section 4.3.2 shows that both strategies are rarely applied in the case of water quality and water quantity problems. This suggests that the extreme property rights rules are indeed infrequently adopted in negative unidirectional externality problems.
- The in-depth analysis of 12 selected agreements shows that not all agreements are 'cooperative' agreements in the sense that they realize gains of cooperation (Section 4.4.2). Instead in a number of cases, the purpose of the agreement is to establish a framework for cooperation with the objective of identifying benefits of cooperation later on in the process or it is the purpose of the respective organization to determine rights. This raises the question whether it is expedient to negotiate a framework agreement and to establish a commission first or whether countries should seek to negotiate a substantive 'cooperative' agreement right away. For instance in 1999 the Nile riparian countries agreed on what they call a transitional institutional arrangement, and they are involved in an ongoing simultaneous process of negotiating specific projects and a legal framework. While this question cannot be answered in this book, the empirical evidence hints at the fact that an agreement on property rights will not necessarily be the first step in a process of collaboration (although it is still necessary for the realization of benefits).
- Other agreements do contain substantive provisions on property rights and infrastructure measures, which would be closer to the assumption of economic theory that agreements are stricken if they realize gains of cooperation (Section 4.4.2). However more detailed analyses show that given the long-term ramification of these provisions, sometimes these provisions have been found not to be flexible enough (e.g. in the

Colorado-Rio Grande or Jordan River Basins). However it should also be noted that in these cases property rights were not tradable as suggested by economic theory.

The existing state practice shows that there is no easy way to resolve disputed property rights to water. However it does raise the question whether it is recommendable to seek to settle property rights issues as a first step in the negotiation process.

Enforcement – theoretical considerations
In terms of enforcement, economic theory argues that externality problems that take the structure of a Prisoner's Dilemma (PD) situation rely on a monitoring and enforcement mechanism in order to sustain cooperation (Section 5.1.2). A PD-type situation is characterized by the fact that in principal players would be better off if they cooperated, but due to free-riding behavior no cooperation can be expected in the one-shot game. Cooperation can only be expected (1) if the game is repeated and the players do not know whether there will be an end game, (2) if the parties install a monitoring and credible punishment mechanism (e.g. through the Grim or Getting-even strategy), (3) if the discount rate is sufficiently small, and (4) if the number of players is sufficiently small. These conditions apply to agreements on negative and positive reciprocal externality problems as well as on negative unidirectional externality problems if they take the structure of a Prisoner's Dilemma, but also if they take the structure of a Chicken or a Rambo II game. In contrast in the case of coordination games (e.g. Assurance, Chicken or Battle of the Sexes) an agreement on one of the Nash equilibria is self-enforcing and no enforcement mechanism is required (Section 5.1.2). However in the case of coordination games with distributional conflict (Chicken or Battle of the Sexes) an agreement on one of the equilibria may be difficult to reach through negotiations, and in the case of the infinitely repeated Chicken game the disadvantaged party may instead enforce the cooperative solution through a punishment strategy.

As such the game-theoretic reconstruction of different externality problems in international water management indicates under which conditions cooperation among rational self-interested players relies on the set up of an enforcement mechanisms and under which conditions such an enforcement mechanism is not required. To the knowledge of the author this has so far not been developed systematically for international water management problems.

Enforcement – empirical evidence

The empirical analysis in Section 4.4.2 shows that almost 50 percent of 86 agreements have neither monitoring nor enforcement mechanisms, and only 10 percent have some kind of enforcement mechanism in place. Only one of the 12 agreements reviewed in greater detail contains explicit enforcement provisions, and none foresees negative sanctions. As argued above not all existing treaties are indeed 'cooperative agreements' in the sense that they seek to realize gains of cooperation and ask their signatories to cooperate, and not all are cooperation problems. Hence not all treaties require enforcement mechanisms. However for those treaties that tackle PD-type cooperation problems and that do not have enforcement mechanisms in place the question is what the implications for cooperation are. Do these treaties fail due to the lack of enforcement, or is enforcement not as important as assumed by economic theory? The necessity of enforcement rests on the assumption of self-interested rational behavior. The question is whether this assumption applies to state behavior. Some authors argue that states generally tend to comply with their treaty obligations. In order to determine whether enforcement is indeed as important as assumed by economic theory a more systematic analysis of the effectiveness of existing agreements would be required. This, however, would be a major research effort on its own (see Section 4.5). At the same time it can be argued that even if an empirical analysis confirmed that riparian states tend to abide by their treaty obligations, credible punishment threats would not harm (unless the introduction of threats is being perceived as a breach of trust).

Table 8.3   Institutional Implications of Different Problem Structures

Type of externality	Reciprocal	Unidirectional
Negative	Type 1: For Prisoner's Dilemma game: • Agreement on water rights in mutual interest • Enforcement problem	Type 3: For Prisoner's Dilemma side-payment game: • Water rights allocation problematic as it has distributional implications • Enforcement problem
Positive	Type 2: For Prisoner's Dilemma game: • No water rights problem • Enforcement problem	Type 4: For Coordination/Battle of the Sexes game: • No water rights problem • No enforcement problem

Source: Own presentation

Problem structure and the likelihood of cooperation

Theoretical considerations

The theoretical analysis of the four types of externality problems suggests that cooperation is more likely in the case of reciprocal than in the case of unidirectional externality problems and more likely in the case of positive unidirectional than of negative unidirectional externality problems (Chapter 5).[219] The reason is that in an ideal reciprocal externality situation, cooperation is principally in the interest of the players involved and only hinges on the set up of an enforcement mechanism. In contrast in the case of unidirectional externalities, the party that is advantaged by the status quo does not necessarily have an immediate interest to cooperate. In the case of negative unidirectional externality the realization gains of cooperation hinges on the explicit or implicit agreement on property rights which, however, has distributional implications. In the case of positive unidirectional externality problems downstream can be expected to cooperate if it has an interest to participate in upstream infrastructure design and operation. As such this book confirms Marty's (2001) hypotheses with respect to the likelihood of cooperation in international water management and underpins them theoretically.

Empirical evidence

Unfortunately, these hypotheses could not be tested empirically in a systematic fashion in the context of this book. A systematic empirical test would have required the characterization of problem structures in a large number of international river basins and an examination whether countries do or do not cooperate. Such a characterization of problem structures at the level of river basins would, however, be a major research effort on its own, given that issues may vary within a basin. To the knowledge of the author there is no database readily available that could have been drawn upon.

Policy implications

From a policy perspective, the typology of international water management problems developed in this book provides a differentiated view on possible problems and on the institutional requirements to achieve and sustain cooperation depending on the underlying problem structure. The 'good news' of this differentiation is that not all international water management

---

[219] In the case of reciprocal externality problems, the likelihood of cooperation does not differ between positive and negative externality problems.

problems represent property rights and enforcement problems in a narrow sense. The 'generic' policy recommendation is to conclude 'Fs' that realize benefits of cooperation or to coordinate in order to avoid undesirable outcomes. Depending on the problem, this requires agreement on property rights and the set up of enforcement mechanisms. For the definition of property rights international law encourages an equitable solution. In procedural terms, the empirical evidence raises the question whether an agreement on property rights must necessarily be a first step in the cooperation process. Furthermore given that enforcement mechanisms are largely absent in international water agreements, the question is how important enforcement really is in practice, and if it is found to be important, how the enforcement of existing agreements can be improved.

8.1.3 The Role of Issue Linkage for the Resolution of Negative Unidirectional Externality Problems

General role

Theoretical considerations
It is often argued in the literature that instead of carrying out side-payments, negative unidirectional externality problems may be resolved through issue linkage. Section 6.1 found that issue linkage may indeed be perceived as a pragmatic solution to asymmetric water problems. At the same time, issue linkage does not 'resolve' disputed property rights as it always relies on the implicit or explicit recognition of a certain property rights regime (usually the status quo) as a starting point for negotiations. In economic terms issue linkage may be considered as a side-payment in kind, which implies that the problems associated with side-payments in the case of negative unidirectional externality problems also apply to issue linkage. But psychologically, it may be easier to agree to issue linkage as this may not entail the image of being a weak negotiator where the affected party 'bribes' the party 'causing' the externality to cooperate. In that sense issue linkage represents a pragmatic solution to simultaneous asymmetric interdependencies, but it does not represent a solution to disputed property rights.[220] This finding puts the problem-solving capacity of issue linkage into perspective.

---

[220] The only case where linkage may be conducive towards a mutual delimitation of property rights to water is if river basins with reversed riparian positions are linked.

Empirical evidence

The analysis of 506 international water treaties in Section 4.3.2 showed that only 9 percent included a capital transfer or side-payment and only 6 percent included a 'non-water issue linkage'. This pattern was by and large reproduced for the 86 international river basin organizations analyzed in this book. While these analyses do not differentiate between different problem structures, it is remarkable that explicit side-payments and non-water issue linkages are not overly common, and that issue linkages are even less common than side-payments. There may be different explanations for these findings:

1. The rejection of the theories of absolute territorial sovereignty or absolute territorial integrity as a starting point for negotiations by many riparian states implies that side-payments and issue linkage are not 'required'. In other words, their acceptability is not overly high as they rely on the acceptance of one of the absolute doctrines.
2. Some issue linkages may be implicit. Examples referred to in Chapter 6 include the Columbia River treaty in 1961, IBWC Minute 242 on the Colorado between the USA and Mexico in 1973 or the Scheldt and Meuse River treaties in 1994.
3. There may not be enough opportunities for issue linkage.
4. Due to transaction costs, issue linkage is rather sought within than outside the water sector.

The question how acceptable side-payments and issue linkage are in the management of international waters, and whether one strategy is more acceptable than the other, would require further empirical research, for instance, in the form of expert interviews.

Opportunities for intra-water sector issue linkages

Theoretical considerations

Chapter 6 furthermore examined opportunities for issue linkages within the water sector. One reason is that if such opportunities exist a more integrated management of the resource may be in the rational self-interest of the parties involved. At a theoretical level it was argued that while some opportunities for intra-water issue linkage exist, they remain limited. Within a river basin, there may be some opportunities for linking water uses controlled by the upstream riparian (such as water withdrawal or pollution) with water uses controlled by the downstream riparian (such as navigation or fish migration, Section 6.2.1). Sometimes it may be possible to balance effects that are directed downstream (such as water withdrawal or pollution) and effects directed upstream (such as a dam flooding upstream, Section 6.2.2). At least under the doctrine of absolute territorial sovereignty there are no opportunities for the off-setting of negative and positive downstream effects (Section 6.2.3). The linking of river basins with reversed riparian positions may be conducive towards cooperation and a mutual delimitation of property rights to water (Section 6.2.4).

The analysis of opportunities for intra-water sector issue linkage shows to what extent integration is the interest of the riparian states, but also hints at the limits of interest-based integration. As such the analysis informs the concept of Integrated Water Resources Management (IWRM).

Empirical evidence

Selected examples referred to in Section 6.2 show that states indeed make use of opportunities for intra-water sector issue linkage. In addition in some basins intra-water sector and inter-sector linkages are carried out simultaneously. This suggests that riparian states use all bargaining leverage they have. It also implies that the hypothesis that intra-water water issue linkages may involve lower transaction costs than inter-sector issue linkages would be difficult to test empirically.

The review of the substantive scope of respective agreements in Section 4.3.2 indicates that two thirds of the 86 water agreements analyzed cover two and more issue areas. It might be worthwhile to explore the rationale for the existing scope of these agreements and to determine to what extent the uses covered can be seen as complementary, i.e. to what extent the scope is determined by (narrow) self-interest and to what extent it is motivated by principles of Integrated Water Resources Management or others.

Policy implications

In principal, the analysis carried out in the context of this book encourages the use of opportunities for issue linkage, including those within the water sector, as a pragmatic solution to unidirectional externality problems. At the same, it cautions that issue linkage usually requires the acceptance of the status quo as starting point for negotiation and as such cannot be seen as a strategy to 'resolve' disputed property rights. Furthermore the analysis shows what opportunities for intra-sector linkage may exist. The use of issue linkages within the water sector can be seen as a contribution towards the concept of Integrated Water Resources Management (if the latter is accepted as a norm).

8.1.4   The Role of Organizations for Cooperation

Set up of formal organizations

Theoretical considerations
From a legal perspective, a formal international organization is established by international agreement under international law and consists of at least one organ with a will distinct from its member states (Section 3.2.1). In this book an international river basin organization is an international organization pertaining to the management of an international river basin or portions thereof. Chapter 7 analyzed to what extent arguments from transaction cost economics and actor-centered institutionalism can explain the rationale for the set up of international river basin organizations. As such it sought to contribute towards the development of an economic theory of international river basin organizations. This relied on both the consideration of theoretical arguments and of empirical phenomena.

Overall the study found that from an economic perspective the purpose of organizations is to lower transaction costs by facilitating search information, bargaining, monitoring and enforcement problems. They facilitate information problems by organizing the exchange of information, bargaining problems by serving as an agenda setter (e.g. through an international secretariat), monitoring problems by collecting (and publishing) reports on implementation by the member states and enforcement problems by creating an expectation of future interaction, thus decreasing the states' discount rates. However the set up and operation of organizations also comes at a cost – hence it is prima facie unclear whether the set up of an international organization is economically expedient.

Transaction cost economics (TCE, Section 7.1) distinguishes five discrete governance structures, i.e. markets, hybrids (long-term contracts), private firms, regulation and public bureaus. The choice of the economically most expedient governance structure depends on the underlying transaction costs which again are a function of the attributes of the transaction, such as asset specificity, uncertainty, frequency of interaction and probity concerns. TCE tends to support the set up of hybrids with contractual safeguards, such as information disclosure, monitoring, enforcement and dispute resolution mechanisms or, if this does not suffice, hierarchies for problems of high asset specificity arguing that hierarchical direction may resolve some of the ex ante and the ex post bargaining problems involved in long-term contracts. Given that the definition of property rights and investments at international waters has long-term ramifications, in principle the attribute of high asset specificity can be assumed to apply. However in view of the fact that international organizations do not resolve the negotiation problem through hierarchical direction, it remains difficult to fit them into the TCE framework of governance structures. In the terminology of TCE even an international organization remains a 'hybrid' that relies on negotiated decision-making. At the same time, the organization adds structure, and the functions of international organizations can be understood as contractual safeguards. The advantages and disadvantages of negotiated versus hierarchical solutions were further explored by drawing upon the theoretical framework of actor-centered institutionalism, which incorporates different theories within the New Institutional Economics and within the political sciences (Section 7.2). While hierarchical direction within a hierarchical river basin organization could theoretically lead to efficient and fair outcomes if an omniscient and benevolent dictator was in place, it remains difficult to conceive how information and motivation problems of a hierarchical river basin organization could be overcome and its accountability be ensured. Therefore negotiations continue to play a key role, despite the limited capacity of negotiations under quasi anarchical conditions to deal with social dilemmata (both at a resource and at an informational level) and to solve problems of distribution (Section 7.2.2). However opportunistic behavior in negotiations can be reduced through further institutionalization, including the building of network-like structures and trust, through the formal set up of a negotiation regime, through the involvement of an agenda setter or even through the set up of an association or organization (Section 7.2.3). The question remains which form of institutionalization is warranted in a given case.

Empirical evidence
Empirical evidence shows that almost 60 percent of the basins with agreements also have a joint organ in place (Section 4.2.2). This is a somewhat mixed result in terms of the perceived need for the set up of formal organizations. This finding can prima facie be understood to support the ambivalence reflected by economic theory.

At the same time, the analysis of typical functions of the existing organizations (Section 4.4.2) principally supports the transaction cost hypothesis. In virtually all cases, these functions include the planning and implementation of measures and the exchange and management of data. In addition in some cases they also comprise the definition of property rights, monitoring, dispute settlement and, in rare cases, explicit enforcement mechanisms. In particular the definition of property rights, the exchange of data and information, monitoring and enforcement can be explained economically. Dispute settlement can be understood as a typical 'regime' function, i.e. the provision of fair procedures if no agreement can be reached, but it can also be interpreted economically as a threat point.

Powers of organizations

Theoretical considerations

If a formal organization is being established, a fundamental question is how much power member states should transfer to the organization, and whether the organization should be able to take decisions that are binding on the member states and their constituencies within the basin. While transaction cost economics (Section 7.1) is relatively optimistic with regard to the coordinative and conflict resolution capacities of hierarchies (in particular in industrial organization in which owner and manager coincide in the same person), in international relations such a transfer of power will usually be perceived as contradictory to sovereignty. Thus as was argued in Section 7.2 a transfer of substantive powers is not very likely in international water management. Furthermore even if it took place, it would raise issues of accountability, i.e. how to create a circular relationship between the 'governors' and those governed. The problem is that a lack of accountability may result in unresponsive and inefficient decisions.

However even for 'regular' international organizations that rely on negotiated decision-making within a plenary organ, the question remains whether its decisions should be binding on member states or not. While binding decisions may under ideal circumstances allow the organization to impose an efficient and fair solution on member states, it can be argued that a provision that decisions are binding could complicate negotiations at the international level. If the decisions are only recommendations to the member states, it may be easier to reach an agreement at the international level, but there is less certainty whether or in what way it will be implemented. At the same time, non-binding decisions leave more leeway for states to come up with flexible solutions.

Empirical evidence

Empirical evidence indicates that the powers of existing international river basin organizations tend to be limited (Section 4.4.1). Interestingly, the international river basin organization with the broadest range of powers, the Organization for the Development of the Senegal River (OMVS), which is also empowered to take decisions that are binding on its member states, is located in the developing world. In contrast industrialized democratic countries appear to be careful to transfer too much power to respective river basin commissions. For instance the decisions of the International Commission for the Protection of the Rhine (ICPR) are recommendations only; yet it is considered as comparatively successful as the member states remain flexible in the implementation of these recommendations (Holtrup 1999: 150 f.). It would be of interest to compare the effectiveness of these two institutions in view of their organizational differences, although this is also no easy endeavor as the settings of these two organizations differ significantly.

Organs and decision-making modus

Theoretical considerations

The form of an international organization is inter alia reflected by the number of its organs and its decision-making modus. From a theoretical perspective different decision-making or interaction modi can be distinguished ranging from unilateral action over negotiated agreement (consensual decision-making or formal unanimity vote) and majority vote to hierarchical direction (Section 7.2). In an international organization the main decision-making organ is usually a plenary organ in which all member states are represented. The plenary organ tends to take decisions on the basis of unanimity, the consensus principle or in rare cases on the basis of a majority vote (Section 3.3.2). Under the unanimity vote or the consensus principle every state has a veto. While this is conducive towards consensual decision-making, it may lead to a situation where those who are advantaged by the status quo may block decisions that could make the group collectively better off. Such a 'joint decision trap' may be prevented by a majority vote (Section 7.2.3). The disadvantage of a majority vote is that the majority may be able to take decisions at the expense of a minority. Therefore, it would be wrong to believe that majority vote will systematically increase (productive) efficiency and distributional justice. At the same time, in committees the threat of a majority vote has been found conducive towards consensual decision-making (Section 3.2.2).

The plenary organ may be supported by various committees and by an international secretariat as non-plenary administrative organ. Thus international organizations that are composed of various organs usually combine consensual decision-making at the inter-state level with forms of hierarchical direction within the organization. Within the organization the mandate of the upper echelon can be expected to facilitate the negotiation process within subordinate committees and working groups, in which case negotiations take place in the 'shadow of hierarchy' (Section 7.2.3).

Empirical evidence

Existing international river basin organizations almost exclusively work on the basis of unanimity or the consensus principle (Section 4.4.1). This reflects their will not to infringe on sovereignty and is typical for international organizations with few members (Section 3.2.2). While some organizations are composed of one plenary organ only, others consist of a hierarchy of organs. In the case of the International Commission for the Protection of the Rhine (ICPR) the plenary assembly provides the mandate for lower level technical working groups to negotiate substantive issues. These negotiations thus take place in the 'shadow of hierarchy'.

Set up of international secretariats

Theoretical considerations
The staff of an international secretariat is supposed to serve solely the objectives of the organization (Section 3.2.2). Thus from a theoretical perspective an international secretariat can be perceived as an agenda setter. An agenda setter supports the negotiating parties in the discovery of technically feasible and mutually acceptable solutions (Section 7.2.3). As such the secretariat may help the parties to manage bargaining problems related to asymmetric information and the 'Negotiator's Dilemma' (Section 7.2.2). In addition it may address problems of information uncertainty by facilitating the exchange of data and possibly the set up of a decision-support system. Last, but not least, it may monitor the implementation process and thus support the enforcement of agreements. At the same time, the set up of a secretariat as a permanent administrative organ also involves costs, including staff and office costs. Hence the question is, whether it is worthwhile for riparian states to 'invest' into an international secretariat and if so, what its size and functions should be.

Empirical evidence
Among the 12 organizations analyzed in greater detail five have international secretariats in place (Section 4.4.1). While the global prevalence of international secretariats has not been examined in the context of this book, this finding is probably biased towards the existence of international secretariats, as it was obvious to include organizations that are known from the literature to have international secretariats in place. Hence it appears that the set up of international secretariats is not overly common.

The existing secretariats can be grouped into two types, larger secretariats with broad project planning (and partly also implementation) functions and smaller secretariats with purely coordinative functions (Section 4.4.1). In the latter case, the substantive work tends to be carried out in inter-governmental technical working groups. The latter type is usually being perceived as more efficient and effective since those who are responsible for the implementation of a decision in the member countries are directly involved in the decision-making process. It is also less costly in terms of staff and office costs.

Policy implications

Overall the state practice appears to confirm theoretical arguments that support the set up of organizations in order to reduce transaction costs, but it also supports arguments that are skeptical about too powerful international organizations. At the same time, our knowledge about the effectiveness of the existing state practice remains limited. It would therefore be wrong to believe that we have conclusive answers to the expedient design of international river basin organizations, and it remains difficult to come up with general policy recommendations: Is the set up of an international organization with several organs including an international secretariat with coordinative functions desirable? The most appealing theoretical argument for the set up of organizations with international secretariats is the management of information and bargaining problems – however as said before, in principle this may also be resolved through other means, and a secretariat involves operational costs. In the literature, the structure and mode of operation of the International Commission for the Protection of the Rhine (ICPR) is often quoted as good practice. In principle the theoretical considerations in this book underpin these findings. This does, however, not necessarily mean that it is an adequate model for other cases.

Given that there is almost no economic work on the role of international river basin organizations, the analysis in this book may be perceived as a first step.

8.1.5 Conclusions on the Relationship of Theoretical and Empirical Findings

Overall there is considerable but no complete congruence between the theoretical and empirical findings of this book. In a number of cases, the theoretical analysis creates needs for additional empirical analyses, the most prominent being the analysis of the effectiveness of a large number of international water management institutions. In some cases the empirical analysis raises detailed design questions that have not been covered by the theoretical part (in particular the detailed treatment of the expedient membership in multiparty basins, see Section 8.3).

An interesting empirical finding of this book is that side-payments and issue linkages in the case of negative unidirectional externality problems are relatively seldom, and that enforcement in Prisoner's Dilemma-type situations is very rare. The question remains whether this suggests that the theory is not appropriate or that states do not get it 'right' yet. With respect to side-payments, it can be argued that their application relies on a successful agreement on the underlying property rights. The rare application of side-payment in the case of negative unidirectional externality problems may be taken as an indication that states do not tend to adopt the extreme property rights doctrines. With respect to enforcement, as discussed above, the determination whether enforcement is indeed as important as assumed by economic theory would require a more systematic analysis of the effectiveness of existing agreements. However irrespectively of the findings of such an analysis, the design of adequate enforcement mechanisms would probably not harm. With respect to organizational aspects, there appears to be a relatively large congruence between theoretical considerations and empirical findings.

8.2   INTERNATIONAL LAW AND ECONOMICS

One finding of this book is that the law of international watercourses and an economic analysis of the cooperation problem on international waters are closely interrelated and clearly inform each other: (1) Economics informs international law by analyzing under which conditions it is in the interest of respective riparian states to cooperate (Section 8.2.1). (2) International law informs economics about what may be considered as an equitable allocation of property rights and as due process in view of the prevailing state practice (Section 8.2.2).

8.2.1   Economics Informs International Law

In particular McCaffrey's (2003a) interpretation of the legal theory of a community of interests is rooted in economic thinking (Section 3.1.2). The theory of community of interests maintains that interrelated interests in international watercourses may give rise to collective action and institutionalization. In addition the emerging customary obligation to cooperate in good faith is underpinned by the fact that in many situations cooperation is in the self-interest of the riparian states involved (Section 3.1.3). McCaffrey (2003a) argues that this applies to Prisoner's Dilemma-type situations in the case of contiguous rivers as well as to successive rivers where options for a mutual exchange of concessions (issue linkage) exist.

The economic theory presented in Part II of this book can inform the legal discourse on the conditions under which interest-led cooperation can be expected, and how institutions must be designed in order to realize and sustain cooperation (see also Section 8.1). It points at the importance of enforcement in PD-type situations as well as at the opportunities and limits of issue linkage (including intra-water sector issue linkage). It supports the notion that interrelated interests give rise to collective action problems (at least in reciprocal settings). It furthermore points out that some negotiation problems such as those stemming from information uncertainty and asymmetry may be alleviated through a further institutionalization in the form of the involvement of an agenda setter and a decision-support system. While this may take the form of a formal international organization, this does not necessarily need to do so.[221]

8.2.2 International Law Informs Economics

As was shown in Chapter 3, the law of international watercourses informs the economic analysis of the cooperation problem by specifying legal perspectives on the (initial) allocation of property rights to international waters. It rejects the theories of absolute territorial sovereignty and absolute territorial integrity (and thus both the laissez-faire and the liability rule in the Coase theorem) and instead supports the theory of limited territorial sovereignty according to which the right to use an international watercourse is associated with an obligation to do so in a manner that takes account of the interests of other watercourse states (Section 3.1.2). It argues that the theory of limited territorial sovereignty is supported by the weight of state practice.

The theory of limited territorial sovereignty is underpinned by the principle of equitable and reasonable utilization in the 1997 UN Watercourse Convention (Section 3.1.3). At the international level, the utilization of water can be considered as equitable if it balances the uses, needs and interests of the respective riparian states. What constitutes an equitable utilization cannot be established in abstract, but has to be determined by the respective watercourse states in a process of claim and counter-claim, by balancing the factors that are relevant in a given case. As such international watercourse law informs the economic analysis about due process in establishing property rights to water. However given that the list of factors to be considered also includes economic considerations, economics in turn has something to contribute towards the establishment of an equitable utilization.

More specifically, in view of the theory of limited territorial sovereignty and the principle of equitable utilization, international watercourse law takes a clear stand with respect to the property rights regime that underlies the payment of side-payments (Section 3.1.3). It calls for the payment of compensation from the harming to the harmed state to the extent that its harm was not reasonable (i.e. harm to legally protected interests). As such

---

[221] The latter argument is in line with Article 24 of the 1994 ILC Draft Articles, which refers to 'joint management mechanisms' instead of organizations in order to allow for less formal means of management.

international law provides guidance in the negotiation process, whether or not the respective parties adhere to this guidance.

This means that whenever 'cooperation' involves distributional bargaining on property rights, customary law may contribute towards overcoming a narrow perception of self-interest by spelling out customary norms and considerations about due process. However whether customary norms will indeed influence individual state behavior in a given situation remains an open question. The problem is that international law does not have the capacity to enforce a solution. This notwithstanding Barrett (1996) argues that states find it in their interest to comply with customary norms, and that compliance with customary norms can be considered as equilibrium behavior (Section 5.3.5).

8.2.3 Conclusions

In conclusion, economic and legal perspectives on international water management clearly complement each other. Economics allows for a sober analysis of interests and incentives in a specific situation and points at opportunities and obstacles for cooperation. As such it is able to explain why, under certain conditions, cooperation does not come about and to point at possible institutional mechanisms to remedy these obstacles (e.g. through the definition of property rights, the set up of enforcement mechanisms and possibly organizations).

However the economic analysis also makes clear that (narrow) self-interest alone may not suffice to bring cooperation about: if the actors do not agree on an allocation of property rights they cannot realize gains of cooperation. By indicating factors of an equitable utilization and due process, international law shows the 'high road' out and may motivate equitable behavior, but at the same time remains toothless.

Neither non-cooperative game theory nor international law is particularly suitable to address power issues, which represent an additional important factor in explaining negotiation outcomes. Even if the weight of existing treaties reflects the doctrine of limited territorial sovereignty, this does not imply that all existing treaties may necessarily be considered as equitable or fair; instead it can be argued that they often rather reflect the balance of powers between the respective states.

Overall the above considerations can be understood as a contribution to the discourse on 'law and economics'. While the latter is usually discussed in the context of domestic policy making, in this book it was applied to phenomena at the international level. To the knowledge of the author this has not been done before for the case of international water management.

8.3 IMPLICATIONS FOR INTEGRATED WATER RESOURCES MANAGEMENT

As was argued in Chapter 1 the concept of Integrated Water Resources Management (IWRM) plays a predominant role in the prevailing multidisciplinary policy discourse on water resources management. IWRM calls for an integrated management of water resources at the river basin level, ideally taking all relevant water uses into account. In addition it is often argued that it may be desirable to set up special river basin organizations. IWRM can be understood as the prevailing policy consensus (Section 1.1.3).

However as demonstrated in Chapter 4, the empirical evidence shows that the majority of existing institutions are only partially integrated. Only 20 percent of all multipartite river basins feature multilateral agreements, and only seven are basin-wide (Section 4.3.1). Up to 60 percent of all international water agreements only include one or two issue areas (Section 4.3.2). Only about 60 percent all basins with agreements have organizations in place (Section 4.2.2).

This gap between policy discourse and empirical evidence raises the question how much integration in terms of the membership, substantive scope and form of international water management institutions can be considered as economically expedient.

As argued in Section 1.4 expediency can be evaluated in terms of the Pareto or the welfare criterion. In this book the conceptual analysis of the expedient degree of integration was carried out in terms of the Pareto criterion, asking how much integration can be expected, if boundedly rational, self-interested behavior is assumed. In doing so, the study mainly addressed the question of substantive scope and form (see also Section 8.1). This notwithstanding some initial conclusions regarding membership can also be made. However in principal the outcome of such a Paretean analysis does not necessarily imply that the result is expedient in terms of the welfare criterion, i.e. from the perspective of the 'society in the basin as whole'.

The following will briefly summarize relevant findings (Section 8.3.1) and then discuss policy implications (Section 8.3.2).

8.3.1 Summary of Findings

Membership

In terms of membership the study showed for 2x2 games that in all four types of externality problems considered in this book cooperation can principally be expected to be in the interest of the players involved (with some qualifications with regard to positive unidirectional externalities), however, depending on the problem, cooperation hinges on an agreement on property rights to water and the set up of enforcement mechanisms (Sections 5.2 and 5.3). The latter implies that cooperation remains problematic in the case of negative unidirectional externality problems.

The question is to what extent these findings also apply to multilateral negotiations in multipartite river basins. For multilateral negotiations it may under certain conditions pay for a party or sub-group not to participate or to form a coalition and to cooperate at the expense of other affected parties. For symmetric multiparty Prisoner's Dilemma-type situations it was argued that the minimum and maximum number of signatories N that can be expected to sign an agreement depends on the underlying cost and benefit functions c and b with $c/b < N \leq (c/b) + 1$ (Section 5.1.2). Thus in the case of a symmetric common pool resource, full participation of all riparian countries is not necessarily in the interest of the countries involved. Further research would be required on membership considerations in upstream-downstream settings (negative unidirectional externality problems) with three and more riparian states.

In principal, midstream countries can be assumed to be in a situation that is akin to a reciprocal setting as they are both in a downstream and in an upstream riparian position, and, at least under the assumption of relatively homogenous players, side-payments would effectively equalize each other. Thus in a multiparty negative unidirectional externality problem, the midstream riparians effectively play a reciprocal PD-type game without side-payments, and only the most upstream and the most downstream riparian play a side-payment game. These considerations would have to be developed further. A possible starting point is Barrett (1996) (see Section 5.3.5).

Substantive scope

In terms of the substantive scope of international water management institutions, integration can be expected to be in the interest of riparian states to the extent that opportunities for the linkage of different water uses exist (Section 6.2). For unidirectional externality problems, the study identified the possibility to link (1) water uses controlled by the upstream riparian with water uses controlled be the downstream user, (2) water uses with downstream effects with water uses with upstream effects and (3) river basins with reversed riparian positions. Thus in principal some opportunities for the linkage of different water uses exist, however, they remain limited. Therefore, also in terms of substantive scope 'full' integration cannot necessarily be expected, at least in the case of unidirectional externality problems. In the case of reciprocal externality problems at border rivers or shared lakes there may be more options for the linking of different water uses as different uses affect both parties simultaneously.

Form

In terms of form it was concluded that the set up of an international organization may reduce transaction costs. The central argument for the set up of an organization with an international secretariat in place is the management of information and bargaining problems by supporting the identification of technically feasible and mutually agreeable solutions. However this involves cost for permanent staff and offices (Section 7.3). Thus whether the set up of an international secretariat is deemed expedient depends on its expected benefits and costs. Again the theoretical considerations show opportunities for and limits of integration in terms of the form of international water management institutions.

8.3.2 Policy Implications

In this book it is assumed that states 'integrate' if they are able to realize gains of cooperation, thus if another set of actions represents a Pareto improvement vis-à-vis the status quo. The results show that 'full' integration in the sense that all riparian states become members of an international river basin organization with broad discretionary powers covering a large spectrum of water uses is not necessarily in the interest of the players involved. Economic theory would therefore usually predict incomplete integration. This finding can be interpreted as a potential explanation why many existing international water management institutions are not 'fully' integrated.[222]

These results are 'positive' in the sense that they predict certain outcomes under the assumption that states behave boundedly rational and maximize their utility. At the same time, they are 'normative' in the sense that it is recommended that states should realize gains of cooperation where such gains exist, i.e. if a Pareto improvement is possible. The question is what the implications of these findings for the concept of IWRM are. Two observations are in order:

1. As argued in Section 1.3.1 in order to ensure that the gains of cooperation are maximized, it is important that the actor-oriented analysis of individual interests be underpinned by a system analysis that seeks to

---

[222] This does, however, not say that all existing arrangements reflect the 'optimal' degree of integration.

maximize the aggregated benefits of water for the 'society in the basin as a whole', i.e. for all users in the river basin.[223] The determination of the cooperation potential in the basin may rely on Whittington et al.'s (2005) concept of the 'system value of water', understood as the total value of water in the river basin (Sections 1.2 and 1.3.1).

2. The outcome of voluntary negotiations is not necessarily equivalent to the optimal outcome under a welfare economic perspective which seeks to maximize the aggregated benefits for the 'society in the basin as a whole'. Given that externalities are an expression of an inefficient allocation of scarce resources, from a welfare economic perspective it can be argued the expedient degree of integration in a river basin is a function of the spatial reach of the externalities involved. This, however, implies that all riparian states that are affected should have a seat at the negotiation table and should be included in an agreement. This is in line with legal considerations on participation in international water agreements (Section 3.1.3).

Thus for determining the cooperation potential it is conducive to take a basin-wide perspective and to consider all relevant uses. However this does not imply that at the end all riparian states necessarily have to participate in an agreement, given that not all may be affected. From a Pareto perspective, only those who are at least as well off as in the status quo can be expected to participate. From a welfare economic perspective, all those who are affected should be included. However even from a welfare economic perspective, a basin-wide approach may not necessarily be required, but the economically expedient membership, scope and form relies on the underlying cost and benefit functions.

With regard to the concept of Integrated Water Resources Management this implies that economics does not support a general imperative to integrate, but what may be considered as the expedient degree of integration depends on the case at hand and the underlying evaluation criterion.[224]

---

[223] In Part II of this book it is implicitly assumed that the respective games are underpinned by a system analysis, but no such analysis has been carried out.

[224] This is in line with the GWP (2000) definition of IWRM according to which the purpose of IWRM is to maximize the value of cooperation in an equitable manner, taking ecological constraints into account (see Section 1.1.3).

8.4 CONCLUDING REMARKS

At the center of this book was the question under which conditions cooperation is in the interest of the riparian states sharing international water resources, and how institutions must be designed to realize gains of cooperation. This research question was developed both from a practical policy discourse as well as on the basis of theoretical and methodological considerations.

In the study hydrological phenomena were translated into the economic language of the theory of external effects and game theory. In particular the game-theoretic reconstruction enabled the study to show opportunities for cooperation, but also to identify factors that inhibit cooperation, thus informing the discourse on conflict and cooperation in the social sciences. While the existing literature on international water management in the political sciences focuses on the likelihood of cooperation, the game-theoretic reconstruction in this book showed how institutions, including agreements, property rights, enforcement mechanisms and organizations must be designed to manage social dilemmata and bring cooperation about. Thus the study provided a differentiated view on possible problems and respective policy responses.

Organizational aspects of international water management were addressed by drawing upon transaction cost economics and a special version of actor-centered institutionalism. As such the study contributed to an enhanced understanding of the advantages and disadvantages of different forms of organization and to the explanation of the empirical findings.

From an empirical perspective, the innovation of this book was to consider a large number of international water agreements and organizations worldwide, thus providing an indication of variation in institutional design. The cross-country review was complemented by a more in-depth analysis of selected examples as appropriate. This approach allowed – at least in parts – for the iterative consideration of empirical evidence and theoretical considerations. At the same time, due to the study's overall focus on theory, not all theoretical considerations could be validated empirically. In that sense the emphasis of the study was on improving the quality of hypotheses.

The study furthermore showed how international law and an economic analysis of international water management problems can inform each other. Overall it may therefore be considered as an interdisciplinary contribution at the interface of hydrology, law and economics.

A further focus of this book was the concept of Integrated Water Resources Management (IWRM) which plays a predominant role in the prevailing multi-disciplinary policy discourse on water. The study informs this discourse on in two ways. First the empirical analysis shows that the degree of integration of the majority of existing international water management institutions is relatively low. Second the economic analysis does not support a general imperative to integrate, but what may be considered as the expedient degree of integration depends on the case at hand.

While the study seeks to inform the ongoing policy discourse as explained above, overall the study's emphasis has been on explanation and prediction as opposed to prescription. The value added of the actor-oriented game-theoretic economic analysis is that it explains and predicts outcomes if rational self-interested behavior is assumed. Its prescriptive contribution is confined to the recommendation to realize gains of cooperation where such gains exist.

In two areas further research it deemed particularly valuable. First the empirical analysis shows that in international water management states rarely set up enforcement mechanisms on the basis of negative sanctions. This raises the question whether enforcement is indeed as important as argued by economic theory for Prisoner's Dilemma-type situations. This question would require the analysis of the effectiveness of a large number of international water agreements.

Second the empirical findings show that only 20 percent of all multipartite river basins feature multilateral agreements. This raises the question under which conditions the participation in multilateral agreements can be expected to be in the interest of the riparian states of multipartite rivers. This question could be further pursued on the basis of game theory.

References

Abreu, Dilip (1986), 'Extremal Equilibria of Oligopolistic Supergames', *Journal of Economic Theory*, **39**, 191-228.

Ahlert, Marlies (2004), *A New Theory of Bargaining. An Axiomatic Approach to Bounded Rationality in Negotiations – Agreements by Aspiration Balancing*, Volkswirtschaftliche Diskussionsbeiträge Nr. 36, Wirtschaftswissenschaftliche Fakultät, Martin-Luther-Universität Halle-Wittenberg.

Alchian, Armen and Harold Demsetz (1972), 'Production, Information Costs, and Economic Organization', *American Economic Review*, **62**, 777-795.

Allan, John A. (1996), 'The Political Economy of Water: Reasons for Optimism but Long Term Caution', in John A. Allan (ed.), *Water, Peace and the Middle East. Negotiating Resources in the Jordan Basin*, London: I.B. Tauris, pp. 75-120.

Allan, John A. (2001), *The Middle East Water Question. Hydropolitics and the Global Economy*, London: I.B. Tauris.

Allan, John A. (2003), *IWRM/IWRAM: A New Sanctioned Discourse?*, Occasional Paper 50, SOAS Water Issues Study Group, London: University of London.

Ambec, Stefan and Yves Sprumont (2002), 'Sharing a River', *Journal of Economic Theory*, **107**, 453-462.

Axelrod, Robert (1984), *The Evolution of Cooperation*, New York: Basic Books.

Barnard, Chester (1938), *The Functions of the Executive*, Cambridge, MA: Harvard University Press.

Barrett, Scott (1994a), 'Self-enforcing International Environmental Agreements', *Oxford Economic Papers*, **46**, 878-894.

Barrett, Scott (1994b), *Conflict and Cooperation in Managing International Water Resources*, Policy Reserach Working Paper 1303, Washington, DC: The World Bank.

Barrett, Scott (1996), 'Building Property Rights for Transboundary Resources', in Susan S. Hanna, Carl Folke and Karl-Göran Mäler (eds), *Rights to Nature: Cultural, Economic, Political, and Economic Principles of Institutions for the Environment*, Washington, DC: Island Press, pp. 265-284.

Barrett, Scott (2003), *Environment and Statecraft. The Strategy of Environmental Treaty-Making*, Oxford: Oxford University Press.

Barzel, Yoram (1989), *Economic Analysis of Property Rights*, Cambridge: Cambridge University Press.

Becker, Nir and Edna T. Loehman (2004), *Groundwater Management in a Hydro-Economic Commons: Application to Israel and the West Bank*, Draft.

Becker, Nir and Naomi Zeitouni (1998), 'A Market Solution for the Israeli-Palestinian Water Dispute', *Water International*, **23** (4), 238-243.

Bennett, Lynne L., Shannon E. Ragland and Peter Yolles (1998), 'Facilitating International Agreements through an Interconnected Game Approach: The Case of River Basins', in Richard E. Just and Sinaia Netanyahu (eds), *Conflict and Cooperation on Trans-Boundary Water Resources*, Boston: Kluwer Academic Publishers, pp. 61-85.

Bernauer, Thomas (1996), 'Protecting the Rhine River against Chloride Pollution', in Robert O. Keohane and Marc A. Levy (eds), *Institutions for Environmental Aid: Pitfalls and Promise*, Cambridge, MA: The MIT Press, pp. 201-232.

Bernauer, Thomas (1997), 'Managing International Rivers', in Oran R. Young (ed.), *Global Governance: Drawing Insights from the Environmental Experience*, Cambridge, MA: The MIT Press, pp. 155-195.

Bernauer, Thomas (2002), 'Explaining Success and Failure in International River Management' *Aquatic Sciences*, **64**, 1-19.

Bernauer, Thomas and Peter Moser (1996), 'Reducing Pollution of the Rhine River: The Influence of International Cooperation', *Journal of Environment & Development*, **5** (4), 389-415.

Blatter, Joachim and Helen Ingram (2000), 'States, Markets and Beyond: Governance of Transboundary Water Resources', *Natural Resources Journal*, **40** (2), 439-473.

Bower, Blair T., Remy Barré, Jochen Kühner and Clifford S. Russell (1981), *Incentives in Water Quality Management. France and the Ruhr Area*, Baltimore: The Johns Hopkins University Press.

Bromley, Daniel W. (1991), *Environment and Economy. Property Rights and Public Policy*, Cambridge, MA: Blackwell Publishing.

Browder, Greg and Leonard Ortolano (2000), 'The Evolution of an International Water Resources Management Regime in the Mekong River Basin', *Natural Resources Journal*, **40** (3), 499-531.

Buchanan, James M. and Gordan Tullock (1962), *The Calculus of Consent*, Indianapolis: Liberty Fund.

Burchi, Stefano and Melvin Spreij (2003), *Institutions for International Freshwater Management*, IHP-VI Technical Documents in Hydrology. PC->CP Series No. 3, Paris: UNESCO, IHP, WWAP.

Caflisch, Lucius (1992), 'Règles Générales du Droit des Cours d'Eau Internationaux', *Recueil des Cours de l'Académie de Droit International de La Haye*, **219** (1989-VII), 9-225.

Caflisch, Lucius (1998), 'Regulation of the Uses of International Watercourses', in Salman M. A. Salman and Laurence Boisson-de-Chazournes (eds), *International Watercourses: Enhancing Cooperation and Managing Conflict: Proceedings of a World Bank Seminar, World Bank Technical Paper No. 414*, Washington, DC: The World Bank, pp. 3-16.

Cech, Thomas V. (2003), *Principles of Water Resources: History, Development, Management, and Policy*, New York: Wiley.

Challen, Ray (2000), *Institutions, Transaction Costs and Environmental Policy: Institutional Reform for Water Resources*, Cheltenham, UK: Edward Elgar.

Chayes, Abram and Antonia Chayes (1993), 'On Compliance', *International Organization*, **47** (2), 175-205.

Chenoweth, Jonathan L. and Eran Feitelson (2001), 'Analysis of Factors Influencing Data and Information Exchange in International River Basins. Can Such Exchanges be used to Build Confidence in Cooperative Management?', *Water International*, **26** (4), 499-512.

Coase, Ronald H. (1937), 'The Nature of the Firm', in Ronald H. Coase (ed.), *The Firm, the Market, and the Law. 1988*, Chicago: The University of Chicago Press, pp. 33-55.

Coase, Ronald H. (1960), 'The Problem of Social Cost', *The Journal of Law and Economics*, **3**, 1-44.

Coase, Ronald H. (1988a), 'Notes on the Problem of Social Cost', in Ronald H. Coase (ed.), *The Firm, the Market, and the Law. 1988*, Chicago: The University of Chicago Press, pp. 157-185.

Coase, Ronald H. (1988b), 'The Firm, the Market, and the Law', in Ronald H. Coase (ed.), *The Firm, the Market, and the Law. 1988*, Chicago: The University of Chicago Press, pp. 1-31.

Commons, John R. (1932), 'The Problem of Correlating Law, Economics and Ethics', *Wisconsin Law Review*, **8**, 3-26.

Demsetz, Harold (1967), 'Towards a Theory of Property Rights', *American Economic Review*, **57**, 347-359.

Dinar, Ariel and Aaron T. Wolf (1994), 'International Markets for Water and the Potential for Regional Cooperation: Economic and Political Perspectives in the Western Middle East', *Economic Development and Cultural Change*, **43** (1), 43-66.

Dombrowsky, Ines (1995), *Wasserprobleme im Jordanbecken. Perspektiven einer gerechten und nachhaltigen Nutzung internationaler Ressourcen*, Frankfurt: Peter Lang Verlag.

Dombrowsky, Ines (2003), 'Water Accords in the Middle East Peace Process: Moving towards Co-operation?', in Hans G. Brauch, Antonio Marquina, Mohammed Selim, Peter H. Liotta and Paul Rogers (eds), *Security and the Environment in the Mediterranean. Conceptualising Security and Environmental Conflicts*, Berlin: Springer-Verlag, pp. 729-744.

Dombrowsky, Ines (2004), 'Is Water a Public Good?', in Ines Dombrowsky, Heidi Wittmer and Felix Rauschmayer (eds), *Institutionen in Naturschutz und Ressourcenmanagement - Beiträge der Neuen Institutionenökonomik. Ergebnisse eines Workshops am 26./27. Juni 2003 am Umweltforschungszentrum (UFZ) in Leipzig. UFZ-Bericht Nr. 7/2004*, Leipzig: UFZ-Umweltforschungszentrum Leipzig-Halle, pp. 54-71.

Dombrowsky, Ines (2005a), 'Integriertes Wasserressourcen-Management als Koordinationsproblem', in Susanne Neubert, Waltina Scheumann, Annette v. Edig and Walter Huppert (eds), *Integriertes Wasserressourcen-Management (IWRM). Ein Konzept in die Praxis überführen*, Baden-Baden: Nomos, pp. 61-82.

Dombrowsky, Ines (2005b), 'The Role of Intra-water Sector Issue Linkage in the Resolution of International Water Conflicts', in G. N. Mathur and A.S. Chawla (eds), *Proceedings of the XII World Water Congress*, 22-25 November 2005, New Delhi, India, Vol. 1, New Delhi: Central Board of Irrigation, pp. 1-9-1-17.

Dombrowsky, Ines and David Grey (2002), 'The Status of International River Management in Africa', in Ismail Al Baz, Volkmar Hartje and Waltina Scheumann (eds), *Co-operation on Transboundary Rivers*, Baden-Baden: Nomos, pp. 83-99.

Dombrowsky, Ines and Robert Holländer (2004), 'Erfahrungen im integrierten Management grenzüberschreitender Flüsse in Europa: Das Beispiel des Rheins', *Zeitschrift für Angewandte Umweltpolitik*, **15/16** (Sonderausgabe aus Heft 3-5 (2003/04)), 443-459.

Downs, George, David M. Rocke and Peter Barsoom (1996), 'Is the Good News about Compliance Good News about Cooperation?', *International Organization*, **50** (3), 379-406.

Durth, Rainer (1996), *Grenzüberschreitende Umweltprobleme und regionale Integration. Zur Politischen Ökonomie von Oberlauf-Unterlauf-Problemen an internationalen Flüssen*, Baden-Baden: Nomos.

Elhance, Arun P. (1999), *Hydropolitics in the Third World. Conflict and Cooperation in International River Basins*, Washington, DC: United States Institute of Peace.

Elmusa, Sharif (1995), 'The Jordan-Israel Water Agreement: A Model or an Exception?', *Journal of Palestine Studies*, **24** (3), 63-73.

Endres, Alfred (1977), 'Die Coase-Kontroverse', *Journal of Institutional and Theoretical Economics*, **133** (4), 637-651.

Erlei, Mathias, Martin Leschke and Dirk Sauerland (1999), *Neue Institutionenökonomik*, Stuttgart: Schäffer-Poeschel.

EU (2000), 'Directive 2000/60/EC of the European Parliament and of the Council of 23 October 2000 establishing a framework for Community action in the field of water policy', *Official Journal of the European Communities*, **L 327**, 1-72.

FAO (1978), *Systematic Index of International Water Resource Treaties, Declarations, Acts and Cases by Basin*, Rome: Food and Agriculture Organization of the United Nations.

FAO (1984), *Systematic Index of International Water Resource Treaties, Declarations, Acts and Cases by Basin. Volume 2*, Rome: Food and Agriculture Organization of the United Nations.

Feess, Eberhard (1998), *Umweltökonomie und Umweltpolitik, 2. Auflage*, München: Verlag Vahlen.

Feitelson, Eran and Marwan Haddad (1998), 'A Stepwise Open-Ended Approach to the Identification of Joint Management Strucure for Shared Aquifers', *Water International*, **23** (4), 227-237.

Fischhendler, Itay, Eran Feitelson and David Eaton (2004), 'The Short-term and Long-term Ramifications of Linkages Involving Natural Resources: the US-Mexico Transboundary Water Case', *Environment and Planning C: Government and Policy*, **22**, 633-650.

Fisher, Franklin (1995), 'The Economics of Water Dispute Resolution, Project Evaluation and Management: An Application to the Middle East', *International Journal of Water Resources Development*, **11** (4), 377-390.

Folmer, Henk P. and Aart de Zeeuw (2000), 'International Environmental Problems and Policy', in Henk P. Folmer and Landis H. Gabel (eds), *Principles of Environmental and Resource Economics. A Guide for Students and Decision-Makers*, Cheltenham, UK: Edward Elgar, pp. 447-478.

Folmer, Henk P. and Pierre von Mouche (2000), 'Transboundary Pollution and International Cooperation', in Tom Tietenberg and Henk P. Folmer (eds), *The International Yearbook of Environmental and Resource Economics 2000/2001*, Cheltenham, UK: Edward Elgar, pp. 231-266.

Folmer, Henk P., Pierre von Mouche and Shannon E. Ragland (1993), 'Interconnected Games and International Environmental Problems', *Environmental and Resource Economics*, **3**, 313-335.

Fudenberg, Drew and Jean Tirole (1991), *Game Theory*, Cambridge, MA: The MIT Press.

Furubotn, Eirik G. and Rudolf Richter (1997), *Institutions and Economic Theory. The Contribution of the New Institutional Economics*, Ann Arbor: The University of Michigan Press.

German Federal Government (2001), *International Conference on Freshwater, Bonn, 3-7 December 2001. Ministerial Declaration. The Bonn Keys. Recommendations for Action*, Bonn: Lemmens Verlags & Mediengesellschaft mbH.

Gleick, Peter H. (1993), 'Water and Conflict: Fresh Water Resources and International Security', *International Security*, **18**, 79-112.

Gleick, Peter H. (2000), *The World's Water 2000-2001. The Biennal Report on Freshwater Resources*, Washington, DC: Island Press.

Godana, Bonaya A. (1985), *Africa's Shared Water Resources. Legal and Institutional Aspects of the Nile, Niger and Senegal River Systems*, London: Frances Printers.

Grieco, Joseph M. (1988), 'Anarchy and the Limits of Cooperation: A Realist Critique of the Newest Liberal Institutionalism', *International Organization*, **42** (3), 485-507.

Grossekettler, Heinz (1991), 'Die Versorgung mit Kollektivgütern als ordnungspolitisches Problem', in Hans O. Lenel, Helmut Gröner and Walter Hamm (eds), *ORDO. Jahrbuch für die Ordnung von Wirtschaft und Gesellschaft*, Suttgart: Gustav Fischer Verlag, pp. 69-89.

Grossman, Sanford J. and Oliver D. Hart (1983), 'An Analysis of the Principal-Agent Problem', *Econometrica*, **51**, 7-45.

Guariso, Giorgio and Dale Whittington (1987), 'Implications of Ethiopian Water Development for Egypt and Sudan', *Water Resources Development*, **3** (2), 105-114.

GWP (2000), *Integrated Water Resources Management*, GWP Technical Advisory Committee Background Papers No. 4, Stockholm: Global Water Partnership.

Haddadin, Munther (2000), 'Negotiated Resolution of the Jordan Israel Water Conflict', *International Negotiation*, **5** (2), 263-288.

Haftendorn, Helga (2000), 'Water and International Conflict', *Third World Quarterly*, **21** (1), 51-68.

Hamner, Jesse and Aaron T. Wolf (1998), 'Patterns in International Water Resource Treaties: The Transboundary Freshwater Dispute Database', *Colorado Journal of International Environmental Law and Policy*, 1997 Yearbook.

Hanley, Nick and Clife L. Spash (1993), *Cost-Benefit Analysis and the Environment*, Cheltenham, UK: Edward Elgar.

Hansjürgens, Bernd (2000), 'Ronald Coase - Wegbereiter der institutionenorientierten Umweltökonomik', in Ingo Pies and Martin Leschke (eds),

Ronald Coase' Transaktionskosten-Ansatz, Tübingen: Mohr Siebeck, pp. 96-103.

Hansjürgens, Bernd (2001), *Äquivalenzprinzip und Staatsfinanzierung*, Berlin: Duncker und Humblot.

Hansjürgens, Bernd and Frank Messner (2002), 'Die Erhebung kostendeckender Preise in der EU-Wasserrahmenrichtlinie', in Stephan v. Keitz and Michael Schmalholz (eds), *Handbuch der EU-Wasserrahmenrichtlinie. Inhalte, Neuerungen und Anregungen für die nationale Umsetzung*, Berlin: Erich Schmidt Verlag, pp. 293-319.

Hartje, Volkmar (2002), 'International Dimensions of Integrated Water Management', in Ismail Al Baz, Volkmar Hartje and Waltina Scheumann (eds), *Co-operation on Transboundary Rivers*, Baden-Baden: Nomos, pp. 7-34.

Hauer, Grant and Ford C. Runge (1999), 'Trade-Environment Linkages in the Resolution of Transboundary Externalities', *The World Economy*, **22** (1), 25-39.

Hayek, Friedrich A. (1945), 'The Use of Knowledge in Society', *The American Economic Review*, **35** (4), 519-530.

Holm, Karin (1988), *Wasserverbände im internationalen Vergleich. Eine ökonomische Analyse der französischen Agences Financières de Bassin und der deutschen Wasserverbände im Ruhrgebiet*, München: Ifo-Institut für Wirtschaftsforschung e.V.

Holtrup, Petra (1999), *Der Schutz grenzüberschreitender Flüsse in Europa - zur Effektivität internationaler Umweltregime*, Programmgruppe Technologieforschung Kenn-Nr. Jül-3642 D 5 (Diss. Universität Bonn), Jülich: Forschungszentrum Jülich.

Holzinger, Katharina (2003), *The Problems of Collective Action: A New Approach*, Bonn: Max-Planck-Projektgruppe Recht der Gemeinschaftsgüter. http://www.mpp-rdg.mpg.de/holzilit.html (August 23, 2005).

Homann, Karl and Andreas Suchanek (2000), *Ökonomik. Eine Einführung*, Tübingen: Mohr Siebeck.

Homer-Dixon, Thomas F. (1994), 'Environmental Scarcities and Violent Conflict. Evidence from Cases', *International Security*, **19** (1), 5-40.

Homer-Dixon, Thomas F. (1999), *Environment, Scarcity, and Violence*, Princeton: Princeton University Press.

Huber, Max (1907), 'Ein Beitrag zur Lehre von der Gebietshoheit an Grenzflüssen', *Zeitschrift für Völkerrecht und Bundesstaatsrecht*, **1**, 29-52.

ICPR (1998), *Action Plan on Flood Defence*, Koblenz: International Commission for the Protection of the Rhine.

ICPR (2003), *Rules of Procedure and Financial Regulations of the ICPR as last Amended by the 69th Plenary Assembly of the ICPR 1st July 2003 in Bonn*, Koblenz: International Commission for the Protection of the Rhine.

ICWE (1992), *International Conference on Water and the Environment: Development Issues for the 21st Century. 26-31 January 1992, Dublin, Ireland. Report of the Conference*, Geneva: World Meteological Organization.

IDGEC (1999), *Institutional Dimensions of Global Enviromental Change - Science Plan*, IHDP Report No. 9, International Human Dimensions Programme on Global Environmental Change.

IKGB (2005), *Internationale Gewässerschutzkommission für den Bodensee*, http://www.igkb.de/ (March 7, 2005).

IKSE (2003), *Aktionsplan Hochwasserschutz Elbe*, Magdeburg: Internationale Kommission zum Schutz der Elbe.

ILC (1994), *Report of the International Law Commission on the Work of Its Forty-Sixth Session*, General Assembly Official Records, Forty-nineth Session Supplement No. 10, UN doc. A/49/10, New York: United Nations.

Ipsen, Knut (1999), *Völkerrecht. Ein Studienbuch*, München: C.H. Beck'sche Verlagsbuchhandlung.

Kahlenborn, Walter and R.A. Kraemer (1999), *Nachhaltige Wasserwirtschaft in Deutschland*, Berlin: Springer-Verlag.

Kilgour, D.M. and Ariel Dinar (1995), *Are Stable Agreements for Sharing International River Waters Now Possible?*, Policy Research Working Paper 1474, Washington, DC: The World Bank.

Kilgour, D.M. and Ariel Dinar (2001), 'Flexible Water Sharing within an International River Basin', *Environmental and Resource Economics*, **18** (1), 43-60.

Kirmani, Syed S. and Robert Rangeley (1990), 'Water, Peace and Conflict Management: The Experience of the Indus and Mekong River Basins', *Water International*, **15** (4), 200-205.

Klabbers, Jan (2002), *An Introduction to International Institutional Law*, Cambridge: Cambridge University Press.

Klare, Michael T. (2001), 'The New Geography of Conflict', *Foreign Affairs*, **80** (3), 49-61.

Kliot, Nurit, Deborah Shmueli and Uri Shamir (1997), *Institutional Frameworks for Management of Transboundary Water Resources: Volume One: Institutional Frameworks as Reflected in Thirteen River Basins, Second Printing: September 1998*, Haifa: Water Research Institute.

Kneese, Allen V. and Blair T. Bower (1968), *Managing Water Quality. Economics, Technology, Institutions, Second Paperback Printing, 1985*, Washington, DC: The Johns Hopkins University Press and Resources for the Future.

Krasner, Stephen D. (1983), 'Structural Causes and Regime Consequences: Regimes as Intervening Variables', in Stephen D. Krasner (ed.), *International Regimes*, Ithaca: Cornell University Press, pp. 1-22.

Kroll, Stephan, Charles F. Mason and Jason F. Shogren (1998), 'Environmental Conflicts and Interconnected Games: An Experimental Note on Institutional Design', in Nick Hanley and Henk P. Folmer (eds), *Game Theory and the Environment*, Cheltenham, UK: Edward Elgar, pp. 204-218.

Krutilla, John V. (1967), *The Columbia River Treaty: The Economics of an International River Basin Development*, Baltimore: The Johns Hopkins Press for Resource for the Future.

Lax, David A. and James K. Sebenius (1986), *The Manager as Negotiator. Bargaining for Cooperation and Competitive Gain*, New York: The Free Press.

LeMarquand, David G. (1977), *International Rivers. The Politics of Cooperation*, Vancouver: Westwater Research Center, University of British Columbia.

Libecap, Gary D. (1989), *Contracting for Property Rights*, Cambridge: Cambridge University Press.

Liebrand, Wim B. (1983), 'A Classification of Social Dilemma Games', *Simulation and Games*, **14** (2), 123-138.

Lipnowski, Irwin and Shlomo Maital (1983), 'Voluntary Provision of a Pure Public Good as the Game of Chicken', *Journal of Public Economics*, **20**, 381-386.

Locke, John (1983), *Über die Regierung (The Second Treaties of Government), In der Übersetzung von Dorothee Tidow. Revidierte Fassung der 1966 erstmals publizierten Ausgabe*, Stuttgart: Philipp Reclam Jun.

Luce, Duncan R. and Howard Raiffa (1957), *Games and Decisions. Introduction and Critical Survey*, New York: Dover Publications.

Mäler, Karl-Göran (1990), 'International Environmental Problems', *Oxford Review of Economic Policy*, **6** (1), 80-107.

Marty, Frank (2001), *The Management of International Rivers - Problems, Politics and Institutions*, Frankfurt: Peter Lang.

Mas-Colell, Andreu, Michael D. Whinston and Jerry R. Green (1995), *Microeconomic Theory*, New York: Oxford University Press.

Mayntz, Renate and Fritz W. Scharpf (1995), 'Der Ansatz des akteurzentrierten Institutionalismus', in Renate Mayntz and Fritz W. Scharpf (eds), *Steuerung und Selbstorganisation in staatsnahen Sektoren*, Frankfurt: Campus, pp. 39-72.

McCaffrey, Stephen (1993), 'Water, Politics and International Law', in Peter Gleick (ed.), *Water in Crisis. A Guide to the World's Fresh Water Resources*, Oxford: Oxford University Press, pp. 92-103.

McCaffrey, Stephen (1998), 'International Watercourses', in René-Jean Dupuy (ed.), *Manuel sur les organisations internationales. A Handbook on International Organizations*, Dordrecht: Martinus Nijhoff Publishers, pp. 725-751.

McCaffrey, Stephen (2003a), *The Law of International Watercourses. Non-Navigational Uses, Paperback Edition*, Oxford: Oxford University Press.

McCaffrey, Stephen (2003b), 'The Need for Flexibility in Freshwater Treaty Regimes', *Natural Resources Forum*, **27**, 156-162.

McGinnis, Michael D. (1986), 'Issue Linkage and the Evolution of International Cooperation', *Journal of Conflict Resolution*, **30** (1), 141-170.

Mcneil, Ian R. (1978), 'Contracts: Adjustments of Long-term Economic Relations under Classical, Neoclassical, and Relational Contract Law', *Northwestern University Law Review*, **72**, 854-906.

Meijerink, Sander V. (1999), *Conflict and Cooperation on the Scheldt River Basin: A Case Study of Decision Making on International Scheldt Issues between 1967 and 1997*, Boston: Kluwer Academic Publishers.

Missfeldt, Fanny (1999), 'Game-Theoretical Modelling of Transboundary Pollution', *Journal of Economic Surveys*, **13** (3), 287-321.

Mitchell, Robert C. and Richard T. Carson (1989), *Using Surveys to Value Public Goods: The Contingent Valuation Method*, Washington, DC: Resources for the Future.

Moe, Terry (1997), 'The Positive Theory of Public Bureaucracy', in Dennis Mueller (ed.), *Perspectives on Public Choice: A Handbook*, New York: Cambridge University Press, pp. 455-480.

Moss, Timothy (2003), 'Raumwissenschaftliche Perspektiverweiterung zur Umsetzung der EU-Wasserrahmenrichtlinie', in Timothy Moss (ed.), *Das Flussgebiet als Handlungsraum. Institutionenwandel durch die EU-Wasserrahmenrichtlinie aus raumwissenschaftlichen Perspektiven*, Münster: Lit Verlag, pp. 21-43.

Mostert, Erik (2003), *Conflict and Co-operation in the Management of International Freshwater Resources: A Global Review*, IHP-VI Technical Documents in Hydrology. PC->CP Series No. 19, Paris: UNESCO, IHP, WWAP.

Mostert, Erik (N.d.), *Case Study: International Co-operation in the Scheldt and Meuse River Basins*, http://gwpforum.netmasters05.netmasters.nl/en/content/case_EC1B5C0D-FF65-4F33-9FEF-21835CCAF6C5.html (July 11, 2005).

Musgrave, Richard A., Peggy B. Musgrave and Lore Kullmer (1994), *Die öffentlichen Finanzen in Theorie und Praxis. 1, 6. Auflage*, Stuttgart: UTB.

Myerson, Roger B. and Mark A. Satterthwaite (1983), 'Efficient Mechanisms for Bilateral Trading', *Journal of Economic Theory*, **29**, 265-281.

NBI (1999), *Nile Basin Initiative. Policy Guidelines for a Nile Basin Strategic Action Programme*, Entebbe: Nile Basin Initiative Secretariat.

Netanyahu, Senaia (1998), *Bilateral Cooperation on Transboundary Water Resources: The Case of the Israeli-Palestinian Mountain Aquifer*, Ph.D. diss. University of Maryland, College Park.

Newson, Malcolm (1992), *Land, Water and Development: River Basin Systems and their Sustainable Management*, London: Routledge.

Niskanen, William (1971), *Bureaucracy and Representative Government*, Chicago: Aldine.

North, Douglass C. (1990), *Institutions, Institutional Change and Economic Performance*, Cambridge: Cambridge University Press.

Ohl, Cornelia (2003), *Staatliche Umweltregime und transnationales Risikomanagement*, Frankfurt: Campus Verlag.

Olson, Mancur (1965), *The Logic of Collective Action. Public Goods and the Theory of Groups*, Cambridge, MA: Harvard University Press.

Olson, Mancur (1969), 'The Principle of "Fiscal Equivalence": The Division of Responsibilities among Different Levels of Government', *American Economic Review*, **59**, 479-487.

Ostrom, Elinor (1990), *Governing the Commons. The Evolution of Institutions for Collective Action. Political Economy of Institutions and Decisions*, Cambridge: Cambridge University Press.

Ostrom, Elinor, Roy Gardner and James Walker (1994), *Rules, Games, & Common Pool Resources*, Ann Arbor: The University of Michigan Press.

Ostrom, Vincent and Elinor Ostrom (1977), 'Public Goods and Public Choices', in Michael D. McGinnis (ed.), *Polycentricity and Local Public Economies: Readings from the Workshop in Political Theory and Policy Analysis. 1999*, Ann Arbor: The University of Michigan Press, pp. 75-103.

Petry, Daniel and Ines Dombrowsky (N.d.), 'River Basin Management in Germany – Past Experiences and Challenges Ahead', in John Erickson, Frank Messner and Irene Ring (eds), *Ecological Economics of Sustainable Watershed Management*, Amsterdam: Elsevier Publishers, Forthcoming.

Pies, Ingo (2000), *Ordnungspolitik in der Demokratie. Ein ökonomischer Ansatz diskursiver Politikberatung*, Tübingen: Mohr Siebeck.

Pies, Ingo (2001), 'Können Unternehmen Verantwortung tragen? - Ein ökonomisches Kooperationsangebot an die philosophische Ethik', in Josef Wieland (ed.), *Die moralische Verantwortung kollektiver Akteure*, Heidelberg: Physica-Verlag, pp. 171-199.

Pigou, Arthur C. (1920), *The Economics of Welfare*, London: Macmillan Press.

Rapoport, Anatol and Albert M. Chammah (1969), 'The Game of Chicken', in Ira R. Buchler and Hugo G. Nutini (eds), *Game Theory in the Behavioral Sciences*, Pittsburgh: University of Pittsburgh Press, pp. 151-175.

Rapoport, Anatol and Melvin J. Guyer (1966), 'A Taxonomy of 2 x 2 Games', *General Systems*, **9**, 203-214.

Rasmusen, Eric (2001), *Games and Information. An Introduction to Game Theory*, *Third Edition*, Malden, MA: Blackwell Publishing.

Requate, Till (N.d.), 'Umweltökonomik. Skript zur Vorlesung WS 1996/97'.

Richards, Alan and Nirvikar Singh (2001), 'No Easy Exit: Property Rights, Markets, and Negotiations over Water', *Water Resources Development*, **17** (3), 409-425.

Rob, Rafael (1989), 'Pollution Claim Settlements under Private Information', *Journal of Economic Theory*, **47**, 307-333.

Rogers, Peter (1993), 'The Value of Cooperation in Resolving International River Basin Disputes', *Natural Resources Forum*, **17** (May), 117-131.

Rogers, Peter (1997), 'International River Basins: Pervasive Unidirectional Externalities', in Partha Dasgupta, Karl-Göran Mäler and Alessandro Vercelli (eds), *The Economics of Transnational Commons*, Oxford: Carendon Press, pp. 35-76.

Rogers, Peter and Alan W. Hall (2003), *Effective Water Governance*, GWP Technical Committee Report No. 7, Stockholm: Global Water Partnership.

Rubinstein, Ariel (1982), 'Perfect Equilibrium in a Bargaining Model', *Econometrica*, **50** (1), 97-109.

Sadoff, Claudia W. and David Grey (2002), 'Beyond the River: The Benefits of Cooperation on International Rivers', *Water Policy*, 4, 389-403.

Sadoff, Claudia W., Dale Whittington and David Grey (2002), *Africa's International Rivers. An Economic Perspective*, Directions in Development, Washington, DC: The World Bank.

Saleth, R.M. and Ariel Dinar (2004), *The Institutional Economics of Water. A Cross-country Analysis of Institutions and Performance*, Cheltenham, UK and Washington, DC: Edward Elgar and The World Bank.

Scharpf, Fritz W. (1997), *Games Real Actors Play. Actor-Centered Institutionalism in Policy Research*, Boulder: Westview Press.

Schermers, Henry G. (1980), *International Institutional Law*, Alphen aan den Rijn: Sijthoff & Noordhoff.

Schermers, Henry G. and Niels M. Blokker (1995), *International Institutional Law. Unity within Diversity*, *Third Revised Edition*, The Hague: Martinus Nijhoff Publishers.

Schulte-Wülwer-Leidig, Anne (2003), *Interview with Anne Schulte-Wülwer-Leidig*, Deputy Secretary General of ICPR, March 20, 2003, ICPR Secretariat, Koblenz, Germany.

Schweizer, Urs (1988), 'Externalities and the Coase Theorem: Hypothesis or Result?', *Journal of Institutional and Theoretical Economics*, **144**, 245-266.

Sebenius, James K. (1983), 'Negotiation Arithmetic: Adding and Subtracting Issues and Parties', *International Organization*, **37** (2), 281-316.

Selten, Reinhard (1978), 'The Chain-Store Paradox', *Theory and Decision*, **9** (April), 127-159.

Serageldin, Ismail, Norman Borlaug, Henry Kendall, Ingvar Carlsson and Mikhail Gorbatchev (2000), 'A Report of the World Commission on Water for the 21st Century', *Water International*, **25** (2), 284-302.

Sharma, Narendra P., Torbjorn Damhaug, Edeltraut Gilgan-Hunt, David Grey, Valentina Okaru and Daniel Rothberg (1995), *African Water Resources: Challenges and Opportunities for Sustainable Development*, World Bank Technical Paper No. 331, Washington, DC: The World Bank.

Sigman, Hilary (2002), 'International Spillovers and Water Quality in Rivers: Do Countries Free Ride?', *The American Economic Review*, **92** (4), 1152-1159.

Simon, Herbert A. (1957), *Models of Man*, New York: John Wiley & Sons.

Sohmen, Egon (1992), *Allokationstheorie und Wettbewerb, 2. Auflage*, Tübingen: Mohr Siebeck.

Starr, Joyce R. (1991), 'Water Wars', *Foreign Policy*, **82** (Spring), 17-36.

Stein, Arthur A. (1982), 'Coordination and Collaboration: Regimes in an Anarchic World', *International Organization*, **36** (2), 299-324.

Stigler, George J. (1966), *The Theory of Price, 3rd edn*, New York: Macmillan.

Teclaff, Ludwik A. (1967), *The River Basin in History and Law*, The Hague: Martinus Nijhoff Publishers.

Teclaff, Ludwik A. (1996), 'Evolution of the River Basin Concept in National and International Water Law', *Natural Resources Journal*, **36**, 359-392.

Tollison, Robert D. and Thomas D. Willett (1979), 'An Economic Theory of Mutually Advantageous Issue Linkages in International Negotiations', *International Organization*, **33** (4), 425-449.

Toset, Hans P.W., Nils P. Gleditsch and Havard Hegre (2000), 'Shared Rivers and Interstate Conflict', *Political Geography*, **19** (8), 971-996.

Tugendhat, Ernst (1993), *Vorlesungen über Ethik*, Frankfurt: Suhrkamp-Taschenbuch Wissenschaft.

Turton, Anthony R. (2000), 'Water Wars: Enduring Myth or Impeding Reality?', in Hussein Solomon and Anthony R. Turton (eds), *Water Wars: En-*

during Myth or Impeding Reality, Africa Dialogue Monograph Series No.2, Durban: African Centre for the Constructive Resolution of Disputes, pp. 165-176.

Turton, Anthony R. (2005), *A Critical Assessment of the Basins at Risk in the Southern African Hydrological Complex*, CSIR Report Number: ENV-P-CONF 2005-001, Council for Scientific and Industrial Research (CSIR).

UN (1958), *Integrated River Basin Development*, UN Publications, sales no. 58.II.B.3, New York: United Nations.

UN (1975), *Management of International Water Resources: Institutional and Legal Aspects. Report of the Panel of Experts on the Legal and Institutional Aspects of International Water Resources Development*, Department of Economic and Social Affairs. Natural Resources/Water Series No. 1, New York: United Nations.

UN (1978), *Register of International Rivers*, Prepared by the Centre for Natural Resources, Energy and Transport of the Department of Economic and Social Affairs of the United Nations, Oxford: Pergamon Press for the United Nations.

UN (1983), *Experiences in the Development and Management of International River and Lake Basins. Proceedings of the United Nations Interregional Meeting of International River Organizations, Dakar, Senegal, 5-14 May 1981*, Department of Technical Co-operation for Development. Natural Resources/Water Series No. 10, New York: United Nations.

UN (2002), *Report on the World Summit on Sustainable Development. Johannesburg, South Africa, 26 August-4 September 2002*, A/CONF. 199/20*, New York: United Nations.

UNCED (1992), *United Nations Conference on Environment and Development, 3-14 June 1992, Rio de Janeiro, Brazil, Agenda 21*, New York: United Nations. http://www.sidsnet.org/docshare/other/Agenda21_UNCED.pdf (August 23, 2005).

UNEP (2002), *Atlas of International Freshwater Agreements*, Nairobi: United Nations Environment Programme.

Verweij, Marco (2000), *Transboundary Environmental Problems and Cultural Theory. The Protection of the Rhine and the Great Lakes*, Hampshire, UK: Palgrave.

Voigt, Stefan and Eli Salzberger (2002), 'Choosing Not to Choose: When Politicians Choose to Delegate Powers', *Kyklos*, **55** (2), 247-268.

Waltz, Kenneth N. (1979), *Theory of International Politics*, New York: Random House.

Waterbury, John (1979), *Hydropolitics of the Nile Valley*, Syracuse: Syracuse University Press.

Waterbury, John (1994), 'Transboundary Water and the Challenge of International Cooperation in the Middle East', in Peter Rogers and Peter

Lydon (eds), *Water in the Arab World: Perspectives and Prognoses*, Cambridge, MA: Harvard University Press, pp. 39-64.

Waterbury, John (1997), 'Between Unilateralism and Comprehensive Accords: Modest Steps toward Cooperation in International River Basins', *International Journal of Water Resources Development*, **13** (3), 279-289.

Waterbury, John and Dale Whittington (1998), 'Playing Chicken on the Nile? The Implications of Microdam Development in the Ethiopian Highlands and Egypt's New Valley Project', *Natural Resources Forum*, **22** (3), 155-163.

Weber, Max (1947), *The Theory of Social and Economic Organization, Translated by A.M. Henderson and Talcott Parsons*, New York: Free Press.

Weimann, Joachim (1995), *Umweltökonomik. Eine theorieorientierte Einführung, 3. Auflage*, Berlin: Springer-Verlag.

Whittington, Dale, Xun Wu and Claudia W. Sadoff (2005), 'Water Resources Management in the Nile Basin: The Economic Value of Cooperation', *Water Policy*, **7**, 227-252.

Williamson, Oliver E. (1971), 'The Vertical Integration of Production: Market Failure Considerations', *American Economic Review*, **61** (2), 112-123.

Williamson, Oliver E. (1985), *The Economic Institutions of Capitalism*, New York: The Free Press.

Williamson, Oliver E. (1991), 'Comparative Economic Organization: The Analysis of Discrete Structural Alternatives', *Administrative Science Quarterly*, **36** (2), 269-296.

Williamson, Oliver E. (1998), 'Transaction Cost Economics: How It Works; Where It Is Headed', *De Economist*, **146** (1), 23-58.

Williamson, Oliver E. (1999), 'Public and Private Bureaucracies: A Transaction Cost Economics Perspective', *The Journal of Law, Economics, & Organization*, **15** (1), 306-342.

Wirkus, Lars and Volker Böge (2005), *Afrikas internationale Flüsse und Seen. Stand und Erfahrungen im grenzüberschreitenden Wassermanagement in Afrika an ausgewählten Beispielen*, Discussion Paper 7/2005, Bonn: Deutsches Institut für Entwicklungspolitik.

Wittfogel, Karl A. (1957), *Oriental Despotism. A Comparative Study of Total Power*, New Haven: Yale University Press.

Wolf, Aaron T. (1997), 'International Water Conflict Resolution: Lessons from Comparative Analysis', *International Journal of Water Resources Development*, **13** (3), 333-365.

Wolf, Aaron T. (1998), 'Conflict and Cooperation along International Waterways', *Water Policy*, **1**, 251-265.

Wolf, Aaron T., Jeffrey A. Natharius, Jeffrey J. Danielson, Brian S. Ward and Jan K. Pender (1999), 'International River Basins of the World', *International Journal of Water Resources Development*, **15** (4), 387-427.

Wolf, Aaron T., Shira B. Yoffe and Mark Giordano (2003), 'International Waters: Identifying Basins at Risk', *Water Policy*, **5**, 29-60.

World Bank (1993), *Water Resources Management. A World Bank Policy Paper*, Washington, DC: The World Bank.

World Bank (2004), *Water Resources Sector Strategy. Strategic Directions for World Bank Engagement*, Washington, DC: The World Bank.

WWC (2000), *Second World Water Forum & Ministerial Conference, 17-22 March 2000, The Hague, Final Report*, World Water Council. www.worldwaterforum.net/Ministerial/declaration.html (September 11, 2002).

Young, Oran R. (2002), *The Institutional Dimensions of Environmental Change. Fit, Interplay, and Scale*, Cambridge, MA: The MIT Press.

Young, Oran R. and Levy A. Marc (1999), 'The Effectiveness of International Environmental Regimes', in Oran R. Young (ed.), *The Effectiveness of International Environmental Regimes. Causal Connections and Behavioral Mechanisms*, Cambridge, MA: The MIT Press, pp. 1-32.

Young, Peyton H. (1994), *Equity in Theory and Practice*, Princeton: Princeton University Press.

Zeitouni, Naomi, Nir Becker and Mordechai Shechter (1994), 'Water Sharing Through Trade in Marekts for Water Rights: An Illustrative Application to the Middle East', in Jad Isaac and Hillel Shuval (eds), *Water and Peace in the Middle East*, Amsterdam: Elsevier B.V., pp. 399-412.

Zürn, Michael (1992), *Interessen und Institutionen in der internationalen Politik. Grundlegung und Anwendung des situationsstrukturellen Ansatzes*, Opladen: Leske + Budrich.

Annex 1

Convention on the Law of the Non-navigational Uses of International Watercourses

The Parties to the present Convention,

Conscious of the importance of international watercourses and the non-navigational uses thereof in many regions of the world,

Having in mind Article 13, paragraph 1 (a), of the Charter of the United Nations, which provides that the General Assembly shall initiate studies and make recommendations for the purpose of encouraging the progressive development of international law and its codification,

Considering that successful codification and progressive development of rules of international law regarding non-navigational uses of international watercourses would assist in promoting and implementing the purposes and principles set forth in Articles 1 and 2 of the Charter of the United Nations,

Taking into account the problems affecting many international watercourses resulting from, among other things, increasing demands and pollution,

Expressing the conviction that a framework convention will ensure the utilization, development, conservation, management and protection of international watercourses and the promotion of the optimal and sustainable utilization thereof for present and future generations,

Affirming the importance of international cooperation and good-neighbourliness in this field,

Aware of the special situation and needs of developing countries, Recalling the principles and recommendations adopted by the United Nations Conference on Environment and Development of 1992 in the Rio Declaration and Agenda 21,

Recalling also the existing bilateral and multilateral agreements regarding the non-navigational uses of international watercourses,

Mindful of the valuable contribution of international organizations, both governmental and non-governmental, to the codification and progressive development of international law in this field,

Appreciative of the work carried out by the International Law Commission on the law of the non-navigational uses of international watercourses,

Bearing in mind United Nations General Assembly resolution 49/52 of 9 December 1994,

Have agreed as follows:

PART I
INTRODUCTION

Article 1
Scope of the present Convention

1. The present Convention applies to uses of international watercourses and of their waters for purposes other than navigation and to measures of protection, preservation and management related to the uses of those watercourses and their waters.

2. The uses of international watercourses for navigation is not within the scope of the present Convention except insofar as other uses affect navigation or are affected by navigation.

Article 2
Use of terms

For the purposes of the present Convention:

(a) 'Watercourse' means a system of surface waters and ground waters constituting by virtue of their physical relationship a unitary whole and normally flowing into a common terminus;

(b) 'International watercourse' means a watercourse, parts of which are situated in different States;

(c) 'Watercourse State' means a State Party to the present Convention in whose territory part of an international watercourse is situated, or a Party that is a regional economic integration organization, in the territory of one or more of whose Member States part of an international watercourse is situated;

(d) 'Regional economic integration organization' means an organization constituted by sovereign States of a given region, to which its member States have transferred competence in respect of matters governed by this Convention and which has been duly authorized in accordance with its internal procedures, to sign, ratify, accept, approve or accede to it.

Article 3
Watercourse agreements

1. In the absence of an agreement to the contrary, nothing in the present Convention shall affect the rights or obligations of a watercourse State arising from agreements in force for it on the date on which it became a party to the present Convention.

2. Notwithstanding the provisions of paragraph 1, parties to agreements referred to in paragraph 1 may, where necessary, consider harmonizing such agreements with the basic principles of the present Convention.

3. Watercourse States may enter into one or more agreements, hereinafter referred to as 'watercourse agreements', which apply and adjust the provisions of the present Convention to the characteristics and uses of a particular international watercourse or part thereof.

4. Where a watercourse agreement is concluded between two or more watercourse States, it shall define the waters to which it applies. Such an agreement may be entered into with respect to an entire international watercourse or any part thereof or a particular project, programme or use except insofar as the agreement adversely affects, to a significant extent, the use by one or more other watercourse States of the waters of the watercourse, without their express consent.

5. Where a watercourse State considers that adjustment and application of the provisions of the present Convention is required because of the characteristics and uses of a particular international watercourse, watercourse States shall consult with a view to negotiating in good faith for the purpose of concluding a watercourse agreement or agreements.

6. Where some but not all watercourse States to a particular international watercourse are parties to an agreement, nothing in such agreement shall affect the rights or obligations under the present Convention of watercourse States that are not parties to such an agreement.

Article 4
Parties to watercourse agreements

1.   Every watercourse State is entitled to participate in the negotiation of and to become a party to any watercourse agreement that applies to the entire international watercourse, as well as to participate in any relevant consultations.

2.   A watercourse State whose use of an international watercourse may be affected to a significant extent by the implementation of a proposed watercourse agreement that applies only to a part of the watercourse or to a particular project, programme or use is entitled to participate in consultations on such an agreement and, where appropriate, in the negotiation thereof in good faith with a view to becoming a party thereto, to the extent that its use is thereby affected.

PART II
GENERAL PRINCIPLES

Article 5
Equitable and reasonable utilization and participation

1.   Watercourse States shall in their respective territories utilize an international watercourse in an equitable and reasonable manner. In particular, an international watercourse shall be used and developed by watercourse States with a view to attaining optimal and sustainable utilization thereof and benefits therefrom, taking into account the interests of the watercourse States concerned, consistent with adequate protection of the watercourse.

2.   Watercourse States shall participate in the use, development and protection of an international watercourse in an equitable and reasonable manner. Such participation includes both the right to utilize the watercourse and the duty to cooperate in the protection and development thereof, as provided in the present Convention.

Article 6
Factors relevant to equitable and reasonable utilization

1. Utilization of an international watercourse in an equitable and reasonable manner within the meaning of article 5 requires taking into account all relevant factors and circumstances, including:

(a) Geographic, hydrographic, hydrological, climatic, ecological and other factors of a natural character;

(b) The social and economic needs of the watercourse States concerned;

(c) The population dependent on the watercourse in each watercourse State;

(d) The effects of the use or uses of the watercourses in one watercourse State on other watercourse States;

(e) Existing and potential uses of the watercourse;

(f) Conservation, protection, development and economy of use of the water resources of the watercourse and the costs of measures taken to that effect;

(g) The availability of alternatives, of comparable value, to a particular planned or existing use.

2. In the application of article 5 or paragraph 1 of this article, watercourse States concerned shall, when the need arises, enter into consultations in a spirit of cooperation.

3. The weight to be given to each factor is to be determined by its importance in comparison with that of other relevant factors. In determining what is a reasonable and equitable use, all relevant factors are to be considered together and a conclusion reached on the basis of the whole.

Article 7
Obligation not to cause significant harm

1. Watercourse States shall, in utilizing an international watercourse in their territories, take all appropriate measures to prevent the causing of significant harm to other watercourse States.

2. Where significant harm nevertheless is caused to another watercourse State, the States whose use causes such harm shall, in the absence of agreement to such use, take all appropriate measures, having due regard for the provisions of articles 5 and 6, in consultation with the affected State, to eliminate or mitigate such harm and, where appropriate, to discuss the question of compensation.

Article 8
General obligation to cooperate

1. Watercourse States shall cooperate on the basis of sovereign equality, territorial integrity, mutual benefit and good faith in order to attain optimal utilization and adequate protection of an international watercourse.

2. In determining the manner of such cooperation, watercourse States may consider the establishment of joint mechanisms or commissions, as deemed necessary by them, to facilitate cooperation on relevant measures and procedures in the light of experience gained through cooperation in existing joint mechanisms and commissions in various regions.

Article 9
Regular exchange of data and information

1. Pursuant to article 8, watercourse States shall on a regular basis exchange readily available data and information on the condition of the watercourse, in particular that of a hydrological, meteorological, hydrogeological and ecological nature and related to the water quality as well as related forecasts.

2. If a watercourse State is requested by another watercourse State to provide data or information that is not readily available, it shall employ its best efforts to comply with the request but may condition its compliance upon payment by the requesting State of the reasonable costs of collecting and, where appropriate, processing such data or information.

3. Watercourse States shall employ their best efforts to collect and, where appropriate, to process data and information in a manner which facilitates its utilization by the other watercourse States to which it is communicated.

Article 10
Relationship between different kinds of uses

1. In the absence of agreement or custom to the contrary, no use of an international watercourse enjoys inherent priority over other uses.

2. In the event of a conflict between uses of an international watercourse, it shall be resolved with reference to articles 5 to 7, with special regard being given to the requirements of vital human needs.

PART III
PLANNED MEASURES

Article 11
Information concerning planned measures

Watercourse States shall exchange information and consult each other and, if necessary, negotiate on the possible effects of planned measures on the condition of an international watercourse.

Article 12
Notification concerning planned measures with possible adverse effects

Before a watercourse State implements or permits the implementation of planned measures which may have a significant adverse effect upon other watercourse States, it shall provide those States with timely notification thereof. Such notification shall be accompanied by available technical data and information, including the results of any environmental impact assessment, in order to enable the notified States to evaluate the possible effects of the planned measures.

Article 13
Period for reply to notification

Unless otherwise agreed:

(a) A watercourse State providing a notification under article 12 shall allow the notified States a period of six months within which to study and evaluate the possible effects of the planned measures and to communicate the findings to it;

(b) This period shall, at the request of a notified State for which the evaluation of the planned measures poses special difficulty, be extended for a period of six months.

Article 14
Obligations of the notifying State during the period for reply

During the period referred to in article 13, the notifying State:

(a) Shall cooperate with the notified States by providing them, on request, with any additional data and information that is available and necessary for an accurate evaluation; and

(b) Shall not implement or permit the implementation of the planned measures without the consent of the notified States.

Article 15
Reply to notification

The notified States shall communicate their findings to the notifying State as early as possible within the period applicable pursuant to article 13. If a notified State finds that implementation of the planned measures would be inconsistent with the provisions of articles 5 or 7, it shall attach to its finding a documented explanation setting forth the reasons for the finding.

Article 16
Absence of reply to notification

1. If, within the period applicable pursuant to article 13, the notifying State receives no communication under article 15, it may, subject to its obligations under articles 5 and 7, proceed with the implementation of the planned measures, in accordance with the notification and any other data and information provided to the notified States.

2. Any claim to compensation by a notified State which has failed to reply within the period applicable pursuant to article 13 may be offset by the costs incurred by the notifying State for action undertaken after the expiration of the time for a reply which would not have been undertaken if the notified State had objected within that period.

Article 17
Consultations and negotiations concerning planned measures

1. If a communication is made under article 15 that implementation of the planned measures would be inconsistent with the provisions of articles 5 or 7, the notifying State and the State making the communication shall enter into consultations and, if necessary, negotiations with a view to arriving at an equitable resolution of the situation.

2. The consultations and negotiations shall be conducted on the basis that each State must in good faith pay reasonable regard to the rights and legitimate interests of the other State.

3. During the course of the consultations and negotiations, the notifying State shall, if so requested by the notified State at the time it makes the communication, refrain from implementing or permitting the implementation of the planned measures for a period of six months unless otherwise agreed.

Article 18
Procedures in the absence of notification

1. If a watercourse State has reasonable grounds to believe that another watercourse State is planning measures that may have a significant adverse effect upon it, the former State may request the latter to apply the provisions of article 12. The request shall be accompanied by a documented explanation setting forth its grounds.

2. In the event that the State planning the measures nevertheless finds that it is not under an obligation to provide a notification under article 12, it shall so inform the other State, providing a documented explanation setting forth the reasons for such finding. If this finding does not satisfy the other State, the two States shall, at the request of that other State, promptly enter into consultations and negotiations in the manner indicated in paragraphs 1 and 2 of article 17.

3. During the course of the consultations and negotiations, the State planning the measures shall, if so requested by the other State at the time it requests the initiation of consultations and negotiations, refrain from implementing or permitting the implementation of those measures for a period of six months unless otherwise agreed.

Article 19
Urgent implementation of planned measures

1. In the event that the implementation of planned measures is of the utmost urgency in order to protect public health, public safety or other equally important interests, the State planning the measures may, subject to articles 5 and 7, immediately proceed to implementation, notwithstanding the provisions of article 14 and paragraph 3 of article 17.

2. In such case, a formal declaration of the urgency of the measures shall be communicated without delay to the other watercourse States referred to in article 12 together with the relevant data and information.

3. The State planning the measures shall, at the request of any of the States referred to in paragraph 2, promptly enter into consultations and negotiations with it in the manner indicated in paragraphs 1 and 2 of article 17.

PART IV
PROTECTION, PRESERVATION AND MANAGEMENT

Article 20
Protection and preservation of ecosystems

Watercourse States shall, individually and, where appropriate, jointly, protect and preserve the ecosystems of international watercourses.

Article 21
Prevention, reduction and control of pollution

1. For the purpose of this article, 'pollution of an international watercourse' means any detrimental alteration in the composition or quality of the waters of an international watercourse which results directly or indirectly from human conduct.

2. Watercourse States shall, individually and, where appropriate, jointly, prevent, reduce and control the pollution of an international watercourse that may cause significant harm to other watercourse States or to their environment, including harm to human health or safety, to the use of the waters for any beneficial purpose or to the living resources of the watercourse. Watercourse States shall take steps to harmonize their policies in this connection.

3. Watercourse States shall, at the request of any of them, consult with a view to arriving at mutually agreeable measures and methods to prevent, reduce and control pollution of an international watercourse, such as:

(a) Setting joint water quality objectives and criteria;

(b) Establishing techniques and practices to address pollution from point and non-point sources;

(c) Establishing lists of substances the introduction of which into the waters of an international watercourse is to be prohibited, limited, investigated or monitored.

Article 22
Introduction of alien or new species

Watercourse States shall take all measures necessary to prevent the introduction of species, alien or new, into an international watercourse which may have effects detrimental to the ecosystem of the watercourse resulting in significant harm to other watercourse States.

Article 23
Protection and preservation of the marine environment

Watercourse States shall, individually and, where appropriate, in cooperation with other States, take all measures with respect to an international watercourse that are necessary to protect and preserve the marine environment, including estuaries, taking into account generally accepted international rules and standards.

Article 24
Management

1. Watercourse States shall, at the request of any of them, enter into consultations concerning the management of an international watercourse, which may include the establishment of a joint management mechanism.

2. For the purposes of this article, 'management' refers, in particular, to:

> (a) Planning the sustainable development of an international watercourse and providing for the implementation of any plans adopted; and

> (b) Otherwise promoting the rational and optimal utilization, protection and control of the watercourse.

Article 25
Regulation

1. Watercourse States shall cooperate, where appropriate, to respond to needs or opportunities for regulation of the flow of the waters of an international watercourse.

2. Unless otherwise agreed, watercourse States shall participate on an equitable basis in the construction and maintenance or defrayal of the costs of such regulation works as they may have agreed to undertake.

3. For the purposes of this article, 'regulation' means the use of hydraulic works or any other continuing measure to alter, vary or otherwise control the flow of the waters of an international watercourse.

Article 26
Installations

1. Watercourse States shall, within their respective territories, employ their best efforts to maintain and protect installations, facilities and other works related to an international watercourse.

2. Watercourse States shall, at the request of any of them which has reasonable grounds to believe that it may suffer significant adverse effects, enter into consultations with regard to:

> (a) The safe operation and maintenance of installations, facilities or other works related to an international watercourse; and

> (b) The protection of installations, facilities or other works from wilful or negligent acts or the forces of nature.

PART V
HARMFUL CONDITIONS AND EMERGENCY SITUATIONS

Article 27
Prevention and mitigation of harmful conditions

Watercourse States shall, individually and, where appropriate, jointly, take all appropriate measures to prevent or mitigate conditions related to an international watercourse that may be harmful to other watercourse States, whether resulting from natural causes or human conduct, such as flood or ice conditions, water-borne diseases, siltation, erosion, salt-water intrusion, drought or desertification.

Article 28
Emergency situations

1. For the purposes of this article, 'emergency' means a situation that causes, or poses an imminent threat of causing, serious harm to watercourse States or other States and that results suddenly from natural causes, such as floods, the breaking up of ice, landslides or earthquakes, or from human conduct, such as industrial accidents.

2. A watercourse State shall, without delay and by the most expeditious means available, notify other potentially affected States and competent international organizations of any emergency originating within its territory.

3. A watercourse State within whose territory an emergency originates shall, in cooperation with potentially affected States and, where appropriate, competent international organizations, immediately take all practicable measures necessitated by the circumstances to prevent, mitigate and eliminate harmful effects of the emergency.

4. When necessary, watercourse States shall jointly develop contingency plans for responding to emergencies, in cooperation, where appropriate, with other potentially affected States and competent international organizations.

PART VI
MISCELLANEOUS PROVISIONS

Article 29
International watercourses and installations in time of armed conflict

International watercourses and related installations, facilities and other works shall enjoy the protection accorded by the principles and rules of international law applicable in international and non-international armed conflict and shall not be used in violation of those principles and rules.

Article 30
Indirect procedures

In cases where there are serious obstacles to direct contacts between watercourse States, the States concerned shall fulfil their obligations of cooperation provided for in the present Convention, including exchange of data and information, notification, communication, consultations and negotiations, through any indirect procedure accepted by them.

Article 31
Data and information vital to national defence or security

Nothing in the present Convention obliges a watercourse State to provide data or information vital to its national defence or security. Nevertheless, that State shall cooperate in good faith with the other watercourse States with a view to providing as much information as possible under the circumstances.

Article 32
Non-discrimination

Unless the watercourse States concerned have agreed otherwise for the protection of the interests of persons, natural or juridical, who have suffered or are under a serious threat of suffering significant transboundary harm as a result of activities related to an international watercourse, a watercourse State shall not discriminate on the basis of nationality or residence or place where the injury occurred, in granting to such persons, in accordance with its legal system, access to judicial or other procedures, or a right to claim compensation or other relief in respect of significant harm caused by such activities carried on in its territory.

Article 33
Settlement of disputes

1.   In the event of a dispute between two or more Parties concerning the interpretation or application of the present Convention, the Parties concerned shall, in the absence of an applicable agreement between them, seek a settlement of the dispute by peaceful means in accordance with the following provisions.

2.   If the Parties concerned cannot reach agreement by negotiation requested by one of them, they may jointly seek the good offices of, or request mediation or conciliation by, a third party, or make use, as appropriate, of any joint watercourse institutions that may have been established by them or agree to submit the dispute to arbitration or to the International Court of Justice.

3.   Subject to the operation of paragraph 10, if after six months from the time of the request for negotiations referred to in paragraph 2, the Parties concerned have not been able to settle their dispute through negotiation or any other means referred to in paragraph 2, the dispute shall be submitted, at the request of any of the parties to the dispute, to impartial fact-finding in accordance with paragraphs 4 to 9, unless the Parties otherwise agree.

4.   A Fact-finding Commission shall be established, composed of one member nominated by each Party concerned and in addition a member not having the nationality of any of the Parties concerned chosen by the nominated members who shall serve as Chairman.

5.   If the members nominated by the Parties are unable to agree on a Chairman within three months of the request for the establishment of the Commission, any Party concerned may request the Secretary-General of the United Nations to appoint the Chairman who shall not have the nationality of

any of the parties to the dispute or of any riparian State of the watercourse concerned. If one of the Parties fails to nominate a member within three months of the initial request pursuant to paragraph 3, any other Party concerned may request the Secretary-General of the United Nations to appoint a person who shall not have the nationality of any of the parties to the dispute or of any riparian State of the watercourse concerned. The person so appointed shall constitute a single-member Commission.

6. The Commission shall determine its own procedure.

7. The Parties concerned have the obligation to provide the Commission with such information as it may require and, on request, to permit the Commission to have access to their respective territory and to inspect any facilities, plant, equipment, construction or natural feature relevant for the purpose of its inquiry.

8. The Commission shall adopt its report by a majority vote, unless it is a single-member Commission, and shall submit that report to the Parties concerned setting forth its findings and the reasons therefor and such recommendations as it deems appropriate for an equitable solution of the dispute, which the Parties concerned shall consider in good faith.

9. The expenses of the Commission shall be borne equally by the Parties concerned.

10. When ratifying, accepting, approving or acceding to the present Convention, or at any time thereafter, a Party which is not a regional economic integration organization may declare in a written instrument submitted to the Depositary that, in respect of any dispute not resolved in accordance with paragraph 2, it recognizes as compulsory ipso facto and without special agreement in relation to any Party accepting the same obligation:

> (a) Submission of the dispute to the International Court of Justice; and/or

> (b) Arbitration by an arbitral tribunal established and operating, unless the parties to the dispute otherwise agreed, in accordance with the procedure laid down in the annex to the present Convention.

A Party which is a regional economic integration organization may make a declaration with like effect in relation to arbitration in accordance with subparagraph (b).

PART VII
FINAL CLAUSES

Article 34
Signature

The present Convention shall be open for signature by all States and by regional economic integration organizations from 21 May 1997 until 20 May 2000 at United Nations Headquarters in New York.

Article 35
Ratification, acceptance, approval or accession

1. The present Convention is subject to ratification, acceptance, approval or accession by States and by regional economic integration organizations. The instruments of ratification, acceptance, approval or accession shall be deposited with the Secretary-General of the United Nations.

2. Any regional economic integration organization which becomes a Party to this Convention without any of its member States being a Party shall be bound by all the obligations under the Convention. In the case of such organizations, one or more of whose member States is a Party to this Convention, the organization and its member States shall decide on their respective responsibilities for the performance of their obligations under the Convention. In such cases, the organization and the member States shall not be entitled to exercise rights under the Convention concurrently.

3. In their instruments of ratification, acceptance, approval or accession, the regional economic integration organizations shall declare the extent of their competence with respect to the matters governed by the Convention. These organizations shall also inform the Secretary-General of the United Nations of any substantial modification in the extent of their competence.

Article 36
Entry into force

1. The present Convention shall enter into force on the ninetieth day following the date of deposit of the thirty-fifth instrument of ratification, acceptance, approval or accession with the Secretary-General of the United Nations.

2. For each State or regional economic integration organization that ratifies, accepts or approves the Convention or accedes thereto after the deposit of the thirty-fifth instrument of ratification, acceptance, approval or accession, the Convention shall enter into force on the ninetieth day after the

deposit by such State or regional economic integration organization of its instrument of ratification, acceptance, approval or accession.

3. For the purposes of paragraphs 1 and 2, any instrument deposited by a regional economic integration organization shall not be counted as additional to those deposited by States.

Article 37
Authentic texts

The original of the present Convention, of which the Arabic, Chinese, English, French, Russian and Spanish texts are equally authentic, shall be deposited with the Secretary-General of the United Nations.

ANNEX

ARBITRATION

Article 1

Unless the parties to the dispute otherwise agree, the arbitration pursuant to article 33 of the Convention shall take place in accordance with articles 2 to 14 of the present annex.

Article 2

The claimant party shall notify the respondent party that it is referring a dispute to arbitration pursuant to article 33 of the Convention. The notification shall state the subject matter of arbitration and include, in particular, the articles of the Convention, the interpretation or application of which are at issue. If the parties do not agree on the subject matter of the dispute, the arbitral tribunal shall determine the subject matter.

Article 3

1. In disputes between two parties, the arbitral tribunal shall consist of three members. Each of the parties to the dispute shall appoint an arbitrator and the two arbitrators so appointed shall designate by common agreement the third arbitrator, who shall be the Chairman of the tribunal. The latter shall not be a national of one of the parties to the dispute or of any riparian State of the watercourse concerned, nor have his or her usual place of residence in the territory of one of these parties or such riparian State, nor have dealt with the case in any other capacity.

2.   In disputes between more than two parties, parties in the same interest shall appoint one arbitrator jointly by agreement.

3.   Any vacancy shall be filled in the manner prescribed for the initial appointment.

Article 4

1.   If the Chairman of the arbitral tribunal has not been designated within two months of the appointment of the second arbitrator, the President of the International Court of Justice shall, at the request of a party, designate the Chairman within a further two-month period.

2.   If one of the parties to the dispute does not appoint an arbitrator within two months of receipt of the request, the other party may inform the President of the International Court of Justice, who shall make the designation within a further two-month period.

Article 5

The arbitral tribunal shall render its decisions in accordance with the provisions of this Convention and international law.

Article 6

Unless the parties to the dispute otherwise agree, the arbitral tribunal shall determine its own rules of procedure.

Article 7

The arbitral tribunal may, at the request of one of the Parties, recommend essential interim measures of protection.

Article 8

1.   The parties to the dispute shall facilitate the work of the arbitral tribunal and, in particular, using all means at their disposal, shall:

> (a) Provide it with all relevant documents, information and facilities; and

> (b) Enable it, when necessary, to call witnesses or experts and receive their evidence.

2. The parties and the arbitrators are under an obligation to protect the confidentiality of any information they receive in confidence during the proceedings of the arbitral tribunal.

Article 9

Unless the arbitral tribunal determines otherwise because of the particular circumstances of the case, the costs of the tribunal shall be borne by the parties to the dispute in equal shares. The tribunal shall keep a record of all its costs, and shall furnish a final statement thereof to the parties.

Article 10

Any Party that has an interest of a legal nature in the subject matter of the dispute which may be affected by the decision in the case, may intervene in the proceedings with the consent of the tribunal.

Article 11

The tribunal may hear and determine counterclaims arising directly out of the subject matter of the dispute.

Article 12

Decisions both on procedure and substance of the arbitral tribunal shall be taken by a majority vote of its members.

Article 13

If one of the parties to the dispute does not appear before the arbitral tribunal or fails to defend its case, the other party may request the tribunal to continue the proceedings and to make its award. Absence of a party or a failure of a party to defend its case shall not constitute a bar to the proceedings. Before rendering its final decision, the arbitral tribunal must satisfy itself that the claim is well founded in fact and law.

Article 14

1. The tribunal shall render its final decision within five months of the date on which it is fully constituted unless it finds it necessary to extend the time limit for a period which should not exceed five more months.

2. The final decision of the arbitral tribunal shall be confined to the subject matter of the dispute and shall state the reasons on which it is based. It shall contain the names of the members who have participated and the date of the

final decision. Any member of the tribunal may attach a separate or dissenting opinion to the final decision.

3.   The award shall be binding on the parties to the dispute. It shall be without appeal unless the parties to the dispute have agreed in advance to an appellate procedure.

4.   Any controversy which may arise between the parties to the dispute as regards the interpretation or manner of implementation of the final decision may be submitted by either party for decision to the arbitral tribunal which rendered it.

Adopted by the UN General Assembly in resolution 51/229 of 21 May 1997. Text: U.N. Doc. A/51/869

Annex 2

Table A-1   International River Basin Organizations

Int'l River Basin after TFDD*	Basin States	Area	Treaty Basins	Basin States	Organization	Foundation	Member States		Issue Areas	
	No.	000 km²		No.		Year		No.		No.
Amazon	8	5.866,1	Amazon	8	Amazonian Cooperation Council	1978	Bolivia, Brazil, Colombia, Ecuador, Guyana, Peru, Surinam, Venezuela	8	Ecology, Economic Development, Water Quality	3
Amur	4	2.085,9	Bulgan, Halah, Bor Nor, Lake, Kerulen/ Herlen He		Joint Committee on Transboundary Waters	1994	China, Mongolia	2	Ecology, Fishing, Flood Control, Infrastructure, Water Quality, Water Quantity	6
Aral Sea	8	1.231,4	Aral Sea, Amu Darya, Syr Darya	8	Interstate Council for the Aral Sea Basin Crisis with Standing Tashkent-based Executive Committee, Coordinating Commission on Water Resources, Commission of Social and Economic Development and Cooperation in Scientific, Technical, and Ecological Spheres	1993	Kazakhstan, Kyrgyzstan, Tajikistan, Turkmenistan, Uzbekistan; Russia as observer	5	Water Quality, (Water Quantity)	1+
Asi/Orontes	3	37,9	Al Asi, Orontes	3	Joint Technical Committee	1994	Lebanon, Syria	2	Infrastructure, Water Quality	2

Table A-1 (continued)

Int'l River Basin after TFDD*	Basin States	Area	Treaty Basins	Basin States	Organization	Foundation	Member States	No.	Issue Areas	No.
	No.	000 km²		No.		Year		No.		No.
Candelaria	2	12,8	Candelaria, Coatan Achute, Grijalva, Hondo, Schuchiate	2	International Borders and Waters Commission	1987	Guatemala, Mexico	2	Ecology, Water Quality	2+
Coatan Achute	2	2,0								
Grijalva	2	126,8								
Hondo	2	14,6								
Suchiate	2	1,6								
Colorado	2	655,0	Colorado, Rio Grande, Tijuana*, Rio Bravo del Norte*	2	International Boundary and Water Commission	1889/ 1944*	Mexico, USA	2	Border Issues, Fishing, Hydropower, Irrigation, Navigation, Water Quality, Water Quantity	7+
Rio Bravo/ Rio Grande	2	656,1								
Tijuana	2	4,4								
Columbia	2	668,4	Columbia, Fraser, Mississippi, Nelson-Saskatchewan, Skagit, St. Croix, St. John, St. Lawrence	2	International Joint Commission	1909	Canada, USA	2	Ecology, Flood Control, Hydropower, Infrastructure, Irrigation, Navigation, Water Quality, Water Quantity	8+
Fraser	2	239,7								
Mississippi	2	3.226,3								
Nelson-Saskatchewan	2	1.109,4								
St. Croix	2	4,6								
St. John	2	55,1								
St. Lawrence	2	1.055,2								

Table A-1 (continued)

Int'l River Basin after TFDD*	Basin States	Area	Treaty Basins	Basin States	Organization	Foundation	Member States		Issue Areas	
	No.	000 km²		No.		Year		No.		No.
Danube	17	790,1	Danube	12	Danube Commission	1948	Austria (since 1960), Bulgaria, Czechoslovakia, Hungary, Romania, Ukraine, USSR, Yugoslavia	8	(Hydropower), Navigation	1
			Danube	17	International Commission for the Protection of the Danube River	1994	Austria, Bulgaria, Croatia, Czech Republic*, Germany, Hungary, Moldova, Romania, Serbia and Montenegro*, Slovakia, Slovenia*, Ukraine and EU* (1994-)	12	Ecology, Flood Control, Hazard Prevention, Hydropower, Water Quality, Water Quantity	6+

333

Int'l River Basin after TFDD*	Ba-sin Sta-tes	Area	Treaty Basins	Ba-sin Sta-tes	Organization	Foun-dation	Member States		Issue Areas	
	No.	000 km²		No.		Year		No.		No.
Danube	17	790,1	Sava		International Sava River Basin Commission	2002	Bosnia and Herzegovina, Croatia, Slovenia, Yugoslavia	4	Hazard Prevention, Navigation	2+
			Salzach, Inn	2	Austrian-Bavarian Power Plant Company (Österreich-Bayrische Kraftwerke AG)	1950	Austria, Germany	2	Hydropower	1
			Danube		Multiple bilateral commissions					
Daugava	4	58,7	Zapadnaya, Dvina, Daugava	4	Ad hoc International Zapadnaya Dvina/Daugava River Commission	1997	Belarus, Latvia, Russia	3	Water Quality	1
Douro/Duero	2	96,2	Douro	2	Joint Commission	1927/ 1951	Portugal, Spain	2	Hydropower	1
Guadiana	2	65,7	Agueda, Aravil, Barranco de Raia, Caya, Chanza, Cuncos, Erjas, Guadiana, Limia, Mino, Perna Seca, Ponsul, Sever,	2	Spanish-Portuguese International Border Commission	1968	Portugal, Spain	2	Hydropower, (Irrigation), Water Quantity	2+

Table A-1 (continued)

Int'l River Basin after TFDD*	Ba-sin Sta-tes	Area	Treaty Basins	Ba-sin Sta-tes	Organization	Foun-dation	Member States		Issue Areas	
	No.	000 km²		No.		Year		No.		No.
Guadiana	2	65,7	Tajo, Troncoso/ Trancoso							
Lima	2	2,3	Douro/Duero, Guadiana, Lima, Minho, Tagus/Tejo	2	Joint Commission for the Protection and Sustainable Use of Portuguese-Spanish Hydrological Basins	1998	Portugal, Spain	2	Ecology, Hydrological Monitoring, Water Quality	2+
Mino/Minho	2	16,6								
Tagus/Tejo	2	69,9								
Elbe	4	139,5	Elbe	4	International Commission for the Protection of the Elbe	1990	Czech Republic, Germany, EU; Austria as observer	2	Ecology, Water Quality, (Irrigation)	2+
			Elbe, Eder		German-Czech Commission on Boundary Waters	1974/ 1995	Czech Republic, Germany	2	Flood Control, Hazard Prevention, Hydrological Monitoring, Infrastructure, Melioration, Water Quality, Water Quantity	7+
Fenney	2	2,8	Frontier waters	2	Joint Committee of Experts	1985/ 1986	Bangladesh, India	2	Water Quantity	1
Karnaphuli	3	12,5								

Int'l River Basin after TFDD*	Ba-sin Sta-tes	Area	Treaty Basins	Ba-sin Sta-tes	Organization	Foun-dation	Member States		Issue Areas	
	No.	000 km²		No.		Year		No.		No.
Gambia	3	69,9	Gambia	3	Gambia River Basin Development Organization	1978	Gambia, Guinea, Senegal	3	Economic Development	1
Ganges-Brahmaputra-Meghna	6	1634,9	Kosi		Coordination Committee for the Kosi Project	1954	India, Nepal	2	Erosion Control, Flood Control, Hydropower, Irrigation	4
			Ganges-Brahmaputra		Indo-Bangladesh Joint River Commission	1972	Bangladesh, India	2	Flood Control, Irrigation	2+
			Ganges		Joint Committee (Farakka agreements)	1977/ 1996	Bangladesh, India	2	River Regulation, Water Quantity	2
			Mahakali		Mahakali River Commission	1996	India, Nepal	2	Flood Control, Hydropower, Irrigation, Water Quantity	4
Garonne	3	55,8	Lake Lanoux		Joint Commission, Joint Supervisory Committee	1958/ 1970	France, Spain	2	Hydropower, Water Quantity	2
			Garonne	3	Commission of Mixed Technical Experts	1963	France, Spain	2	Hydropower, Water Quantity	2
Helmand	3	353,5	Helmand	3	Helmand River Delta Commission	1950	Afghanistan, Iran	2	Water Quantity	1

Table A-1 (continued)

Int'l River Basin after TFDD*	Basin States	Area	Treaty Basins	Basin States	Organization	Foundation	Member States		Issue Areas	
	No.	000 km²		No.		Year		No.		No.
Incomati	3	46,7	Incomati and shared waters	3	Tripartite Permanent Technical Committee	1983	Mozambique, South Africa, Swaziland	3	River Regulation, Water Quantity	2+
			Komati, Maputo		Joint Water Commission	1992	South Africa, Swaziland	2	River Regulation, Water Quantity	3+
			Komati		Komati Basin Water Authority	1992	South Africa, Swaziland	2	Hydropower, Water Quantity	2
Indus	5	1.138,8	Indus	5	Permanent Indus Commission	1960	India, Pakistan, World Bank	2	Flood Control, Hydropower, Irrigation, Water Quantity	4+
Jordan	5	42,8	Yarmouk	3	Joint Syro-Jordanian Commission	1953/ 1987	Jordan, Syria	2	Hydropower, River Regulation, Water Quantity	3
			Jordan, Yarmouk, Araba/Arava groundwater	5	Joint Water Committee	1994	Israel, Jordan	2	Infrastructure, River Regulation, Water Quality, Water Quantity	3

Table A-1 (continued)

Int'l River Basin after TFDD*	Ba-sin Sta-tes	Area	Treaty Basins	Ba-sin Sta-tes	Organization	Foun-dation	Member States		Issue Areas	
	No.	000 km²		No.		Year		No.		No.
Jordan	5	42,8	(Jordan), West Bank Aquifer, Coastal Aquifer	(5) 2	Joint Water Committee	1995	Israel, Palestine Liberation Organization	2	Infrastructure, Water Quality, Water Quantity	3
La Plata	5	2954,5	Uruguay	2	Salto Grande Joint Technical Commission (CTM)	1946	Argentina, Uruguay	2	Fishing, Hydro-power, Irrigation, Navigation, Water Quality	5
			La Plata	5	Intergovernmental Coordinating Committee of the River Plate Basin Countries (CIC)	1967/ 1969	Argentina, Bolivia, Brazil, Paraguay, Uruguay	5	Ecology, Economic Development, Navigation, River Regulation	4
			Uruguay	2	Uruguay River Management Commission (CARU)	1975	Argentina, Uruguay	2	Ecology, Fishing, Navigation	3+
			Uruguay, Pepiri-Guazu	2	Coordinating Commission	1980/ 1983	Argentina, Brazil	2	Ecology, Hydropower, Infrastructure, Navigation	4+
			Parana	3	Joint Argentine-Paraguayan Technical Commission	1958	Argentina, Paraguay	2	Hydropower, Navigation	2+

Table A-1 (continued)

Int'l River Basin after TFDD*	Basin States	Area	Treaty Basins	Basin States	Organization	Foundation	Member States		Issue Areas	
	No.	000 km²		No.		Year		No.		No.
La Plata	5	2954,5	Parana	3	Brazilian-Paraguayan Joint Technical Commission, ITAIPU as binational electricity entity	1967/ 1973/ 1979	Brazil, Paraguay, Argentina* (*1979-)	(2) 3	Hydropower, Water Quantity	2
			Cuareim	2	Mixed Commission	1991	Brazil, Uruguay	2	Ecology, Economic Development, Erosion Control, Flood Control, Hydropower, Irrigation, Melioration, Navigation	8+
			Bermejo, Grande de Tarija	2	Binational Commission	1995	Argentina, Bolivia	2	Ecology, Economic Development, Flood Control, Hydropower, Joint Management, Water Quality	6+
			Pilcomayo	3	Tri-national Commission for the Development of the Riverbed of the Rio Pilcomayo	1995	Argentina, Bolivia, Paraguay	3	Joint Management	1

Int'l River Basin after TFDD*	Basin States	Area	Treaty Basins	Basin States	Organization	Foundation	Member States		Issue Areas	
	No.	000 km²		No.		Year		No.		No.
Lagoon Mirim	2	55,0	Lagoon Mirim	2	Joint Commission for the Development of the Mirim Lagoon	1963/ 1977	Brazil, Uruguay	2	Economic Development, Navigation	2+
Lake Chad	9	2.388,7	Lake Chad	9	Lake Chad Basin Commission	1964	Cameroon, Chad, Niger, Nigeria	4	Ecology, Navigation, Water Quality, Water Quantity	4+
Lake Titicaca	3	111,8	Lake Titicaca	2	Joint Peruvian-Bolivian Commission	1955/ 1957	Bolivia, Peru	2	Fishing, Hydro-power, Irrigation, Navigation	4
			Titicaca, Desaguadero, Sal ar de Coipasa, Poopo	2	Binational Authority	1993	Bolivia, Peru	2	Joint Management	1
Limpopo	4	414,8	Limpopo	4	Tripartite Permanent Technical Committee	1983	Mozambique, South Africa, Swaziland	3	Water Quantity	1

Table A-1 (continued)

Int'l River Basin after TFDD*	Ba-sin Sta-tes	Area	Treaty Basins	Ba-sin Sta-tes	Organization	Foun-dation	Member States		Issue Areas	
	No.	000 km²		No.		Year		No.		No.
Mekong	6	787,8	Mekong	6	Committee for Coordination of Investigations of the Lower Mekong Basin/Interim Committee for Coordination of Investigations of the Lower Mekong Basin/Mekong River Commission	1957/ 1978/ 1995	Cambodia, Laos, Thailand, Vietnam; China and Myanmar as observers	(3) 4	Fishing, Flood Control, Hydropower, Irrigation, Navigation, Recreation/Touri sm, Timber Floating, Water Quantity	8
Narva	4	53,0	Narva, Lake Peipsi/ Chudskoe	2	Joint Estonian-Russian Commission on the Protection and Rational Use of Transboundary Waters	1997	Estonia, Russia	2	Water Quality	1+
Neman	5	90,3	Neman, Daugava	2	Permanent Working Group for the Protection of Transboundary Watercourses and International Lakes	1995	Belarus, Lithuania	2	Water Quality	1+
Nestos	2	10,2	Nestos and transboundary waters	2	Greek-Bulgarian Joint Programming and Follow-up Committee	1994/ 1995	Bulgaria, Greece	2	Water Quantity	1+

Table A-1 (continued)

Int'l River Basin after TFDD*	Basin States	Area	Treaty Basins	Basin States	Organization	Foundation	Member States		Issue Areas	
	No.	000 km²		No.		Year		No.		No.
Niger	11	2113,2	Niger	11	Niger River Basin Commission/Niger Basin Authority	1964/ 1980/ 1987	Benin, Burkina Faso, Cameroon, Chad, Cote d'Ivoire, Guinea, Mali, Niger, Nigeria	9	Ecology, Economic Development, Erosion Control, Fishing, Flood Control, Infrastructure, Irrigation, Melioration, Water Quality	9+
			Niger	11	Joint Technical Committee	1988	Mali, Niger	2	Joint Management	1
			Niger	11	Nigeria-Niger Joint Commission for Cooperation – A joint hydropower institution	1990/ 1999	Niger, Benin	2	Hydropower	1+
Nile	10	3038,1	Nile	10	Joint Permanent Technical Committee	1959	Egypt, Sudan	2	Water Quantity	1
			Nile	10	Nile Basin Initiative	1999	Burundi, DR Congo, Egypt, Ethiopia, Kenya, Rwanda, Sudan, Tanzania, Uganda; Eritrea as observer	9	Ecology, Econ. Development, Erosion Control, Flood Control, Hydropower, Infrastructure, Irrigation, River Regulation	10+

Table A-1 (continued)

Int'l River Basin after TFDD*	Ba-sin Sta-tes	Area	Treaty Basins	Ba-sin Sta-tes	Organization	Foun-dation	Member States		Issue Areas	
	No.	000 km²		No.		Year		No.		No.
Nile	10	3038,1	Kagera	4	Organization for the Management and Development of the Kagera River Basin	1977/ 1981	Burundi, Rwanda, Tanzania, Uganda	4	Multi-purpose	12+
			Lake Victoria	5	Regional Policy and Steering Committee	1994	Kenya, Tanzania, Uganda	3	Ecology, Fishing, Hydrological Monitoring, Joint Management, Water Quality	5
Ob	4	2.950,8	Ishim, Irtysh, Pu Lun T'o, Tobol, Ural	2	Joint Commission	1992	Kazakhstan, Russia	2	Joint Management	1+
Oder/Odra	4	122,4	Oder	4	Permanent Commission on Boundary Waters	1992	Germany, Poland	2	Ecology, Flood Control, Hydrol. Monitoring, Infrastructure, Melioration, Navigation, Water Quality, Water Quantity	8

Table A-1 (continued)

Int'l River Basin after TFDD*	Ba-sin Sta-tes	Area	Treaty Basins	Ba-sin Sta-tes	Organization	Foun-dation	Member States		Issue Areas	
	No.	000 km²		No.		Year		No.		No.
Oder/Odra	4	122,4	Oder	4	International Commission for the Protection of the Oder River from Pollution	1996	Czech Republic, Germany, Poland, EU	3	Ecology, Water Quality	2+
Okavango	4	706,9	Okavango		Okavango River Basin Water Commission	1994	Angola, Botswana, Namibia	3	Water Quantity	1
Orange	4	945,5	Orange, Senqu	4	Joint Permanent Technical Commission/Lesotho Highlands Water Commission, Lesotho Highlands Development Authority, Trans-Caledon Tunnel Authority	1986/ 1999	Lesotho, South Africa	2	Economic Development, Fishing, Hydropower, Infrastructure, Irrigation, Recreation/Touri sm, Water Quantity	7+
			Frontier waters		Permanent Water Commission	1992	Namibia, South Africa	2	Ecology, Erosion Control, Water Quality, Water Quantity	3+
Po	4	87,1	Transboundary Waters	2	Mixed Commission for the Protection of Italo-Swiss Waters against Pollution (Italy, Switzerland)	1972	Italy, Switzerland	2	Water Quality	1

Table A-1 (continued)

Int'l River Basin after TFDD*	Ba-sin Sta-tes	Area	Treaty Basins	Ba-sin Sta-tes	Organization	Foun-dation	Member States		Issue Areas	
	No.	000 km²		No.		Year		No.		No.
Po	4	87,1	Transboundary Waters	2	*Various bilateral water projects between Italy and Switzerland and France and Italy*					
Rhine	9	172,9	Rhine	9	Central Commission for the Navigation on the Rhine	1815/ 1868	Belgium, France, Germany, the Netherlands, Switzerland	5	Navigation	1+
			Rhine	9	International Commission for the Protection of the Rhine	1963/ 1999	France, Germany, Luxembourg, the Netherlands, Switzerland, EU	5	Ecology, Flood Control, Hazard Prevention, Water Quality	4+
			Lake Constance	4	International for Commission for the Protection of Lake Constance	1960	Austria, Baden-Württemberg, Bavaria, Liechtenstein, Switzerland	4	Ecology, Water Quality	2+

Table A-1 (continued)

Int'l River Basin after TFDD*	Ba-sin Sta-tes	Area	Treaty Basins	Ba-sin Sta-tes	Organization	Foun-dation	Member States		Issue Areas	
	No.	000 km²		No.		Year		No.		No.
Rhine	9	172,9	Meuse	5	International Commission for the Protection of the Meuse against Pollution/International Commission for the Meuse	1994/ 2002	Brussels Capital R., France, Flemish R., the Netherlands, Walloon R. Germany*, Luxembourg* (*2002-)	5	Ecology, Flood Control, Water Quality	3
			Moselle	3	International Commission for the Protection of the Moselle	1961	France, Germany, Luxembourg	3	Water Quality	1
			Saar	3	International Commission for the Protection of the Saar	1961	France, Germany	2	Water Quality	1
			Alpine Rhine	3	International Commission for the Regulation of the Rhine/Joint Rhine Commission	1892/ 1936	Switzerland, Austria	2	Flood Control, River Regulation	2
			Rhine		*Various other commissions*					
Rhone	3	100,2	Lake Geneva	2	International Commission for the Protection of the Waters of Lake Geneva against Pollution	1962	France, Switzerland	2	Water Quality	1
			Emosson	2	Permanent Commission	1967	France, Switzerland	2	Hydropower	1

Table A-1 (continued)

Int'l River Basin after TFDD*	Basin States	Area	Treaty Basins	Basin States	Organization	Foundation	Member States		Issue Areas	
	No.	000 km²		No.		Year		No.		No.
Rhone	3	100,2	Lake Leman	2	Lake Leman Council	1987	France, Switzerland	2	Ecology, Economic Development, Hydropower, Infrastructure, Tourism	5+
Schelde	3	17,1	Scheldt	3	International Commission for the Protection of the Scheldt against Pollution	1994	Brussels R., France, Flemish R., Netherlands, Walloon R.	3	Water Quality	1+
			Escaut/Scheldt, Espierre, Haine, Lys	3	Tripartite Standing Committee on Polluted Waters	1950	Belgium, France, Luxembourg	3	Water Quality	1
Senegal	4	436,0	Senegal	4	Organization for the Management of the Senegal River	1972/ 1978/ 1982	Mali, Mauritania, Senegal, Guinea as observer	3	Ecology, Economic Development, Hydropower, Irrigation, Navigation, River Regulation, Water Quality, Water Quantity	8

Table A-1 (continued)

Int'l River Basin after TFDD*	Basin States No.	Area 000 km²	Treaty Basins	Basin States No.	Organization	Foundation Year	Member States	No.	Issue Areas	No.
Struma	4	15,0	Axios, Dojran, Prespa	4	Permanent Yugoslav-Greek Hydro-Economic Commission	1959	Greece, Yugoslavia	2	Economic Development	1
Tana	2	15,6	Frontier waters, incl. Rajajoki, Ski-etshamjokka, Enare, Tana	2	Finnish-Norwegian Boundary Waters Commission	1980	Finland, Norway	2	'Detrimental effects'	
Tigris-Euphrates-Shatt al Arab	6	789	Tigris-Euphrates-Shatt al Arab		Joint Technical Committee	1989	Iraq, Syria	2	Water Quantity	1
			Tib, Cham, Alvend, Gangir, Kanjan, Duverij, Qurahtu, Bnava Suta		Permanent Technical Commission	1975	Iran, Iraq	2	Border Issues, Water Quantity	2
			Shatt al'Arab		Mixed Iranian-Iraqi Commission	1975	Iran, Iraq	2	Border Issues	1
Torne	3	37,3	Konkama, Muonio, Tome	3	Finnish-Swedish Frontier River Commission	1971	Finland, Sweden	2	Ecology, Fishing, Infrastructure, River Regulation, Timber Floating, Water Quality	6

Table A-1 (continued)

Int'l River Basin after TFDD*	Basin States	Area	Treaty Basins	Basin States	Organization	Foundation	Member States		Issue Areas	
	No.	000 km²		No.		Year		No.		No.
Umbeluzi	3	10,9	Umbeluzi	3	Tripartite Permanent Technical Committee	1983	Mozambique, South Africa, Swaziland	3	River Regulation, Water Quantity	2+
Zambezi	9	1.385,3	Zambezi	9	Zambezi River Authority	1987	Zambia-Zimbabwe	2	Hydropower	1

*TFDD: Transboundary Freshwater Dispute Database, see http://ocid.nacse.org/cgi-bin/qml

+: The number refers to the minimum number of issue areas mentioned in the agreement.

Source: Own compilation

Table A-2   Analysis of Selected International River Basin Organizations

Name	Organization for the Development of the Senegal River (OMVS)
Foundation	1972/1978/1982
Member states	Mali, Mauritania, Senegal, Guinea as observer
Geographical scope	Senegal river in the territory of Mali, Mauritania and Senegal.
Issue areas	Ecology, Economic Development, Hydropower, Irrigation, Navigation, River Regulation, Water Quality, Water Quantity
Mandate	To promote and coordinate the studies and construction works of the development of the Senegal River Basin on the territory of the member States.
Treaty organs	Conference of the Heads of State; Council of Ministers; High Commission; Permanent Water Commission.
Additional institutions	Two consultative bodies; three national offices; Inter-State Commission supervising joint infrastructure; Interstate public companies SOGED and SOGEM.
Staffing of the secretariat	5 executives, about 15 technical staff, 30 supporting staff. High Commissioner, Secretary-General, 4 Directors, 3 Chiefs of common services.
Financing	Regular budget: member states on equal basis. Studies: donors. Investments: financial institutions. Cost-sharing in proportion of benefits: MAU 22.6%, SEN 42.1%, MALI 35.3%.
Decision-making	Decisions are taken by unanimity. The quorum equals full membership. Decisions by the Conference and the Council are binding to the member states.
Legal status and powers of the organization	Full legal personality. Power to enter into contracts; acquire and dispose of property; receive grants and other financial gifts; subscribe to bonds; apply for technical assistance; go to court. Common ownership of infrastructure.
Functions of the organization	To implement the Convention concerning the Statute of the Senegal River; to promote and coordinate the studies and construction works for the development of the Senegal River Basin; to carry out all other economic and technical tasks entrusted by the member states.
Functions of the secretariat	Represents OMVS between Council sessions and vis-à-vis donors. Manages data bases; prepares work program and budget; undertakes studies; submits proposed projects to Council; seeks financing.
Definition of property rights	Permanent Water Commission defines the principles and modalities of water allocation among the countries and the water using sector (industry, agriculture, transport).
Prior notification	Yes
Monitoring and enforcement	High Commission reports regularly on implementation. High Commissioner may be empowered by one or several states to carry out checks and controls on the development works achieved.
Dispute settlement	Disputes to be settled through conciliation and mediation, otherwise submission for arbitration by the Organization of African Unity. International Court of Justice as last appeal tribunal.
Agreements	Convention concerning the Statute of the Senegal River, March 11, 1972/Convention establishing the Organization for the Development of the Senegal River (OMVS), March 11, 1972/Convention on the Legal Status of the Common Works, Dec. 21, 1978/Convention on the Financing of the Common Works, May 12, 1982.
Other sources	Godana (1985), Burchi and Spreij (2003).

Table A-2 (continued)

Name	International Commission for the Protection of the Rhine (ICPR)
Foundation	1963/1999
Member states	France, Germany, Luxembourg, the Netherlands, Switzerland, EU
Geographical scope	Rhine between Lake Constance and North Sea (main stream); groundwater and ecosystems interacting with the Rhine; Rhine catchment insofar as it is important for pollution and flood control.
Issue areas	Ecology, Flood Control, Hazard Prevention, Water Quality
Mandate	Sustainable development of the Rhine ecosystem; improvement of water and sediment quality; flood control; help restore the North Sea.
Treaty organs	Commission (represented by Chairman); Coordination Group*; Secretariat; Working Groups* (*according to rules of procedure).
Additional institutions	Conference of Rhine Ministers (meets irregularly); partly national coordination units.
Staffing of the secretariat	1963-1987: 5 staff; 1987-2001: 10 staff ; since 2001: 13 staff.
Financing	Member states bear costs of representation and of studies and actions within their territory. Contributions to operational budget: NL: 32.5%, F: 32.5%, D: 32.5%, CH: 12%, L: 2.5%, EU: 2.5%.
Decision-making	Decisions are taken unanimously. Quorum: 4 member state delegations. Decisions are recommendations to member states. Outside plenary sessions, decisions may be taken in writing.
Legal status and powers of the organization	Yes. Enjoys the legal capacity conferred on legal persons in the member states. German law governs labor legislation.
Functions of the organization	Prepare international measuring program; make proposals for measures; coordinate warning and alert plans; evaluate effectiveness of decided actions; any other tasks entrusted to it.
Functions of the secretariat	Carries out the tasks entrusted to it by the Commission; invites to meetings on behalf of the Chairman; takes minutes; drafts annual budget.
Definition of property rights	Framework agreement. 1976-1987: definition of binding thresholds proofed difficult. Since 1987: political targets, member state define appropriate measures.
Prior notification	No provisions. (Requirement to notify in case of accidents or extreme events.)
Monitoring and enforcement	Member states report regularly to Commission on results of measures, and possible problems. Commission may decide to assist in the implementation. Commission evaluates effectiveness of its decisions, prepares annual activity report and informs the public about its results.
Dispute settlement	Disputes to be settled through negotiation or other forms of dispute settlement; otherwise submission to arbitration according to Annex.
Agreements	Agreement on the International Commission for the Protection of the Rhine against Pollution, Apr. 29, 1963/Convention on the Protection of the Rhine, Apr. 12, 1999.
Other sources	Holtrup (1999); IKSR (2001); Wulwer-Schulte-Leidig (2003); Burchi and Spreij (2003).

Table A-2 (continued)

Name	International Commission for the Protection of the Elbe (ICPE)
Foundation	1990
Member states	Czech Republic, Germany, EU; Austria and Poland as observers
Geographical scope	The Elbe as its drainage area/The territories in which the Treaty establishing the EEC is applicable and under the terms of that Treaty, on the one hand, and in the territory of the Czech and Slovak Federal Republic, on the other hand.
Issue areas	Ecology, Water Quality (Irrigation)
Mandate	To cooperate in the International Commission for the Protection of the Elbe, to prevent the pollution of the Elbe and its drainage area.
Treaty organs	Commission (each delegation 5 commissioners); Working Parties for specific tasks; Secretariat.
Additional institutions	Not known.
Staffing of the secretariat	8
Financing	Each party bears costs of representation and investigations in its territory. Costs of the secretariat are divided as follows: Germany: 65%, Czech Republic: 32.5%; EU: 2.5%.
Decision-making	Decisions shall be adopted unanimously. Rules of procedure may provide for a written procedure. The order of the agenda shall be decided by majority decision.
Legal status and powers of the organization	Not specified.
Functions of the organization	Determine work programs for the reduction of pollution. Identify point and non-point sources; propose emission limits and quality objectives; coordinate measurement programs; propose a warning system; discuss planned types of water utilization, prepare regulations, etc.
Functions of the secretariat	Prepare, implement and support the Commission's work.
Definition of property rights	Prepare emission limits and water quality standards. Discuss planned, and upon request, existing water utilization.
Prior notification	Discuss planned water utilization.
Monitoring and enforcement	Commission provides the parties with an activity report at least every two years and, as required, with further reports setting out the results of investigations and their assessments.
Dispute settlement	No provisions.
Agreements	Convention between the Federal Republic of Germany and the Czech and Slovak Federal Republic and the European Economic Community on the International Commission for the Protection of the Elbe, Oct. 8, 1990.
Other sources	N/A

Table A-2 (continued)

Name	**Mekong River Commission (MRC)**
Foundation	1957/1975/1978/1995
Member states	Cambodia, Laos, Thailand, Vietnam; China and Myanmar as observers
Geographical scope	Water and related resources in the Lower Mekong River Basin.
Issue areas	Fishing, Flood Control, Hydropower, Irrigation, Navigation, Recreation/Tourism, Timber Floating, Water Quantity
Mandate	To cooperate in the sustainable development, utilization, conservation and management of the Mekong River Basin water and related resources.
Treaty organs	Council; Joint Committee; Secretariat.
Additional institutions	National Mekong Committees and National Mekong Committee Secretariats.
Staffing of the secretariat	Almost 50 staff (administrative and technical including international staff on secondment by donors). Secretariat has 7 divisions.
Financing	Equal contribution from member states plus donor contributions, mainly for projects; annual budget secretariat: US$ 10 million.
Decision-making	Decisions by unanimous vote except as provided by Rules of Procedure; Council members are empowered to make decisions on behalf of their government.
Legal status and powers of the organization	Enjoys status of an international body. Power to enter into agreements with donors and the international community.
Functions of the organization	Implementation of the objectives of the agreement, in particular development of rules for water utilization and inter-basin diversion and of a basin development plan and joint projects/programs to be implemented.
Functions of the secretariat	Carries out decisions and tasks by Council; assists Joint Committee in implementation of projects; maintains databases and information; etc.
Definition of property rights	Framework agreement: Joint Committee to prepare rules for water utilization and inter-basin diversions for wet and dry seasons.
Prior notification	Yes. Differentiation between notification and consultation requirements.
Monitoring and enforcement	No provisions.
Dispute settlement	Commission shall seek to resolve the issue, otherwise reference to the Governments; Governments may by mutual agreement seek mediation.
Agreements	Agreement on the cooperation for the sustainable development of the Mekong River Basin.
Other sources	Burchi and Spreij (2003).

Table A-2 (continued)

Name	Nile Basin Initiative (NBI)
Foundation	1999
Member states	Burundi, DR Congo, Egypt, Ethiopia, Kenya, Rwanda, Sudan, Tanzania, Uganda; Eritrea as observer
Geographical scope	Nile Basin water resources.
Issue areas	Ecology, Economic Development, Erosion Control, Flood Control, Hydropower, Infrastructure, Irrigation, River Regulation
Mandate	To achieve sustainable socio-economic development through the equitable utilization of, and benefit from, the common Nile Basin water resources.
Treaty organs	Transitional set up consisting of Council of Ministers of Water Affairs in the Nile Basin States (Nile-COM); Technical Advisory Committee (Nile-TAC); NBI Secretariat (Nile-SEC).
Additional institutions	National NBI offices. Eastern Nile Subsidiary Action Program Team. Eastern Nile Technical Regional Office. Nile Equatorial Lakes Technical Advisory Committee, etc.
Staffing of the secretariat	About 10 core staff (incl. office support) plus project related staff (as of 2003).
Financing	Regular budget: member states on equal basis. Studies and projects: donors.
Decision-making	Nile-TAC takes decisions by consensus. Quorum: 2/3 of member states. Nile-COM: no formal Rules of Procedure, decision by consensus.
Legal status and powers of the organization	On Feb. 14, 2002, Nile-COM agreed to invest NBI, on a transitional basis, with legal personality in all member states. On Nov. 6, 2002, a Headquarter Agreement was signed with Uganda.
Functions of the organization	Nile-COM prepares policy guidance for cooperation and the Nile Basin Strategic Action Program. Nile-TAC prepares and reviews Shared Visions projects; coordinates activities and other Nile projects; provides support and advice to Nile-COM; heads the national NBI office; etc.
Functions of the secretariat	Coordination of the NBI process; logistical support; secretariat services; financial management; communications and PR; overall responsibility for delivery of Shared Vision projects.
Definition of property rights	No, given the transitional character.
Prior notification	No.
Monitoring and enforcement	No formal provision. Nile-SEC submits annual report.
Dispute settlement	No provisions.
Agreements	Agreed Minutes of the Extra-ordinary Meeting of the Nile Basin Council of Ministers and Policy Guidelines for a Nile River Basin Strategic Action Program, Feb. 22, 1999 (copy on file with author).
Other sources	http://www.nilebasin.org; Burchi and Spreij (2003).

Table A-2 (continued)

Name	International Boundary and Water Commission United States and Mexico (IBWC)
Foundation	1889/1944
Member states	Mexico, USA
Geographical scope	Border ('limitrophe') parts of the Rio Grande/Rio Bravo and Colorado Rivers, land boundary between the member states and works located upon the boundary. Each member state retains jurisdiction upon works within its territory.
Issue areas	Border Issues, Fishing, Hydropower, Irrigation, Navigation, Water Quality, Water Quantity
Mandate	Studies, plans for works, construction, operation, etc. (see functions).
Treaty organs	Commission consists of a US and a Mexican Section, each headed by an Engineer Commissioner.
Additional institutions	Not known.
Staffing of the secretariat	Minimum: 1 commissioner, 2 principal engineers, 1 legal advisor, 1 secretary. US section consists of engineering, operations and administration department.
Financing	Each government bears its expenses. Joint expenses shall be born equally by the two governments, unless agreed otherwise. Project costs are shared in proportion of benefits.
Decision-making	Decisions are taken in the form of minutes. These are binding on member states, unless a member state objects within 30 days.
Legal status and powers of the organization	Status of an international body (consisting of two sections). Commissioners and staff enjoy certain privileges and immunities. Works and equipment is exempt from custom duties.
Functions of the organization	To initiate investigations and develop plans for works; to construct, operate and maintain agreed works; to regulate and exercise other rights and obligations assumed by the member states; to furnish the information requested by the two governments; to settle differences concerning the Treaty.
Functions of the secretariat	Not defined in the treaty.
Definition of property rights	Yes. Detailed provisions for allocation of Rio Grande/Rio Bravo and Colorado Rivers. Commission to prepare recommendations for equitable distribution of Tijuana River.
Prior notification	No.
Monitoring and enforcement	IBWC submits an annual report on its activities to the member states.
Dispute settlement	IBWC shall settle differences that may arise. If either Government disapproves a decision of the Commission, the two Governments seek agreement through diplomatic channels.
Agreements	Boundary Convention, March 1, 1899/Treaty relating to the utilization of the waters of the Colorado and Tijuana Rivers and of the Rio Grande, Feb. 3, 1944.
Other sources	Burchi and Spreij (2003).

Table A-2 (continued)

Name	International Joint Commission United States and Canada (IJC)
Foundation	1909
Member states	Canada, USA
Geographical scope	The lakes, rivers and connecting waterways (or portions thereof) along which the boundary between the US and Canada passes or the waters flowing across the boundary. Excluded are tributaries flowing into and waters flowing from these waters.
Issue areas	Ecology, Flood Control, Hydropower, Infrastructure, Irrigation, Navigation, Water Quality, Water Quantity
Mandate	Provides the principles and mechanisms to help prevent and resolve disputes, primarily those concerning water quality along the boundary between the two countries.
Treaty organs	Each country appoints three commissioners; US and Canada sections of the commission, each with a small secretariat; Headquarter offices in Ottawa, Ontario and Washington DC.
Additional institutions	Boards with equal representation. IJC is supported by task forces. Great Lakes Commission (8 US States plus Ontario and Quebec as associated members).
Staffing of the secretariat	30 administrators and specialists. 2 full-time Co-Chairmen. Control Board: 10 members (UNDP).
Financing	Each member state bears the costs of its commissioners and secretariat. Member states contribute on an equal basis to all reasonable and necessary joint expenses of the IJC.
Decision-making	Decisions may be taken by majority (consensus as decision-making goal). Quorum: 4 commissioners.
Legal status and powers of the organization	No provisions. (IJC has the power to employ engineers and clerical assistants). Power to administer oaths to witnesses and to take evidence on oath.
Functions of the organization	Issues orders of approval for the use, obstruction or diversions of waters; investigates specific issue when requested and makes recommendations; decides on differences jointly referred to by the member states. Overseas the implementation of the Great Lakes Water Quality (1978) and Air Quality Agreement (1991).
Functions of the secretariat	Not defined in the treaty.
Definition of property rights	Commission as regulator: issues orders of approval in response to applications for the use, obstruction or diversion of boundary and or transboundary waters.
Prior notification	Yes.
Monitoring and enforcement	No provisions.
Dispute settlement	Matters of difference are referred to IJC for examination and report, or binding decision if both Governments consent (not yet used). If IJC is evenly divided, Governments may refer the matter to an umpire for decision.
Agreements	Treaty relating to boundary waters and questions arising between the United States and Canada, Jan. 11, 1909.
Other sources	IJC; Burchi and Spreij (2003).

Table A-2 (continued)

Name	Permanent Indus Commission (PIC)
Foundation	1960
Member states	India, Pakistan, World Bank
Geographical scope	Waters of the Indus Basin, including tributaries and connecting lakes.
Issue areas	Flood Control, Hydropower, Irrigation, Water Quantity
Mandate	The treaty apportions the three eastern and three western rivers of the Indus basin to the two parties.
Treaty organs	Commission consisting of one Commissioner per party meeting at least once per year and when requested by one Commissioner.
Additional institutions	Not known.
Staffing of the secretariat	Not applicable.
Financing	Each party bears the costs of its Commissioner and ordinary staff. Indus Basin Development Fund (1960/1964), Development fund for Tarbela Dam (1968). Apparently not active any more.
Decision-making	Not specified
Legal status and powers of the organization	Commissioners enjoy UN equivalent privileges and immunities.
Functions of the organization	Commissioners represent the parties in matters arising from the treaty and promote cooperation. Functions: to exchange information and data provided for in the treaty; to study and report on problems; to carry out inspections; to settle differences.
Functions of the secretariat	Not applicable
Definition of property rights	Yes. Allocation of the tributaries of the Indus River between the two parties.
Prior notification	Yes
Monitoring and enforcement	Every five years, the Commission undertakes a tour inspection. The same is done promptly on request of either Commissioner. Each year the Commission submits a report to the Parties.
Dispute settlement	Questions are referred to the Commission. If Commission does not reach agreement, either reference to a Neutral Expert (for matters specified in the treaty) or to a court of arbitration.
Agreements	Indus waters treaty 1960 between the government of India, the government of Pakistan and the International Bank for Reconstruction and Development, Sep. 19, 1960.
Other sources	Burchi and Spreij (2003).

Table A-2 (continued)

Name	Joint Water Committee Israel and Jordan (ISR-JOR JWC)
Foundation	1994
Member states	Israel, Jordan
Geographical scope	Jordan and Yarmouk River waters (on Israeli and Jordanian territory) and Wadi Araba/Arava ground water.
Issue areas	Infrastructure, River Regulation, Water Quality, Water Quantity
Mandate	Implementation of Annex II 'Water Related Matters' of the Peace Treaty.
Treaty organs	Joint Water Committee comprised of three members from each country. JWC may set up specialized sub-committees, including a northern and a southern sub-committee.
Additional institutions	Not known.
Staffing of the secretariat	Not applicable.
Financing	Financing of JWC not specified in the treaty. Treaty specifies financial responsibility for some of the projects mentioned in the treaty.
Decision-making	Not specified in treaty (JWC specifies its work procedures.) De facto has each party a veto (=unanimity).
Legal status and powers of the organization	Not specified.
Functions of the organization	Implementation of Annex II 'Water Related Matters' of the Peace Treaty; exchange of relevant data on water resources; cooperation in developing plans for increasing water supplies and improving water use efficiency.
Functions of the secretariat	Not applicable.
Definition of property rights	Yes. By and large confirms Israeli uses and defines measures to increase water supply to Jordan.
Prior notification	Yes.
Monitoring and enforcement	No provisions.
Dispute settlement	No provisions.
Agreements	Treaty of peace between the state of Israel and the Hashemite Kingdom of Jordan, Oct. 26, 1994.
Other sources	Haddadin (2000).

Table A-2 (continued)

Name	Joint Water Committee Israel and the Palestinian Authority (ISR-PAL JWC)
Foundation	1995
Member states	Israel, Palestine Liberation Organization
Geographical scope	Water and sewage resources and systems in the West Bank and in the Gaza Strip.
Issue areas	Infrastructure, Water Quality, Water Quantity
Mandate	Implementation of Article 40 of the Oslo B Interim Agreement.
Treaty organs	Joint Water Committee (for the interim period) comprised of an equal number of representatives from each side. (For the Gaza strip, a 'Council' had been installed prior to the agreement.)
Additional institutions	Not known.
Staffing of the secretariat	Not applicable.
Financing	Financing of JWC not specified in the treaty. The agreement specifies who has to bear the costs for which measures.
Decision-making	Decisions are taken by consensus. Note that JWC only deals with water in the West Bank, but not in Israel. Thus JWC provides Israel with a veto for Palestinian activities.
Legal status and powers of the organization	Not specified.
Functions of the organization	JWC deals with all water issues in the West Bank: coordinated management of water resources and water and sewage systems; protection of water resources; exchange of information relating to water laws and regulations; overseeing the JSETs; approval of water extraction licenses and new projects.
Functions of the secretariat	Not applicable.
Definition of property rights	Yes. Confirms Israeli uses and recognizes Palestinian water rights in the West Bank to be negotiated in permanent status negotiations. Defines 'future Palestinian needs'.
Prior notification	De facto for Palestinians.
Monitoring and enforcement	Set up of 5 Joint Supervision and Enforcement Teams (JSETs). In case of infringement, the JSET shall take necessary measures to reinstate the status quo ante; otherwise matter is referred to the 2 Chairmen of JWC.
Dispute settlement	JWC shall resolve all water and sewage related disputes.
Agreements	Israeli-Palestinian interim agreement on the West Bank and the Gaza Strip, with Annexes I to VII, Sep. 28, 1995.
Other sources	Feitelson and Haddad (1998).

Table A-2 (continued)

Name	German-Czech Commission on Boundary Waters (CBW)
Foundation	1974/1995
Member states	Czech Republic, Germany
Geographical scope	Boundary waters and transboundary surface and ground water within 15 m of the boundary. Areas flooded by boundary waters; surface and ground water where measures lead to significant impact on boundary waters; water infrastructure that crosses the boundary.
Issue areas	Flood Control, Hazard Prevention, Hydrological Monitoring, Infrastructure, Melioration, Water Quality, Water Quantity
Mandate	Maintenance, restoration and coordinated management of transboundary waters, and improvement of their water quality.
Treaty organs	German-Czech Boundary Commission (9 members per delegation). Permanent Bavarian Committee. Permanent Saxonian Committee.
Additional institutions	Commission and Permanent Committee may establish task forces with equal members on each side.
Staffing of the secretariat	Not applicable.
Financing	Each delegation carries its own costs. Costs of measures are born depending on whose interests they serve. Maintenance costs are compensated in kind unless agreed otherwise.
Decision-making	Decisions require the consent of both delegations.
Legal status and powers of the organization	Commission makes recommendations on measures (water quality, regulation and ecosystem protection); determines scope for the Permanent Committees; coordinates collaboration of administrations. Materials for measures are toll exempt.
Functions of the organization	Planning and implementation of measures; maintenance of watercourses and water-related infrastructure; evaluation of services; monitoring of water quality and quantity and exchange of data; early warning systems on floods, icing and pollution; coordination of procedures.
Functions of the secretariat	Not applicable.
Definition of property rights	No. Treaty has no implications on existing water rights and related obligations.
Prior notification	Yes.
Monitoring and enforcement	Monitoring and evaluation of services related to common works.
Dispute settlement	Not specified.
Agreements	Treaty between the Federal Republic of Germany and the Czech Republic concerning cooperation on the management of boundary waters, Dec. 12, 1995.
Other sources	N/A

Table A-2 (continued)

Name	Permanent Water Commission Namibia and South Africa (PWC)
Foundation	1992
Member states	Namibia, South Africa
Geographical scope	Water resources of common interest to the parties.
Issue areas	Ecology, Erosion Control, Water Quality, Water Quantity
Mandate	To act as a technical advisor to the Parties on matters relating to the development and utilization of water resources of common interest.
Treaty organs	Commission consisting of two delegations with up to three members.
Additional institutions	Not known.
Staffing of the secretariat	Not applicable.
Financing	Each party bears its costs of representation. Other costs are shared equally unless agreed otherwise.
Decision-making	By consensus. Quorum: at least two members per delegation.
Legal status and powers of the organization	Not specified.
Functions of the organization	Advice on: measurement of supply, demand, criteria for allocation, investigations, pollution control, potential measures. Power to appoint consultants.
Functions of the secretariat	Not applicable.
Definition of property rights	No. Commission shall advise the parties on the criteria to be adopted in the allocation and utilization of common water resources.
Prior notification	No provisions.
Monitoring and enforcement	No provisions.
Dispute settlement	In the event of failing to reach consensus, the matter shall be referred to the Parties for further negotiation.
Agreements	Agreement between the government of the Republic of Namibia and the government of the Republic of South Africa on the establishment of a permanent water commission, Sep. 14, 1992.
Other sources	N/A

Source: Own compilation

Index

The index contains references to central subjects covered in the book. Definitions are indicated by **bold** page references.